GROWING OLD IN AMERICA

Cornelia Blair

INFORMATION PLUS REFERENCE SERIES
Formerly published by Information Plus, Wylie, Texas

GALE GROUP

Detroit
New York
San Francisco
London
Boston
Woodbridge, CT

GROWING OLD IN AMERICA
was produced for the Gale Group by Information Plus, Wylie, Texas

Information Plus Staff:

Cornelia Blair, Author

Jacquelyn Quiram, Designer

Editorial: Abbey Begun, Barbara Klier, Nancy R. Jacobs, Virginia Peterson, Mei Ling Rein, Mark A. Siegel

The Gale Group Staff:

Editorial: Rita Runchock, Managing Editor; John F. McCoy, Editor

Graphic Services: Randy Bassett, Image Database Supervisor; Robert Duncan, Senior Imaging Specialist

Product Design: Michelle DiMercurio, Senior Art Director; Michael Logusz, Graphic Artist

Production: NeKita McKee, Buyer; Dorothy Maki, Manufacturing Manager

GROWING OLD IN AMERICA

CHAPTER I

OLDER AMERICANS — A DIVERSE AND GROWING POPULATION

AMERICA GROWS OLDER

Old age is the most unexpected of all the things that happen to a man. — Leon Trotsky (1879-1940)

While America began the twentieth century young, America begins the twenty-first century aging and aging rapidly. The elderly population (age 65 and older) increased elevenfold from 1900 to 1994, compared to a threefold increase for those under age 65. Fewer children per family and longer life spans have transformed the aging from a small to a sizable portion of the U.S. population. The large baby boom generation is expected to swell the elderly population until, by mid-century, 1 in 4 Americans — almost 80 million — will be 65 or older (Figure 1.1). The growth in the number of America's older residents will likely be among the most important developments in the United States in the twenty-first century.

WHO IS OLD?

According to Webster, the word "old" means "having lived or been in existence for a long time." This definition works well for a car or a piece of pottery, but when applied to people, it reveals only a small part of a much larger picture — it indicates only the number of years a person has been alive.

Life expectancy (the anticipated average length of life) has changed throughout history. The average life expectancy of an ancient Greek was 18 years. Native Americans in the pre-Columbian Southwest could expect to live 33 years. The low life expectancy was based on a high infant mortality rate. Once a child survived through childhood, however, he or she had a better chance of making it into his or her fifties or sixties. In 1900, the life expectancy of the average American was 47 years. By 1999, the average American female born could expect to live more than 79 years, and a male, 73 years.

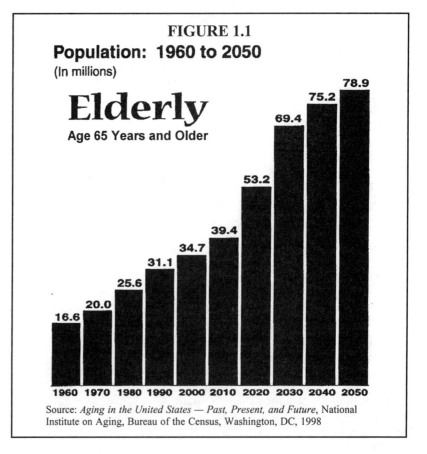

FIGURE 1.1
Population: 1960 to 2050
(In millions)

Elderly
Age 65 Years and Older

Source: *Aging in the United States — Past, Present, and Future,* National Institute on Aging, Bureau of the Census, Washington, DC, 1998

WHAT IS OLD?

There are many ways to characterize an aging person, and everyone has an idea of what old means. Aside from the obvious measure of number of birthdays, people may be labeled old because of their appearance, their physical functioning, their mental capacity, or their lifestyle.

A Working Definition

In 1995, the American Association of Retired Persons (AARP), in its study *Images of Aging in America*, conducted by FGI Research, tried to determine knowledge and attitudes regarding aging in American society. In both its 1981 and 1994 studies, when asked to define "old," most people defined the point of becoming old by a specific chronological number of years. In contrast, in the earlier 1974 sampling, respondents had tended to give non-chronological or event-driven criteria for being old, such as retirement, menopause, or disability. (See Table 1.1.)

Old age does not happen overnight; aging is a process that begins before birth and ends with death. At what point does this aging make a person become "old"? The problem of defining old age is reflected in the terminology used to describe those who are no longer "young" adults: for example, middle-aged, elder, older, aged, mature, or senior. Some researchers distinguish between various stages of the later years: young-old, middle-old, and oldest-old. In the AARP study, most people thought old age began around 60 to 69, although a significant proportion thought it began around 70 to 79.

For statistical and legislative purposes, however, some definition of "old age" is necessary.

TABLE 1.1

AGE AT WHICH THE AVERAGE PERSON BECOMES OLD
(Opinions of Americans)

	Average Man			Average Woman		
	1974	1981	1994	1974	1981	1994
N =	4,254	3,427	1,200	4,254	3,427	1,200
	%	%	%	%	%	%
Under 40	1	1	2	1	2	2
40 to 49	4	4	5	5	5	7
50 to 59	11	13	14	11	14	16
60 to 69	23	36	35	18	35	31
70 to 79	13	24	24	12	20	22
80 or older	1	5	5	2	5	6
Never	2	1	1	2	2	2
It depends/event	40	14	9	43	13	8
Not sure	5	2	5	6	2	7
Mean	--	--	63	--	--	62
Median	63	66	65	62	65	65
Chronological (cited specific age)	58	83	85	49	86	84
Non-chronological (cited event/it depends)	42	17	15	51	14	17

NOTE: means and medians are based only on ages expressed in years, as opposed to events.

Source: Kathy Speas and Beth Obenshain, *Images of Aging in America*, AARP/FGI Integrated Marketing, Chapel Hill, NC, 1995

The United States government initially assigned a person's sixty-fifth birthday as the age when U.S. citizens become eligible for government benefits such as full Social Security and Medicare. The number 65 was not selected by any scientific process; it followed a precedent set by German Chancellor Otto von Bismark in 1899. In that year, Germany became the first western government to assume financial support of its older citizens by passing the Old Age and Survivors Pension Act. Chancellor von Bismark arbitrarily decided that eligibility for benefits would begin at age 65 (although he himself was an active and vigorous 74 years old at the time).

In this book, the terms "old," "older," and "elderly" are used interchangeably to describe people ages 65 and older, although in a few specific cases, the ages 55 and older may be used. The term "oldest old" refers to people 85 and older. Centenarians are those over the age of 100. Of note is the fact that the United Nations Population Division has adjusted its definition of "elderly" to mean those 85 and older, rather than 65 and up.

THE "AGE WAVE"

Why is America getting older? One of the main reasons is that in the 20 years after World War II (1945-1965), as soldiers returned home eager to start families, as the world political climate stabilized, and as the U.S. economy prospered, there was an explosion of births. Children born during these years make up what is called the "baby-boom generation." The baby boomers, who are now heading into their forties and fifties, will begin to turn 65 around 2010. The 65+ population will increase dramatically between 2010 and 2030 as the baby boomers complete their transition from "not-old" to "old."

Figure 1.2 shows the movement of the swell in the numbers of Americans as these boomers age. Initially, the baby boom generation reduced the median age (half of the people were over that age and half were younger than that age) by the presence of so many young. As it grows older, it is moving the median age upward in what is being termed an "age wave." The national median age was 16.7 years in 1820. It took 130 years for the median age to reach 30 years. In 1987, it exceeded 32 years, and in 1999, the median age of Americans reached 35.6 years. In November 1999, of an estimated U.S. population of 273.8 million people, 34.7 million (13 percent) were over the age of 65. (See Table 1.2.)*

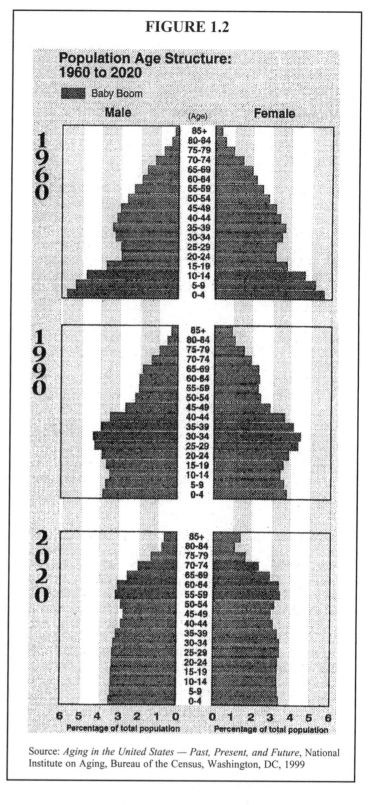

FIGURE 1.2

Population Age Structure: 1960 to 2020

Source: *Aging in the United States — Past, Present, and Future*, National Institute on Aging, Bureau of the Census, Washington, DC, 1999

---

*Under the Constitution of the United States, the Census Bureau must conduct a count every 10 years to determine the population of the nation. Census counts are used to apportion representation in the U.S. House of Representatives, draw legislative boundaries, formulate public policy, and assist with planning and decision-making in the private sector. Although a census is to be conducted in 2000, the data will not be available for a time. The statistics used in any discussion of population numbers are, therefore, necessarily based on dated 1990 census counts or on later estimates.

The Oldest Old

Even more dramatic than the growth of the 65+ population is the increase in the number of Americans over the age of 85, the "oldest old." In 1999, 4.2 million Americans (1.5 percent) were 85 years old or older, and the number of people over 85 will continue to grow through 2050 (Figure 1.3). By 2050, the 85+ age group will make up 5 percent of the total U.S. population and 22 percent of the 65+ age group. Among the oldest old, women outnumber men by a ratio of 5 to 2. Because women will continue to live longer into the middle of the next century, they will make up an even larger proportion of the older population and thereby a larger percentage of the total population in the future.

The 100 Club

It is becoming increasingly hard to win a televised 100th birthday greeting from Willard Scott, who mentions 12 centenarians every week on the *Today Show*. Every week, due to their increasing numbers, about 90 new centenarians are disappointed. (Figure 1.4 shows the historical events in the lives of those over 100.)

Within the next 60 years, America will experience a "centenarian boom." The chances of living to age 100 have increased 40 times since 1900. The centenarian population more than doubled during the 1980s to reach 62,000 in 1999 (Table 1.2). The U.S. Census Bureau predicts that America will have 131,000 centenarians by 2010 (middle series projection) and 834,000 by 2050 (Table 1.3), a phenomenal growth when compared to the 4,000 centenarians living in the United States in 1960. Not surprisingly, most centenarians live past the age of 100 by only a few years, the vast majority (90 percent) not reaching 105 years of age.

TABLE 1.2

Resident Population Estimates of the United States by Age and Sex: April 1, 1990 to November 1, 1999

(Numbers in thousands. Consistent with 1990 Decennial Census enumeration.)

	Nov. 1, 1999	July 1, 1999	July 1, 1998	July 1, 1997	July 1, 1996	July 1, 1995
BOTH SEXES						
Population, all ages	273,866	272,878	270,299	267,744	265,190	262,765
Summary indicators						
Median age.........	35.6	35.5	35.2	34.9	34.7	34.4
Mean age...........	36.4	36.4	36.2	36.1	35.9	35.8
Five-year age groups						
Under 5 years.......	18,909	18,918	18,966	19,097	19,289	19,529
5 to 9 years........	19,913	19,957	19,921	19,749	19,435	19,092
10 to 14 years......	19,661	19,554	19,242	19,091	19,001	18,849
15 to 19 years......	19,846	19,762	19,539	19,140	18,704	18,200
20 to 24 years......	18,188	18,061	17,674	17,483	17,504	17,978
25 to 29 years......	18,159	18,240	18,588	18,812	18,927	18,899
30 to 34 years......	19,620	19,750	20,186	20,732	21,309	21,821
35 to 39 years......	22,523	22,556	22,626	22,629	22,549	22,293
40 to 44 years......	22,372	22,278	21,894	21,376	20,809	20,257
45 to 49 years......	19,581	19,363	18,859	18,465	18,428	17,456
50 to 54 years......	16,730	16,452	15,726	15,157	13,927	13,641
55 to 59 years......	13,081	12,883	12,407	11,755	11,356	11,085
60 to 64 years......	10,566	10,526	10,269	10,062	9,996	10,046
65 to 69 years......	9,457	9,455	9,593	9,775	9,900	9,925
70 to 74 years......	8,771	8,779	8,802	8,753	8,789	8,830
75 to 79 years......	7,385	7,337	7,218	7,086	6,891	6,700
80 to 84 years......	4,857	4,823	4,734	4,664	4,575	4,478
85 to 89 years......	2,664	2,629	2,556	2,480	2,415	2,351
90 to 94 years......	1,165	1,151	1,117	1,080	1,043	1,017
95 to 99 years......	355	344	324	305	291	268
100 years and over..	62	60	57	54	51	48
Special age categories						
5 to 13 years.......	35,659	35,618	35,389	34,996	34,597	34,188
14 to 17 years......	15,720	15,661	15,517	15,495	15,210	14,826
18 to 24 years......	26,229	26,056	25,470	24,973	24,837	25,107
16 years and over...	211,518	210,627	208,277	205,919	203,666	201,492
18 years and over...	203,578	202,682	200,426	198,156	196,094	194,222
15 to 44 years......	120,709	120,647	120,508	120,171	119,803	119,449
65 years and over...	34,716	34,578	34,401	34,198	33,955	33,618
85 years and over...	4,246	4,184	4,054	3,919	3,800	3,684

Source: Population Estimates Program, Population Division, Bureau of the Census, Washington, DC, 1999

FIGURE 1.3

Oldest Old (in millions)

0.9 (1960) 1.4 (1970) 2.2 (1980) 3.0 (1990) 4.3 (2000) 5.7 (2010) 6.5 (2020) 8.5 (2030) 13.6 (2040) 18.2 (2050)

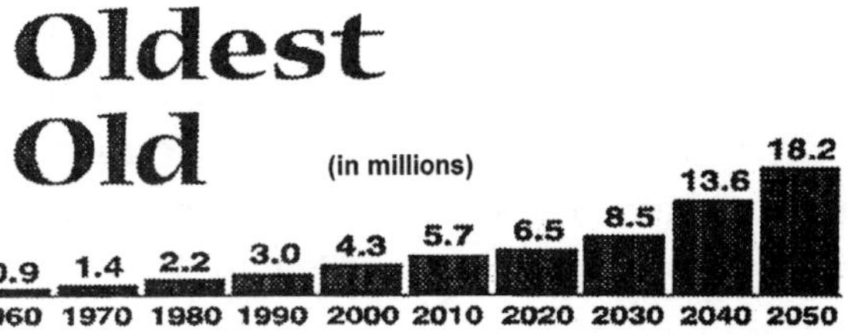

Source: *Aging in the United States — Past, Present, and Future*, National Institute on Aging, Bureau of the Census, Washington, DC, 1999

How Long Do You Want to Live?

In 1999, the American Association of Retired Persons (AARP) conducted a telephone survey regarding attitudes on longevity. Despite medical advances that have extended life, most Americans do not want to live to 100. Sixty-three percent of respondents opted for fewer than 100 years. Survey respondents reported they would like to live to an average of 91 years, but expect to live to be 80. Eighty percent claimed they did things to stay healthy, such as exercise, watch their diets and weight, and maintain a positive attitude. Despite those measures, however, most people were still worried about their futures if they should live to be 100. Forty-six percent worried about declining health; 38 percent, lack of money; 13 percent, loss of mental faculties; 12 percent, having to depend on others; 11 percent, becoming a burden to family; 9 percent, being isolated or alone; and 8 percent, living in a nursing or "old age" home.

RACIAL CHARACTERISTICS

The older population is becoming more ethnically and racially diverse, although at a slower pace than the overall population of the United States. In 1997, of the total population over 65, about 85 percent were non-Hispanic White; 8 percent, Black; 0.4 percent, American Indian; 2 percent, Asian/Pacific Islander; and 5 percent, of Hispanic origin.

These differences in racial proportions are expected to continue into the next century, when the minority elderly are predicted to increase more rapidly than the White population, especially among Hispanics and Asian/Pacific Islanders.

FOREIGN-BORN ELDERLY

Although the total foreign-born population in the United States is growing much faster than the total American population, the percentage of elderly who were born in foreign countries declined from about 11.7 percent in 1980 to 8.6 percent in 1994 (Figure 1.5). This general decrease in per-

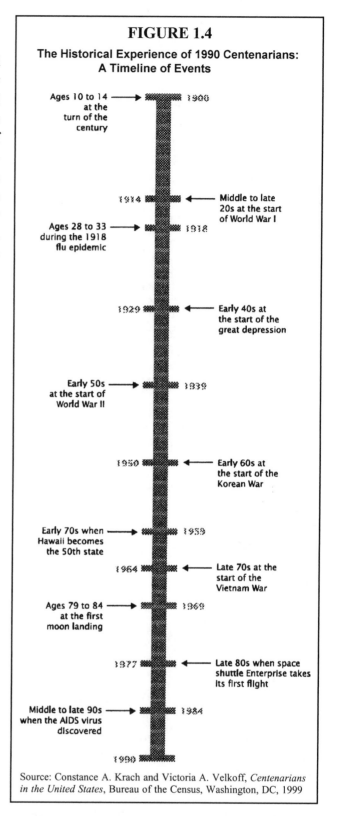

FIGURE 1.4

The Historical Experience of 1990 Centenarians: A Timeline of Events

Ages 10 to 14 at the turn of the century — 1900

1914 — Middle to late 20s at the start of World War I

Ages 28 to 33 during the 1918 flu epidemic — 1918

1929 — Early 40s at the start of the great depression

Early 50s at the start of World War II — 1939

1950 — Early 60s at the start of the Korean War

Early 70s when Hawaii becomes the 50th state — 1959

1964 — Late 70s at the start of the Vietnam War

Ages 79 to 84 at the first moon landing — 1969

1977 — Late 80s when space shuttle Enterprise takes its first flight

Middle to late 90s when the AIDS virus discovered — 1984

1990

Source: Constance A. Krach and Victoria A. Velkoff, *Centenarians in the United States*, Bureau of the Census, Washington, DC, 1999

centage of foreign-born among the elderly has resulted from the deaths of the large volume of immigrants who entered the United States in the early 1900s. More recent immigration has been generally among the young.

TABLE 1.3

Projected Number of Centenarians in the United States by
Sex, Race, and Hispanic Origin: 2000 to 2050[1]

Year	Total (lowest series)[2]	Total (middle series)	Total (highest series)[3]	Percent male[4]	Percent female	Percent Hispanic[5]	Percent Non-Hispanic			
							White	Black	American Indian, Eskimo, and Aleut	Asian and Pacific Islander
2000	69,000	72,000	81,000	16.7	83.3	5.6	77.8	12.5	1.4	2.8
2010	106,000	131,000	214,000	15.3	84.7	7.6	72.5	14.5	2.3	2.3
2020	135,000	214,000	515,000	15.4	84.6	9.8	69.2	13.1	2.8	4.7
2030	159,000	324,000	1,074,000	16.4	83.6	14.5	62.3	12.7	2.8	8.0
2040	174,000	447,000	1,902,000	17.4	82.8	17.7	56.2	13.2	2.7	10.5
2050	265,000	834,000	4,218,000	18.0	82.0	19.2	55.4	12.7	2.2	10.6

[1] Projections are based on a July 1, 1994 estimate of the resident population, which is based on the enumerated 1990 census population modified by age and race. As a result of these modifications, the April 1, 1990 population of centenarians is assumed to be 36,000. For a detailed description of the age modification procedures, see publication CPH-L-74, *Age, Sex, and Hispanic Origin Information from the 1990 Census: A Comparison of Census Results with Results Where Age and Race have been Modified.*
[2] Assumes low fertility, low life expectancy, and low net migration in comparison to the middle series values.
[3] Assumes high fertility, high life expectancy, and high net migration in comparison to the middle series values.
[4] Percentage values are based on middle series projections.
[5] Persons of Hispanic origin may be of any race.
Source: Day, J. C., 1996, *Population Projections of the United States by Age, Sex, Race, and Hispanic Origin: 1995 to 2050,* U.S. Bureau of the Census, Current Population Reports, P25-1130, U.S. Government Printing Office, Washington, DC.

Source: Constance A. Krach and Victoria A. Velkoff, *Centenarians in the United States,* Bureau of the Census, Washington, DC, 1999

In 1960, about one-third of foreign-born persons were elderly; by 1994, only about 12 percent of all foreign-born were elderly. By race, elderly Asian/Pacific Islanders were more likely (71 percent) to be foreign-born, and elderly American Indians, Eskimos, and Aleuts were least likely (2 percent) to be foreign-born. The proportion of elderly among the foreign-born will likely continue to decline until the immigrants of the past few decades begin to reach 65.

awareness of and desire for a healthy lifestyle have helped lengthen the lives of Americans.

WHERE DO OLDER AMERICANS LIVE — AND WHERE ARE THEY GOING?

Nine states have more than 1 million elderly: California, New York, Florida, Pennsylvania, Texas, Illinois, Ohio, Michigan, and New Jersey.

ADDITIONAL REASONS FOR THE AGING OF AMERICA

In addition to the large number of births after World War II, there are a number of additional reasons for the American population's aging. Foremost are medical advances that have greatly reduced infant mortality and death from childhood diseases; people have a greater chance of surviving the first years of life. (An extremely high infant and child mortality rate was the main reason that average life expectancy was so low in early civilizations.) At the other end of life, medical advances, life-sustaining technologies, and a greater

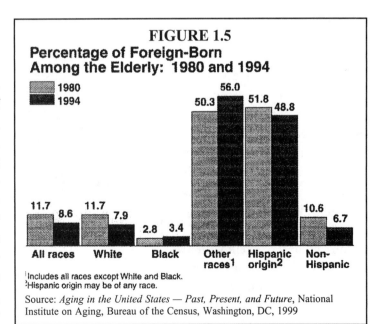

FIGURE 1.5
Percentage of Foreign-Born Among the Elderly: 1980 and 1994

[1]Includes all races except White and Black.
[2]Hispanic origin may be of any race.

Source: *Aging in the United States — Past, Present, and Future,* National Institute on Aging, Bureau of the Census, Washington, DC, 1999

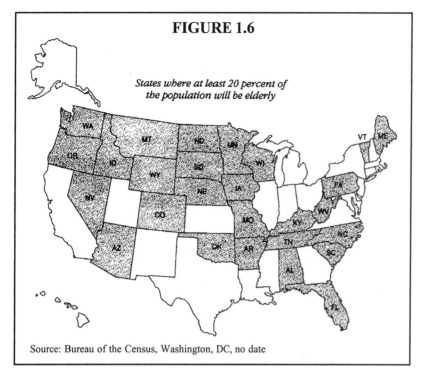

FIGURE 1.6

States where at least 20 percent of the population will be elderly

Source: Bureau of the Census, Washington, DC, no date

To further show the growth in the aging population in 1995, only five states had at least 15 percent of their population in the elderly segment. By 2025, that number is expected to grow to 48 states.

The U.S. Bureau of the Census ("State-By-State Population Changes to 2025," *Census Brief*, December 1996) predicted that, by 2025, 27 states will have at least 1 in 5 (20 percent) people elderly (Figure 1.7). Every state but Alaska and California will have 15 percent or more of their population over the age of 65 in 2025, up from just five states in 1995. Twenty-one states will at least double their elderly population. Except for New Hampshire, these states are in the South or West. In 1980, for the first time in American history, a greater number of elderly people lived in the suburbs than in central cities. These were generally older suburbs known to have lower resident income levels, more

Although California has the largest number of elderly residents, in 1995, Florida had the highest percentage (19 percent) relative to its total population. Alaska had the fewest elderly residents both in number and in percentage (5 percent) of population. Since 1980, most states have experienced a steady rise in the proportion of elderly persons. (Figure 1.6 shows the states where 20 percent or more of the population will be elderly by 2015.)

The number of 65+ residents will increase in all regions of the United States into the next century, with the South gaining the greatest number and the Midwest the fewest. By 2025, Florida is expected to remain the "oldest" state with more than 26 percent of its population age 65 or older. Alaska will still rank as the "youngest' state with 10 percent elderly. (Some states "age" not only due to the in-migration of elderly but also to the out-migration of the young.)

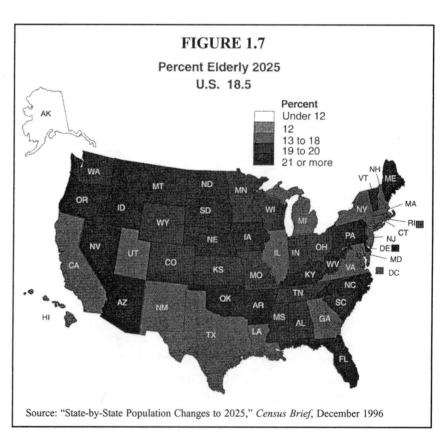

FIGURE 1.7

Percent Elderly 2025
U.S. 18.5

Percent
Under 12
12
13 to 18
19 to 20
21 or more

Source: "State-by-State Population Changes to 2025," *Census Brief*, December 1996

rental housing, lower home values, and higher population densities. In 1996, all but one of the top 10 metropolitan areas having the greatest percentage of people over 65 were in Florida (Table 1.4).

Most older Americans still live in, or have returned to, their native states. Older Americans are less likely than the average American to move across state lines. They tend to remain where they spent their adult lives. In 1997, according to *Americans 55 and Older: A Changing Market* (2nd Edition, New Strategist Publications, Ithaca, New York, 1999), a publisher of reference and demographics materials, 16 percent of all Americans moved — three times the proportion of those 55 and older who moved. Only 7 percent of people 60 to 64 moved in that year, as did 5 percent of those 65 to 69. Mobility was least among those 70 to 74 (3.8 percent) but then rose to above 6 percent at age 85 and older.

Although migration is less common among the elderly, when older citizens do move, they generally move to the Sunbelt states of the South and Western regions, especially Florida, Arizona, Texas, and Washington. Long-distance retirees have become coveted prizes for state economic developers. Some retirement areas get such a rich monthly boost of money from pensions, investments, and Social Security checks that their civic leaders boast of a "mailbox economy." Nonetheless, older people who move to retire make up a small percentage of the elderly. According to the AARP, 84 percent of adults 55 and older report they would prefer to stay in their current homes.

TABLE 1.4

Top 25 Metro Areas – Our Older Population

Percent of the population 65 years old and over: 1996

Rank	Percent	Rank	Percent
1 Punta Gorda, FL MSA	34.3	10 Tampa-St. Petersburg-Clearwater, FL MSA	21.9
2 Sarasota-Bradenton, FL MSA	30.9	11 Scranton–Wilkes-Barre–Hazleton, PA MSA	19.9
3 Fort Myers-Cape Coral, FL MSA	24.8	12 Cumberland, MD-WV MSA	18.9
4 West Palm Beach-Boca Raton, FL MSA	24.3	13 Johnstown, PA MSA	18.7
5 Fort Pierce-Port St. Lucie, FL MSA	23.4	14 Chico-Paradise, CA MSA	18.6
6 Daytona Beach, FL MSA	23.2	15 Lakeland-Winter Haven, FL MSA	18.5
7 Barnstable-Yarmouth, MA NECMA	22.8	16 Wheeling, WV-OH MSA	18.5
8 Naples, FL MSA	22.4	17 Sharon, PA MSA	17.8
9 Ocala, FL MSA	22.1	18 Pittsburgh, PA MSA	17.7
		19 Pittsfield, MA NECMA	17.7
		20 Altoona, PA MSA	17.6

MSA Metropolitan statistical area. NECMA New England county metropolitan area. CMSA Consolidated metropolitan statistical area.

Source: "Metro Areas and Much More — Yours in Brief," *Census and You*, vol. 33, no. 9, September 1998

What retirees want most is easy access to important services — grocery stores, pharmacies, hospitals. Only 40 percent of older adults report that they want to live close to children or grandchildren, although that desire increases with age. Retirement migrants are increasingly concerned about getting away from crime and congestion, one of the reasons that Florida's share of incoming migrants has declined in recent years as the state has grown rapidly.

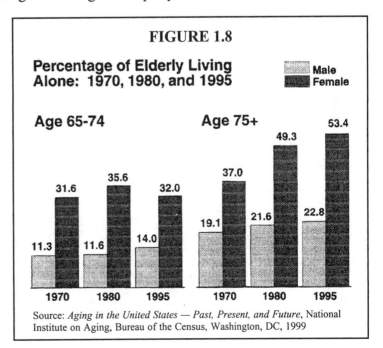

FIGURE 1.8

Percentage of Elderly Living Alone: 1970, 1980, and 1995

Source: *Aging in the United States — Past, Present, and Future*, National Institute on Aging, Bureau of the Census, Washington, DC, 1999

9

Boomer Movers — From Metropolis to Rural America

Many researchers suggest that many baby boomers are making retirement plans that include settling down in rural areas. Upcoming retirees have more income, independence, and motivation for migrating than in the past. As a group they are wealthier, better educated, and younger. They have benefited from the real estate boom of the 1970s and 1980s and a surging 1990s economy. Many are dual-career couples. They generally participate in physical activities longer and may have identified with rural areas since their "hippie" days. In addition, this generation has traveled more for work and education in their lifetimes than have previous generations, and as a result, have been exposed to more places. Rarely do people move to a place previously unknown to them.

Where will these retirees go to retire? The Milken Institute in Santa Monica, California, predicts that the states in the West will lead the nation in elderly migrants beginning around 2010. The states with the greatest growth of people 65 and older from 2000 to 2025 will be Utah, Alaska, Idaho, Wyoming, and Colorado — states with relatively small populations, lots of rural space, and natural beauty. Southern states will likely grow as well, but more slowly than the West.

MARRIED MEN, UNMARRIED WOMEN, AND LIVING ALONE — AGING IS LARGELY A WOMEN'S ISSUE

The good news is that we live longer than men, and the bad news is that we live longer than men. — Judith Lichtman, President of National Partnership for Women and Families

The ratio of women to men varies dramatically by age, with the disparity becoming most marked among the oldest. At age 65, there are 81 men for every 100 women; by age 100, only 27 men are living for each 100 women. (Figure 1.2 demonstrates the moving of the baby boom generation through the population over time. The diagrams illustrate the increase of the population at the oldest ages and the especially noticeable increase in the female elderly.) Higher female life expectancy, combined with the fact that men are generally older than their spouses, contributes to the higher proportions of women living alone — widowed or unmarried.

Most younger elderly are married, but the number decreases with age, especially among women. In 1995, 64 percent of persons age 65 to 74 were married and living with their spouses; 24 percent (14 percent of men and 32 percent of women) were living alone. Among those 75 and older, 22.8 percent of men and 53.4 percent of women lived alone (Figure 1.8). Twenty-one percent of persons 85 and over lived with their spouses, while 54 percent lived alone.

Widowhood increases with age and is greater among women than men. In 1995, 33 percent of women age 65 to 74, 59 percent of those 75 to 84, and 81 percent of women 85 years and over were widowed. Elderly men were much less likely to be widowers: 9 percent of men 65 to 74, 18 percent of those 75 to 84, and 41 percent of men 85 years and older were widowers. Researchers estimate that the average age of widowhood was 68.9 for women and 72.3 years for men. On average, women spend 15.3 years as widows, while men live 8.4 years as widowers.

The large discrepancy between the percentage of elderly men and elderly women who are married results from women living longer than men, men tending to marry women younger than themselves and, therefore, being more likely to die before their spouses, and men who are widowed or divorced remarrying more often than do women in the same situation. As life expectancy increases, the proportion of those widowed may decline. For the immediate future, however, the proportion who are divorced is expected to rise.

ATTITUDES ABOUT AGING

In non-industrialized countries, old people are often held in great respect and esteem. Not only have they weathered years of what may have been harsh living conditions, but also they have accumulated wisdom and knowledge that younger generations need to survive and carry on the traditions of their cultures. In many industrialized societies, such as the United States, a person's worth is measured largely by the type of work he or she does and the amount of wealth accumulated. When people retire from full-time employment, they may lose status because they are no longer working, earning money, or "contributing" to society. People's identity is often bound to their former jobs, and without them, they may feel worthless. Their lifetime of experience may not seem relevant in an ever-changing world where computers become outdated every year.

Until recently, partly in jest and partly reflecting real fears, many people did not acknowledge any birthday from 40 onward and became "39 and holding" — indefinitely. "Old" people were once thought to have wrinkled faces, to walk with canes, to be generally irritable and demanding, to be forgetful, and to spend their waking hours playing bingo and shuffleboard — passing time until they died. While this stereotype was probably never an accurate representation of most older people, it is even less true today. As technology and better living conditions increase the number of years a human being can survive and people actively strive to improve and preserve their health, "old age" becomes harder to portray.

One Definition Does Not Fit All

Individuals age very differently. In fact, the differences between individuals in the latter years of their lives are much greater than in their early years. Although they may have diverse personalities and intellects, most babies and young children

FIGURE 1.9

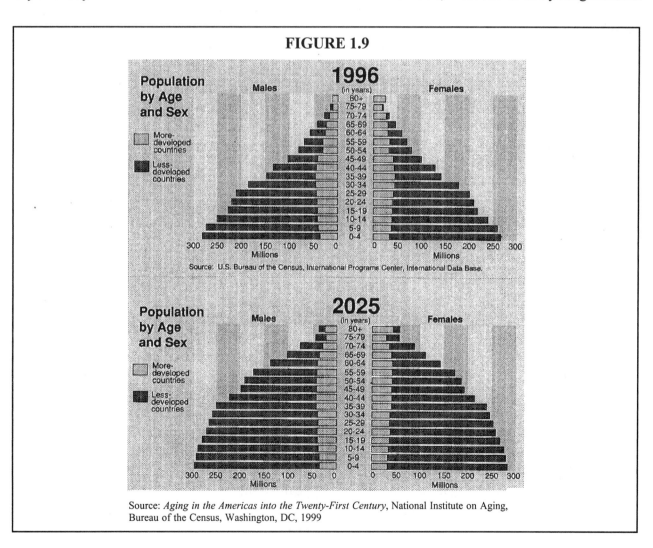

Source: *Aging in the Americas into the Twenty-First Century*, National Institute on Aging, Bureau of the Census, Washington, DC, 1999

behave and develop within fairly predictable patterns. Even our educational system, rightly or wrongly, presupposes a uniformity among children that allows them to be taught and to learn specific materials at specific ages.

On the other hand, one 65-year-old man may go to work every day as he has for the past 40 years, while another requires constant care. One 70-year-old woman may play 18 holes of golf four times a week, while another is crippled with arthritis. One 80-year-old couple may volunteer to be foster grandparents; another spends most of their days in front of the TV.

Challenging the Myth

During the past few years, a revolution has been taking place. Older people are no longer content to be regarded as "old." They want to be recognized as individuals rather than as stereotypes. Most of them are healthier and better educated, and many are wealthier, than at any time in history. They are demanding the respect and recognition they feel they have earned. Older activists are involved in causes ranging from job retraining to long-term care to saving historical buildings to changing the public's perception of old age.

RESHAPING AMERICAN SOCIETY

Baby boomers have radically transformed every stage of life through which they have traveled. We have repeatedly seen that whatever the issues are for boomers at each stage, whether driven by financial, interpersonal, or even hormonal forces, these have become the dominant social, political, and marketplace themes of the time. — Ken Dychtwald, *Age Power*, 1999

The aging of America means much more than just having more old people around. Attitudes about older people are changing as the elderly become more numerous and vocal, and the focus of daily life is shifting from a youth culture to a mature one. This is unfamiliar territory. America has never been old before.

It is little wonder that the United States has been a youth-oriented society for so many years. When the baby boomers were young, their needs dominated society. It was not until 1983 that the number of elderly equaled the number of teenagers for the first time. The complexion of the nation is changing and will change even more dramatically in the years to come.

Changing the Marketplace

I began to see that we had designed our modern world, top to bottom, to match the size, shape, and style of youth — from the height of the steps in our public buildings to the length of time it takes for traffic lights to change, from the size of the typeface in our newspapers and magazines to the auditory range in our telephones and televisions, from the age and style of the models in advertisements to our embarrassment about our birthdays. In thousands of ways ... we were being influenced to like what's young and dislike what's old. — Ken Dychtwald, *Age Power*, 1999

Because spending power has traditionally been in the hands of young adults and their children, manufacturers and retailers targeted these age groups almost exclusively. Now a whole new market is surfacing. Today's older adults worked in the prosperous post-war years, generally earned good wages, and were often conscientious about saving. Having completed child-rearing responsibilities, many now have considerable discretionary money.

Many manufacturers have no idea how to tap this potential market. Older consumers are a very diverse group with wide-ranging interests and needs. Marketing programs sometimes fail because manufacturers promote items designed specifically for "old" people, only to find that older people reject products marketed on the basis of age. It is often harder to develop a product that universally appeals to the old because they are old than one that appeals to the young simply because they are young.

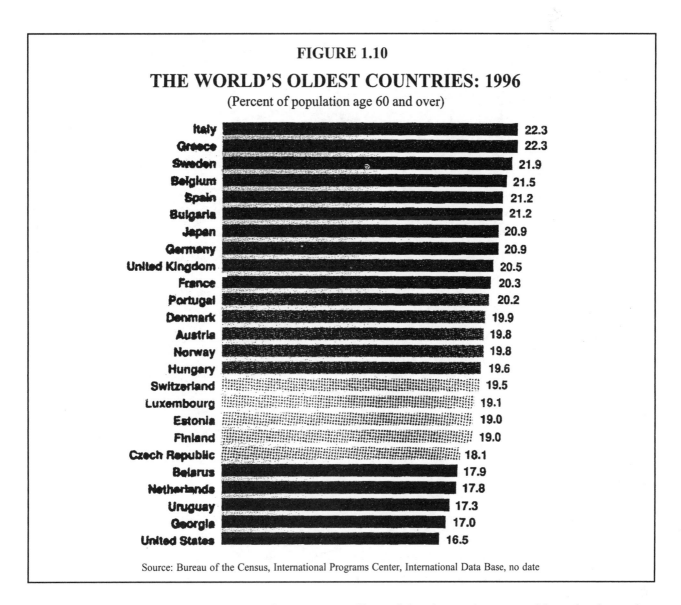

FIGURE 1.10

THE WORLD'S OLDEST COUNTRIES: 1996

(Percent of population age 60 and over)

Country	Percent
Italy	22.3
Greece	22.3
Sweden	21.9
Belgium	21.5
Spain	21.2
Bulgaria	21.2
Japan	20.9
Germany	20.9
United Kingdom	20.5
France	20.3
Portugal	20.2
Denmark	19.9
Austria	19.8
Norway	19.8
Hungary	19.6
Switzerland	19.5
Luxembourg	19.1
Estonia	19.0
Finland	19.0
Czech Republic	18.1
Belarus	17.9
Netherlands	17.8
Uruguay	17.3
Georgia	17.0
United States	16.5

Source: Bureau of the Census, International Programs Center, International Data Base, no date

A Three-Segment Mature Market

Research by one marketing research firm, Media Matrix (New York City), reports that the mature market constitutes not one but three markets — age 55-64, age 65-79, and age 80-plus. The oldest baby boomers, who turned 54 in 2000, are offended by attempts to categorize them as mature. They will not buy products sold to them on that basis nor respond to advertising that appeals to older seniors.

Those age 55-64 constitute the "working mature" market. They are the youngest and most active of the so-called mature market. They are approaching retirement and are at the peak of their earning and spending potential. They are generally anticipating retirement with enthusiasm, but greet age with defiance.

Those ages 65-79 are the "young retirees." They have the highest discretionary income of any age group. Their homes are often paid for, and their children are grown. Although health is beginning to become a concern, they have made their peace with the aging process. They are as active and involved in leisure, volunteer, family, and second career as their health and finances allow.

America's oldest elderly population consists of those 80 and older. They generally view themselves as 10 to 15 years younger than they actually are and view 50-year-olds as nearly as young and naïve as 20-somethings may appear to 50-year-olds.

As a whole, the 21 percent of the population age 55 and older control about 75 percent of the nation's financial assets. Approximately 80 percent of mature Americans own their own homes and are gradually liquidating and spending their assets. They give more than any other age groups to charity, educational organizations, and family members. They spend more on travel, financial services, and health care. They are responsible for 71 percent of all prescription drug purchases. They spend more hours watching television and listening to radio than do younger audiences, and they read more newspapers and magazines. Media Matrix found that retirees spend far more time with their computers than do members of any other age group. Those age 55 to 64 spend more annually on computers and related equipment than do householders overall.

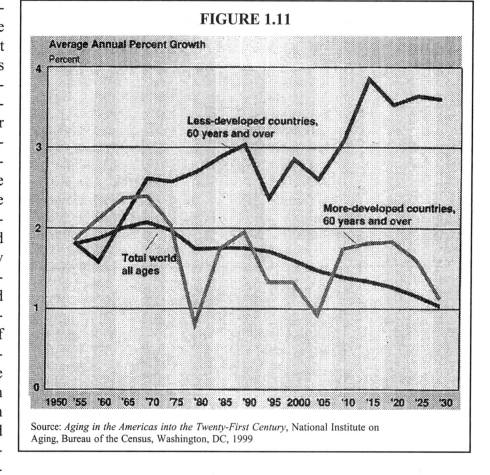

FIGURE 1.11

Source: *Aging in the Americas into the Twenty-First Century*, National Institute on Aging, Bureau of the Census, Washington, DC, 1999

The Need for New Marketing Approaches

Television commercials may look very different in the years ahead. The emphasis on youthfulness may find less acceptance in a generally aging community. Modeling and advertising agencies increasingly demand the over-50 model. Magazines aimed at the mature audience, such as *Modern Maturity*, published by the AARP, almost exclusively use advertisements with older models. Nonetheless, the image of older people in advertising will almost certainly retain the healthy, vital qualities of younger models, while emphasizing the wisdom and experience gained with age.

The increasing number of elderly, the hours they spend watching television and otherwise attuned to the media (See Chapter XI), and the considerable discretionary income available to many of them are making the elderly a prime target for consumer marketing.

The Need for New and Different Housing

Increasingly, the privately owned, one-family residence with a lawn is only one of the housing options preferred by the elderly. Houses that accommodate the physical limitations of the elderly will become more necessary, as will apartment complexes for those no longer able or interested in maintaining a single-unit home for physical, financial, or security reasons. Entire developments devoted to elderly retirees have sprung up in several states. Chapter III explores more fully the housing options for the elderly.

Caring for the Elderly

While many older people are remaining active and independent longer than ever before, many

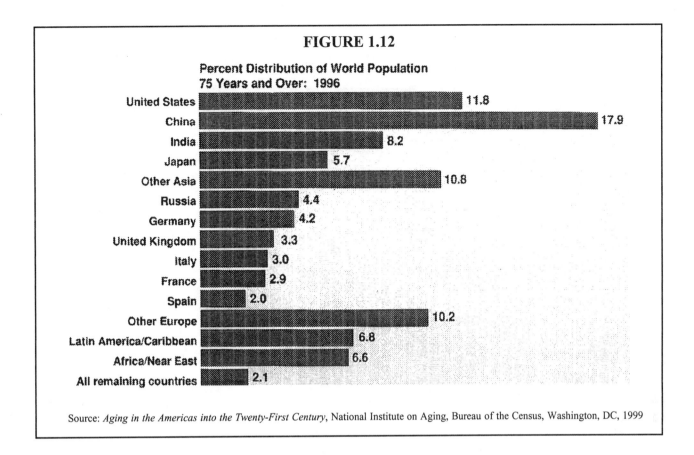

FIGURE 1.12

Percent Distribution of World Population
75 Years and Over: 1996

United States	11.8
China	17.9
India	8.2
Japan	5.7
Other Asia	10.8
Russia	4.4
Germany	4.2
United Kingdom	3.3
Italy	3.0
France	2.9
Spain	2.0
Other Europe	10.2
Latin America/Caribbean	6.8
Africa/Near East	6.6
All remaining countries	2.1

Source: *Aging in the Americas into the Twenty-First Century*, National Institute on Aging, Bureau of the Census, Washington, DC, 1999

others live in poor health and at the brink of poverty. With time even the sturdiest body weakens and faculties may decline. Long or catastrophic illnesses can deplete a lifetime of savings. Almost all of the oldest old require some kind of assistance — financial, physical, or often both — just to survive the day. This assistance must come from somewhere, whether the family, private organizations, or the government. Caring for a much larger older population in the future will require foresight and planning. For more information, see Chapters VIII and IX.

GLOBAL AGING

Unlike with global warming, there can be little debate over whether or when global aging will manifest itself. And unlike with other challenges, even the struggle to preserve and strengthen unsteady new democracies, the costs of global aging will be far beyond the means of even the world's wealthiest nations — unless retirement benefit systems are radically reformed.

Failure to do so, to prepare early and bold enough — will spark economic crises that will dwarf the recent [economic] meltdowns in Asia and Russia. — Peter Peterson, *Gray Dawn: the Global Aging Crisis*, 1999

Population aging is not confined to the United States. The size of the world's population has been growing for centuries. What is new is the accelerated pace of aging. Over the next several decades, countries in the developed world will experience unprecedented growth in the number of their elderly and unprecedented decline in the number of their youth. (See Figure 1.9.)

According to United Nations projections, 1 in 10 persons worldwide will be age 65 or older by 2025 — up from 1 in 15 today. As fertility levels decline throughout the world, all major areas will have a greater share of elderly population. The elderly in Asia and Latin America will nearly double to about 10 percent in 2025. The elderly in North America will increase from 12.5 percent in 1995

15

TABLE 1.5

Life Expectancy and Demographic Characteristics

Country	Years of life expectancy at birth, 1997		Percent widowed age 60 and over		Percent economically active age 60 and over		Percent literate age 60 and over		Percent GDP spent on health 1990
	Male	Female	Male	Female	Male	Female	Male	Female	
Anguilla	77	82	14	32	33	9	(NA)	(NA)	(NA)
Antigua and Barbuda	71	77	13	28	51	23	(NA)	(NA)	6
Argentina	74	79	12	46	39	13	93	91	9
Aruba	77	80	13	37	23	6	(NA)	(NA)	(NA)
Bahamas	74	79	14	44	47	26	(NA)	(NA)	5
Barbados	75	79	14	31	19	9	(NA)	(NA)	6
Belize	69	74	13	33	60	13	[1]45	[1]45	5
Bolivia	60	73	18	44	50	27	59	32	5
Brazil	65	72	13	47	51	21	59	54	6
Canada	79	82	10	40	20	8	(NA)	(NA)	9
Chile	75	80	13	39	40	11	83	82	6
Colombia	70	78	15	46	45	11	73	64	6
Costa Rica	76	78	12	34	41	6	[1]79	[1]78	9
Cuba	75	79	11	36	[1]21	[1]3	(NA)	(NA)	(NA)
Dominica	78	82	15	31	41	14	(NA)	(NA)	6
Dominican Republic	69	77	(NA)	(NA)	[1]79	[1]22	[1]42	[1]37	5
Ecuador	71	79	12	33	71	16	72	61	6
El Salvador	69	78	13	35	62	20	(NA)	(NA)	5
French Guiana	76	81	7	25	26	13	[1]69	[1]73	(NA)
Grenada	71	77	13	31	36	12	(NA)	(NA)	6
Guadeloupe	78	82	11	33	15	8	[1]66	[1]63	(NA)
Guatemala	66	75	12	46	[1]62	[1]7	[1]43	[1]31	3
Guyana	63	58	17	45	46	16	(NA)	(NA)	6
Haiti	51	59	8	27	[1]64	[1]35	[1]21	[1]15	3
Honduras	65	66	9	29	72	19	39	33	6
Jamaica	75	80	13	38	[1]49	[1]23	62	73	4
Martinique	79	82	11	30	14	8	[1]69	[1]72	(NA)
Mexico	71	79	12	37	60	18	71	59	4
Netherlands Antilles	77	80	13	34	20	3	(NA)	(NA)	(NA)
Nicaragua	66	76	[2]10	[2]33	[1]58	[1]11	51	46	5
Panama	74	79	11	32	42	8	72	71	9
Paraguay	72	77	11	30	54	20	79	68	3
Peru	70	78	17	43	60	24	[1]76	[1]49	3
Puerto Rico	74	78	13	40	20	6	[1]75	[1]67	(NA)
St. Kitts and Nevis	67	75	14	25	56	16	93	94	6
St. Lucia	71	77	(NA)	(NA)	47	15	(NA)	(NA)	5
St. Vincent & Grenadines	73	79	14	25	41	12	(NA)	(NA)	6
Suriname	70	77	(NA)	(NA)	15	5	(NA)	(NA)	4
Trinidad and Tobago	70	74	16	41	23	10	90	78	4
United States	76	79	13	47	26	15	91	93	13
Uruguay	75	81	11	43	31	11	[1]85	[1]87	6
Venezuela	72	79	10	35	[1]48	[1]11	[1]75	[1]66	7
Virgin Islands (US)	78	82	11	30	27	[1]12	(NA)	(NA)	(NA)

NA Data not available.
[1] Refers to age 65 and over.
[2] Refers to age 50 and over.

Note: Component population projections are unavailable for the following countries: Bermuda, British Virgin Islands, Cayman Islands, Montserrat, Turks and Caicos.

Source: *Aging in the Americas into the Twenty-First Century*, National Institute on Aging, Bureau of the Census, Washington, DC, 1999

to 18.5 percent; Europe, from 13.8 to 20.2 percent; and Africa, from 3.2 to 4.2 percent. Figure 1.10 shows that, in 1996, the United States was one of the youngest countries in the developed world.

Population aging is occurring in less industrialized countries as well. Uruguay, for example, has a higher percentage of older people than does Canada and the United States. Nearly 80 percent of the increase in 1995 occurred in less-developed countries (Figure 1.11). In 1996, more than 43 percent of those over 75 years lived in just four countries: the People's Republic of China, the United States, India, and Japan. In many countries, such

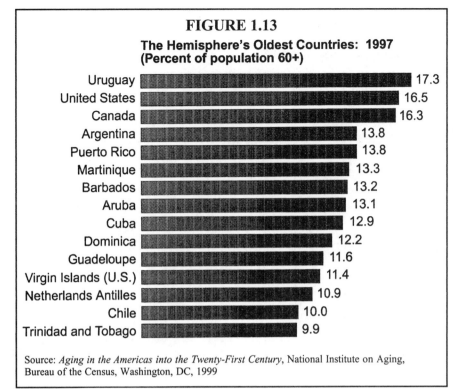

FIGURE 1.13

The Hemisphere's Oldest Countries: 1997
(Percent of population 60+)

Country	Percent
Uruguay	17.3
United States	16.5
Canada	16.3
Argentina	13.8
Puerto Rico	13.8
Martinique	13.3
Barbados	13.2
Aruba	13.1
Cuba	12.9
Dominica	12.2
Guadeloupe	11.6
Virgin Islands (U.S.)	11.4
Netherlands Antilles	10.9
Chile	10.0
Trinidad and Tobago	9.9

Source: *Aging in the Americas into the Twenty-First Century*, National Institute on Aging, Bureau of the Census, Washington, DC, 1999

Aging in the Americas

There is wide variation in the life expectancy and aging in the nations of North, South, and Central America. For example, a woman born in 1997 in the Virgin Islands can expect to live 82 years; a woman born in Haiti, only 59. Over the age of 60, in the United States and Brazil, almost half (47 percent) of women are widowed, compared to about one-quarter in French Guiana, St. Kitts, Haiti, and St. Vincent. (See Table 1.5.)

In 1997, among the countries of the Western Hemisphere, Uruguay (17.3 percent), the United States (16.5 percent), and Canada (16.3 percent) had the largest percentages of population over the age of 60. (See Figure 1.13.)

The percentage of people over the age of 60 in all countries of the Americas is projected to rise by 2025. The median age will increase in virtually all the Americas. (See Table 1.6.)

The Feminization of Aging — Women of the World

Worldwide, the number of women aged 60 and older will more than double, reaching 645 million in the next 25 years. In developed countries, older women now account for 1 in 10 residents; that proportion will rise to 1 in 7 by 2025, and 1 in 6 in countries such as Japan and Italy.

Women are the majority of the older population in virtually all nations. They usually face more special challenges than men do as they age. They are more likely to be widowed, to live alone, and to be poor. They tend to have less education and

as the United States, those 75 and older constituted the fastest-growing segment of the population.

Growth of aging populations around the world reflects major social and economic achievements — declines in infant mortality, declines in fertility, decreases in infectious diseases, and improvements in nutrition and education. This unprecedented growth challenges social planners since the oldest old use disproportionate amounts of health and long-term care services.

The Fastest-Growing Segment

In many countries of the world, those 75 and older are the fastest-growing segment of the elderly population. In 1996, this age group constituted 23 percent of the world's 60-and-over population — 30 percent in developed countries and 19 percent in developing countries. More than 43 percent of those age 75 and over in 1996 lived in just four nations — the People's Republic of China, the United States, India, and Japan. (See Figure 1.12.)

TABLE 1.6

Population Age 60 and Over

Country	Population age 60 and over		Percent age 60 and over		Percent age 75 and over		Percent female in population age 75 and over		Median age (years)	
	1997	2025	1997	2025	1997	2025	1997	2025	1997	2025
Anguilla	1,052	3,229	9.8	19.9	3.7	4.9	61	57	27	38
Antigua and Barbuda	4,693	13,938	7.4	21.3	2.1	2.3	54	64	28	40
Argentina	4,946,759	8,303,040	13.8	17.2	4.0	5.7	62	62	28	33
Aruba	8,916	21,079	13.1	28.6	3.4	8.5	64	65	34	43
Bahamas	21,999	65,265	8.0	17.7	2.2	4.6	62	60	26	35
Barbados	34,047	67,718	13.2	24.3	4.9	6.3	64	63	31	41
Belize	11,909	32,109	5.3	8.4	1.2	1.5	55	55	18	28
Bolivia	488,412	1,202,703	6.4	10.0	1.7	2.6	56	59	20	28
Brazil	12,471,740	32,738,784	7.4	15.6	1.6	4.2	64	63	25	34
Canada	4,947,621	10,521,953	16.3	27.7	5.3	9.1	63	59	36	43
Chile	1,443,223	3,666,275	9.9	20.4	2.4	5.8	63	61	28	38
Colombia	2,522,595	8,089,985	6.7	13.9	1.3	3.1	56	63	24	30
Costa Rica	252,448	773,972	7.1	14.5	1.8	3.4	56	58	24	32
Cuba	1,417,555	2,842,476	12.9	24.3	4.2	7.6	54	59	31	43
Dominica	8,096	12,771	12.2	19.1	4.3	5.3	61	63	26	39
Dominican Republic	508,599	1,456,291	6.5	12.4	1.3	2.9	54	57	22	29
Ecuador	768,147	2,281,085	6.3	12.8	1.7	3.2	56	58	21	3
El Salvador	413,586	934,288	7.3	11.1	1.9	3.1	55	59	21	29
French Guiana	11,953	46,439	7.6	17.4	1.8	4.7	56	52	27	31
Grenada	5,997	11,572	6.3	7.5	1.8	1.1	58	49	18	27
Guadeloupe	47,857	103,328	11.6	20.7	3.6	6.2	60	62	28	40
Guatemala	621,804	1,672,921	5.3	7.5	1.0	1.8	56	58	18	23
Guyana	46,796	95,957	6.6	13.5	1.7	3.1	60	66	23	33
Haiti	418,916	721,246	6.3	7.1	1.5	1.6	54	60	18	25
Honduras	293,703	715,495	5.1	8.3	1.2	2.1	52	60	18	26
Jamaica	238,863	502,256	9.1	15.0	2.8	3.8	59	60	24	35
Martinique	53,670	106,926	13.3	22.2	4.3	6.7	61	63	30	41
Mexico	5,948,491	17,491,716	6.1	12.4	1.3	3.1	58	61	21	31
Netherlands Antilles	23,013	57,902	10.9	23.2	2.9	6.9	62	62	30	40
Nicaragua	184,598	607,172	4.1	7.5	0.7	1.5	59	60	17	26
Panama	216,429	566,295	8.0	14.9	2.2	4.2	53	57	24	33
Paraguay	341,976	984,356	6.6	9.9	1.6	2.3	57	55	20	24
Peru	1,710,218	4,792,645	6.7	12.2	1.4	3.1	57	57	22	30
Puerto Rico	526,307	975,438	13.8	23.1	4.5	8.1	57	61	30	40
St. Kitts and Nevis	3,453	6,525	8.3	10.9	3.4	1.6	60	64	22	32
St. Lucia	10,976	24,667	7.3	12.2	2.2	2.5	65	70	22	34
St. Vincent & Grenadines	9,024	22,186	7.6	14.7	2.4	3.0	60	59	23	37
Suriname	32,698	71,219	7.7	15.5	1.5	3.3	55	60	24	34
Trinidad and Tobago	112,060	231,412	9.9	21.4	2.7	5.0	57	57	27	38
United States	44,158,531	82,501,033	16.5	24.6	5.8	7.9	63	58	35	38
Uruguay	564,878	805,507	17.3	20.6	5.0	7.4	62	62	31	36
Venezuela	1,456,905	4,606,436	6.5	14.2	1.6	3.5	57	58	23	33
Virgin Islands (US)	13,273	36,164	11.4	25.2	2.7	9.4	60	63	29	39

Note: Component population projections are unavailable for the following countries: Bermuda, British Virgin Islands, Cayman Islands, Montserrat, Turks and Caicos.

Source: *Aging in the Americas into the Twenty-First Century*, National Institute on Aging, Bureau of the Census, Washington, DC, 1999

less employment, but more care-giving responsibilities than do older men.

In 1999, the United Nations, noting the sobering projections, named 1999 as the International Year of Older Persons and launched a campaign to raise awareness of the needs of the elderly. The growing needs — and the smaller base of younger people to support those needs — highlight the increasing vulnerability of those societies.

CHAPTER II

THE ECONOMIC STATUS OF OLDER AMERICANS

The economic status of older Americans is more varied than that of any other age group. The elderly were once popularly stereotyped as generally poor, ill, and in need of public and private economic support. Today that image has changed, and some observers now even suggest that because many older people are often financially well off, they do not need as much assistance, especially from the government. Elderly-rights advocates, on the other hand, point out that many older Americans have high out-of-pocket medical expenses and are sharply affected by inflation and the overall economic climate. They have few opportunities to increase, or even maintain, their incomes.

Unfortunately for most elderly retirees who live off their investments, the recent trend in the U.S. economy toward lower interest rates has led to sig-

TABLE 2.1

Family net worth, by selected characteristics of families, 1989, 1992, and 1995

Thousands of 1995 dollars except as noted

Family characteristic	1989			1992			1995		
	Median	Mean	Percentage of families	Median	Mean	Percentage of families	Median	Mean	Percentage of families
All families	**56.5** (n.a.)	**216.7** (n.a.)	**100.0**	**52.8** (3.2)	**200.5** (15.6)	**100.0**	**56.4** (3.3)	**205.9** (14.0)	**100.0**
Income (1995 dollars)[1]									
Less than 10,000	1.6	26.1	15.4	3.3	30.9	15.5	4.8	45.6	16.0
10,000–24,999	25.6	77.9	24.3	28.2	71.2	27.8	30.0	74.6	26.5
25,000–49,999	56.0	121.8	30.3	54.8	124.4	29.5	54.9	119.3	31.1
50,000–99,999	128.1	229.5	22.3	121.2	240.8	20.0	121.1	256.0	20.2
100,000 and more	474.7	1372.9	7.7	506.1	1283.6	7.1	485.9	1465.2	6.1
Age of head (years)									
Less than 35	9.2	66.3	27.2	10.1	50.3	25.8	11.4	47.2	24.8
35–44	69.2	171.3	23.4	46.0	144.3	22.8	48.5	144.5	23.2
45–54	114.0	338.9	14.4	83.4	287.8	16.2	90.5	277.8	17.8
55–64	110.5	334.4	13.9	122.5	358.6	13.2	110.8	356.2	12.5
65–74	88.4	336.8	12.0	105.8	308.3	12.6	104.1	331.6	11.9
75 and more	83.2	250.8	9.0	92.8	231.0	9.4	95.0	276.0	9.8
Education of head									
No high school diploma	28.5	92.1	24.3	21.6	75.8	20.4	26.3	87.2	19.0
High school diploma	43.4	134.4	32.1	41.4	120.6	29.9	50.0	138.2	31.6
Some college	56.4	213.8	15.1	62.6	185.4	17.7	43.2	186.6	19.0
College degree	132.1	416.9	28.5	103.1	363.3	31.9	104.1	361.8	30.5
Race or ethnicity of head									
White non-Hispanic	84.7	261.4	75.1	71.7	237.8	75.1	73.9	244.0	77.5
Nonwhite or Hispanic	6.8	82.1	24.9	16.9	87.9	24.9	16.5	74.4	22.5
Current work status of head									
Professional, managerial	106.6	262.7	16.9	78.8	248.5	16.8	89.3	252.8	15.9
Technical, sales, clerical	40.9	98.9	13.4	48.0	105.4	14.8	43.3	109.3	14.9
Precision production	58.4	94.2	9.6	38.4	85.5	7.0	43.5	79.3	8.2
Machine operators and laborers	23.1	67.2	10.6	23.5	56.8	10.0	37.3	70.0	13.1
Service occupations	9.3	53.2	6.6	15.7	52.9	6.2	15.8	60.0	6.6
Self-employed	200.7	765.4	11.2	155.6	644.3	10.9	152.9	731.5	9.7
Retired	77.5	199.2	25.0	76.3	201.2	26.0	81.6	218.3	25.0
Other not working	0.7	62.9	6.7	5.5	68.5	8.2	4.5	60.4	6.5
Housing status									
Owner	119.9	311.7	63.8	106.1	289.6	63.9	102.3	295.4	64.7
Renter or other	2.4	49.4	36.2	3.6	42.7	36.1	4.5	42.2	35.3

1. For the calendar year preceding the survey.

Source: Arthur B. Kennickell et al., "Family Finances in the U.S.: Recent Evidence from the 1995 Survey of Consumer Finances," *Federal Reserve Bulletin*, January 1997

nificant cuts in their monthly incomes, sometimes by several hundreds, and even many thousands of dollars. In addition, changes in governmental programs, such as Medicare and Social Security, may threaten the economic stability of many elderly and soon-to-be-elderly persons.

The elderly are well represented in every economic bracket — affluence, middle class, and poverty. The major questions are how many elderly are in each segment, how wealth and poverty are defined, and how severe poverty is among the poor elderly.

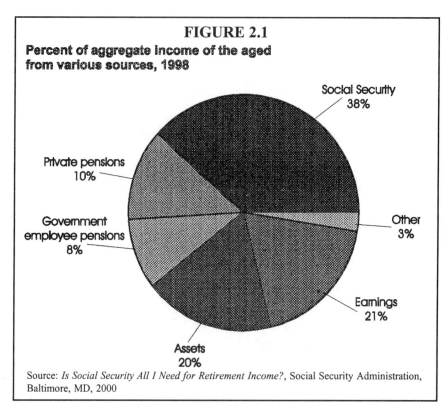

FIGURE 2.1

Percent of aggregate income of the aged from various sources, 1998

Social Security 38%

Private pensions 10%

Government employee pensions 8%

Other 3%

Earnings 21%

Assets 20%

Source: *Is Social Security All I Need for Retirement Income?*, Social Security Administration, Baltimore, MD, 2000

NET WORTH

A person's net worth is the sum of all his or her financial resources, including assets (items of value) and income, minus all debts and liabilities.

Are the Elderly Worth More?

The median net worth of families headed by a person 65 to 74 years old in 1995 (the latest data available), including home equity (the market value of the home less the amount remaining on the mortgage), was $104,100, the highest of any age group except those persons 55 to 64 years of age ($110,800). Those over the age of 75 had a median net worth of $95,000. (See Table 2.1.) These figures seem to support the argument that the elderly are generally more wealthy than the non-elderly. However, many elderly people have fixed incomes, about three-quarters of their equity is in their home, and what they own cannot always be easily converted into cash if needed. Older people often have higher per person living costs.

As shown in Table 2.1, net worth increased for each successive age group through age 64, and then declined. This increase is largely due to the fact that at some time during their lives most people work outside the home, and a working person generally earns more money and accumulates more assets as he or she gets older. By age 65, however, most people are retired from the work force. They must then rely on fixed resources, such as interest income, Social Security, and pension benefits, or compensate by tapping other, perhaps non-replaceable resources, such as savings accounts and investments.

What About the Next Elderly Generation — the Baby Boomers?

These 50+ men and women currently earn almost $2 trillion in annual income, own more than 70 percent of all financial assets in America, and represent 50 percent of all discretionary spending power. — Ken Dychtwald, *Age Power*, 1999

Many people wonder about the condition — financial and otherwise — of those who will be the nation's next senior generation. Ken Dychtwald, in *Age Power: How the 21st Century*

TABLE 2.2

Distribution of Measured Net Worth by Age of Householder and Asset Type: 1993 and 1991

[Excludes group quarters]

Asset type	1993						1991					
	Total	Less than 35 years	35 to 44 years	45 to 54 years	55 to 64 years	65 years and over	Total	Less than 35 years	35 to 44 years	45 to 54 years	55 to 64 years	65 years and over
Total measured net worth	100.0	100.0	100.0	100.0	100.0	100.0	100.0	100.0	100.0	100.0	100.0	100.0
Interest-earning assets at financial institutions	11.4	10.9	7.9	7.7	9.6	16.7	14.3	12.3	9.6	9.5	12.2	21.1
Other interest-earning assets	4.0	2.1	2.5	2.6	4.1	6.1	5.0	1.9	3.0	3.7	5.1	7.3
Checking accounts	0.5	1.2	0.7	0.5	0.4	0.4	0.5	1.2	0.7	0.4	0.4	0.4
Stocks and mutual fund shares	8.3	8.9	6.4	8.1	8.8	9.1	7.1	4.7	5.9	5.4	6.7	9.4
Own home	44.4	43.8	47.7	45.3	42.4	43.6	42.1	42.1	45.3	41.0	41.2	41.6
Rental property	6.7	5.3	6.4	7.2	9.1	5.2	6.5	6.0	7.7	9.1	6.6	4.4
Other real estate	4.6	5.1	5.0	5.5	4.9	3.6	5.4	6.2	5.4	6.8	6.3	4.0
Vehicles	6.4	18.2	8.8	6.5	4.9	3.7	6.4	18.1	8.8	6.4	5.2	3.5
Business or profession.....	6.4	10.6	9.5	9.0	6.1	2.4	7.3	13.5	11.6	10.8	6.8	2.1
U.S. savings bonds........	0.8	1.0	1.2	0.7	0.7	0.8	0.6	0.7	0.5	0.5	0.7	0.6
IRA or Keogh accounts	6.7	3.9	6.3	7.4	8.8	5.7	5.2	3.2	5.7	5.8	7.1	3.8
Other financial investments[1]	3.0	3.6	2.9	2.6	3.0	3.2	3.0	3.5	1.7	4.1	4.3	2.4
Unsecured liabilities[2]	-3.4	-14.5	-5.3	-3.3	-2.8	-0.6	-3.4	-13.6	-5.8	-3.7	-2.6	-0.5

[1]Includes mortgages held from sale of real estate, amount due from sale of business, unit trusts, and other financial investments.
[2]Since net worth is the value of assets less liabilities, unsecured liabilities are subtracted from the distribution of net worth and are shown as negative.

Source: T. J. Eller and Wallace Fraser, *Asset Ownership of Households, 1993*, Bureau of the Census, Washington, DC, 1995

Will Be Ruled by the New Old (1999), reported that in 1995, those 55 to 64 represented the greatest mean net worth ($356,000) of all age groups, compared to $331,000 for those 65 to 74, $277,800 for those 45 to 54, and $276,000 for those 75 and over. Other experts disagree and express concern about what they deem a lack of preparedness of baby boomers (those born between 1946 and 1964) for retirement. (See below.)

SOURCES OF INCOME

Unlike younger people, who may get almost all their income from regular paychecks, the elderly rely on a variety of sources to meet the expenses of daily living. Usually unable to improve their incomes through work, they often are vulnerable to circumstances beyond their control, such as the death of a spouse, health problems, Social Security and Medicare changes, and inflation.

As a group, in 1998, the elderly derived 38 percent of their income from Social Security benefits, 20 percent from assets (returns on stock in-vestments, interest from savings accounts, etc.), 21 percent from earnings, 18 percent from government and private employee pensions, and 3 percent from "other" sources. (See Figure 2.1.) Very few elderly people receive income from all these sources at any one time. In addition, many elderly receive favorable treatment in taxes and government in-kind transfers, such as Medicare, Medicaid, food stamps, and housing assistance.

Social Security

The elderly depend on Social Security for their incomes more than on any other source. In 1998, the Social Security program paid benefits to 90 percent of those over 65. For 63 percent of the elderly, Social Security provided more than 50 percent of their income, and for 18 percent of the elderly, Social Security was their only source of income. As the number of elderly increases in the next decades, the number of Social Security participants will rise. (For more information on Social Security, see below.)

FIGURE 2.2

Retirees with Income from Assets have Higher Retirement Income

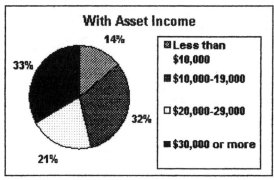

With Asset Income

- ☒ Less than $10,000
- ▨ $10,000-19,000
- ☐ $20,000-29,000
- ■ $30,000 or more

14%
33%
32%
21%

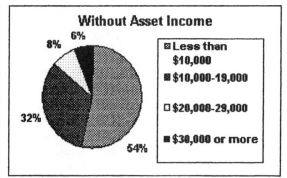

Without Asset Income

- ☒ Less than $10,000
- ▨ $10,000-19,000
- ☐ $20,000-29,000
- ■ $30,000 or more

6%
8%
32%
54%

Source: Income of the Aged Chartbook, 1996

Source: *Is Social Security All I Need for Retirement Income?*, Social Security Administration, Baltimore, MD, 2000

Assets and Earnings

The percentage of employed men age 65 and older has declined over the past few decades. In 1997, there were 3.8 million employed people over 65. (For more information on employment among the elderly, see Chapter IV.)

The trend toward earlier retirement has led to a decline in the role of earnings in supporting the aged. As earnings account for a smaller proportion of income, assets and pensions have become more important. Assets represent one-fifth of the income of the elderly. It must be emphasized that this is an average figure; while some elderly have large assets, one-third of the elderly have *no* income from assets.

The elderly hold more assets than the non-elderly because of people's tendency to accumulate savings, home equity, and property over their lifetimes. Older Americans will usually have a greater percentage of their assets in bank accounts (23.2 percent) than the non-elderly (Table 2.2).

In all age groups, home equity accounts for most of the household's net worth. In 1993 (the latest Census Bureau data available), it represented 43.6 percent of net worth of households headed by an elderly householder. Nevertheless, regardless of how valuable a home might be, it cannot be used for daily expenses. Generally, the only time a house provides any monetary value to the owner is when it is sold, and even then, new accommodations must be found and paid for. Many older people have lived in their homes for a long time and do not want to move. Money can often be borrowed against the value of a home, but elderly people may be reluctant to take on any new debt, especially if they are on a fixed income, and they may fear losing their home.

Although the elderly maintain the greatest percentages in bank accounts, these assets are not "fixed" in the strict sense because they do represent available cash. Many older people, however, are reluctant to "touch their savings" except in an extreme emergency. They know that one major or prolonged illness can use up a lifetime of savings. Many elderly reserve their savings for illness or long-term care, such as residence in a nursing home — costs that can wipe out all their financial reserves.

Changing Assets

Numbers such as net worth do not always accurately describe the condition of elderly people. Some older people in the United States are, indeed, very rich. When their wealth is averaged into in-

TABLE 2.3
NUMBER OF RETIREMENT PLANS 1950–1997

	1950	1960	1970	1975	1980	1985	1990	1994	1997
Private Industry	a	a	a	311,094	488,901	632,135	712,308	690,344	700,000
Defined benefit	a	a	a	103,346	148,096	170,172	113,062	74,422	53,000
Defined contribution	a	a	a	207,748	340,805	461,963	599,245	615,922	647,000
State and Local Governments[b]	a	2,346	2,304	3,075	3,075	2,589	2,387	a	a
Federal Government	2	2	2	2	2	2	4	4	4

[a]Data not available.

[b]Because of data availability, past years for state and local governments do not match with other categories. The data years for state and local governments apply to the years in the table headings: 1960 is represented with 1962 data, 1970 is represented with 1971–1972 data, and 1975 is represented with 1976–1977 data, 1980 is represented with 1981 data.

Source: *Facts from EBRI*, Employee Benefit Research Institute, Washington, DC, www.ebri.org

come and asset statistics, it masks the fact that a large number of old people live below the poverty level (see below).

Retirees who have income from assets generally have higher retirement income, sometimes twice as much. Among those with asset income in 1996, 33 percent had annual incomes of $30,000 or more, while 14 percent received less than $10,000. For those with no asset income, only 6 percent received annual incomes of $30,000 or more, and 54 percent had annual incomes of less than $10,000. (See Figure 2.2.)

Pension (Retirement) Funds

Many large companies, along with most local and state governments and the federal government, offer pension plans. (The first employer-provided retirement plan in the United States was started in 1875.) Employees are eligible for pension benefits when they retire or leave a company if they have worked for the company for a designated number of years and/or have reached a specified age. A pension benefit is usually money in the form of a monthly check beginning at retirement and ending at death. A few companies pay for 100 percent of pension benefits, but more commonly, companies provide a portion of the benefits, and employees contribute a percentage of their salaries to the pension fund during their working years.

Employers are not required to provide pensions. In addition, pension plans do not have to include all workers; they may exclude certain jobs and/or individuals. Before 1976, pension plans could require an employee to work a lifetime for one company before being eligible for pension

TABLE 2.4
TOTAL RETIREMENT PLAN PARTICIPANTS 1950–1997

	1950	1960	1970	1975	1980	1985	1990	1994	1997[a]
					(millions)				
Private Industry	b	b	b	44.5	57.9	74.7	76.9	85.1	86.0
Defined benefit	b	b	b	33.0	38.0	39.7	38.8	40.3	40.0
Defined contribution	b	b	b	11.5	19.9	35.0	38.1	44.8	46.0
State and Local Governments[c]	b	5.4	9.1	11.0	14.7	15.2	16.9	13.3	b
Federal Government	b	b	b	b	6.4[d]	8.6	10.7	10.8	b

[a]Estimates.

[b]Data not available.

[c]Because of data availability, past years for state and local governments do not match with other categories. The data years for state and local governments apply to the years in the table headings: 1960 is represented with 1962 data, 1970 is represented with 1971–1972 data, 1975 is represented with 1976–1977 data, and 1980 is represented with 1981 data.

[d]Data are for 1981.

Source: *Facts from EBRI*, Employee Benefit Research Institute, Washington, DC, www.ebri.org

TABLE 2.5

ACTIVE RETIREMENT PLAN PARTICIPANTS AS A PERCENTAGE OF THE WORK FORCE 1950–1994

	1950	1960	1970	1975	1980	1985	1990	1994
Private Industry	25.0%	40.8%	45.1%	45.1%	45.9%	45.8%	44.8%	45.1%
Defined benefit	a	a	a	39.4	38.0	32.7	27.8	24.3
Defined contribution	a	a	a	5.8	7.9	13.1	17.0	20.7
State and Local Governments[b]	a	72.4	76.7	77.2	78.8	75.8	74.3	72.0

[a]Data not available.

[b]Because of data availability, past years for state and local governments do not match with other categories. The data years for state and local governments apply to the years in the table headings: 1960 is represented with 1962 data, 1970 is represented with 1971–1972 data, 1975 is represented with 1976–1977 data, and 1980 is represented with 1981 data.

Source: *Facts from EBRI*, Employee Benefit Research Institute, Washington, DC, www.ebri.org

benefits. As required by the Employee Retirement Income Security Act of 1974 (ERISA — see below), as of 1976, an employee becomes eligible after 10 years of service. Most current plans require five years of work before an employee becomes vested (eligible for benefits).

The Social Security Administration reports that, in 1962, private pensions accounted for 3 percent of the income for the elderly. By 1998, private pensions supplied 10 percent of older persons' income. (The spouse of a person who actually participated in a pension plan is also considered a recipient.) Government employee pensions also provided 8 percent of the total income of the aged. (See Figure 2.1.)

The number of private and federal pension plans have risen. In 1975, private industry offered 311,094 retirement plans; by 1997, employees were covered by 700,000 private pensions. (See Table 2.3.) Total participation in private retirement plans rose from 44.5 million persons in 1975 to approximately 86 million people in 1997 (Table 2.4). The percentage of pension participants in the labor force has remained relatively stable since 1970 — about 45 percent in private pension plans and 72 percent in state and local government plans (Table 2.5).

Employees in larger firms were more likely than those in smaller firms to be covered. Highly paid workers were more likely to have coverage, as were workers in industries covered by union contracts. White-collar workers were somewhat more likely to receive pensions than blue-collar.

Pension coverage is greater among Whites than Blacks or Hispanics and is strongly related to a worker's wage level. Also, employer pensions are more prevalent in goods-producing industries than in service-producing industries. There are fewer government pension plans than private plans, but average benefits are substantially larger.

Women over the age of 65 are much less likely to have worked outside the home than are younger women; therefore, they are less likely to have access to pension and Social Security income in their own name. The U.S. Department of Labor, in *Retirement Benefits of American Workers* (1995), reported the percentage of people receiving pension benefits in 1994 and the median amounts. The older the recipient, the lower the amount of pension received. The median annual amount for an 80-year-old woman was $1,356; a man that age received $4,140 a year. (See Table 2.6.) This is likely to change, however, because of the large increase in the number of women who have entered the labor force over the past two decades. In the future, it is expected that many women over 65 will have earned their own pension and Social Security benefits.

Unlike Social Security, most pension plans do not provide automatic cost-of-living adjustments, which can gradually erode retirees' incomes. Persons receiving pensions from the military, the government, or Railroad Retirement were more likely to receive increases than were those receiving pensions from the private sector.

The proportion of retirees receiving pension benefits is expected to rise over the next 20 to 30 years because of growth in coverage and vesting. By 2018, the percentage of elderly households receiving pension benefits is projected to reach 88 percent. This growth will reflect the increasing coverage of women by pension plans due to the continually increasing numbers of women in the labor force. However, some sources contend that downsizing efforts by many companies may reduce benefits.

Federal Pension Laws

A company that has a pension plan will often invest the money put into the plan in an investment fund (for example, stocks or bonds), much as a bank does with its depositors' money. If the investment choice is a good one, the company makes a profit on the money in the fund; a bad investment results in a loss. During the early 1970s, several major plans collapsed, leaving retirees without benefits even though they had contributed to a plan for many years.

These collapses led to the passage in 1974 of the Employment Retirement Income Security Act (ERISA; PL 93-406). ERISA established participation and vesting (eligibility for benefits) guidelines and standards to ensure that funds are managed in the best interest of plan participants. It also created the Pension Benefit Guaranty Corporation, a federal agency, to take over benefit payments when underfunded plans are terminated. (See Table 2.7 for laws relating to pensions.)

Before 1983, some plans paid lower monthly benefits to women because, statistically, women lived longer than men and, on average, collected pension benefits for a longer period of time. In 1983, the Supreme Court, in *Arizona Governing Committee for Tax Deferred Annuity and Deferred Compensation Plan v. Natalie Norris* (463 U.S. 1073), ruled that pension plans must make payments based on gender-neutral actuarial tables (statistical calculations for insurance purposes).

The Retirement Equity Act of 1984 (PL 98-397) requires pension plans to pay a survivor's benefit to the spouse of a deceased vested plan participant. Prior to 1984, some spouses received no benefits unless the employee was near retirement age at the time of death. Under the 1984 law, pension vesting begins at age 21 or after five years on the job, and employees who have a break in employment for reasons such as maternity leave will not lose any time already accumulated.

TABLE 2.6

Private Pension Annuity Recipients and Median Annual Pension Benefit by Sex, Race, and Age, September 1994[1]

| | Women Receiving Annuities | | Men Receiving Annuities | |
	Percentage	Median Amount (in dollars)	Percentage	Median Amount (in dollars)
Distribution by age				
40–54	5.0	9,600	4.9	12;000
55–59	6.5	4,620	7.6	11,784
60–64	15.2	4,032	16.6	10,860
65–69	24.0	3,204	25.3	9,000
70–74	22.2	3,576	20.1	7,140
75–79	14.5	2,112	14.1	6,000
80 and over	12.7	1,356	11.3	4,140
Distribution by race				
White	89.8	3,000	94.6	7,800
Black	8.3	3,240	4.0	6,000
All other races	1.9	—	1.4	—
Distribution by education level				
Not high school graduate	23.8	1,476	27.3	5,280
High school graduate	44.3	3,300	32.9	7,200
Some college but less than a bachelor's degree	21.8	3,600	20.5	10,800
Bachelor's degree	6.8	5,088	11.9	12,000
Master's degree or more	3.2	—	7.4	14,400
Total number (in thousands)	2,249	3,000	4,945	7,800

[1]Percentages may not 100.0 due to rounding.

Source: U.S. Department of Labor, *Retirement Benefits of American Workers*, 1995, Table D1.

Source: Anne J. Stone and Jennifer E. Griffith, *Older Women: The Economics of Aging*, Women's Research & Education Institute, Washington, DC, 1998

TABLE 2.7

Significant federal legislation affecting retirement income plans:

- 1921—The Revenue Act of 1921 exempted from current taxation interest income on trusts holding stock bonus or profit-sharing plans. Under this act, trust income was taxed as it was distributed to employees only to the extent that it exceeded employees' own contributions. The act did not authorize deductions for past service contributions.
- 1926—The Revenue Act of 1926 exempted income of pension trusts from current taxation.
- 1928—The Revenue Act of 1928 allowed employers to take tax deductions for reasonable amounts paid into a qualified trust in excess of the amount required to fund current liabilities. It changed the taxation of trust distributions that are attributable to employer contributions and earnings.
- 1935—The Social Security Act was signed into law.
- 1942—The Revenue Act of 1942 tightened standard qualifications for pension plans, limited allowable deductions, and allowed integration of plans with Social Security.
- 1948—The National Labor Relations Board ruled that Congress intended pensions to be part of wages and to fall under "conditions of employment" mentioned in the act, although the term was not specifically defined.
- 1974—The Employee Retirement Income Security Act of 1974 (ERISA) was passed. It was designed to secure the benefits of participants in private pension plans through participation, vesting, funding, reporting, and disclosure rules, and established the Pension Benefit Guaranty Corporation (PBGC). ERISA provided added pension incentives for the self-employed (through changes in Keoghs) and for persons not covered by pensions (through individual retirement accounts (IRAs)). It established the legal status of employee stock ownership plans (ESOPs) as an employee benefit, codified stock bonus plans under the Internal Revenue Code (IRC), and established requirements for plan implementation and operation.
- 1978—The Revenue Act of 1978 established qualified deferred compensation plans (sec. 401(k)) under which employees are not taxed on the portion of income they elect to receive as deferred compensation rather than direct cash payments. It created simplified employee pensions (SEPs) and changed IRA rules.
- 1996—The Small Business Job Protection Act of 1996 created the savings incentive match for employees (SIMPLE) for small establishments.
- 1997—The Taxpayer Relief Act of 1997 created a new, nondeductible IRA, the Roth IRA, which can be used to save for retirement, first-time home purchase, and college expenses. More individuals are eligible for a Roth IRA than for a deductible IRA.

Source: *Facts from EBRI*, Employee Benefit Research Institute, Washington, DC, www.ebri.org

Problems with Pension Management

A variety of flaws bedevil the American pension system, some of which may deprive retired workers of part, or all, of their pensions. A 1995 audit by the federal Pension Benefit Guaranty Corporation, a Washington, DC-based advocacy group, found an 8 percent error rate in the administration of pension payments, and some sources believe it is higher.

A major trouble spot arises from corporate mergers and downsizings. Employees may lose out when dissimilar pension plans are consolidated. Problems also arise when widows and divorced spouses fail to get a rightful share of their spouses' pensions. Spouses are often entitled to pension benefits, but terms must be included in divorce decrees or filed with a plan administrator. Divorce lawyers or judges may fail to include pensions when dividing assets, or wives may unknowingly sign away their rights. Pension calculations are often very complicated, and errors are easily made in calculating amounts due.

IRAs and 401(k)s — The Shift Toward Self-Reliance

Individual Retirement Accounts (IRAs) were first established in 1974 as a means of retirement savings for those not covered by pensions. Another thrift plan, which is employer-provided, is the 401(k). An employee may have both a pension and a 401(k).

During and immediately following the Great Depression, when so many people felt vulnerable to poverty, America developed a "one-for-all" or "we're all in this together" economic system. New government safety nets, such as Social Security, came into existence, and corporations took on new responsibilities for the well-being of their workers. This communal system is giving way to a do-it-yourself approach that increasingly asks Americans to make their own way. (Other signs are the trends in Americans assuming more responsibility for their own health insurance premiums, once covered by corporations, and new more demanding hurdles to staying on welfare.) Consequently, many workers are increasingly financing their own retirements by means of savings plans such as 401(k)s and IRAs.

The Investment Company Institute (ICI), a national association of investment industry groups, reported in 1999 that in companies offering 401(k) plans, approximately 77 percent of their employees were enrolled. Eighty-nine percent of companies match employees' contributions, most commonly at the rate of $0.50 per dollar. An estimated 30 million households — 30 percent — had IRAs in 1998.

The Employee Benefit Research Institute (EBRI), a non-profit organization that researches

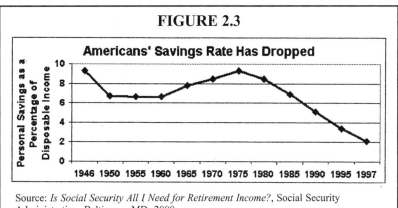

FIGURE 2.3

Source: *Is Social Security All I Need for Retirement Income?*, Social Security Administration, Baltimore, MD, 2000

economic policy, conducted a study with the ICI (*The EBRI-ICI 401(k) Plan Participant-Directed Retirement Plan Data Collection Project*) on worker pension investments. EBRI reported, in 1999, that 401(k) plans provided substantial retirement income for workers with long participation in the plans. For example, workers in their 60s with 30 years tenure had an average account balance in excess of $156,000. Those in their 50s had balances in excess of $117,000.

Family Support

While the contribution by the family, both in financial support and the value of the care and time they give to an elderly parent or relative, has not been statistically determined, numerous studies suggest that it is substantial. According to these

TABLE 2.8

Comparison of Summary Measures of Income by Selected Characteristics: 1989, 1997, and 1998

[Households and people as of March of the following year. For meaning of symbols, see text]

Characteristics	1998			Median income in 1997 (in 1998 dollars)		Median income in 1989ʳ (in 1998 dollars)		Percent change in real income 1997 to 1998		Percent change in real income 1989ʳ to 1998	
		Median income									
	Number (1,000)	Value (dollars)	90-percent confidence interval (+/–) (dollars)	Value (dollars)	90-percent confidence interval (+/–) (dollars)	Value (dollars)	90-percent confidence interval (+/–) (dollars)	Percent change	90-percent confidence interval (+/–)	Percent change	90-percent confidence interval (+/–)
HOUSEHOLDS											
All households	103,874	38,885	378	37,581	286	37,884	344	*3.5	0.6	*2.6	0.8
Age of Householder											
15 to 24 years.	5,770	23,564	730	22,935	822	24,401	755	2.7	2.4	–3.4	2.6
25 to 34 years.	18,819	40,069	696	38,769	755	39,041	603	*3.4	1.3	*2.6	1.5
35 to 44 years.	23,968	48,451	730	47,081	637	49,310	675	*2.9	1.0	–1.7	1.2
45 to 54 years.	20,158	54,148	877	52,683	727	54,575	893	*2.8	1.1	–0.8	1.4
55 to 64 years.	13,571	43,167	989	42,000	763	40,569	878	*2.8	1.5	*6.4	2.0

Source: *Money Income in the United States, 1998*, Bureau of the Census, Washington, DC, 1999

TABLE 2.9

Median Income of People by Selected Characteristics: 1998, 1997, and 1996

[People 15 years old and over as of March of the following year. An asterisk (*) preceding percent change indicates statistically significant change at the 90-percent confidence level. For meaning of symbols, see text]

Characteristic	1998			1997			1996			Percent change in real median income (1997-1998)
	Number with income (1,000)	Median income		Number with income (1,000)	Median income		Number with income (1,000)	Median income		
		Value (dollars)	Standard error (dollars)		Value (dollars)	Standard error (dollars)		Value (dollars)	Standard error (dollars)	
TOTAL										
Male										
All males	94 948	26 492	128	94 168	25 212	123	93 439	23 834	157	* 3.5
Age										
Under 65 years	81 447	28 355	226	80 860	26 629	129	80 265	25 548	130	* 4.8
15 to 24 years	14 079	8 190	222	13 905	7 468	154	14 016	6 960	127	* 8.0
25 to 34 years	18 330	28 117	379	18 936	25 996	179	19 354	25 179	194	* 6.5
35 to 44 years	21 539	35 177	287	21 456	32 851	444	21 181	32 167	216	* 5.4
45 to 54 years	16 821	38 922	587	16 203	37 624	436	15 748	36 232	312	1.9
55 to 64 years	10 678	32 776	627	10 361	31 157	393	9 966	29 526	583	* 3.6
65 years and over	13 501	18 166	224	13 308	17 768	228	13 173	16 684	221	0.7
65 to 74 years	7 902	19 734	329	7 843	19 651	311	7 947	18 605	338	−1.1
Female										
All females	98 694	14 430	102	97 447	13 703	108	96 558	12 815	106	* 3.7
Age										
Under 65 years	80 501	16 096	119	79 354	15 408	112	78 532	14 476	130	* 2.9
15 to 24 years	13 875	6 534	120	13 626	6 342	110	13 502	5 881	116	1.4
25 to 34 years	17 773	18 257	281	18 081	17 647	235	18 481	16 384	224	1.9
35 to 44 years	20 970	20 285	224	20 809	18 706	310	20 637	18 447	288	* 6.8
45 to 54 years	16 915	21 588	244	16 231	20 534	236	15 693	19 046	284	* 3.5
55 to 64 years	10 968	14 675	309	10 607	14 376	332	10 220	13 316	335	0.5
65 years and over	18 193	10 504	114	18 093	10 062	112	18 026	9 626	84	* 2.8
65 to 74 years	9 545	10 453	185	9 571	10 141	182	9 642	9 656	128	1.5

Source: *Money Income in the United States, 1998*, Bureau of the Census, Washington, DC, 1999

studies, income from Social Security plays a minor role compared to the amount of support contributed by family members. When elderly persons outlive their family members, they are often faced with serious problems of financial security and personal care.

Although nobody knows the exact extent of financial support given to aging parents by their children, most sources believe that 10 to 12 percent of the work force is caring for older parents in some capacity. Andrew Scharlach, professor at the University of California at Berkeley, predicts that, by 2020, 1 in 3 people will have to provide care for an elderly parent, much of that in the form of financial assistance. The Conference Board, a business research group, estimates as many as 40 percent will be affected during the early twenty-first century. (For more information on elder care, see Chapter VIII.)

Personal Savings

The more personal savings put aside for retirement, the higher the retirement income. Personal savings rates in the United States have fallen since World War II — from 9.3 percent of disposable income in 1946 to 2.1 percent in 1997 (Figure 2.3).

Many sources have claimed that baby boomers, who will be entering retirement within the next two decades, are not saving adequately for retirement. The American Association of Retired Persons (AARP), in *Do Baby Boomers Save and, If So, What For?* (Washington, DC, 1999), studied the savings practices of baby boomers. The study concluded that while the typical boomer has accumulated just over $40,000 in total net worth, not including Social Security and pension wealth, they will be better off than their parents. The AARP believes that boomers are closer to reaching attainable retirement savings targets than many have suggested primarily because of their involvement in the stock market surge.

MEDIAN INCOME

In 1998, the elderly had the lowest median incomes of all age groups. The median income for a household headed by someone 65 years and older

TABLE 2.10

Women's Income as a Percent of Men's Income: 1947 to 1997

[People 15 years old and over beginning with March 1980, and people 14 years old and over as of March of the following year for previous years]

Year	Percent	Year	Percent	Year	Percent	Year	Percent
1997	54.4	1984	44.0	1971 [12]	34.9	1958	31.4
1996	53.8	1983	43.2	1970	33.5	1957	32.6
1995	53.8	1982	42.2	1969	33.2	1956	31.9
1994	52.8	1981	40.5	1968	33.8	1955	33.4
1993	52.3	1980	39.3	1967 [11]	32.4	1954	36.3
1992	52.4	1979	36.9	1966 [10]	30.9	1953	36.2
1991	51.2	1978	37.2	1965 [9]	30.3	1952 [6]	36.9
1990	49.6	1977	38.9	1964	31.2	1951	35.4
1989	48.4	1976	37.9	1963	30.4	1950	37.1
1988	47.0	1975	38.2	1962 [8]	30.7	1949 [5]	40.9
1987	46.6	1974	36.5	1961 [7]	30.5	1948	42.1
1986	44.5	1973	34.7	1960	30.9	1947 [4]	45.6
1985	44.2	1972	34.9	1959	30.6		

Source: *Measuring 50 years of Economic Change*, Bureau of the Census, Washington, DC, 1998

was $21,729, just half the income of those 55 to 64 years of age ($43,167) (Table 2.8). The median income of individuals over the age of 65 was $18,166 for males and $10,054 for females. Income typically declines after age 65 as people retire and are not receiving income from a job. (See Table 2.9.) Among men 75 and older, median income was $16,479; for women of 75 and older, $10,545.

Income Inequality Between the Sexes

Women of all ages lag behind men in wages and income. In 1997, women's wages were about 54.4 percent of men's earnings. (See Table 2.10.) The wage gap, however, increases with age.

The already lower women's income increases until age 45, the peak of a woman's earnings, while men's income peaks a decade later. This results in substantial differences in male and female income among the elderly and in differences in pensions and Social Security payments, which are based on earnings.

Many factors contribute to this wage gap, among them differences in education, experience, and union affiliation. The lower incomes of older women are, to some extent, associated with their greater likelihood of lifelong economic dependence on men. Women traditionally have had broken work histories, with time spent out of the labor force while they raise families and the correspond-

ing lower wages and seniority. Many sources, however, believe that the primary reason is job segregation. Older women often work in more traditional "women's occupations," which are generally lower paying. More than half of women hold jobs in sales, clerical, and service jobs, and that is particularly so among older women. In addition, unflattering stereotypes of older women as weak, incapable, and inflexible also encourage discrimination against women from mid-life on.

The Older Women's League reported that, in 1995, among retired workers receiving Social Security benefits based on their own work records, women's average monthly benefits were $538, compared to an average of $858 for men. In addition, just 13 percent of women over 65 had private pensions, compared to 33 percent of older men. The mean private pension for women was $3,940 a year, compared to $7,468 for men.

EXPENSES

The elderly tend to spend their money differently from younger people. Older households spend less than younger households because they have less money to spend, fewer people to support, and different needs and values. In 1998, the annual expenditure for those older than 65 was $24,721, lower than all other age groups except those under the age of 25. Those over 75 spent only $20,987, the least of all the elderly. The greatest amounts

TABLE 2.11

Age of reference person: Shares of average annual expenditures and sources of income, Consumer Expenditure Survey, 1998

Item	All consumer units	Under 25	25-34	35-44	45-54	55-64	65 and over	65-74	75 and over
Number of consumer units (in thousands)	107,182	8,255	19,969	24,241	20,058	12,829	21,830	11,874	9,957
Consumer unit characteristics:									
Income before taxes [1]	$41,622	$16,839	$41,782	$50,894	$58,705	$44,238	$24,011	$27,037	$20,229
Income after taxes [1]	38,358	15,973	38,430	46,762	53,257	40,834	22,892	25,654	19,442
Age of reference person	47.6	21.4	29.7	39.5	49.2	59.4	74.7	69.3	81.0
Average number in consumer unit:									
Persons	2.5	1.8	2.8	3.3	2.7	2.2	1.7	1.9	1.5
Children under 18	.7	.4	1.1	1.4	.6	.2	.1	.1	([2])
Persons 65 and over	.3	([2])	([2])	([2])	([2])	.1	1.4	1.4	1.3
Earners	1.3	1.2	1.5	1.7	1.8	1.3	.4	.6	.2
Vehicles	2.0	1.1	1.8	2.2	2.5	2.3	1.5	1.8	1.2
Percent distribution:									
Sex of reference person:									
Male	58	52	58	59	63	61	51	57	45
Female	42	48	42	41	37	39	49	43	55
Housing tenure:									
Homeowner	64	10	43	69	77	78	80	83	76
With mortgage	39	7	37	58	57	38	15	21	9
Without mortgage	26	3	6	11	20	40	65	63	67
Renter	36	90	57	31	23	22	20	17	24
Race of reference person:									
Black	12	12	14	14	12	11	9	10	7
White and other	88	88	86	86	88	89	91	90	93
Education of reference person:									
Elementary (1-8)	7	2	3	3	4	9	17	14	21
High school (9-12)	39	33	36	39	32	45	46	47	45
College	54	65	62	58	63	46	36	38	33
Never attended and other	([3])	([4])	([3])	([3])	([3])	1	1	1	1
At least one vehicle owned or leased	87	67	88	91	93	90	81	87	75
Average annual expenditures	$35,535	$19,436	$34,779	$42,154	$45,475	$37,329	$24,721	$27,830	$20,987
Food	13.5	15.8	13.2	13.6	13.2	13.1	14.0	13.9	14.1
Food at home	7.8	7.8	7.3	7.9	7.5	7.6	9.2	8.8	9.7
Cereals and bakery products	1.2	1.2	1.1	1.2	1.1	1.1	1.5	1.4	1.6
Cereals and cereal products	.4	.4	.4	.4	.4	.3	.5	.4	.5
Bakery products	.8	.7	.7	.8	.7	.8	1.0	.9	1.1
Meats, poultry, fish, and eggs	2.0	1.8	1.8	2.1	2.0	2.1	2.4	2.3	2.4
Beef	.6	.6	.6	.6	.6	.6	.7	.7	.7
Pork	.4	.3	.3	.4	.4	.5	.5	.5	.6
Other meats	.3	.2	.2	.3	.2	.2	.3	.3	.3
Poultry	.4	.3	.4	.4	.4	.4	.4	.4	.4
Fish and seafood	.3	.2	.2	.3	.3	.3	.3	.4	.3
Eggs	.1	.1	.1	.1	.1	.1	.1	.1	.1
Dairy products	.8	.9	.8	.9	.8	.8	1.0	.9	1.1
Fresh milk and cream	.3	.4	.3	.4	.3	.3	.4	.4	.5
Other dairy products	.5	.5	.5	.5	.5	.5	.6	.6	.6
Fruits and vegetables	1.3	1.3	1.2	1.2	1.3	1.4	1.7	1.6	1.9
Fresh fruits	.4	.4	.4	.4	.4	.5	.6	.5	.6
Fresh vegetables	.4	.4	.4	.4	.4	.4	.5	.5	.6
Processed fruits	.3	.3	.3	.3	.3	.3	.4	.3	.4
Processed vegetables	.2	.2	.2	.2	.2	.2	.3	.3	.3

See footnotes at end of table.

(continued)

were spent on housing (including utilities), food, transportation, and health care. Not surprisingly, the elderly spent more of their money on health care than any other age group, both in actual dollars and in percentage of expenditures. They spent less on entertainment, tobacco and smoking products, alcoholic beverages, apparel, food eaten away from home, and vehicle-related items than other groups. (See Table 2.11.)

One measure of the economic differences among the elderly is shown in those who have dis-

TABLE 2.11 (Continued)

Age of reference person: Shares of average annual expenditures and sources of income, Consumer Expenditure Survey, 1998 — Continued

Item	All consumer units	Under 25	25-34	35-44	45-54	55-64	65 and over	65-74	75 and over
Other food at home	2.4	2.7	2.4	2.5	2.3	2.3	2.6	2.5	2.7
Sugar and other sweets	.3	.3	.3	.3	.3	.3	.4	.4	.4
Fats and oils	.2	.2	.2	.2	.2	.2	.3	.3	.3
Miscellaneous foods	1.1	1.3	1.1	1.1	1.0	.9	1.1	1.1	1.2
Nonalcoholic beverages	.6	.8	.6	.7	.6	.6	.7	.7	.7
Food prepared by consumer unit on out-of-town trips	.2	.1	.1	.1	.2	.2	.2	.2	.1
Food away from home	5.7	8.0	5.8	5.8	5.7	5.5	4.8	5.1	4.3
Alcoholic beverages	.9	1.6	1.1	.8	.8	.8	.8	.8	.7
Housing	33.0	31.6	34.5	33.6	31.1	32.1	33.9	32.6	36.0
Shelter	18.8	19.5	20.8	19.9	17.8	16.9	17.3	16.5	18.5
Owned dwellings	11.9	2.1	10.1	14.1	12.9	12.0	11.4	11.8	10.8
Mortgage interest and charges	6.9	1.3	7.2	9.5	7.8	6.0	2.7	3.2	1.8
Property taxes	2.9	.4	1.8	2.8	3.1	3.3	4.4	4.3	4.5
Maintenance, repairs, insurance, other expenses	2.2	.4	1.2	1.9	2.1	2.7	4.3	4.2	4.5
Rented dwellings	5.6	16.2	9.9	4.8	3.2	3.3	4.4	3.1	6.6
Other lodging	1.3	1.2	.8	1.0	1.7	1.6	1.5	1.7	1.1
Utilities, fuels, and public services	6.8	5.9	6.4	6.4	6.4	7.0	8.8	8.5	9.2
Natural gas	.8	.5	.7	.7	.7	.9	1.2	1.0	1.4
Electricity	2.6	2.1	2.3	2.4	2.4	2.7	3.6	3.5	3.7
Fuel oil and other fuels	.2	.1	.2	.2	.2	.3	.4	.4	.5
Telephone services	2.3	2.9	2.6	2.2	2.2	2.2	2.4	2.4	2.4
Water and other public services	.8	.3	.6	.8	.8	.9	1.2	1.1	1.3
Household operations	1.5	1.0	2.0	1.7	1.1	1.2	1.9	1.4	2.7
Personal services	.7	.7	1.4	1.0	.3	.2	.5	.2	1.0
Other household expenses	.8	.3	.5	.7	.8	1.0	1.4	1.2	1.7
Housekeeping supplies	1.4	1.0	1.1	1.3	1.2	2.0	1.6	1.5	1.7
Laundry and cleaning supplies	.3	.3	.3	.3	.3	.3	.4	.4	.4
Other household products	.7	.5	.4	.6	.5	1.3	.7	.7	.7
Postage and stationery	.4	.3	.3	.4	.3	.4	.5	.5	.5
Household furnishings and equipment	4.5	4.3	4.4	4.3	4.7	5.0	4.4	4.7	3.9
Household textiles	.3	.2	.3	.3	.3	.4	.4	.5	.2
Furniture	1.1	.8	1.3	1.1	1.0	1.1	.9	1.0	.8
Floor coverings	.4	5.1	.1	.3	.6	.4	.6	.7	.6
Major appliances	.5	.5	.4	.5	.4	.5	.5	.5	.5
Small appliances, miscellaneous housewares	.2	.3	.2	.2	.2	.3	.2	.3	.2
Miscellaneous household equipment	2.1	2.3	2.1	1.9	2.1	2.4	1.7	1.8	1.6
Apparel and services	4.7	5.8	5.1	5.2	4.8	4.0	3.3	3.7	2.6
Men and boys	1.1	1.3	1.2	1.3	1.2	.9	.7	.8	.5
Men, 16 and over	.9	1.1	.9	.9	1.0	.8	.6	.7	.5
Boys, 2 to 15	.2	.1	.3	.4	.2	.1	.1	.1	(2)
Women and girls	1.8	2.1	1.7	2.0	2.0	1.6	1.5	1.5	1.3
Women, 16 and over	1.5	2.0	1.3	1.6	1.8	1.4	1.4	1.4	1.2
Girls, 2 to 15	.3	.2	.4	.5	.2	.1	.1	.1	.1
Children under 2	.2	.5	.4	.2	.1	.1	.1	.1	5.1
Footwear	.8	1.1	.8	.9	.8	.6	.5	.6	.4
Other apparel products and services	.8	.9	1.0	.7	.8	.8	.5	.6	.4
Transportation	18.6	21.3	19.3	18.7	18.7	19.0	16.3	17.9	13.8
Vehicle purchases (net outlay)	8.3	10.7	8.9	8.8	8.2	8.2	6.4	7.3	5.1
Cars and trucks, new	3.9	2.5	3.4	4.2	4.2	4.4	3.3	3.3	3.2
Cars and trucks, used	4.3	7.7	5.3	4.5	3.9	3.8	2.9	3.6	1.8
Other vehicles	.1	5.6	.1	.1	.1	(2)	5.3	5.4	5.1
Gasoline and motor oil	2.9	3.4	2.9	2.9	2.9	2.9	2.6	2.9	2.2

See footnotes at end of table.

(continued)

cretionary income, that is, money left over after the person has paid everything needed to maintain his or her standard of living. Many sources believe that those over the age of 65 have a smaller percentage of discretionary income than all groups except persons under 24, although most experts estimate that at least one-quarter of the elderly have some discretionary income. In 1999, the Conference Board, a marketing research firm, estimated that those 45 to 54 accounted for 19 percent of all households and 20 percent of all discretionary income. Those 55 to 64 made up 13 percent of households and held 13 percent of discretionary income. Americans 65 to 74 were 11 percent of households

TABLE 2.11 (Continued)

Age of reference person: Shares of average annual expenditures and sources of income, Consumer Expenditure Survey, 1998 — Continued

Item	All consumer units	Under 25	25-34	35-44	45-54	55-64	65 and over	65-74	75 and over
Other vehicle expenses	6.2	6.0	6.5	6.1	6.4	6.4	5.6	5.9	5.2
Vehicle finance charges	.9	1.1	1.2	.9	.9	.8	.5	.6	.2
Maintenance and repairs	1.8	1.8	1.6	1.8	1.9	1.9	1.9	1.9	1.9
Vehicle insurance	2.1	2.0	2.0	1.9	2.2	2.2	2.2	2.3	2.1
Vehicle rental, leases, licenses, other charges	1.4	1.2	1.7	1.5	1.4	1.6	1.0	1.1	.9
Public transportation	1.2	1.2	1.1	.9	1.2	1.5	1.6	1.8	1.3
Health care	5.4	2.3	3.4	4.0	4.8	5.8	11.9	10.5	14.0
Health insurance	2.6	1.1	1.7	1.9	2.1	2.7	6.2	5.6	7.2
Medical services	1.5	.7	1.1	1.3	1.6	1.7	2.4	2.1	2.9
Drugs	1.0	.4	.4	.6	.8	1.2	2.7	2.4	3.2
Medical supplies	.3	.1	.2	.2	.3	.3	.6	.5	.8
Entertainment	4.9	5.0	5.1	5.3	4.7	5.1	4.2	4.7	3.5
Fees and admissions	1.3	1.4	1.2	1.2	1.4	1.2	1.2	1.2	1.1
Television, radios, sound equipment	1.5	2.1	1.6	1.5	1.4	1.5	1.4	1.4	1.4
Pets, toys, and playground equipment	.9	.7	1.0	1.0	.9	.9	.9	.9	.8
Other entertainment supplies, equipment, and services	1.2	.9	1.2	1.5	1.1	1.5	.8	1.2	.2
Personal care products and services	1.1	1.3	1.1	1.0	1.1	1.1	1.3	1.2	1.5
Reading	.5	.3	.4	.4	.5	.5	.7	.6	.7
Education	1.6	5.9	1.4	1.4	2.3	1.0	.4	.5	.2
Tobacco products and smoking supplies	.8	1.0	.7	.8	.7	.9	.6	.7	.4
Miscellaneous	2.4	1.5	2.2	2.3	2.3	3.1	2.8	2.9	2.6
Cash contributions	3.1	1.1	1.9	2.4	3.3	3.4	6.2	5.3	7.5
Personal insurance and pensions	9.5	5.4	10.5	10.5	11.6	10.0	3.6	4.3	2.4
Life and other personal insurance	1.1	.3	.7	1.0	1.3	1.7	1.3	1.4	1.2
Pensions and Social Security	8.4	5.0	9.8	9.5	10.4	8.3	2.3	3.0	1.2
Sources of income and personal taxes: [1]									
Money income before taxes	$41,622	$16,839	$41,782	$50,894	$58,705	$44,238	$24,011	$27,037	$20,229
Wages and salaries	79.0	86.4	92.3	89.5	87.6	72.2	20.6	27.9	8.5
Self-employment income	5.4	2.2	4.0	6.2	6.2	7.9	2.2	2.5	1.8
Social Security, private and government retirement	11.1	[5].3	.5	1.2	2.8	14.9	67.2	60.6	78.2
Interest, dividends, rental income, other property income	2.1	1.6	.6	.6	1.6	2.8	8.1	7.1	9.8
Unemployment and workers' compensation, veterans' benefits	.5	.5	.4	.4	.5	.8	.3	.4	.3
Public assistance, supplemental security income, food stamps	.8	2.3	.9	.8	.5	.8	.8	.8	.7
Regular contributions for support	.6	3.8	.8	.8	.3	.3	.3	.1	.5
Other income	.5	3.0	.5	.6	.3	.3	.5	.6	.2
Personal taxes	7.8	5.1	8.0	8.1	9.3	7.7	4.7	5.1	3.9
Federal income taxes	5.9	4.0	6.2	6.2	7.2	5.7	3.1	3.5	2.6
State and local income taxes	1.5	1.1	1.7	1.6	1.8	1.5	.6	.7	.4
Other taxes	.4	([2])	.2	.3	.3	.5	.9	.9	.9
Income after taxes	92.2	94.9	92.0	91.9	90.7	92.3	95.3	94.9	96.1

[1] Components of income and taxes are derived from "complete income reporters" only; see glossary.
[2] Value less than 0.05.

[3] Value less than 0.5.
[4] No data reported.
[5] Data are likely to have large sampling errors.

Source: *Consumer Expenditures in 1998*, Bureau of the Census, Washington, DC, 1999

and had 10 percent of the discretionary income. Even among those 75 and over, who were 10 percent of households, had 8.5 percent of all discretionary income.

Spending by Older Householders Grows

Some sources believe that householders 65 and older are spending more. New Strategist Publications, in *Americans 55 and Older: A Changing Market* (1999), a study designed to promote marketing among older Americans, reported that while average annual spending per household actually fell 0.1 percent from 1990-1997 and spending by householders 55 to 64 grew just 1 percent, spending by those 65 to 74 grew 8.3 percent, and that of those 75 and older grew 6.9 percent. Older householders spent more than ever before on a number of categories for which the average householder's spending dropped. For example, while the average household spent 14 percent less on alcoholic beverages in 1997 than in 1990, those headed by people 65 to 74 and 75-plus spent 32 percent and 27 percent more, respectively. Entertainment expenses among people 75 and above increased 66 percent, while for the population as a whole, it rose just 4 percent.

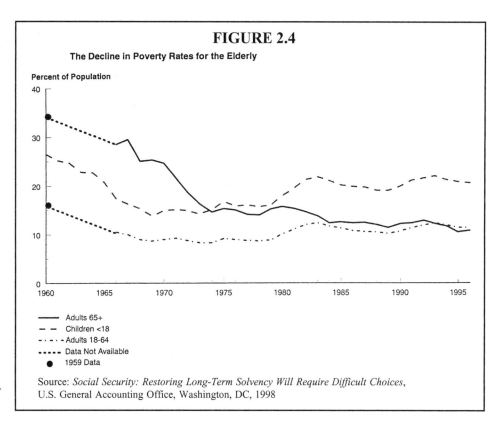

FIGURE 2.4

The Decline in Poverty Rates for the Elderly

Percent of Population

——— Adults 65+
– – Children <18
– · – · – Adults 18-64
· · · · · Data Not Available
● 1959 Data

Source: *Social Security: Restoring Long-Term Solvency Will Require Difficult Choices*, U.S. General Accounting Office, Washington, DC, 1998

Smaller Households Are More Expensive to Run

Almost all elderly households are made up of fewer persons than younger households. Generally, while larger households, in general, cost more to operate, they are less expensive on a per capita basis. For example, the Bureau of the Census reports that the basic cost of living for two people is

TABLE 2.12

People and Families in Poverty by Selected Characteristics: 1989, 1997, and 1998

[Numbers in thousands. For an explanation of confidence intervals (C.I.), see "Standard errors and their use" in Appendix C]

Characteristic	Below poverty, 1998				Below poverty, 1997				Below poverty, 1989			
	Number	90-pct. C.I. (±)	Percent	90-pct. C.I. (±)	Number	90-pct. C.I. (±)	Percent	90-pct. C.I. (±)	Number	90-pct. C.I. (±)	Percent	90-pct. C.I. (±)
PEOPLE												
Total	34,476	920	12.7	0.3	35,574	931	13.3	0.3	32,415	859	13.1	0.3
Age												
Under 18 years...............	13,467	487	18.9	0.7	14,113	495	19.9	0.7	13,154	462	20.1	0.7
18 to 64 years	17,623	674	10.5	0.4	18,085	681	10.9	0.4	15,950	617	10.4	0.4
18 to 24 years...............	4,312	201	16.6	0.8	4,416	204	17.5	0.8	4,132	189	15.4	0.7
25 to 34 years...............	4,582	214	11.9	0.6	4,759	219	12.1	0.6	4,873	212	11.2	0.5
35 to 44 years...............	4,082	202	9.1	0.5	4,251	207	9.6	0.5	3,115	171	8.3	0.5
45 to 54 years...............	2,444	158	6.9	0.4	2,439	158	7.2	0.5	1,873	133	7.5	0.5
55 to 59 years...............	1,165	110	9.2	0.9	1,092	107	9.0	0.9	971	97	9.5	0.9
60 to 64 years...............	1,039	104	10.1	1.0	1,127	109	11.2	1.1	986	97	9.4	0.9
65 years and over	3,386	179	10.5	0.6	3,376	179	10.5	0.6	3,312	171	11.4	0.6

Source: *Poverty in the United States, 1998*, Bureau of the Census, Washington, DC, 1999

less than twice as much as the cost for one person living alone; the living cost of four people is significantly less than four times that of someone living alone.

Larger, younger households often have multiple incomes. Repairing a leaky roof or buying a new refrigerator costs the same for both households, but the larger the household, the less the cost *per person* as a percentage of total income. Buying small quantities of food for one or two persons may be almost as expensive as buying in bulk for three or four. Because the elderly often have limited mobility, they may be forced to buy food and other necessities at small neighborhood stores that generally charge more than supermarkets.

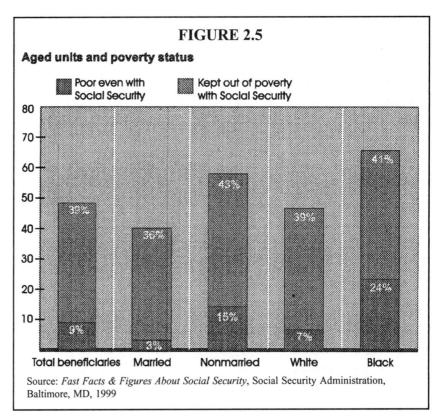

FIGURE 2.5

Aged units and poverty status

Source: *Fast Facts & Figures About Social Security*, Social Security Administration, Baltimore, MD, 1999

Expenditures of Retired and Nonretired Elderly

R. M. Rubin and Z. M. Nieswiadomy, in "Expenditure Patterns of Retired and Nonretired Persons" (U.S. Department of Labor, *Monthly Labor Review*, vol. 117, no.4, 1994), reported a survey of retirees and nonretirees age 50 or older about their income and expenses. They found that the income of retired married couples was 58 percent that of employed couples. Retired women had 53 percent of the income of employed single women, and retired men had 48 percent of the income of employed single men. Retired single women received only half as much pension income as retired single men and less than one-third as much as retired married couples. Similar patterns existed for financial assets.

Nonretired married couples spent 45 percent more than retired couples, while nonretired single men spent 65 percent more than retired men, and nonretired women spent 50 percent more than retired women. All retired groups spent a signifi-

cantly larger share of their total expenditures on food at home, utilities, and health care than did nonretired groups but less on food away from home and entertainment. Working couples and single women allocated more to work-related apparel and services, transportation, alcoholic beverages, and insurance.

THE ELDERLY POOR

Poverty standards are based on the "Economy Food Plan," developed by the U.S. Department of Agriculture (USDA) in the 1960s. The plan calculates the cost of a minimally adequate household food budget for different types of households by age of householder. Since USDA surveys showed that the average family spends one-third of its income on food, it was decided that a household with an income three times the amount needed for food was living fairly comfortably. The poverty level, then, is calculated by multiplying the cost of a minimally adequate food budget by three.

The overall economic position of those 65 and over has improved significantly in recent decades

TABLE 2.13

Poverty Thresholds in 1998, by Size of Family and Number of Related Children Under 18 Years

[Dollars]

Size of family unit	Weighted average thresholds	Related children under 18 years								
		None	One	Two	Three	Four	Five	Six	Seven	Eight or more
One person (unrelated individual) ..	8,316									
Under 65 years	8,480	8,480								
65 years and over..............	7,818	7,818								
Two people	10,634									
Householder under 65 years.....	10,972	10,915	11,235							
Householder 65 years and over..	9,862	9,853	11,193							
Three people	13,003	12,750	13,120	13,133						
Four people	16,660	16,813	17,088	16,530	16,588					
Five people.....................	19,680	20,275	20,570	19,940	19,453	19,155				
Six people......................	22,228	23,320	23,413	22,930	22,468	21,780	21,373			
Seven people...................	25,257	26,833	27,000	26,423	26,020	25,270	24,395	23,435		
Eight people....................	28,166	30,010	30,275	29,730	29,253	28,575	27,715	26,820	26,593	
Nine people or more.............	33,339	36,100	36,275	35,793	35,388	34,723	33,808	32,980	32,775	31,513

Source: *Poverty in the United States, 1998*, Bureau of the Census, Washington, DC, 1999

(Figure 2.4). In 1966, more than 1 in every 4 elderly Americans lived in poverty. During the 1960s and early 1970s, the average income of the elderly increased. This was largely due to increases in Social Security and pension benefits. As a result, by 1989, the poverty rate of those 65 and older had dropped to 11.4 percent and, in 1998, to 10.5 percent (Table 2.12). The poverty rate of the nation's population in 1998 as a whole was 12.7 percent. However, the elderly were more likely than the nonelderly to have incomes just above the poverty level, to be "near poor."

Social Security has played a significant role in reducing poverty among the aged. In 1998, more than two-fifths of the aged were kept out of poverty by their Social Security benefits. Overall, 9 percent of the aged receiving Social Security were poor; without Social Security, the overall poverty rate would have been 48 percent. (See Figure 2.5.)

The Debate — Old-Poor vs. Young-Poor

In 1998, the poverty rate among the elderly was below that of the general population and well below that of those younger than 18 (18.9 percent), which was almost twice the elderly poverty rate (Table 2.12). Many people use these statistics to support the argument that the elderly do not need as much support, especially from the government,

as they currently receive. Some people assert that the elderly get benefits at the expense of the young. Other sources vigorously challenge this claim, noting that many elderly people have incomes that barely cover their needs (if it covers them at all) and that the oldest old are among the poorest poor. In addition, many elderly are near-poor.

A Different Standard for the Old

The Economy Food Plan used in determining poverty levels assumes that a healthy elderly person has lower nutritional requirements than a younger person and, therefore, an elderly person needs less money for food. This assumption has resulted in different poverty standards for the old and for the young. For example, in 1998, the Census Bureau's statistical poverty level for a single adult under 65 years of age was $8,480; for a single adult 65 or older, it was $7,818. A 64-year-old woman, then, with a yearly income of $7,900 is poor, but on her 65th birthday, she becomes "not poor." (See Table 2.13.)

This method of defining poverty does not recognize the specialized problems of the elderly. For example, no household costs other than food are counted, even though the elderly spend a much greater percentage of their incomes on health care than younger people do. In addition, the Economy

TABLE 2.14				
POVERTY RATES OF THE FEMALE POPULATION 65 AND OVER BY MARITAL STATUS, 1997[3]				
All Elderly Women	Married	Divorced	Widowed	Never Married
13.1%	4.6%	22.2%	18.0%	20.0%

Source: *Women and Retirement Security*, prepared by the National Economic Council Interagency Working Group on Social Security, October 27, 1998

Food Plan considers only the nutritional needs of a healthy person; many of the elderly are in poor health and may need special diets or nutritional supplements.

When comparing the percentage of old and very young people who live in poverty, it is important to note that the same poverty standard is not applied to both groups. If it were, the percentage of elderly poor would increase relative to the younger poor. In addition, most young people are poor for a limited period of time; as they become old enough to enter the work force, they often have the opportunity to increase their income. Poor older people, on the other hand, have almost no option but to remain poor, and they may be poor for the rest of their lives.

Differences Among the Poor Old

There are significant differences in poverty levels among the elderly. As a group, women over 65 (13.1 percent) were almost twice as likely as men (7.0 percent) to live below the poverty level. Never-married (20 percent), divorced (22.2 percent), and widowed (18 percent) elderly women were much more likely than married women (4.6 percent) to live in poverty (Table 2.14).

Poverty rates are higher among elderly minority groups. In 1997, the poverty rate for Black women age 65 and older was 28.9 percent, compared to 28.1 percent for Hispanic women and 11.7 percent for White women. The poverty rate for Black men 65 and older was 22.2 percent, compared to 23.6 percent for Hispanic men and 6 percent for White men.

The three areas with the highest poverty among the elderly in 1998 were the District of Columbia (20.6 percent), Arkansas (17.1 percent), and Mississippi (16.6 percent). Following were Louisiana (16.3 percent), Texas (15.8 percent), New Mexico (15.7 percent), South Carolina (15.6 percent), Georgia (14 percent), West Virginia (13.9 percent), and Tennessee (13.7 percent).

THE AFFLUENT ELDERLY

Certainly, more older Americans live comfortably today than at any other time in history. People now in their 70s and 80s were children of the Great Depression that began in 1929 and lasted through the 1930s. Many of them learned to economize and save. In their 20s and 30s, the men returned from World War II to inexpensive housing and G.I. bills that provided a free or inexpensive college education. During their 40s and 50s, their peak earning years, they participated in an unprecedented economic expansion. Today, many of them have raised their children, paid off their mortgages, invested wisely, and are in relatively good health. In addition, Social Security payments are larger than ever.

The Center for Social Research in Aging at the University of Miami (Coral Gables, Florida) defines the "comfortably retired" as those who live in households with incomes more than double the poverty level. It estimated, in 1994, that 59 percent of retired 55- to 64-year-olds were comfortably retired, as were 51 percent of retired 65- to 74-year-olds, and 37.5 percent of those 75 years and older. The Center estimated that Hawaii had the highest percentage of comfortably retired persons in all three age groups, while Mississippi and

South Dakota had the lowest percentage of comfortably retired elderly.

THE SOCIAL SECURITY PROGRAM — AMERICA'S MOST POPULAR GOVERNMENT PROGRAM

On January 31, 1940, Vermont resident Ida May Fuller became the first person to receive an old-age monthly benefit check — $22.54 — from Social Security. She would collect a total of $22,889 in Social Security benefits — on her payroll contribution of $24.75 — by the time she died in 1975 at age 100.

Congress passed the Social Security Act in 1935 to provide economic assistance to retirees, the blind, and mothers and their dependent children. It has since been amended innumerable times and is currently composed of many sections, including Medicare (see Chapter VIII) and Supplemental Security Income (see below). The section authorizing the Old-Age, Survivors, and Disability Insurance (OASDI) program provides monthly benefits to retired and disabled workers and their dependents, and to survivors of insured workers.

The Social Security program is funded with a mandatory tax (Federal Insurance Contributions Act — FICA) that is withheld from workers' earnings and is matched by the employer. When a covered worker retires (or is disabled), he or she draws benefits based on the amount he or she has contributed to the fund. The longer the time of employment and the higher the earnings, the larger the benefit. Today, worker and employer each contribute 7.65 percent of the worker's salary to the fund. In 1998, the fund took in $424.8 billion and paid out $332.3 billion. (Figure 2.6 shows how Social Security is funded.)

Although Social Security was not initially presented as a full pension with which a recipient could maintain his or her pre-retirement standard of living, many elderly people depend almost solely on it. Before Social Security was created, the poverty rate for those 65 and over was over 47 percent. The Social Security Administration has concluded that the program enables 38 million Americans to live above the poverty level and that it is the country's most effective anti-poverty program. Today, the average 65-plus couple receives approximately $22,000 each year from Social Security — for life.

Ever since 1940, when Americans first received Social Security benefits, average monthly retirement benefits have steadily increased, but in the early 1970s, they soared. In 1972, the average benefit was indexed to keep up with inflation as reflected by the Consumer Price Index (CPI). This meant that recipients receive periodic "raises" or COLAs (cost of living adjustments) that were based upon the economic situation at that particular time. The 1970s were characterized by growing inflation, and within a few years, the whole system was

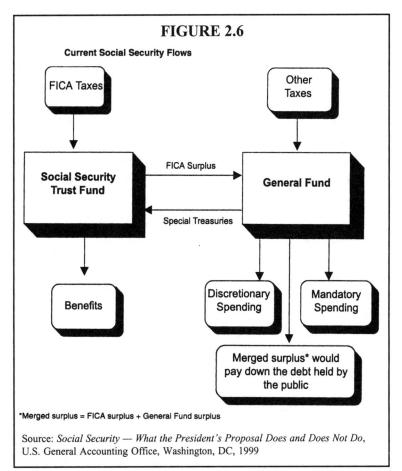

FIGURE 2.6

Current Social Security Flows

Source: *Social Security — What the President's Proposal Does and Does Not Do*, U.S. General Accounting Office, Washington, DC, 1999

facing serious long-range financial troubles, which many observers linked to the 1972 amendments.

Some legislators felt that indexing vastly overcompensated for inflation, causing relative benefit levels to rise higher than at any time in the history of the program. In many cases, if the formula had remained in effect, benefit levels for some future retirees would be higher than their earnings before retirement. In an attempt to prevent future Social Security benefits from rising to what many considered excessive levels, Congress passed the Social Security Amendments of 1977 (PL 95-216) to restructure the benefit plan and design more realistic formulas for benefits.

FIGURE 2.7

Benefit awards, 1998 Type of beneficiary	Total number (in thousands)	Total percent
New awards	3,800	100
Retired workers and dependents	1,992	52
Workers	1,632	43
Spouses and children	361	9
Disabled workers and dependents	1,027	27
Workers	608	16
Spouses and children	419	11
Survivors of deceased workers	781	21

Percent of benefits awarded, 1998

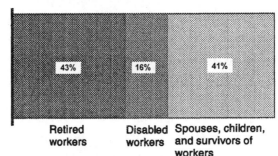

Retired workers	Disabled workers	Spouses, children, and survivors of workers
43%	16%	41%

Source: *Fast Facts & Figures About Social Security*, Social Security Administration, Baltimore, MD, 1999

Benefits and Beneficiaries

More than 3.8 million persons began receiving Social Security benefits in 1998. Forty-three percent of all beneficiaries were retired workers, and 16 percent were disabled workers. The remaining 41 percent were survivors and/or dependents of workers (Figure 2.7). In 1998, Social Security made payments to 48 million persons.

Of all adults receiving monthly Social Security benefits in 1998, 42 percent were men and 58 percent were women. Slightly less than one-fourth of the women received survivor benefits. In 1998, the average Social Security check was $857 for men and $643 for women. Retired workers received the highest amount, and spouses of disabled workers, the least. (See Table 2.15.)

Dual Entitlement

The number of women who are receiving benefits as dependents (based on their husband's earn-ings) has been declining. At the same time, the number of women with dual entitlement (based on both their own earnings and their husbands) has risen from 5 percent in 1960 to 27 percent in 1998. (See Figure 2.8.) This does not mean they get two Social Security payments, but that they are eligible for either and normally will get the larger of the two possibilities.

The Earnings Test

The Social Security program includes a retirement, or earnings, test. Under current law, the test allows beneficiaries ages 62 to 69 to earn income to a specified annual limit without losing their Social Security benefits. When earnings exceed this limit, benefits are reduced $1 for every $3 earned over the limit for those 65 to 69 and $1 for every $2 for those under age 65. The dollar amount depends on the worker's age — $9,600 annually for people under 65 and $15,500 for those 65 to 69. The Social Security Administration has found that workers tend to keep earnings at or below the an-

TABLE 2.15

Average monthly benefits by sex, December 1998

Type of beneficiary	Men	Women
Total	$857	$643
Retired workers	877	676
Spouses	230	402
Disabled workers	823	608
Spouses	137	183
Survivors:		
Nondisabled widows and widowers	549	750
Disabled widows and widowers	333	491
Mothers and fathers	453	549

Source: *Fast Facts & Figures About Social Security*, Social Security Administration, Baltimore, MD, 1999

nual earnings limit. The earnings test may, therefore, depress the income of older workers. (In March 2000, the House of Representatives voted to abolish the earnings test.)

Supplemental Security Income (SSI)

Supplemental Security Income (SSI) is a joint federal-state welfare program designed to supply monthly cash payments to needy aged, blind, or disabled Americans. Instituted in 1974, it replaced many local public assistance programs. SSI benefits are financed from general revenues, not from the Social Security Trust fund, and are issued in addition to Social Security benefits. Individual payments vary from state to state, depending on whether the federal or state government administers the program.

About 6.6 million persons, 20 percent of them elderly, received SSI payments in 1998 (Figure 2.9). The average payment to an aged individual was $272 and for an aged couple, $611. About 60 percent of all SSI payments went to women.

The percentage of SSI recipients under 65 years of age increased between 1974 and 1998, while the percentage of recipients over 65 decreased. Critics of the program believe

that the SSI program could do more to help the elderly. For one thing, it provides only enough income to bring an individual to 70 percent, and a couple to 90 percent, of the poverty level. Its strict assets test excludes many elderly people from receiving benefits, and many low-income people are unaware of the program.

THE FUTURE OF THE SOCIAL SECURITY PROGRAM

Most experts believe that the Social Security program faces a shaky future and that its solvency is threatened in the next decades. In 1982, the OASDI trust fund almost went bankrupt. Then-President Ronald Reagan and Congress instituted higher Social Security taxes, along with increased contributions and a one-time delay in the cost-of-living adjustment.

Social Security is a "pay-as-you-go" program, with contributions of present workers paying the retirement benefits of those currently retired. The program is solvent at this time, the result of a larger

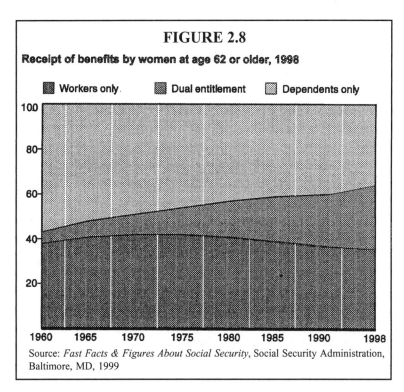

FIGURE 2.8

Receipt of benefits by women at age 62 or older, 1998

■ Workers only   ▨ Dual entitlement   ▤ Dependents only

Source: *Fast Facts & Figures About Social Security*, Social Security Administration, Baltimore, MD, 1999

number of employees contributing funds to the system and fewer retirees than expected. The earliest wave of baby boomers, those individuals who were born between 1946 and 1964, are still in the work force and reaching their peak earning years.

At the same time, people who are now retiring were born during the low birth rate cycle of the Great Depression, so there are now fewer retirees depleting funds than there are workers contributing to it. The federal government has been using some of the current surplus in the Social Security fund to make the federal deficit appear smaller. By using this money to pay current non-Social Security expenses, there will be less money for Americans when they retire.

At the present time, a retiree who has paid approximately $25,000 into the system will have that amount returned in about three years. However, that will not be the case for a retired worker of the future. He or she will have paid considerably more money into the system and get back much less. Furthermore, since there will be a much larger percentage of retirees as the baby boomers reach 65, starting in 2011, the younger generation of workers will face greater financial responsibility for the support and care of an increasing population of older Americans. Figure 2.10 shows the expected growth in the Social Security-age population through the year 2050.

The retirement age is already scheduled to rise from 65 to 67, to be phased in between 2000 and 2027. In 1993, Social Security Commissioner Shirley Sears Chater warned that the retirement age may have to be increased further and that benefits may need to be reduced. Figure 2.11 shows the increasing num-

FIGURE 2.9

Persons receiving federally administered SSI payments

Year	Total number (in thousands)
1974	3,216
1976	4,326
1978	4,217
1980	4,142
1982	3,858
1984	4,029
1986	4,269
1988	4,464
1990	4,817
1992	5,566
1994	6,296
1996	6,614
1998	6,566

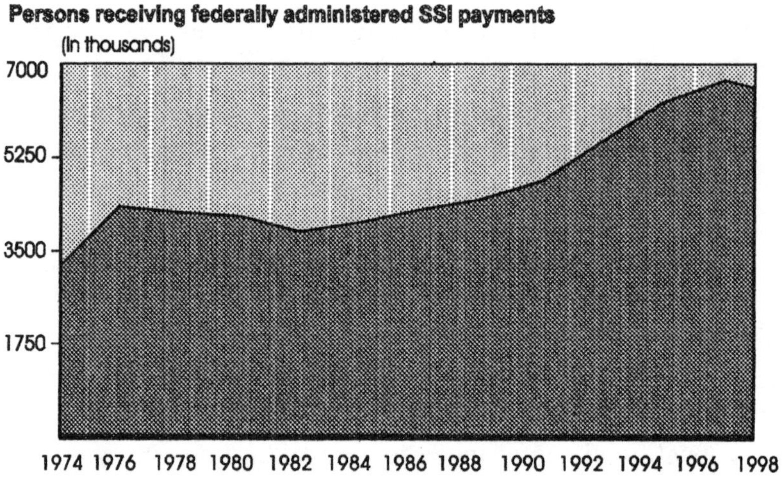

Persons receiving federally administered SSI payments
(in thousands)

Source: *Fast Facts & Figures About Social Security*, Social Security Administration, Baltimore, MD, 1999

bers of years Americans will receive benefits if they retire at the normal retirement age.

At the same time that the elderly population is growing, life expectancy is growing, resulting in even more elderly who will become eligible for Social Security. Additionally, the falling fertility rate caused by fewer children born to couples means there will be fewer workers contributing to Social Security for each aged, disabled, dependent, or surviving beneficiary. (Figure 2.12 shows the declining ratio of workers to beneficiaries.)

Currently, because there are more contributing to the system and fewer elderly to use the funds, contributions to the system exceed expenses paid

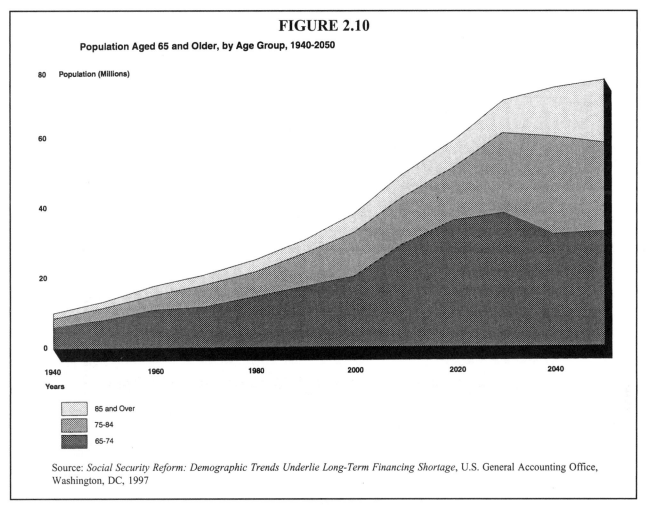

FIGURE 2.10

Population Aged 65 and Older, by Age Group, 1940-2050

Population (Millions)

Years

- 85 and Over
- 75-84
- 65-74

Source: *Social Security Reform: Demographic Trends Underlie Long-Term Financing Shortage*, U.S. General Accounting Office, Washington, DC, 1997

out to the aging by roughly $30 billion each year. That excess goes into a trust fund, which helps reduce the federal budget deficit. The U.S. General Accounting Office predicts, however, that the trust fund will be needed in approximately 17 years (Figure 2.13). So, while most sources predict that Social Security could still pay full benefits to recipients until 2032, the federal budget will be impacted as early as the second decade of the twenty-first century.

Restoring Social Security's long-term financial balance will require a combination of increased revenues and reduced expenditures. Some ways to reduce expenditures include

- Reducing initial benefits to retirees.

- Raising the retirement age.

- Lowering cost-of-living adjustments.

- Limiting benefits based on the beneficiaries' other income and assets.

Ways to increase revenues include

- Increasing Social Security payroll taxes.

- Investing trust funds in securities with potentially higher yields than the government bonds in which they are currently invested.

- Increasing income taxes on Social Security benefits.

In addition to those measures — or a combination of them — some sources suggest it may be possible to return funds to workers in the form of tax rebates, which they could then invest in stock and bond markets through individual accounts, with the proceeds going to finance their retirement benefits, a concept called privatization.

41

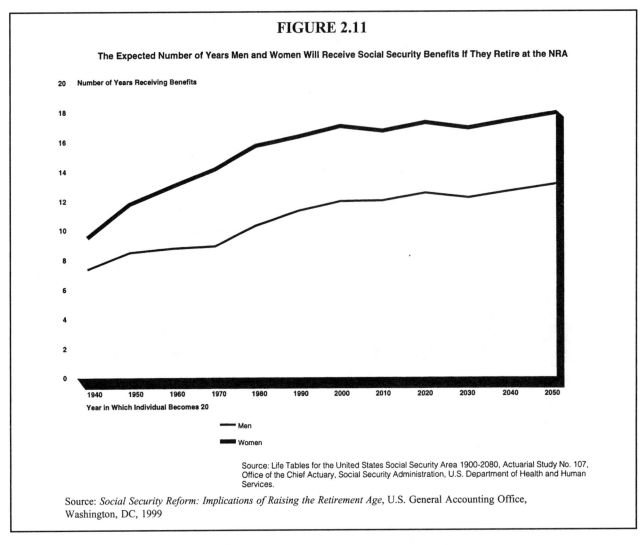

FIGURE 2.11

The Expected Number of Years Men and Women Will Receive Social Security Benefits If They Retire at the NRA

Number of Years Receiving Benefits

Year in Which Individual Becomes 20

— Men

▬ Women

Source: Life Tables for the United States Social Security Area 1900-2080, Actuarial Study No. 107, Office of the Chief Actuary, Social Security Administration, U.S. Department of Health and Human Services.

Source: *Social Security Reform: Implications of Raising the Retirement Age*, U.S. General Accounting Office, Washington, DC, 1999

Linking Social Security in some way to the performance of the stock market is one of the key issues in the current debate about rescuing Social Security. In general, such plans would return to individuals degrees of responsibility for their retirement investments. Critics of such plans point out that many groups, particularly low-income workers and women, would avoid the risks and invest in lower-yielding investments, reducing their earnings. Other sources believe such systems would expose less educated or inexperienced investors to the dangers of investment scams.

A Contract Between the Generations?

A "pay-as-you-go" pension system means that current workers finance the retirement of their elders. Some sources have predicted that with fewer workers to pay for more retirees, young people will have to sacrifice a good part of their own well-being to keep their elders living in the style they expect. They contend that, in most national systems in both Europe and the United States, this "contract between generations" is headed for trouble.

Rethinking the Future of Social Security

The debate over Social Security is not only about how to prevent the retirement system itself from going broke, but also about a number of much bigger questions. Among these questions, do Americans spend too much and save too little? How much burden should the old impose on the working generations? Is it better to continue the "all-for-one-and-one-for-all" notion embodied in Social Security and other benefit programs, or should Americans be asked to assume more responsibility for their own needs?

These are complicated issues. On one side are the longtime supporters of Social Security, who believe a commitment was made to the aging. On the other side are those who argue that Social Security, in its current form, undermines the economy by discouraging Americans from saving more for the future. As Lester C. Thurow, professor at MIT, contends, in *The Future of Capitalism* (William Morrow and Co., 1996), "Today's elderly are bringing down the social welfare state and threatening the nation's economic future."

FACING THE FUTURE — FUNDING RETIREMENT

Retirement income security in the United States has traditionally been based on the so-called three-legged stool: Social Security, private pensions, and personal savings. Since World War II, that formula has served the elderly well — the poverty rate among the elderly fell from 35 percent in 1959 to 11 percent in 1995.... But the future is uncertain....The prospect of a huge generation edging unprepared toward retirement raises worrisome questions about the living standards of the baby boomers in retirement, the concomitant pressure on government policies, and the stability of the nation's retirement system. — William G. Gale, *The Brookings Review*, Summer 1997

The largest federal study of Americans approaching retirement, performed from 1990 to 1993 by the National Institute on Aging, the University of Michigan, and the Alliance for Aging Research, reported that many of the 12,600 respondents ages 51 to 61 or married to someone in that age range could face an uncertain financial future. Although these "fiftysomethings" are better off than their counterparts decades ago, they are often less prepared to face retirement. Among the findings:

- Two of every 10 households had no assets.

- Two of every 5 interviewees had no expectation of receiving pension income of any type other than Social Security.

- One in 7 lacked health insurance, public or private.

- Almost half of those surveyed believed there was a likelihood they could lose their job in the next year and that they might be unable to find a new job in a few months.

Similarly, the Employee Benefit Research Institute (EBRI), a nonprofit public policy research organization, reported, in its 1999 *Retirement Confidence Survey* (RCS), that although many of today's workers are confident of their financial preparations for retirement, many are inaccurate in their calculations and assumptions. Some workers expect to work longer than current retirees actually worked before retiring, some citing not only that they need the money but also that they enjoy working. However, many current retirees report they had to retire earlier than expected for negative reasons — they experienced health problems or

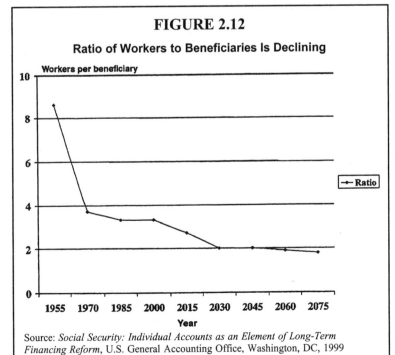

FIGURE 2.12

Ratio of Workers to Beneficiaries Is Declining

Source: *Social Security: Individual Accounts as an Element of Long-Term Financing Reform*, U.S. General Accounting Office, Washington, DC, 1999

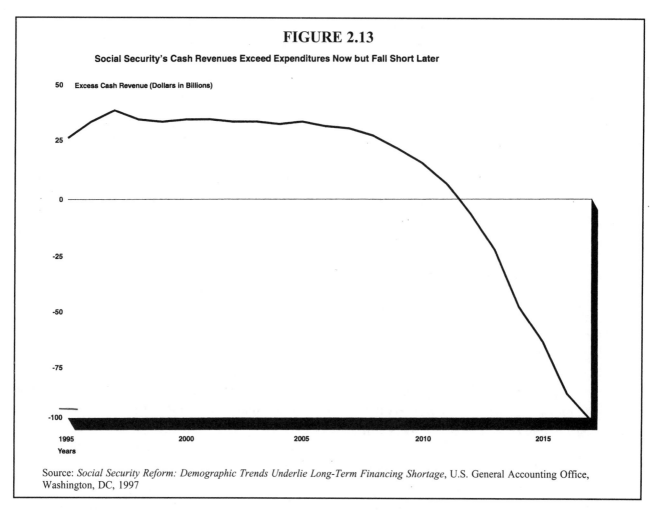

FIGURE 2.13

Social Security's Cash Revenues Exceed Expenditures Now but Fall Short Later

Excess Cash Revenue (Dollars in Billions)

Source: *Social Security Reform: Demographic Trends Underlie Long-Term Financing Shortage*, U.S. General Accounting Office, Washington, DC, 1997

disability or were laid off when companies downsized or closed.

Forty-three percent of current retirees retired earlier than they had planned due to unexpected circumstances. Table 2.16 shows retirees' actual retirement age and workers' expected age of retirement. Sixty-eight percent of workers plan to work for pay after retiring. In 1999, 29 percent of retirees worked after retiring. Table 2.17 shows the reasons current workers cited for wanting to work after they retire and current retirees' actual reasons for working.

Among those people who have already retired, 39 percent reported that Social Security is their primary source of income, followed by employer-funded pensions (30 percent) and personal savings (18 percent). Those who have yet to retire claimed that personal savings will be their primary source of retirement income, with employer pensions sec-

ond (20 percent) and Social Security providing only 12 percent of their income. (See Table 2.18.)

However, many workers were unaware that the retirement age for full Social Security benefits is gradually increasing from age 65 to 67. Fifty-nine percent of workers thought they would be eligible for full benefits before they actually will be. An additional 19 percent admitted they did not know when they will become eligible for full benefits.

The RCS found that 24 percent of all working Americans felt very confident they will have enough money to live comfortably in retirement, and another 45 percent were somewhat confident (Table 2.19). However, this confidence could prove false, considering that

• Only half of workers had tried to determine how much they will actually need before they retire.

44

TABLE 2.16

Workers' *expected* age of retirement and retirees' *actual* retirement age:

	Workers	Retirees
Age 55 or younger	5%	20%
Age 55–59	13	16
Age 60	13	6
Age 61–64	13	29
Age 65	30	14
Age 66 or older	17	12

Source: *The 1999 Retirement Confidence Survey*, Employment Benefit Research Institute, Washington, DC, www.ebri.org

- Only 36 percent had thought about insurance coverage for long-term care or nursing home needs.

- Just 16 percent reported having accumulated $100,000 or more for retirement.

THE AGING CONSUMER — A GROWING MARKET

Today's elderly (and their caregivers) have proven to be a lucrative market for many products. In addition to the products traditionally offered to the aging, such as health and life insurance and burial plots, marketers have discovered the elderly are interested in a new range of products and services. Today's healthier, more affluent aging population desires products that make dressing and routine chores simpler and products that promote health, travel, and recreation. Direct marketers find that elderly consumers readily shop mail-order catalogs. Many older shoppers now expect more attractive and comfortable clothing and footwear.

Mature consumers respond to marketing that reflects autonomy and self-sufficiency, social and spiritual connectedness, altruism, personal growth, and revitalization. Older customers are often suspicious of claims about a product's attributes, are less influenced by peers, less materialistic, and more subjective in their purchasing.

"The Eisenhower Generation"

Americans born during the Great Depression (beginning in 1929) and World War II (1941 - 1945) are now in their most affluent years. They

TABLE 2.17

Major reasons cited by workers expecting to work after retiring and by retirees as reasons they have worked in retirement:

	Workers	Retirees
Enjoy work and want to stay involved	64%	62%
To have money to make ends meet	37	26
To have money to buy extras	36	26
To keep health insurance or other benefits	37	16
To help support children or other household members	18	5
To try a different career	16	5

TABLE 2.18

Most important sources of retirement income (*expected* sources for workers and *actual* sources for retirees):

	Workers	Retirees
Personal savings	49%	18%
Employer-funded plans	20	30
Social Security	12	39
Employment	11	3
Sale of home or business	5	2
Other government programs	1	4
Support from children/family	<1	<1

Source: *The 1999 Retirement Confidence Survey*, Employment Benefit Research Institute, Washington, DC, www.ebri.org

TABLE 2.19

Overall confidence in having enough money to live comfortably throughout retirement:

	Pre-Retirees[a]	Older Boomers[a]	Younger Boomers[a]	Generation X[a]
Very confident	24%	20%	21%	33%
Somewhat confident	45	48	52	41
Not too confident	21	23	19	19
Not at all confident	8	8	9	7

Source: *The 1999 Retirement Confidence Survey*, Employment Benefit Research Institute, Washington, DC, www.ebri.org

often spend freely on grandchildren, new cars, homes, and travel, but many have also been saving for retirement. Marketers have found in the "Ikes" (named for President Dwight Eisenhower) an aging, but definitely not elderly, target.

Approximately 15 percent of the U.S. population is wedged between seniors and baby boomers. They are at the top of their careers as well as earning and spending power. Most of today's corporate leaders come from their ranks. Most of these "Ikes" have the work ethic of their elders and believe in thrift and self-sufficiency. With their housing investments appreciating and pension plans still essentially sound, the "Eisenhowers" may be the last American generation with reasonably bright prospects for retirement. Following generations will have concerns about Social Security and health care, especially costs. They are at a stage in life where they may begin experiencing many life changes, such as grandparenthood, loss of a spouse,

career downshifting or retirement, and traveling. Many have discretionary income and the time to enjoy it, and these events have affected their buying behavior.

The Emerging "Silver" Market

The aging of the boomers will likely change the consumer marketplace. Boomers are more interested in health and in postponing aging than any generation before. They will search for medical, technological, hormonal, and genetic answers to cure ailments and promote vitality and longevity. They invest in foods, medications, and products that promote energy, relaxation, and sexuality.

Boomers have embraced technological advances and financial innovation. They will seek innovation in home design and operations. They are accepting of lifestyle changes. All these suggest that they will be voracious consumers.

CHAPTER III

LIVING ARRANGEMENTS OF THE ELDERLY

ELDERLY HOUSEHOLDS

The Bureau of the Census reports that of the 102.5 million households in the United States in 1998, one in five (21.5 percent) was headed by a person 65 years or older (Table 3.1). This includes both family and non-family households (the members are unrelated to the head of the household). In several states — Rhode Island, Pennsylvania, Iowa, North and South Dakota, Florida, West Virginia, and Arkansas — approximately one-fourth of households were headed by someone 65 and older.

Most elderly prefer to live independently as long as possible. Most elderly Americans are adequately housed, but there is a range of conditions, from the affluent "younger-old" homeowner, to the very elderly and often very poor nursing home resident, to the homeless.

THE "MODIFIED EXTENDED" FAMILY

The "modified extended" family is the dominant form of family organization found in industrialized societies today. It is also the arrangement that most older people say they prefer. In this setting, older and younger generations live in separate households but are in touch with each other on a fairly regular and frequent basis.

LIVING WITH A SPOUSE

The number of elderly people living with their spouses varies greatly between men and women. In 1998, 72.6 percent of all noninstitutionalized men aged 65 or over lived with their spouse, compared to only 40.7 percent of women. The difference is even more dramatic in the 75 to 84 age group: 71 percent of men lived with their spouse, compared to only 32.1 percent of women. By the age of 85, 45.6 percent of men lived with their spouse, while only 10.9 percent of women did. (See Table 3.2.) This occurs because women tend to live longer than men, they are generally younger than the men they marry, and widowers are far more likely to remarry than widows.

LIVING WITH OTHER RELATIVES

In 1998, approximately 13 percent of people over age 65 lived with a relative other than a spouse. Again, the difference between men and women was significant. Sixteen percent of women lived with a relative other than their spouse, but only 7 percent of men did. This would follow naturally since so many more men lived with their spouses.

TABLE 3.1

Percent Distribution of Households by Age of Householder: July 1, 1998

Area	15 to 24 Years	25 to 34 Years	35 to 44 Years	45 to 54 Years	55 to 64 Years	65 Years and Over
United States	5.2	17.5	23.4	19.4	13.0	21.5

Source: Population Estimates Program, Bureau of the Census, Washington, DC, 1999

47

TABLE 3.2

Marital Status of Persons 15 Years and Over, by Age, Sex, Race, Hispanic Origin, Metropolitan Residence, and Region: March 1998

[Numbers in thousands.]

Subject	Total, 15 years and over	15 to 17 years	18 and 19 years	20 to 24 years	25 to 29 years	30 to 34 years	35 to 39 years	40 to 44 years	45 to 54 years	55 to 64 years	65 to 74 years	75 to 84 years	85 years and over	Total, 18 years and over	Total, 65 years and over
UNITED STATES															
All Races															
Both sexes	209 291	11 879	7 587	17 613	18 996	20 358	22 691	21 771	34 057	22 255	17 874	11 281	2 928	197 412	32 082
Never married	58 303	11 742	7 270	13 538	8 511	5 158	4 069	2 771	2 744	1 110	753	485	151	46 561	1 389
Married, spouse present	110 619	57	241	3 313	8 818	12 449	14 573	14 608	23 564	15 613	11 328	5 386	668	110 562	17 382
Married, spouse absent	7 346	51	61	390	699	939	1 170	1 041	1 445	793	423	241	91	7 294	755
Separated	4 922	40	32	244	473	627	901	798	996	504	218	72	16	4 882	306
Other	2 424	11	29	146	227	313	268	243	449	289	205	169	75	2 413	449
Widowed	13 599	5	–	17	45	74	182	216	847	1 801	3 862	4 640	1 910	13 594	10 412
Divorced	19 424	24	15	355	923	1 737	2 697	3 135	5 457	2 937	1 508	529	107	19 400	2 144
Percent	100.0	100.0	100.0	100.0	100.0	100.0	100.0	100.0	100.0	100.0	100.0	100.0	100.0	100.0	100.0
Never married	27.9	98.8	95.8	76.9	44.8	25.3	17.9	12.7	8.1	5.0	4.2	4.3	5.2	23.6	4.3
Married, spouse present	52.9	.5	3.2	18.8	46.4	61.2	64.2	67.1	69.2	70.2	63.4	47.7	22.8	56.0	54.2
Married, spouse absent	3.5	.4	.8	2.2	3.7	4.6	5.2	4.8	4.2	3.6	2.4	2.1	3.1	3.7	2.4
Separated	2.4	.3	.4	1.4	2.5	3.1	4.0	3.7	2.9	2.3	1.2	.6	.6	2.5	1.0
Other	1.2	.1	.4	.8	1.2	1.5	1.2	1.1	1.3	1.3	1.1	1.5	2.6	1.2	1.4
Widowed	6.5	–	–	.1	.2	.4	.8	1.0	2.5	8.1	21.6	41.1	65.2	6.9	32.5
Divorced	9.3	.2	.2	2.0	4.9	8.5	11.9	14.4	16.0	13.2	8.4	4.7	3.7	9.8	6.7
Male	101 123	6 114	3 807	8 826	9 450	10 076	11 299	10 756	16 598	10 673	7 992	4 527	1 006	95 009	13 524
Never married	31 591	6 072	3 706	7 360	4 822	2 939	2 444	1 676	1 481	572	328	145	45	25 518	518
Married, spouse present	55 310	6	61	1 179	3 915	5 925	7 056	7 174	12 015	8 158	6 147	3 216	458	55 303	9 821
Married, spouse absent	3 323	24	30	153	304	420	542	459	650	401	184	111	44	3 298	339
Separated	2 018	21	20	79	166	229	382	350	406	225	91	38	10	1 996	139
Other	1 305	3	11	75	138	191	160	109	244	176	93	73	34	1 302	200
Widowed	2 569	3	–	–	10	20	44	50	150	275	707	888	423	2 567	2 017
Divorced	8 331	9	10	133	398	773	1 213	1 397	2 303	1 266	626	166	36	8 322	828
Percent	100.0	100.0	100.0	100.0	100.0	100.0	100.0	100.0	100.0	100.0	100.0	100.0	100.0	100.0	100.0
Never married	31.2	99.3	97.3	83.4	51.0	29.2	21.6	15.6	8.9	5.4	4.1	3.2	4.5	26.9	3.8
Married, spouse present	54.7	.1	1.6	13.4	41.4	58.8	62.4	66.7	72.4	76.4	76.9	71.0	45.6	58.2	72.6
Married, spouse absent	3.3	.4	.8	1.7	3.2	4.2	4.8	4.3	3.9	3.8	2.3	2.5	4.3	3.5	2.5
Separated	2.0	.3	.5	.9	1.8	2.3	3.4	3.3	2.4	2.1	1.1	.8	1.0	2.1	1.0
Other	1.3	.1	.3	.8	1.5	1.9	1.4	1.0	1.5	1.6	1.2	1.6	3.4	1.4	1.5
Widowed	2.5	–	–	–	.1	.2	.4	.5	.9	2.6	8.8	19.6	42.0	2.7	14.9
Divorced	8.2	.1	.3	1.5	4.2	7.7	10.7	13.0	13.9	11.9	7.8	3.7	3.6	8.8	6.1
Female	108 168	5 765	3 780	8 788	9 546	10 282	11 392	11 015	17 459	11 582	9 882	6 754	1 923	102 403	18 558
Never married	26 713	5 670	3 565	6 178	3 689	2 219	1 626	1 095	1 263	538	425	340	106	21 043	871
Married, spouse present	55 310	51	180	2 135	4 903	6 525	7 517	7 434	11 550	7 455	5 181	2 170	210	55 259	7 561
Married, spouse absent	4 023	27	31	237	395	519	628	582	795	392	239	130	48	3 996	417
Separated	2 904	19	12	165	307	397	520	448	590	279	126	34	7	2 885	167
Other	1 119	8	18	71	89	122	108	134	205	114	112	96	41	1 111	249
Widowed	11 029	2	–	17	35	55	138	166	697	1 526	3 155	3 752	1 487	11 027	8 394
Divorced	11 093	15	5	222	525	964	1 484	1 738	3 154	1 671	882	362	71	11 078	1 316
Percent	100.0	100.0	100.0	100.0	100.0	100.0	100.0	100.0	100.0	100.0	100.0	100.0	100.0	100.0	100.0
Never married	24.7	98.4	94.3	70.3	38.6	21.6	14.3	9.9	7.2	4.6	4.3	5.0	5.5	20.5	4.7
Married, spouse present	51.1	.9	4.8	24.3	51.4	63.5	66.0	67.5	66.2	64.4	52.4	32.1	10.9	54.0	40.7
Married, spouse absent	3.7	.5	.8	2.7	4.1	5.1	5.5	5.3	4.6	3.4	2.4	1.9	2.5	3.9	2.2
Separated	2.7	.3	.3	1.9	3.2	3.9	4.6	4.1	3.4	2.4	1.3	.5	.3	2.8	.9
Other	1.0	.1	.5	.8	.9	1.2	.9	1.2	1.2	1.0	1.1	1.4	2.1	1.1	1.3
Widowed	10.2	–	–	.2	.4	.5	1.2	1.5	4.0	13.2	31.9	55.6	77.4	10.8	45.2
Divorced	10.3	.3	.1	2.5	5.5	9.4	13.0	15.8	18.1	14.4	8.9	5.4	3.7	10.8	7.1

Source: Terry A. Lugalia, *Marital Status and Living Arrangements: March 1998 (Update)*, Bureau of the Census, Washington, DC, 1998

GRANDPARENTS AS PARENTS

Thirty-one percent of adults — about 60 million Americans — are grandparents. With drug addiction, alcoholism, divorce, teen pregnancy, AIDS, family violence, and crime shattering thousands of young American families each year, large numbers of seniors find themselves raising their grandchildren. Over the past 28 years, the number of children living in households headed by grandparents has increased by 80 percent. In 1998, 5.6 percent (4 million) of all children under 18 years of age lived with their grandparents. Some also had one or both of their parents with them in the home of the grandparent, although 35.5 percent did not.

(See Table 3.3.) In addition, another 8 percent of grandparents provided regular day-care for their grandchild(ren).

Half of these families consisted of both a grandmother and grandfather; most of the others (43 percent) had a grandmother with no husband. Half the grandchildren in such families were under age 6. About 27 percent of the grandchildren were poor, and one-third of them had no health insurance.

In cities with substantial drug and crime problems, the numbers of children being raised by grandparents are much greater. In Washington, DC, for example, an estimated 27,000 children — one-

TABLE 3.3

Grandchildren Living in the Home of Their Grandparents: 1970 to Present

(Numbers in thousands)

Year	Total children under 18	Grandchildren				
				With parent(s) present		
		Total	Both parents present	Mother only present	Father only present	Without parent(s) present
1998	71,377	3,989	503	1,827	241	1,417
1997	70,983	3,894	554	1,785	247	1,309
1996	70,908	4,060	467	1,943	220	1,431
1995	70,254	3,965	427	1,876	195	1,466
1994	69,508	3,735	436	1,764	175	1,359
1993	66,893	3,368	475	1,647	229	1,017
1992	65,965	3,253	502	1,740	144	867
1991	65,093	3,320	559	1,674	151	937
1990	64,137	3,155	467	1,563	191	935
1980 Census	63,369	2,306	310	922	86	988
1970 Census	69,276	2,214	363	817	78	957

Source of CPS data: U. S. Bureau of the Census, Current Population Reports, Series P20-514, "Marital Status and Living Arrangements: March 1998 (Update)" and earlier reports.

Source of Decennial Census data: 1980 Census of Population, PC80-2-4B, "Living Arrangements of Children and Adults," table 1. 1970 Census of Population, PC(2)-4B, "Persons by Family Characteristics," table 1.

Source: U.S. Bureau of the Census, Washington, DC, 1999

fourth of all children in the District — live with their grandparents. In some schools in Oakland, California, 50 percent of children are living with their grandparents.

According to the American Association of Retired Persons (AARP) Women's Initiative 1995 survey (*The Real Golden Girls: The Prevalence and Policy Treatment of Midlife and Older People Living in Nontraditional Households*), the average age of grandparent caregivers was 59; the median age was 57. More than 75 percent were between 45 and 64; 23 percent, 65 or older, and 7 percent, 75 or older. Sixty percent were grandmothers, and 40 percent were grandfathers. Three-fourths of the grandparents were married; 13 percent, widowed; and 7 percent, divorced. Sixty-eight percent of grandparents raising their grandchildren were White; 29 percent were Black.

A Strong Bond

The state of American grandparenting is strong.— Gretchen Shaw, AARP Research Group, 2000

Many grandparents "stay in touch" with their grandchildren, spend time with them, and give gifts to them. Despite the belief that generational family relationships have suffered in recent decades, the AARP's *Grandparenting Survey* (January 2000), conducted by ICR Research Group (Media, Pennsylvania), found that most interact with grandchildren and view their relationships as "very positive." Eighty-two percent said they had seen their grandchild in the previous month, and 85 percent said they had talked to that child on the phone in that period. Seventy-two percent had shared a meal in the past month, and an equal number reported they had bought a gift for their grandchild within that month.

The activities most often shared with a grandchild were eating together, watching a TV comedy, staying overnight, shopping for clothes, and engaging in a sport or exercise. When asked about the roles they played when interacting with their grandchildren, 49 percent said they served as companion/friend, and 35 percent reported they gave advice. Approximately one-third each talked about family history, told what their parents did as a child, served as a confidant, or "talked about the old days." Grandparents spent a median of $489 a year on clothes, books, toys, and other items for their grandchildren. The survey found that a typical grandparent had five grandchildren/great grandchildren (one-fourth of grandparents had great-grandchildren).

Grandparents' Rights?

The considerable number of divorces has caused many grandparents to become separated from their grandchildren. As a result, some grandparents are seeking visitation rights to grandchildren. Over the past two decades, more and more cases have made their way into courtrooms, leading most states to develop laws to decide how and when grandparents can see their grandchildren. At issue is whether fit parents can be forced to allow grandparents visits. In most states, grandparents must only show it is in the "best interest of the child." In some states, they must show the child would suffer harm if they were denied visits. Table 3.4 shows the grandparent visitation statutes in the various states and the circumstances under which they may be sought.

In 2000, the U.S. Supreme Court, in *Traxel v. Granville*, heard arguments to decide whether grandparents have a legal right to visit grandchildren over the objections of the child's parents. A final decision is expected in late June 2000.

LIVING ALONE

Most elderly people who live alone have outlived their spouses, and in some cases, their children and siblings. As a result, the percentage of persons living alone increases with age. Thirty percent of women between 65 and 74 and 53 percent of women 75 and over lived alone in 1998. In contrast, only 14 percent of 65- to 74-year-old men and 22 percent of men over 75 lived alone (Table 3.5). These figures reflect the fact that women generally live longer than men, are more likely to be widowed, and less likely to remarry. Nearly half (45.2 percent) of women 65 years and older were widowed. Of those, 70 percent lived alone.

TABLE 3.4
Comparison of Grandparent Visitation Statutes Nationwide

State	FACTORS TO BE CONSIDERED IN EVALUATING PETITION				WHEN PETITION IS PERMITTED		
	Best Interest of Child	Must Show Harm	Prior Grandparent/ Grandchild Relationship	Effect on Parent/ Child Relationship	Any Marital Status of Parents	Parents are Deceased, Divorced and/or Unmarried	After Step-Parent Adoption
AL	✓			✓	✓1		✓
AK	✓		✓		✓		
AZ	✓		✓			✓	✓
AR	✓					✓	
CA	✓		✓	✓		✓	✓
CO	✓					✓	
CT	✓				✓		
DE	✓					✓	
FL	✓		✓	✓	✓1		✓
GA	✓	✓				✓	✓
HI	✓				✓		
ID	✓				✓		
IL	✓					✓	✓
IN	✓		✓			✓	✓
IA	✓		✓		✓1		✓
KS	✓		✓			✓	✓
KY	✓				✓		
LA	✓					✓	✓
ME	✓		✓	✓	✓		

(continued)

Differing Views on Living Alone

Are those elderly who live alone enjoying the freedom and lack of responsibility for others, or are they a sad, lonely group isolated from the rest of the community? Certainly one can find positive and negative examples for every situation and condition. For those in good health, socially active, and financially comfortable, living alone does not have to be a problem. However, this may not be the case with most of those who live alone. On the average, they have lower incomes than older couples, particularly if they are female, are members of a minority group, or are over the age of 85. In addition, a very high proportion of elderly who live alone suffer from chronic health problems and report their health to be only fair or poor.

The combination of poor health, poverty, and solitude is usually not a formula for happy living.

TABLE 3.4 (Continued)

State	FACTORS TO BE CONSIDERED IN EVALUATING PETITION				WHEN PETITION IS PERMITTED		
	Best Interest of Child	Must Show Harm	Prior Grandparent/ Grandchild Relationship	Effect on Parent/Child Relationship	Any Marital Status of Parents	Parents are Deceased, Divorced and/or Unmarried	After Step-Parent Adoption
MD	✓				✓		
MA	✓					✓	✓
MI	✓					✓	✓
MN	✓		✓	✓	✓²		✓
MS	✓		✓		✓¹		✓
MO	✓				✓		✓
MT	✓				✓		✓
NE	✓		✓	✓		✓	
NV	✓		✓	✓		✓	
NH	✓		✓	✓		✓	✓
NJ	✓		✓	✓	✓		
NM	✓		✓		✓²		✓
NY	✓				✓		
NC	✓		✓			✓	✓
ND	✓		✓		✓		✓
OH	✓					✓	✓
OK	✓		✓	✓	✓		✓
OR	✓		✓		✓¹		✓
PA	✓		✓	✓	✓²		✓
RI	✓				✓¹		
SC	✓		✓	✓	✓		
SD	✓				✓		✓
TN	✓		✓	✓		✓	✓
TX	✓		✓		✓²		✓
UT	✓				✓¹		
VT	✓		✓	✓		✓	✓
VA³	✓			✓		✓	
WA	✓		✓	✓	✓		
WV	✓		✓	✓	✓		✓
WI	✓		✓		✓		
WY	✓			✓	✓		✓

[1] Only if denied visitation

[2] Only if child previously resided with grandparent

[3] The Supreme Court of Virginia held that statute could apply to an intact marriage only if there is a finding of harm to the child in the absence of visitation

they would have no one to call on for a period of days, perhaps even weeks.

A Transitional Stage

Living alone is sometimes a transitional stage between living with a spouse or other relative and, as health deteriorates, living in a nursing home or other institution. Most older people prefer to remain independent as long as possible. While some have the physical and financial resources to live alone comfortably, others, especially very elderly women, are often extremely poor.

LIVING IN A NURSING HOME

One of the main reasons for entering a nursing home or similar long-term care facility is to receive medical care. Some experts, however, suggest that between 10 and 60 percent of persons in nursing homes could live in the community if appropriate supportive (primarily nonmedical) services were available. Groups representing the elderly also believe that 30 to 50 percent of those in nursing homes could and would live elsewhere, if such facilities were available.

Only about 5 percent of the older population is living in nursing homes at any one time. The average nursing home resident is very old, female, and unmarried. Most nursing home residents are there because they are sick or disabled and cannot obtain adequate care in the community. Health policy experts generally agree that many people live in nursing homes not because they need medical attention, but because that is the most available, and most likely to be financed, option. (See Chapter IX for a further discussion of nursing homes.)

Respite Care

A concept known as "respite care" offers hope both for the disabled elderly and their families. Respite care involves short-term stays in nursing homes or hospitals. Reasons for choosing temporary care in an institution include vacation needs for adult caregivers, brief medical or therapeutic needs of an elderly person, and relief for both par-

Substantial numbers of elderly persons living alone experience loneliness and fear. Fewer of them consider themselves happy than do those who live with others, and they are generally less satisfied with life. They frequently say that if they needed help,

ties from the caregiver/receiver relationship. Despite the growing need, the number of institutions offering such short-term stays is relatively small (10 percent of hospitals and 30 percent of nursing homes). The cost of respite care is often not reimbursable under private or federal insurance programs or Medicare.

LIVING HOMELESS

Very little research has been conducted on the homeless elderly. Although approximately 12 percent of the population of the United States over 65, only 3 to 5 percent of homeless people who have sought care have been elderly. The relatively low proportion of elderly homeless suggested by this figure may be explained by their access to benefits (Social Security, Medicare, housing), by high death rates once they enter street life, or by their avoidance of high visibility shelters and programs which they fear may be dangerous. (For further information, see *Homeless in America — How Could It Happen Here?*, Information Plus, Wylie, Texas, 1999.)

NONTRADITIONAL LIVING ARRANGEMENTS

For those who have the option of selecting where and how they live, several alternatives to single-family housing have emerged in recent years. There is no perfect alternative; each type of arrangement has its own particular problems and benefits.

Problems Faced by Nontraditional Households

In general, relationships and living arrangements not based on blood, marriage, or adoption are not formally recognized in public policy, leading to less favorable treatment than that accorded traditional family units. Persons in nontraditional relationships usually are not legally recognized as having rights. For example, without a blood or marital relationship, a person does not generally qualify for survivor, pension, or insurance benefits. A person cannot have the benefits of being a spouse or parent without legal standing. In medical matters, persons in nontraditional relationships may not be granted rights given to *family*, such as visitation or making medical decisions for the other person.

Models of Nontraditional Living Arrangements

Assisted Living

Assisted living is emerging as the next century's long-term care model. — Paul Klaassen, CEO of Sunrise Assisted Living

Assisted living housing gets its name from the help provided to residents in the form of housekeeping, meal services, minor medical care, and personal care, such as help getting out of bed, bathing, or dressing. Assisted living sprang up to fill the gap in long-term care — elderly who are frail but not ill and who need some assistance but not around-the-clock medical care.

Assisted living facilities can be large or small, institutional or home-like, expensive or affordable. In response to consumer demand, the private sector is increasingly developing facilities that are more bed-and-breakfast in appearance than nursing homes. Assisted living facilities try to meet the preference for a residential atmosphere with appropriate, individually tailored services. On average, the residents-to-staff ratio in an assisted living home is 3 to 1, compared to 17 to 1 in an active living center, 4 to 1 in a congregate facility (nursing home), and 30 to 1 in an independent living setting.

Assisted living is the fastest growing type of senior housing in the United States, with an estimated 15 to 20 percent annual growth rate over the past few years. The American Association of Homes and Services for the Aging estimated that, in 1999, assisted living accounted for 75 percent of new senior housing.

According to the National Center for Assisted Living, an industry organization, more than 1 million residents are living in 28,000 assisted living

TABLE 3.5

Marital Status and Living Arrangements of Adults 18 Years Old and Over: March 1998

(Numbers in thousands)

Characteristics of adults	Age						
	18 years and over	18 to 24 years	25 to 34 years	35 to 44 years	45 to 64 years	65 to 74 years	75 years over
MARITAL STATUS							
Males	95,009	12,633	19,526	22,055	27,271	7,992	5,533
Married, spouse present	55,303	1,240	9,840	14,230	20,173	6,147	3,674
Married, spouse absent	3,298	183	724	1,001	1,051	184	155
Unmarried	36,407	11,210	8,963	6,823	6,048	1,661	1,704
Never married	25,518	11,066	7,761	4,120	2,053	328	190
Widowed	2,567	-	30	94	425	707	1,311
Divorced	8,322	143	1,171	2,610	3,569	626	202
Females	102,403	12,568	19,828	22,407	29,041	9,882	8,677
Married, spouse present	55,259	2,315	11,428	14,951	19,005	5,181	2,380
Married, spouse absent	3,996	268	914	1,210	1,187	239	178
Unmarried	43,148	9,986	7,486	6,246	8,849	4,462	6,119
Never married	21,043	9,743	5,908	2,721	1,801	425	446
Widowed	11,027	17	90	304	2,223	3,155	5,239
Divorced	11,078	227	1,489	3,222	4,825	882	433
LIVING ARRANGEMENTS							
Males	95,009	12,633	19,526	22,055	27,271	7,992	5,533
Living with relative(s)	75,307	9,988	14,310	17,676	22,560	6,615	4,157
Family householder	45,704	1,286	7,889	11,726	16,663	5,088	3,051
Spouse of householder	12,452	311	2,515	3,405	4,288	1,200	733
Child of householder	12,708	7,399	2,845	1,760	682	22	-
Other, living with relatives	4,443	992	1,061	785	927	305	373
Not living with relatives	19,702	2,645	5,215	4,378	4,712	1,377	1,375
Nonfamily householder	14,122	1,326	3,325	3,208	3,780	1,203	1,280
Living alone	11,000	712	2,222	2,555	3,164	1,111	1,234
Sharing home with nonrelative	3,122	614	1,103	653	616	92	46
Other, not living with relatives	5,580	1,319	1,890	1,170	932	174	95
Females	102,403	12,568	19,828	22,407	29,041	9,882	8,677
Living with relative(s)	80,666	10,020	16,494	19,828	23,649	6,719	3,957
Family householder	25,053	1,609	5,749	7,146	7,418	1,900	1,231
Spouse of householder	41,830	1,564	8,316	11,277	14,672	4,161	1,840
Child of householder	8,917	5,974	1,680	762	477	21	3
Other, living with relatives	4,866	873	749	643	1,082	637	883
Not living with relatives	21,737	2,548	3,334	2,580	5,393	3,163	4,720
Nonfamily householder	17,504	1,068	2,070	1,863	4,758	3,080	4,664
Living alone	15,312	523	1,456	1,499	4,257	2,987	4,590
Sharing home with nonrelative	2,192	545	614	364	501	93	74
Other, not living with relatives	4,233	1,480	1,264	717	635	83	56

- Represents zero or rounds to zero.

Source: Terry A. Lugalia, *Marital Status and Living Arrangements: March 1998 (Update)*, Bureau of the Census, Washington, DC, 1998

facilities. Fifty-three percent of residents moved to assisted living from private residences. The average stay in 1997 was 26 months. The most common reason (44 percent) for discharge was the need for a nursing home stay. Other reasons for discharge included death (26 percent), financial reasons (5 percent), and a move to another assisted living residence (4 percent).

Because of its immense growth, some people have expressed concern about assisted living as an industry. Among the concerns are the potential for serious waste, fraud, and abuse, problems that at times have plagued the nursing home industry and made them among the most regulated of health care components.

In 1996, the Assisted Living Federation of America (ALFA), an industry association, in *Overview of Assisted Living*, studied 286 primarily for-profit assisted living residences in 35 states and Canada, to determine who the facilities served and what their residents felt were important. The study found that 75 percent of residents were single females averaging 84 years of age, 22 percent were single males averaging 82 years, and 3 percent were married couples.

The ALFA study found that 48 percent of those in assisted living facilities suffered some form of mental impairment, 38 percent used a wheelchair or walker, and 30.2 percent were incontinent. Thirty-one percent had been hospitalized before moving into the residence. Among the services the residents felt they most needed help with were medication dispensing (70 percent), bathing (64 percent), medication reminders (50 percent), dressing (46 percent), toileting (32 percent), transferring from bed to chairs or wheelchairs (15.2 percent), and eating (10 percent).

Private units are a critical feature of assisted living that fosters privacy, autonomy, and independence. Some complexes have both private and shared units, but private units are more common. The cost varies depending on services. The ALFA survey found assisted living facility rates lower than nursing homes. The average basic per-day rate, including a private room, was approximately $72, compared to $127 per day for a nursing home. Currently, Medicaid reimburses only the services portion of an assisted living stay, not room and board. A resident eligible for Supplemental Security Income (SSI; see Chapter II) can use those funds to subsidize room and board costs. Many states are, however, trying to incorporate assisted living into their long-term care systems.

Most new assisted living developments are located in major metropolitan areas of the United States. Although seniors often leave the areas where they lived during their child-rearing years to move to retirement meccas like Florida or Arizona, as they age and need more assistance, their children often step in and move them closer to their own homes. In explaining where the developers decide to build, Paul Klaassen, an industry CEO explained, "We go where the daughters are." He revealed that the typical decision-maker is a 53-year old daughter or daughter-in-law who lives near the assisted living facility.

Life-Care Communities

Life-care communities provide their residents with housing, personal care, a variety of social and recreational activities, and, ultimately, nursing care. Typically, residents enter into a lifetime contractual arrangement with the facility for which they pay an entrance fee and a set monthly fee in return for services and benefits. Most facilities are operated by private, non-profit, and/or religious organizations.

Entrance fees in these communities can vary substantially, from $20,000 to $200,000, and monthly fees range from $500 to $2,000 depending on the size of the facility and the quality and number of services. Services usually do not include acute health care needs such as doctor visits and hospitalization and, with few exceptions, are not covered by government or private insurance.

While life-care communities can ensure their residents against rising health care costs and assure daily care, they have come under criticism. Sometimes fee calculations are not based on sound actuarial data, so that a facility may find itself without adequate financial resources. On the other hand, residents may be paying more than necessary for care received. Residents sometimes find that if they decide to leave the community, none of their fees will be refunded. A few states have taken steps to regulate life-care communities, but there is little standardization in regulations between states.

Shared Housing

Some elderly persons share living quarters (and expenses) to reduce costs and responsibilities and also for companionship. Many elderly live in the same homes in which they raised their families. These houses may be too large for the needs of one or two persons. Shared housing can be very cost-effective for those who wish to remain in their own homes and for those who cannot afford a home of their own or the cost of a retirement community. About three-fourths of older home-sharing participants are women.

In its most common form, a single homeowner seeks a roommate to share living space and expenses. Shared housing can also include households with three or more roommates and family-like cooperatives in which large groups of people live together.

Unfortunately, the elderly poor who desire to share housing may lose some of their already meager incomes. Under government regulations, supplemental Social Security eligibility and benefits are computed on the basis of the income of the entire household rather than the individual residents. Savings in living expenses may be more than offset by a reduction in benefits and money for food and medicine. Another barrier to shared housing is zoning restrictions. Some communities restrict people who are not related from sharing living quarters.

Intergenerational home-sharing may fit the needs of younger and older people. While offering the usual benefits of cost-cutting and companionship, home-sharers may exchange services, for example, help with household maintenance in exchange for babysitting.

ECHO Units or "Granny Flats"

Elder Cottage Housing Opportunity (ECHO) units or "granny flats" are small, free-standing, removable housing units that are located on the same lot as a single-family house. Another term used in local zoning is "accessory apartments or units." Generally, they are constructed by a family for an elderly parent or grandparent so that he or she can be nearby while each party maintains a degree of independence. Zoning laws and concerns about property values and traffic patterns are major obstacles to granny flats, although as the elderly survive longer and nursing home costs increase, this concept may gain support.

Retirement Communities

A number of developers have experimented with constructing entire cities just for the elderly. Examples include the Sun City communities in Florida, Arizona, and Texas. The Florida and Arizona locations opened in the 1960s; the Texas site in 1996. Homes in these properties are available only to those families in which at least one member is 55 or older, and no one under age 19 is allowed to stay permanently. Sun City offers clubs, golf courses, social organizations, fitness clubs, and recreational complexes. At the Texas location, 45 percent of the land remains open space and natural areas. Medical facilities are located nearby.

Sun City is not for the poor. Forty percent of its residents have a net worth of $300,000, and 35 percent are worth $400,000 or more. About 60 percent have had at least some college education, compared with 20 percent of all adults aged 65 and older.

While cities devoted to the needs and interests of the elderly may seem ideal, they face a unique challenge: everyone is getting older. The demand for social and health services for the thousands of people with a median age of 80 may prove overwhelming.

Co-Housing and Intentional Communities

Co-housing, which originated in Denmark, is gaining interest in the United States. What distinguishes the arrangements in this category is planning — a group of individuals design and plan a community. Being in better health and living longer, many seniors wish to maintain their own private residences while also benefiting from certain features helpful to their age. They may find apartments or townhouses less strenuous to maintain than single-family homes with lawns. They may also enjoy the camaraderie of others their age and some common areas, such as dining facilities.

For such seniors, many communities — or the seniors themselves — are building apartments, townhouses, and condominiums restricted to those over a specified age. Although acute medical needs are not provided for, many such residences are physically equipped for older residents. Furthermore, because of their specific clientele, these communities can accommodate some specific needs of the elderly, such as common transportation to senior centers, social activities tailored for various stages of aging, and checking on residents when asked. Most of these developments are private enterprises. In fact, in most instances, the seniors plan the community and own not only their own property, but also an interest in the common facilities. There are currently more than 50 co-housing developments in the United States.

Board and Care Facilities

The Subcommittee on Health and Long-term Care of the Select Committee on Aging of the House of Representatives defines a board and care facility as one that "provides shelter, food and protection to frail and disabled individuals." Typically, residents have their own bedroom and bathroom, or share them with one other person, but all other rooms are shared space. While the concept is praiseworthy, all too often, the board and care business is riddled with fraud and abuses. Totally unregulated in many states, these facilities have frequently become dumping grounds for the old, the ill, the mentally retarded, and the disabled.

Medical experts believe that Supplemental Social Security (SSI) is the only form of income for three-fourths of these residents. It is not uncommon for a resident to turn over his or her entire SSI check to the facility's manager and receive less than minimal care in return.

In an attempt to stem abuses, the federal government passed the Keys Amendment in 1978. Under this law, residents living in board and care facilities that do not provide adequate care are subject to reduced SSI income. The facility's owners would then suffer economically as a result of their tenants' reduced income. In fact, in most cases, the only ones who have suffered (even more than before) are the residents. While board and care facilities can provide an alternative living arrangement for the elderly, it is one that very few choose.

THE HIGH COST
OF LIVING ARRANGEMENTS

The graying of America is going to have a significant impact on the nation's housing and will be one of the greatest challenges we face over the next 10 years. — Andrew

Cuomo, Secretary of Housing and Urban Development, 1998

Owning a Home — the American Dream?

In 1998, according to the Bureau of the Census, 79.3 percent of householders 65 and older owned the home in which they lived. Homeownership peaked between the ages of 70 to 74 (82.2 percent). (See Table 3.6.) Home ownership is highest for married-couple families. In 1998, among those 65 and older, 91.4 percent of married couples owned their homes (Table 3.7), compared to the 79.3 percent for all homeowners, 65.2 percent of male one-person households, and 68.5 percent of female one-person households.

More than 1 in 5 householders are elderly. Elderly householders are less likely than those under 65 to have mortgage indebtedness. Eighty percent of elderly homeowners have no mortgage payment. Even where there is no mortgage remaining on the home, however, the homeowner must still pay taxes, insurance, garbage collection, utility bills, and often high repair costs for what is most likely an older home. Although elderly persons spend only half as much for housing as do younger owners, they spend an approximately equal percentage — one-third — of their income for housing.

Nonetheless, failing health and physical disability, often accompanied by reduced or fixed income, can make home ownership a burden. The result is that the proportion of elderly who own their own homes begins to decline at age 65. Most elderly owners have lived in their homes more than 17 years. About half of elderly owners paid less than $20,000 for their homes. About 21 percent of the elderly had four or fewer rooms, while only 11 percent of younger owners' homes were that small. Both of these factors tend to indicate the houses were originally bought a long time ago when houses were less expensive and smaller.

The Bureau of the Census reported that, in 1995, 32 percent of those 65 and older were unable to afford a medium-priced home in their area, compared to 30.9 percent of those 55 to 64 and 40 percent of those 45 to 54. Elderly married couples were the most able (74 percent), compared to older single males (43.6 percent) and single females over 65 (39.2 percent).

Reverse Mortgages

Older homeowners sometimes need spendable cash. An arrangement known as a reverse mortgage allows older homeowners to "cash in" some of their home equity each month for cash, yet still retain ownership of the home. The money is paid out to a homeowner in monthly installments determined by the amount of home equity borrowed against, the interest rate, and the length of the loan. In most cases, no repayment is due until the homeowner dies, sells the house, or permanently moves.

Sale/Leaseback or Life Tenancy

In a sale/leaseback or life tenancy arrangement a homeowner sells the home to an investor, who then leases it back to the homeowner. The former homeowner retains the right to live in the house for life as a renter. The investor pays the former owner in monthly installments and also is responsible for property taxes, insurance, maintenance, and repairs.

Renting Is Even More Expensive

The National Low-Income Housing Coalition, in its study *Out of Reach* (1997), reported that the nationwide median fair market rent for a one-bedroom unit was $449 and for a two-bedroom, $558 (Figures 3.1 and 3.2).

About one-third of elderly households live in rented facilities. Renters generally pay a higher percentage of their incomes for housing than do homeowners. Renters are often faced with several additional drawbacks: mortgage payments on a home generally remain the same over a period of years (often until the entire mortgage is paid off), but rents may increase each year while the renter remains on a fixed income. Also, homeowners have the equity in their homes to fall back on in times

TABLE 3.6

Homeownership Rates for the United States, by Age of Householder

	1997	1998
United States, total............	65.7	66.3
Less than 25 years...........	17.7	18.2
25 to 29 years..............	35.0	36.2
30 to 34 years..............	52.6	53.6
35 to 39 years..............	62.6	63.7
40 to 44 years..............	69.7	70.0
45 to 49 years..............	74.2	73.9
50 to 54 years..............	77.7	77.8
55 to 59 years..............	79.7	79.8
60 to 64 years..............	80.5	82.1
65 to 69 years..............	81.9	81.9
70 to 74 years..............	82.0	82.2
75 years and over...........	75.8	76.2
Less than 35 years........	38.7	39.3
35 to 44 years............	66.1	66.9
45 to 54 years............	75.8	75.7
55 to 64 years............	80.1	80.9
65 years and over.........	79.1	79.3

TABLE 3.7

Homeownership Rates for the United States, by Age of Householder and by Married-couple Families

	1997	1998
Family households		
Married-couple families.......	80.8	81.5
Less than 25 years...........	31.4	33.1
25 to 29 years..............	51.7	54.0
30 to 34 years..............	69.0	70.0
35 to 39 years..............	78.1	78.7
40 to 44 years..............	83.2	83.5
45 to 49 years..............	86.6	86.4
50 to 54 years..............	89.3	89.1
55 to 59 years..............	90.0	90.4
60 to 64 years..............	91.0	92.4
65 to 69 years..............	92.4	92.1
70 to 74 years..............	92.6	92.7
75 years and over...........	90.0	89.7
Less than 35 years........	58.2	59.7
35 to 44 years............	80.6	81.1
45 to 54 years............	87.8	87.7
55 to 64 years............	90.5	91.4
65 years and over.........	91.6	91.4

Source of both tables: *Housing Vacancies and Homeownership Annual Statistics: 1998*, U.S. Bureau of the Census, Washington, DC, 1999

of financial crisis; the renter makes out a monthly check, but none of the money is ever returned as a tangible asset. Finally, mortgage payments are tax-deductible, while rent payments are not.

Four in 10 elderly renters receive some form of housing assistance, either from the government, such as rent control or public or subsidized housing, or some from land-lords who voluntarily lower rents to older renters. About one in 10 renters over 65 years of age paid no cash rent. For many older renters, meals are part of their rental package. The Bureau of the Census estimates that 1 in 10 elderly renters lived in homes where meals were provided as part of their rental agreement. The proportion with a rent-meals arrangement increases with age, reaching 23 percent for renters 85 and older. Most of these elderly renters pay $750 or more per month for this combination of housing and meals.

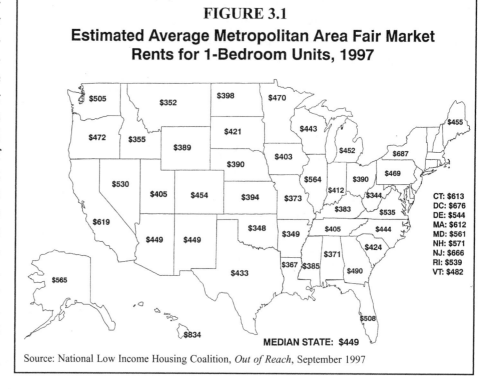

FIGURE 3.1

Estimated Average Metropolitan Area Fair Market Rents for 1-Bedroom Units, 1997

CT: $613
DC: $676
DE: $544
MA: $612
MD: $561
NH: $571
NJ: $666
RI: $539
VT: $482

MEDIAN STATE: $449

Source: National Low Income Housing Coalition, *Out of Reach*, September 1997

A Housing Problem for Older Women

While men may find it hard to find suitable housing, women are disproportionately affected because their retirement incomes are generally much smaller than men's and because they live an average of seven years longer than men. As women age, they are increasingly more likely to live alone because of divorce or death of their spouse. Forty-five percent of older single women have an income of $10,000 a year or less, and nearly one-third of older women renters spend more than half their limited income on housing. On average, women renters spend a third of their income on housing compared to one-fourth for men. Furthermore, almost 30 percent of homeless women are over the age of 50.

A majority of older women live in older suburbs that are falling into decay — homes built in the post-World War II boom that often need major repairs. And although most women in the suburbs are owners rather than renters, their homes are val-ued at less than those owned by single men or couples because single women's incomes often keep them from being able to make repairs. Older women also run a risk of becoming homeless through divorce, abusive marital situations, loss of employment, or the death of their spouses.

ADDITIONAL HOUSING PROBLEMS OF THE ELDERLY

Older Houses and More Maintenance

Many older people live in older houses. It is quite common for elderly owners, especially those over 85, to have lived in their homes for more than 30 years. The age of a house does not necessarily reflect its physical condition, but older houses typically need more frequent and expensive repairs. Building materials become stressed with age. Older houses may be poorly insulated. Owners 65 and older have a greater likelihood of having severe or moderate housing problems than owners 35 to 64 years of age. The elderly and persons living alone are more likely to let maintenance work slide. The elderly constitute more than one-third of those who had not paid for any maintenance recently.

Physical Hazards

Features considered desirable by younger householders may be handicaps to the elderly. For example, the staircase in a two-story house may become a formidable obstacle to someone with osteoporosis or a neuromuscular problem. Narrow halls and doorways cannot be navigated in wheelchairs. High cabinets and shelves may be beyond the reach of an arthritis sufferer. While houses can be modified to meet the physical needs of the elderly, not all older houses can be remodeled to accept such modifications, and installing them may be more costly than some elderly can afford. Condominium owners in Florida, whose "young-old" residents once valued second- and third-floor locations for their breezes and golf-course views, are now being asked to install elevators for residents in their 80s and 90s.

The American Association of Retired Persons (AARP) believes that 85 percent of people over 55 prefer to remain in familiar surroundings, rather than move to alternative housing. As a result, those who are able redesign their homes to accommodate the changes that accompany aging — a concept known as "universal design." Its premise is that homes, from their initial blueprints or as modifications, should be equipped for people with disabilities — functional yet aesthetic.

Anticipating the increase in the elderly population in the coming years, some real estate developers are manufacturing experimental houses designed to meet the needs of the elderly and thus prolong independent living. Such houses include non-skid flooring, walls strong enough to support grab bars, light plugs at convenient heights, levers instead of knobs on doors and plumbing fixtures, and wide doors and hallways.

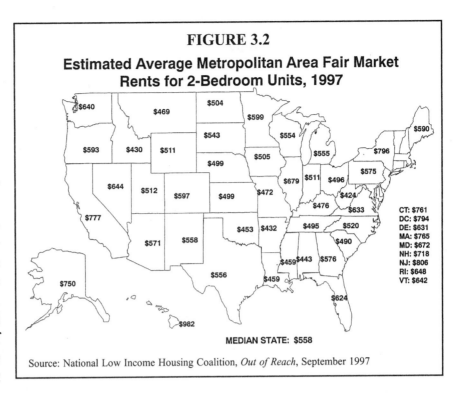

FIGURE 3.2

Estimated Average Metropolitan Area Fair Market Rents for 2-Bedroom Units, 1997

CT: $761
DC: $794
DE: $631
MA: $765
MD: $672
NH: $718
NJ: $806
RI: $648
VT: $642

MEDIAN STATE: $558

Source: National Low Income Housing Coalition, *Out of Reach*, September 1997

Simple adaptations include replacing doorknobs with levers that can be pushed downward with a fist or elbow, requiring no gripping or twisting; replacing light switches with flat, "touch" switches; placing closet rods at adjustable heights; installing stoves with front or side-mounted controls; and marking steps with bright colors. More complex renovations include replacing a bathroom with a wet room, a tiled space with a showerhead, waterproof chair, and sloping floor for a drain, large enough to accommodate a wheelchair; placing electrical receptacles higher than usual along walls; and widening passageways and doors for wheelchairs or battery-operated carts. Family and friends of disabled and elderly people also benefit from universal design.

Lack of Transportation

When an elderly person's vision and physical reflexes decline, driving a car can be difficult and perilous. Older people whose homes are far from shopping centers or public transportation may have to depend on others for transportation or delivery of the basic necessities, or they may simply have to do without. This is a particularly acute problem for the approximately 25 percent of the U.S. elderly who live in rural areas. The rural elderly may be isolated not only from food and clothing stores, but also from health and social services.

PUBLIC HOUSING

In 1937, Congress passed the United States Housing Act (PL 75-412) to create low-income public housing. Prior to 1956, only 10 percent of available units were occupied by persons 65 or older; today, the elderly occupy more than 40 percent of available low-income public housing units.

The federal government makes direct loans to private, non-profit developers to build housing designed specifically for the elderly and the handicapped. At least one-half of the nation's low-income housing units are more than 25 years old. Many were built during the 1930s and 1940s and are in need of major renovation.

Despite federal programs to provide decent, affordable housing, it is still beyond the reach of many millions of elderly. According to the National Council of Senior Citizens (a private advocacy group), the average time on a waiting list for elderly housing is three to five years, and only 1 in 7 elderly poor receives federal housing assistance. For each vacancy in subsidized complexes, there are an estimated eight elderly people on a waiting list.

FUTURE TRENDS

The number of elderly persons living independently has increased significantly, and that trend is expected to continue into the next century. Those now approaching retirement age are more health-conscious than their parents, and they generally had a higher personal income during their working years. While many people still fail to plan adequately for their later years, the importance of such planning is being widely publicized by government agencies and private organizations. The "young-old" and the generation of baby boomers can still take steps to ensure a financially comfortable old age.

The declining birth rate that followed the baby boom has meant that there are fewer children with whom the future elderly can share housing. Because the extended family will likely become even less common than it is now, older people living alone will have to rely more on community services, including senior citizen centers, special transportation, meals, visiting nurses, or day care. A greater proportion of the elderly living alone use community services, a situation that is especially true of the poor.

While the number of elderly living independently will increase, so will the number of those who will become nursing home residents. Since 1980, the number of older Americans in need of long-term care has grown 14 percent, and the number is expected to double by 2020.

The near-universal desire of even the frail and chronically ill elderly to remain at home has fostered a number of alternatives that may enable them, when possible, to stay in familiar surroundings with at least some control of their lives. Among these approaches are adult day care, home repair services, and housekeeping and visiting nurse programs. Telephone reassurance programs telephone frail individuals daily to check their status. Some municipalities now provide free or low-cost transportation to elderly residents, including those with handicaps.

Technology also plays a part; electronic alarm systems and remote control appliances are increasingly being marketed to the aging population. Foster family programs for the elderly have been introduced. The goal of these programs is to enable as many elderly as possible to remain independent, in their own homes, and out of institutions for as long as possible. (For a further discussion of health care, see Chapter IX.)

CHAPTER IV

WORKING — PAID AND UNPAID CONTRIBUTIONS

Millions of older people are ready, willing, and able to increase their productivity, paid and voluntary. Even now, in taking care of spouses, siblings, and grandchildren, the elderly do the work of three million care givers. For many people, retirement is not the end of a productive life but the beginning of a new one. — The MacArthur Foundation, 1998

As far back as 1968, then-Secretary of Labor Willard Wirtz observed, "Senior citizens don't want handouts. They want to continue to make a contribution to their fellow man. They want to continue to be a vital and living part of the American society." Productivity is not the exclusive domain of the young. Genius, creativity, and dedication do not end on a person's sixty-fifth birthday. Older people have made and continue to make significant contributions in all areas.

U.S. Senator John Glenn, the first American to orbit the earth in 1962, returned to space at age 77 as a payload specialist. Rather than retire as Federal Reserve chairman, 71-year-old Alan Greenspan was recently reappointed to oversee the American economy. Benjamin Franklin — writer, scientist, inventor, and statesman — helped draft the Declaration of Independence at the age of 70. Golda Meir was elected Prime Minister of Israel when she was 71. Thomas Alva Edison worked on such inventions as the light bulb, the microphone, and the phonograph until his death at the age of 81. Rear Admiral (Ret.) Grace Hooper, one of the early computer scientists and co-creator of the computer language COBOL, maintained an active speaking and consulting schedule up until her death in her 80s.

Margaret Mead, the noted anthropologist, returned to New Guinea when she was 72 and exhausted a much younger television filming crew as they tried to keep up with her. Albert Einstein, who formulated the theory of relativity, was working on a unifying theory of the universe when he died at age 76. Pablo Picasso and Georgia O'Keefe created masterful paintings when they were each past 80 years of age. And in 1997, President George Bush celebrated his seventy-second birthday with a sky dive over the Arizona desert.

A CHANGING ECONOMY AND CHANGING ROLES

*America today possesses not only the fastest-growing, but the largest, best-educated, and most vigorous collection of older adults in our history. In fact, the senior population may represent the country's only **increasing** natural resource.* — Mark Freedman, *Seniors in National and Community Service: A Report Prepared for The Commonwealth Fund's Americans Over 55 at Work Program*, 1994

From Agricultural ...

In early America, there was little correlation between age and work. In that agricultural society, youngsters were put to work as soon as possible to contribute to the family upkeep. At the other end of the age scale, workers did not retire; they worked as long as they were physically able to do so. Then they were cared for by the younger members of the family. Older people were valued and respected for their accumulated knowledge and experience. They were an integral part of the interconnected family and labor systems.

... to Industrial

The Industrial Revolution took men away from the farm and into manufacturing jobs. The work was physically demanding, the hours long, and the tasks strictly structured. Women labored in factories and at home caring for the family. Older people found themselves without a place in the workforce. Their skills and experience were not relevant to new technologies, nor could they physically compete with the large number of young workers eager to take advantage of new economic opportunities.

As industrial workers matured, some of them were promoted to positions as supervisors and managers. Labor unions provided some job security through the seniority system ("first hired, last fired") for older workers who had been with the same company for many years. However, in an increasingly youth-oriented society, older workers were often pushed aside to make way for younger workers. The problem became so severe that Congress passed the Age Discrimination Act (PL 90-202) in 1967 and the Age Discrimination Act Amendment (PL 95-256) in 1978, prohibiting differential treatment of workers based solely on age. In 1987, Congress amended the act to abolish age-based mandatory retirement for most workers in the private sector as well as those in government employment (see Age Discrimination, below).

... to Service

The American economy continues its dramatic shift away from manufacturing and toward the service sector. Doctors, data entry persons, travel agents, auto mechanics, and teachers far outnumber coal miners, carpenters, and pipefitters. The number of agricultural employees continues to decline, manufacturing jobs are decreasing, and the service industry has doubled in the number of employees since 1970.

Many service jobs are ideally suited for older workers. They usually do not require heavy labor, and the cumulative experience of years of work is an advantage in almost all service fields. Furthermore, at a time when unemployment rates are extremely low, businesses need workers of any age. Nonetheless, bias against older workers still exists.

PARTICIPATION IN THE LABOR FORCE

In 1999, almost 4 million men and women over age 65 participated in the labor force (either by actively working or actively seeking work), compared to approximately 8.9 million people ages 55 to 59 and 4.7 million ages 60 to 64. More than 12 percent of Americans over age 65 were in the labor market. (See Table 4.1.)

Although older women outnumber older men in the general population, a greater percentage of men than women were in the labor force. Most men (67.9 percent) ages 55 to 64 were participants; by age 65, only 16.9 percent participated. About 51.5 percent of women ages 55 to 64 were in the labor force; by age 65, the percentage dropped to 8.9 percent.

Older Women and Work

Women are beginning to realize that by working just a few more years, they can become eligible for good pensions. — Olivia Mitchell, University of Pennsylvania economist, 1997

Most of today's older women spent some time in the labor force when they were younger. The older the woman, however, the less likely she is to have worked. The U.S. Department of Labor reported, in 1995, that half the women over 80 have either never worked or have worked less than five years for one employer, compared with, for example, one-third of women 65 to 69 and one-fifth of the women in their late fifties. (See Figure 4.1.)

American women in their late 50s and early 60s, the first generation to leave their houses to

TABLE 4.1

Employment status of the civilian noninstitutional population by age, sex, and race

(Numbers in thousands)

Age, sex, and race	Civilian noninstitutional population	Civilian labor force		Employed				Unemployed		Not in labor force
		Total	Percent of population	Total	Percent of population	Agriculture	Nonagricultural industries	Number	Percent of labor force	
TOTAL										
16 years and over	207,753	139,368	67.1	133,488	64.3	3,281	130,207	5,880	4.2	68,385
16 to 19 years	16,040	8,333	52.0	7,172	44.7	234	6,938	1,162	13.9	7,706
16 to 17 years	8,060	3,337	41.4	2,793	34.7	107	2,686	544	16.3	4,723
18 to 19 years	7,979	4,996	62.6	4,379	54.9	128	4,251	618	12.4	2,983
20 to 24 years	17,968	13,933	77.5	12,891	71.7	332	12,559	1,042	7.5	4,034
25 to 54 years	118,198	99,414	84.1	96,228	81.4	2,009	94,219	3,186	3.2	18,785
25 to 34 years	37,976	32,143	84.6	30,865	81.3	648	30,218	1,278	4.0	5,833
25 to 29 years	18,339	15,517	84.6	14,836	80.9	318	14,519	681	4.4	2,822
30 to 34 years	19,637	16,626	84.7	16,029	81.6	330	15,699	597	3.6	3,011
35 to 44 years	44,635	37,882	84.9	36,728	82.3	782	35,946	1,154	3.0	6,753
35 to 39 years	22,379	18,937	84.6	18,345	82.0	388	17,957	592	3.1	3,441
40 to 44 years	22,256	18,945	85.1	18,382	82.6	393	17,989	562	3.0	3,311
45 to 54 years	35,587	29,388	82.6	28,635	80.5	580	28,055	753	2.6	6,199
45 to 49 years	19,324	16,330	84.5	15,904	82.3	341	15,563	426	2.6	2,994
50 to 54 years	16,263	13,058	80.3	12,731	78.3	239	12,492	327	2.5	3,205
55 to 64 years	23,064	13,682	59.3	13,315	57.7	422	12,893	367	2.7	9,382
55 to 59 years	12,747	8,895	69.8	8,656	67.9	234	8,422	239	2.7	3,852
60 to 64 years	10,317	4,787	46.4	4,659	45.2	188	4,471	128	2.7	5,530
65 years and over	32,484	4,005	12.3	3,882	11.9	283	3,599	124	3.1	28,478
65 to 69 years	9,281	2,137	23.0	2,065	22.2	120	1,945	72	3.4	7,144
70 to 74 years	8,540	1,116	13.1	1,088	12.7	81	1,007	29	2.6	7,424
75 years and over	14,663	752	5.1	729	5.0	82	648	23	3.0	13,911
Men										
16 years and over	99,722	74,512	74.7	71,446	71.6	2,432	69,014	3,066	4.1	25,210
16 to 19 years	8,167	4,318	52.9	3,685	45.1	188	3,497	633	14.7	3,848
16 to 17 years	4,143	1,732	41.8	1,437	34.7	84	1,353	295	17.0	2,411
18 to 19 years	4,024	2,587	64.3	2,249	55.9	104	2,145	338	13.1	1,437
20 to 24 years	8,899	7,291	81.9	6,729	75.6	259	6,470	562	7.7	1,608
25 to 54 years	57,870	53,093	91.7	51,496	89.0	1,467	50,029	1,597	3.0	4,776
25 to 34 years	18,565	17,318	93.3	16,694	89.9	497	16,198	624	3.6	1,248
25 to 29 years	8,931	8,283	92.7	7,949	89.0	249	7,700	334	4.0	649
30 to 34 years	9,634	9,035	93.8	8,745	90.8	247	8,498	290	3.2	599
35 to 44 years	21,969	20,382	92.8	19,811	90.2	569	19,241	571	2.8	1,587
35 to 39 years	11,026	10,287	93.3	9,999	90.7	301	9,699	288	2.8	739
40 to 44 years	10,942	10,095	92.3	9,811	89.7	269	9,543	283	2.8	848
45 to 54 years	17,335	15,394	88.8	14,991	86.5	401	14,590	403	2.6	1,942
45 to 49 years	9,444	8,532	90.3	8,302	87.9	240	8,062	229	2.7	912
50 to 54 years	7,892	6,862	87.0	6,689	84.8	160	6,528	173	2.5	1,029
55 to 64 years	11,008	7,477	67.9	7,274	66.1	297	6,977	203	2.7	3,531
55 to 59 years	6,123	4,799	78.4	4,671	76.3	160	4,511	128	2.7	1,324
60 to 64 years	4,885	2,678	54.8	2,603	53.3	136	2,466	75	2.8	2,207
65 years and over	13,779	2,333	16.9	2,263	16.4	222	2,041	70	3.0	11,446
65 to 69 years	4,279	1,218	28.5	1,177	27.5	94	1,083	40	3.3	3,062
70 to 74 years	3,776	657	17.4	642	17.0	64	578	15	2.3	3,119
75 years and over	5,724	458	8.0	444	7.8	63	380	14	3.1	5,266
Women										
16 years and over	108,031	64,855	60.0	62,042	57.4	849	61,193	2,814	4.3	43,175
16 to 19 years	7,873	4,015	51.0	3,487	44.3	46	3,440	529	13.2	3,858
16 to 17 years	3,917	1,606	41.0	1,357	34.6	23	1,334	249	15.5	2,312
18 to 19 years	3,955	2,410	60.9	2,130	53.9	23	2,107	280	11.6	1,546
20 to 24 years	9,089	6,643	73.2	6,163	68.0	74	6,089	480	7.2	2,426
25 to 54 years	60,329	46,321	76.8	44,732	74.1	542	44,190	1,588	3.4	14,008
25 to 34 years	19,411	14,826	76.4	14,171	73.0	151	14,020	654	4.4	4,585
25 to 29 years	9,408	7,235	76.9	6,888	73.2	68	6,819	347	4.8	2,173
30 to 34 years	10,003	7,591	75.9	7,284	72.8	83	7,201	307	4.0	2,412
35 to 44 years	22,666	17,501	77.2	16,917	74.6	212	16,705	584	3.3	5,166
35 to 39 years	11,352	8,650	76.2	8,346	73.5	87	8,259	304	3.5	2,702
40 to 44 years	11,314	8,850	78.2	8,571	75.8	125	8,446	279	3.2	2,464
45 to 54 years	18,251	13,994	76.7	13,644	74.8	179	13,465	350	2.5	4,257
45 to 49 years	9,880	7,798	78.9	7,602	76.9	100	7,501	197	2.5	2,082
50 to 54 years	8,371	6,196	74.0	6,042	72.2	78	5,964	154	2.5	2,175
55 to 64 years	12,056	6,204	51.5	6,041	50.1	126	5,915	163	2.6	5,851
55 to 59 years	6,624	4,096	61.8	3,985	60.2	74	3,911	110	2.7	2,528
60 to 64 years	5,432	2,109	38.8	2,056	37.8	52	2,004	53	2.5	3,323
65 years and over	18,705	1,673	8.9	1,619	8.7	61	1,558	54	3.2	17,032
65 to 69 years	5,002	920	18.4	888	17.7	26	862	32	3.5	4,082
70 to 74 years	4,764	459	9.6	446	9.4	17	429	13	2.9	4,305
75 years and over	8,939	294	3.3	286	3.2	18	267	9	2.9	8,645

Source: *Employment and Earnings*, vol. 47, no. 1, January 2000

63

work in large numbers, are approaching retirement. If they are single, widowed, or divorced, they often continue to work to support themselves or because they do not have enough Social Security credits to retire.

Going in Separate Directions

As the share of men 55 to 64 in the labor force has declined, the share of older married women has increased. The result is a growing number of older women working after their husbands retire, breaking with the practice of sharing their husband's retirement. Older husbands and wives are increasingly going in opposite directions. Among the reasons cited are

- They have their own careers.

- They need to secure their retirement and avoid the poverty that has historically come with widowhood.

- Their income helps maintain the family living standards, particularly if the husband has been pushed out of his job by forced retirement.

- They enjoy the sociability. Building friendships has been found to be more important to women than to men, and women often find retirement more isolating.

Today, only 33 percent of married women are entitled to higher pensions than their spousal benefits. The Social Security Administration predicts that if current trends continue, by 2015, nearly 60 percent of married women will be entitled to higher pensions upon retirement than the spousal benefits

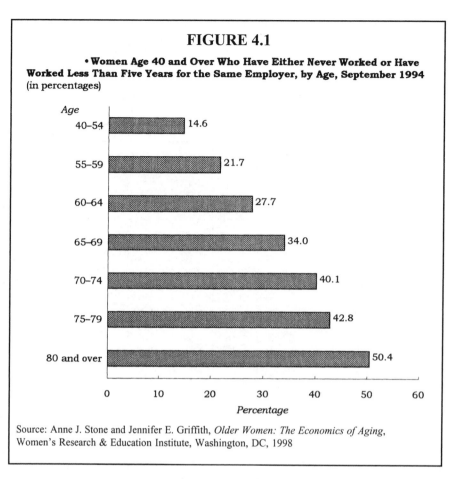

FIGURE 4.1

• Women Age 40 and Over Who Have Either Never Worked or Have Worked Less Than Five Years for the Same Employer, by Age, September 1994 (in percentages)

Source: Anne J. Stone and Jennifer E. Griffith, *Older Women: The Economics of Aging*, Women's Research & Education Institute, Washington, DC, 1998

they would receive under their husbands' Social Security. Furthermore, 20 percent of the women will qualify for pensions higher than their husbands, up from less than 10 percent today.

The result of these changes is not always positive for a marriage. Many men, who looked forward to retirement and travel, find themselves alone. They sometimes find the husband/wife roles have changed — she becomes the breadwinner, and he ends up doing domestic chores.

Changing Job Choices

Women have always been more concentrated than men in fewer occupational fields, primarily service and administrative support that typically pay lower than average wages and are less likely to provide benefits, such as pensions. In recent years, there has been some shift in the occupational distribution of women workers, including those 45 and older. From 1983 to 1995, women of all ages worked less in the administrative support and service sectors and more in executive and managerial and professional jobs, although women 65 and over generally experienced less change than other age groups. (See Table 4.2.)

Part-Time Work

Older people forced to leave their occupations sometimes feel unproductive and worthless. They may suffer emotional and financial hardship or become bored or lonely. It is increasingly common to find retired workers re-entering the workforce or remaining in the workforce by working part-time. In 1999, 25 percent of workers 55 and older who were working had part-time jobs (Table 4.3).

For employers, hiring part-time older workers is often an attractive alternative to hiring younger, full-time workers, partly because of older workers' dependability and experience. In addition, companies often pay older workers (or part-time workers, in general) lower wages and do not provide benefits such as health insurance, pensions, profit-sharing, etc.

Older persons receiving Social Security benefits may choose part-time work to supplement their incomes, although they lose part of their Social Security benefits if their earnings are too great. In 1998, the threshold for benefit retention for 62- to 64-year-old workers was raised to $9,600 annually (after which they lose $1 for every $2 they earn), and to $15,500 (after which they lose $1 for every $3 they earn) for workers 65 to 69.

RETIREMENT

Increasing longevity means that people spend more time in all phases of their lives — education, work, and retirement. In 1900, the average person spent only 1.2 years in retirement; by 1980, he was retired an average of 13.6 years. In

1997, the typical person 65 years of age could expect to live yet another 17.3 years, probably in retirement, an increase from 3 percent to approximately 20 percent of one's life span. Retirement has become an institution in the life span of the American citizen.

The age of 65 has traditionally been considered "normal retirement age" since the Social Security legislation of 1935 set that age for receipt of Social Security benefits. However, many persons choose to leave the labor force before that time for a variety of reasons — health, the retirement of a spouse, the availability of Social Security or pension benefits, or the opportunity for leisure activities. Downturns in the economy, mergers, layoffs, down-sizing, and bankruptcies can also result in unplanned early retirement. Some companies have reduced staff by offering attractive retirement packages to older workers.

The result has been a declining retirement age, from around 68 in 1950 to 63 in 1995, although the decline has leveled off in the past few years. (Figure 4.2 shows the decline in labor force participation of people 55 and older in some developed nations.) However, some elderly, because of improved health, a slight raising of Social Secu-

TABLE 4.2

• Employed Women Age 45 and Over by Occupation and Age, 1983 and 1995 (percent distributions)[1]

Occupation	Age 45–54 1983	Age 45–54 1995	Age 55–64 1983	Age 55–64 1995	Age 65 and over 1983	Age 65 and over 1995
Executive, administrative, managerial	9.1	15.3	8.3	12.8	7.3	10.7
Professional	14.3	19.5	10.9	14.8	10.3	11.3
Technicians and related	2.5	3.2	2.3	2.4	1.6	1.0
Sales	11.5	10.3	12.1	11.6	16.6	16.0
Administrative support including clerical	30.0	26.1	29.7	27.0	23.3	27.4
Service	17.1	14.3	20.4	18.6	29.6	22.1
Precision production, craft, repair	2.6	2.3	2.6	2.1	2.5	1.5
Machine operators	9.1	5.5	9.8	6.0	4.8	3.3
Transportation	0.8	1.0	0.7	0.9	0.2	0.9
Handlers, equipment cleaners, laborers	1.4	1.2	1.6	1.7	1.0	1.6
Farming, forestry, fishing	1.5	1.3	1.7	1.9	2.8	4.4
Total percentage	100.0	100.0	100.0	100.0	100.0	100.0
Total number (in thousands)	6,678	11,421	4,628	5,163	1,157	1,558

[1]Percentages may not total 100.0 due to rounding.

Source: Anne J. Stone and Jennifer E. Griffith, *Older Women: The Economics of Aging*, Women's Research & Education Institute, Washington, DC, 1998

TABLE 4.3

Employed and unemployed full- and part-time workers by age, sex, and race

(Numbers in thousands)

Age, sex, and race	1999 Employed[1] Full-time workers				Employed[1] Part-time workers				Unemployed	
		At work				At work[2]				
	Total	35 hours or more	1 to 34 hours for economic or noneconomic reasons	Not at work	Total	Part time for economic reasons	Part time for noneconomic reasons	Not at work	Looking for full-time work	Looking for part-time work
TOTAL										
Total, 16 years and over	110,302	96,276	10,079	3,947	23,186	2,216	19,509	1,461	4,669	1,211
16 to 19 years	2,386	2,007	326	53	4,786	277	4,322	187	575	587
16 to 17 years	353	279	62	11	2,440	64	2,287	90	158	386
18 to 19 years	2,033	1,727	264	42	2,346	213	2,035	97	417	201
20 years and over	107,917	94,270	9,754	3,893	18,399	1,939	15,187	1,273	4,094	624
20 to 24 years	9,568	8,424	909	235	3,323	419	2,753	152	876	167
25 years and over	98,349	85,846	8,845	3,658	15,076	1,520	12,434	1,122	3,218	458
25 to 54 years	85,529	74,991	7,515	3,023	10,699	1,336	8,605	758	2,867	319
55 years and over	12,820	10,855	1,330	635	4,376	184	3,829	363	351	139
Men, 16 years and over	63,930	57,034	4,971	1,924	7,516	946	6,178	392	2,548	518
16 to 19 years	1,416	1,208	182	27	2,269	137	2,051	81	327	307
20 years and over	62,514	55,827	4,790	1,897	5,247	809	4,127	311	2,222	211
20 to 24 years	5,371	4,823	441	107	1,357	211	1,091	55	488	74
25 years and over	57,142	51,004	4,348	1,790	3,890	598	3,036	256	1,733	137
25 to 54 years	49,428	44,351	3,636	1,441	2,068	511	1,441	116	1,526	71
55 years and over	7,715	6,653	712	350	1,822	87	1,595	140	207	66
Women, 16 years and over	46,372	39,242	5,108	2,022	15,670	1,270	13,330	1,069	2,121	693
16 to 19 years	969	799	144	26	2,517	139	2,271	107	248	280
20 years and over	45,403	38,443	4,964	1,996	13,152	1,131	11,059	962	1,872	413
20 to 24 years	4,196	3,601	468	128	1,966	208	1,661	97	387	93
25 years and over	41,207	34,842	4,496	1,868	11,186	922	9,398	866	1,485	320
25 to 54 years	36,101	30,641	3,878	1,582	8,631	825	7,164	642	1,341	248
55 years and over	5,106	4,202	618	286	2,555	97	2,234	224	145	72

[1] Employed persons are classified as full- or part-time workers based on their usual weekly hours at all jobs regardless of the number of hours they are at work during the reference week. Persons absent from work also are classified according to their usual status.

[2] Includes some persons at work 35 hours or more classified by their reason for working part time.

NOTE: Beginning in January 1999, data reflect revised population controls used in the household survey.

Source: *Employment and Earnings*, vol. 47, no. 1, January 2000

rity retirement age (from 65 to 67), and economic need caused by possible cuts in Social Security pension and health insurance benefits may feel they need and want to work longer. In addition, with fewer younger workers available and unemployment rates low, many businesses need older workers.

Some labor economists feel that early retirements deprive the nation of skilled workers needed for robust growth. The government also loses the revenue that those workers would have contributed in income and payroll taxes. For those elderly who must work for economic reasons, forced retirement and unemployment are serious problems. Older workers often experience difficulty in being re-hired, and the duration of their unemployment is longer.

Working Retirement

A worker's first retirement may not be his last. Early retirement is often triggered by the onset of pension benefits. These retirees may be back at work at another job within a year, either full- or part-time, although those jobs often last no more than two or three years. Since people are living longer and experiencing less disability, some retirees find that they miss the work environment, and some use retirement as an opportunity to embark on a second career. Some retirees choose to work but also want more flexibility to pursue outside interests, hence, a job that requires fewer hours. Rather than retire altogether, they choose to "phase down" their work lives.

In 1999, the University of Michigan's *Study on Health, Retirement, and Aging* found that, of

12,600 workers ages 51 to 61, 73 percent reported they would prefer to continue doing some work, while 27 percent wanted to stop work entirely. When asked if they thought their employer would allow an older worker to move to a less demanding job, however, 66 percent said "probably not."

Similarly, in 1997, the Gallup Poll Monthly asked people who were not yet retired about their plans for retirement. They found that 76 percent of respondents wanted to continue to work part time or full time; only 23 percent said they wanted to stop work altogether. (See Table 4.4.)

MYTHS AND MISPERCEPTIONS ABOUT OLDER WORKERS

Often, older workers are stereotyped by the common misperception that performance declines with age. Performance studies, however, show that older workers perform intellectually as well as or better than workers 30 or 40 years younger. They maintain their IQ levels, vocabulary, and creative thinking skills well into their sixties and sometimes beyond.

Many of today's jobs do not require physical stamina or strength; yet, older people are sometimes seen as too frail or sickly to work. However, corporate studies indicate that older workers have better attendance records and do as much work as younger employees. Poor health is cited as a reason for leaving a job in only a small number of workers over 50.

A concern about high health insurance costs and generally higher salaries of older workers, coupled with the notion of an older person's low productivity,

may lead an employer to believe that it is not cost-effective to hire or retain older employees. However, in most cases, this is not true. Very small companies may see higher insurance and benefit costs for older workers, but lower turnover rates, specialized skills, and job experience may more than offset these costs. Employee turnover is very costly for a company because the company often puts considerable time and money into training each new employee, and there is a learning period before a new employee becomes fully productive.

A Good Investment

Companies are recognizing all the brain power and corporate memory they lost

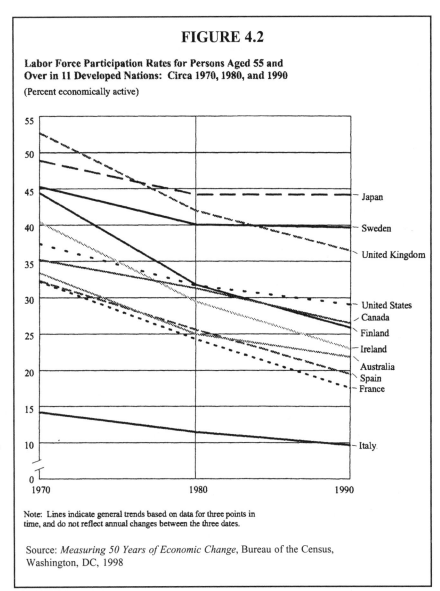

FIGURE 4.2

Labor Force Participation Rates for Persons Aged 55 and Over in 11 Developed Nations: Circa 1970, 1980, and 1990

(Percent economically active)

Note: Lines indicate general trends based on data for three points in time, and do not reflect annual changes between the three dates.

Source: *Measuring 50 Years of Economic Change*, Bureau of the Census, Washington, DC, 1998

when older employees left. — John Challenger, spokesperson for an out-placement firm, 1998

A major study of American businesses, *America over 55 at Work Program*, commissioned by the Commonwealth Fund from 1988-1993, concluded that older workers are good investments for employers. Older workers had a rate of absenteeism 39 percent less than younger employees and a turnover rate 6 times lower. Firms that employed older workers had half the loss in theft and damage and an 18 percent higher profit. The study also found that older workers could be trained in new technologies and were often better salespeople than younger workers. The report concluded that the employment of older people made good business sense.

A 1993 survey by the American Association of Retired Persons (AARP) and the Society for Human Resource Management concluded that older workers are underutilized and undervalued. Businesses indicated that although older workers offer numerous advantages to employers (Figures 4.3 and 4.4), 67 percent of respondents did not actively recruit older workers. What, then, explains the failure of American industry to hire, train, and retain older workers?

Dr. Robert Atchley, of Miami University of Ohio's Scripps Gerontology Center, in *The Challenge of an Aging Work Force in an Aging Population* (1993), observed that the data have existed for a long time documenting the productivity of the older worker. He attributed the hesitancy of business to make use of older workers to a number of myths. Among those myths were the belief that older workers are 1) less productive, 2) sickly, 3) expensive in terms of insurance and other benefits, 4) not as bright as younger workers, and that 5) old age is unattractive (i.e.

other employees do not like to be reminded of their own mortality).

The Myth of Lower Productivity

All things considered, the older person is in many respects the perfect employee.— Jeanette Takamira, U.S. Department of Health and Human Services, 1999

In fact, research overwhelmingly shows that experience is more predictive of performance than age. Sara Rix, in *Older Workers: Choices and Challenges* (1990), reported that the question, "Can older workers remain competitive?" is not the issue facing America, but rather, "How do you convince corporate America that older workers are and can remain competitive?"

Numerous studies have found no decline in productivity; indeed, older employees performed as well as or better than younger ones (see above), except in jobs requiring substantial physical exertion. Dr. Atchley's study (above) concluded that productivity does not peak until the 50s and 60s. The "incompetence model" of aging focuses on the deficits some older people have relative to youth and contributes to self-fulfilling prophesies. Other advantages to hiring older workers are their decreased time off for child-care responsibilities and less need for supervision.

Studies have been conducted to determine whether age was correlated to job performance in public safety jobs, such as police and fire officers, pilots and air traffic controllers, or to determine if

---

TABLE 4.4

(Based on those who are not retired) After you reach retirement age, would you like to continue to do some kind of work, whether part-time or fulltime, or would you like to stop working altogether?

Continue	76%
Stop	23
No opinion	1
	100%

Source: *The Gallup Poll Monthly*, March 1997

68

mandatory retirement at a specific age was necessary to ensure public safety. They have invariably concluded that chronological age was a poor predictor of job performance and limitation, even in situations where public safety was concerned, and the studies have, in general, recommended abolition of mandatory retirement.

Furthermore, the MacArthur Foundation, in a decade-long study of seniors, announced, in 1999, that society is not giving older people credit for doing unpaid work. Researchers concluded, "In taking care of spouses, siblings, and grandchildren, the elderly do the work of 3 million care givers. For many people, retirement is not the end of a productive life but the beginning of a new one."

The Myth of Declining Health, Increased Absenteeism, and Injury

Aging is sometimes associated with wheelchairs, medication, dentures, and infirmity, especially in the minds of employers. In fact, absentee rates are lower for those 50 to 65 years of age than for the 33- to 44-year-old group. And, although, in the year of Atchley's study, older workers (55 and older) made up 13.6 percent of the labor force, they accounted for only 9.7 percent of workplace injuries. Also, numerous studies have confirmed that absenteeism among older workers is lower than among younger workers and that, although many people assume that a large segment

of the elderly suffer from serious health problems, only one-fifth of older respondents report debilitation by health problems. Even those who claim to have chronic, controlled health issues are not necessarily limited or bothered by them.

The National Institute on Aging reports that many of the problems of old age are not due to old age at all, but rather to improper care of the body over a lifetime, in other words, to lifestyle. And

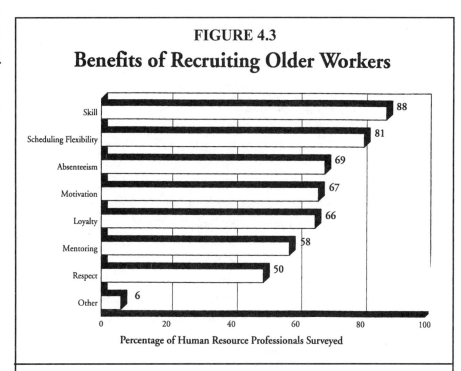

FIGURE 4.3
Benefits of Recruiting Older Workers

Percentage of Human Resource Professionals Surveyed

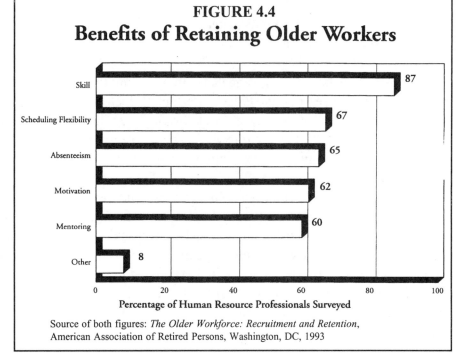

FIGURE 4.4
Benefits of Retaining Older Workers

Percentage of Human Resource Professionals Surveyed

Source of both figures: *The Older Workforce: Recruitment and Retention*, American Association of Retired Persons, Washington, DC, 1993

overwhelmingly, studies show that older workers are more likely to be on the job even when ill than younger people and are generally more dedicated and committed to their jobs than younger workers.

Furthermore, disability rates among the elderly have declined during the 1980s and 1990s (see Chapter VIII). As the number of elderly grew, the number of elderly requiring personal assistance has dropped. Disability is not an inevitable part of aging.

Higher Benefit Costs

While the costs of some benefits, primarily insurance, increase as a person ages, most increased costs of benefits associated with age are linked more to seniority and salary. In general, male workers 50 and older are more expensive in their health insurance claims than male workers under 50. On the other hand, female employees over 50 are less expensive to insure than female workers under 50, primarily due to the high costs associated with maternity and child-rearing. The rate of insurance claims for workers over 50 are generally higher than for younger workers. On the other hand, older workers generally do not have as many dependents and are often already covered by other health or pension plans, including Medicare.

The Myth That Older Workers Are Expensive to Train

Atchley's study (see above) found that employers sometimes believed that the elderly are more expensive to train because 1) they are not as bright as young people and 2) they have fewer years to return the employer's investment in training costs.

First, of Americans over the age of 65, only 10 percent showed any significant loss of memory, and fewer than half of those were seriously impaired. Most of those losses in mental capacity happened to the very old, not to those in their 60s and 70s, and were due not to age itself but to depression, drug effects, treatable illnesses, or lack of exercise.

Research suggests that older employees value and, therefore, focus not on bits of information but on overall relationships. Older employees bring to their jobs a lifetime of learning that does not have to be taught and which is valuable to themselves, their co-workers, and their employers. They have an "organizational" memory — they understand why organizations have evolved in the ways they have. Psychological skills, such as the ability to adapt and find life satisfaction, do not vary by age. Although older workers are somewhat more resistant to change, they can and do adapt; in fact, their greater life experiences have nurtured greater long-term resiliency.

Second, older employees tended to stay at their jobs longer than younger workers. Employees over the age of 45 rarely change jobs unless forced to do so by external circumstances. Training and retraining older workers is a fiscally sound investment for employers.

The Belief That Old People Are Unattractive

While inaccurate, stereotypes about older workers impel younger workers and the elderly themselves to become fearful of growing old. They can even foster ageism.
— Noreen Hale, *The Older Worker*, 1990

Webster's Ninth New Collegiate Dictionary defines stereotype as a "standardized mental picture that is held in common by members of a group and that represents an oversimplified opinion, affective attitude, or judgment." The nation's preoccupation with youth undermines the contribution of experience and knowledge of older workers.

America is a youth-oriented culture, and many people shun the physical appearances and reminders of aging — wrinkles, baldness, and assumed sexlessness. Many prospective hirees report they have been hired only after they colored their hair. Physical attractiveness pays. Researchers suggest that managers, employers, and co-workers do not like to be reminded of their own mortality.

AGE DISCRIMINATION — ILLEGAL YET PERVASIVE

The 1967 Age Discrimination in Employment Act (ADEA, PL 90-202) and a 1978 amendment were enacted to promote the employment of older workers based on their ability and to ban discrimination against workers between 40 and 65 years of age. The law made it illegal for employers to discriminate because of age in hiring, discharging, and compensating employees. It also prohibited companies from coercing older workers into accepting incentives to early retirement. In 1987, the act was amended to lift the 65-year-old age limit, making it illegal to discriminate against any worker over 40 years of age and eliminating mandatory retirement at any age.

In 1990, the Supreme Court (*Public Employees Retirement System of Ohio v. Betts*, [492 U.S. 158]) spelled out the terms under which employee benefits may be provided to older workers. In the case before the court, an employee had been denied disability retirement benefits and was forced instead to accept a less generous early retirement benefit because of her age. The court ruled that employers may not withhold benefits from older workers although they may adjust levels of benefits to offset the higher cost of providing those benefits to older workers.

Although age discrimination in the workplace is against the law, it still exists. More than 15,000 claims of age discrimination were filed between 1994 and 1999, a number that is expected to multiply by 2005, when half of all U.S. workers will be over 40 years of age. Although most cases involve older workers who believe they were terminated unfairly, a number of the cases involve people who feel they have met discrimination in hiring practices.

Some workers begin to experience negative attitudes about their age when they are in their 50s, and by the time they reach 60, age discrimination may be obvious. There are many ways an employer (and fellow employees) can exert pressure on an older employee to retire or resign. Age discrimination may be overt, but it can also be covert, subtle, or even unintentional.

Discrimination in Hiring

Older people often have a difficult time finding employment because of their age. Even with equal credentials, it generally takes older workers longer to get a job. Many people report rejections even before the interview process.

The Pressure to Retire

Corporations base employment decisions not only on how much an employee contributes to the company, but on how much salary and benefits the company must pay the employee *relative to the cost of other employees*. Since salary tends to increase with longevity on the job, older workers usually receive higher wages than younger ones. Thus, if two employees are equally productive, but the older one has a higher salary, a company has an economic incentive to encourage the older worker to take early retirement or to lay him or her off.

Employees in this situation find themselves in a difficult position. Early retirement benefits are almost always less than regular retirement benefits, and they may not provide enough financial support to allow a retiree to live comfortably without working. Finding a new job is more difficult for an older person than for a younger one, and older persons are usually unemployed for longer periods of time than are younger ones. If they refuse to accept early retirement, they may find themselves without jobs at all, perhaps with no pension and no severance pay.

The 1990 Older Workers Benefit Protection Act (PL 101-433) strengthens the Age Discrimination in Employment Act. It provides that an employee's waiver of the right to sue for age discrimination, a clause sometimes included in severance packages, is invalid unless "voluntary and knowing."

Suing the Company

It is costly to file an age discrimination suit. In addition, employers are reluctant to hire someone who has filed a discrimination suit against a former employer. Workers caught in this position can suffer emotional and financial damage which may adversely affect them for the rest of their lives. Nonetheless, more older workers are choosing to sue their employers. The main classes of issues affecting older workers involve

- Whether "over-qualification" can be grounds (or pretext) for refusing to hire an older person.

- Whether a senior worker's higher salary can be used as a basis for discharge.

- What pre-conditions can employers demand from older workers prior to hiring (for example, hiring an older worker with special exemptions from benefits).

However, a number of sources report that an aging population, coupled with low unemployment, strong demand for experienced workers, and managers who are themselves older are making age less of an issue in the marketplace. Providing the economy stays strong, older workers have a factor in their favor: the technology gap between younger and older workers is narrowing as personal computers become easier to use.

A CHANGING FUTURE FOR OLDER WORKERS?

The U.S. Bureau of Labor Statistics (BLS) predicts that as America's population grows older, so will its workforce. During the early years of the twenty-first century, as the baby boomers mature, the median age will increase dramatically. At the same time, the number of workers between the ages of 16 and 24 will decline.

Graying of the Workforce

Within at least the next six or seven years, we'll turn over the entire workforce here.
— Herb Stone, Plant manager, General Motors, 1999

Many American companies face a major turnover of its employees. As baby boomers near retirement, companies will be forced to replace them with younger, less experienced workers. In the process, industry will lose important talent. Many experts contend that it is a time for corporations to "rethink their structure." While employers are glad to see older workers replaced with cheaper younger workers, this is a bad time economically for them to have to do so. At present, the supply of young, high-tech production workers cannot keep up with job openings, and that situation will worsen in decades ahead. As Dennis Coleman, of Pricewaterhouse Coopers in New Jersey, concluded, "There are not enough baby busters [children of baby boomers] following in the footsteps of too many baby boomers who are going to want to retire."

Some companies are beginning to take notice of the shift. In 1999, the Committee of Economic Development, a New York-based public policy association, issued a call to business and lawmakers to launch a "pro-work agenda" for older workers. It urged the federal government to eliminate rules that discourage Social Security recipients from working and advised employers to rethink pension plans that encourage early retirement. It called on employers to make it more attractive for older workers to stay on the job.

Why Aging Boomers Will Continue to Work

The role of the older worker in America's future is difficult to predict. As fewer young people enter the labor force, industry may have no choice but to retain or hire older workers. There is a general feeling that today's young workers are less skilled and less educated than their mature counterparts, making older workers more desirable employees. In addition, as the age for receiving Social Security benefits is raised and private pensions become more rare, more elderly may need to work longer.

Many sources believe baby boomers are likely to stay in the labor force longer than their parents did. More-educated workers tend to have longer work lives, and boomers are the most educated generation in U.S. history. A study of workers in Wisconsin, "Older Workers in the 21st Century: Active and Educated, a Case Study" (*Monthly Labor Review*, June, 1996), found a clear association between educational attainment and labor force participation. Although labor force participation among older adults, especially men, has declined for many years, recent evidence suggests that the trend has slowed and may be reversing, and some experts have projected a modest rise by 2005 and an even greater rise over the following decades. Among explanations offered for the decline in labor force participation among older adults, especially men, in past decades are:

- Restructuring of the economy has cut the number of blue-collar workers, whose productivity is most likely to decline with advancing age.

- Job growth is concentrated in white-collar and service occupations, in which age matters less.

Among the factors that will likely cause growth in the proportions of older workers are:

- The proportions of women of all ages in the labor force has been increasing, creating a larger pool of older women to work.

- Divorce rates among boomers are higher, so many will not have a spouse's pension income to rely on. In addition, many married couples are finding they need or want the income.

- Higher-educated workers tend to command higher salaries, making a monthly Social Se-

curity check a poor substitute for a paycheck. (A typical college-educated worker sacrifices more income by retiring than does a worker who failed to finish high school. Higher education thus creates a financial incentive to remain in the labor force.)

- Intangible benefits, such as greater job satisfaction, and tangible factors, such as cleaner and safer work conditions, serve to bolster labor force participation among better-educated workers.

Suddenly in Demand

The Bureau of Labor Statistics reported in late 1999 that 55-plus workers were finding new jobs faster than people in their 30s, a stunning, possibly temporary, situation. The median time spent job hunting was 7.9 weeks for workers 55 and older, compared with 8.2 weeks for those 35 to 44. Just two years earlier, it took 55-plus workers 15.5 weeks to find a job, compared to 7.9 weeks for younger job seekers. Other positive signs for older workers were that the unemployment rate for workers 55 and older was 2.8 percent in January 2000, far below the 4.8 percent in 1992. Whether this will continue in a less vital economy is unknown.

A New Model — Will Retirement Be "Out"?

The idea of retiring at 65 is obsolete; it is based on an outdated life expectancy. — Betty Friedan, Cornell University, 1997

In the past century, people have come to believe that retirement is a right written into the constitution of almost every developed nation. Economists worldwide now contend that earlier and earlier retirement is undermining the economic survival of these countries. Peter G. Petersen, chairman of the Institute for International Economics, said, "Unless people can be persuaded to work longer into old age, developed countries will have to accept a loss of productivity, creativity, and even general economic health. Or they will be forced to accept waves of immigration from poorer nations."

He contends that in the United States, a major hurdle is ageism, a youth culture that pervades many American companies.

Furthermore, with longer life spans, less disability, and more need and desire to work among many of today's elder, some sources are predicting that the notion of retirement is fast becoming obsolete. In fact, many studies have found that people stay healthier when they work. Many people claim that workers can have two or three careers, lasting until one's 80s. Extending the work years would also mesh with proposals to finance Social Security not just by delaying payment but also by extending productive years and payments into the system.

VOLUNTEERING —
THE UNPAID CONTRIBUTION

In recent decades, these needs [of religious and service organizations] have become harder to fill because the women who used to do volunteer work as part of their traditional "at home" roles are instead entering the paid work force in record numbers. To offset this loss in potential volunteers, one particularly promising and growing group comprises the older, retired members of society. Because Americans are retiring at younger ages, and are in better health and better educated than earlier cohorts of retirees, they are very likely to have the time, skills, and energy to contribute to society through volunteer work.
— A. Regula Herzog and James N. Morgan, *Achieving a Productive Aging Society*, 1993

One of the reasons some older people become depressed and frustrated when they retire from the work force is they sense that they are no longer making meaningful contributions — that they are not an important part of society. But every day, millions of older Americans participate through volunteer work.

Older persons make ideal volunteers. They have time in a world where time is at a premium; they have wisdom and experience that years of living can bring; they have compassion from having encountered many of the same problems with which they are helping others cope.

Volunteering by older people is a relatively new phenomenon. Historically, the elderly were seen as the segment of society most in need of care and support. However, as medical technology enables people to live longer, healthier lives and stereotypes about aging crumble, the elderly are now recognized as a valuable asset for every type of volunteer activity. Increased education and affluence among the elderly suggest they may be more able and available for volunteer work.

Independent Sector, a national coalition of philanthropic organizations, reported, in *America's Senior Volunteers* (Washington, DC, 1998), that in 1996, almost 44 percent of people 55 and older volunteered at least once a year. Among those 55 to 64, 48 percent volunteered; of those 65 to 74, 44.7 percent; and among those 75 and older, 33.7 percent did volunteer work. These volunteers worked an average of 4.4 hours per week. The 24 million senior volunteers contributed approximately 5.5 billion hours of their time, a value of $70.5 billion to nonprofit organizations and other causes in the United States.

Who Volunteers?

Older people do not usually do volunteer work merely because they have nothing else to do. The strongest influence on volunteer activity is a person's general activity. The more involved they were in other activities, the more seniors volunteered. More than 47 percent of senior volunteers 55 to 64 who were still working on a part-time or full-time basis volunteered over four hours a week. Forty-two percent gave over five hours a week. Among those 55 to 64 who were retired, 34 percent reported doing volunteer work. Once over the age of 65, the participation rate became almost identical for those who were retired and those who worked.

Seniors pursued a wide variety of volunteer activities. The largest portion (22 percent) worked for religious causes, followed by informal volunteering in their neighborhoods and health organizations (13 percent each), education (8 percent), human services (7 percent), arts and youth (6 percent each). (See Figure 4.5.)

Volunteer Programs

Volunteer activities take many forms. Many older volunteers work through their churches and community centers or help friends and neighbors informally on a regular basis. Others work with established government and private programs. In 2000, 476 Americans ages 50 and older (7 percent of the total number of Peace Corps volunteers) were serving as Peace Corps volunteers in 77 countries throughout the world. The oldest is 79 years of age. Senior volunteers assignments are similar to those of younger volunteers. Age is no handicap to bringing assistance and knowledge to those needing help worldwide.

Thousands of senior citizens provide volunteer service through national and local non-government programs. In some cities, retired physicians and nurses donate their time to run clinics. Senior volunteers helped the City of Virginia Beach's police department expand its services by maintaining and purging files, checking suspects through the national Crime Information Center, and collecting, collating, and coding reports.

Some metropolitan communities around the country have implemented programs in which senior citizens earn credit for volunteer work. These service credits are earned by performing services for others, ranging from child care to hospital visits. Credits are redeemed when the volunteer needs assistance, which is provided by another volunteer (who in turn receives service credits). Volun-

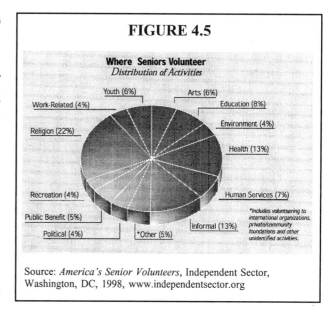

FIGURE 4.5

Where Seniors Volunteer
Distribution of Activities

Youth (6%) — Arts (6%)
Work-Related (4%) — Education (8%)
Environment (4%)
Religion (22%)
Health (13%)
Recreation (4%)
Human Services (7%)
Public Benefit (5%)
Political (4%) — *Other (5%) — Informal (13%)

*Includes volunteering to international organizations, private/community foundations and other unidentified activities.

Source: *America's Senior Volunteers*, Independent Sector, Washington, DC, 1998, www.independentsector.org

teers are thus rewarded for their service, yet there is no expense for either government or private agencies.

The Future of Senior Volunteering

Not only does volunteer work benefit society, it also gives the volunteer worker a sense of worth and purpose. In the future, the increasing number of baby-boom elderly with greater discretionary income will likely lead to a rise in the participation of the elderly in volunteer work.

There are indications that more older adults are looking for opportunities to serve. The U.S. Administration on Aging reported that 14 million Americans over 65 (37 percent of the senior population) might be willing to come forward if asked, while 4 million current volunteers say they would like to volunteer more time. Forty percent of those interviewed say the government should be doing more to promote service opportunities. Some older persons cannot afford the minimal cost associated with volunteering, even with the reimbursement for expenses offered by some programs. As the value of older volunteers receives wider recognition, perhaps resources will become available to help more of them in their desire to help others.

CHAPTER V

EDUCATION AND VOTING BEHAVIOR

EDUCATION LEVELS OF OLDER AMERICANS

At the turn of the last century, most children were not educated beyond the eighth grade. Today's elderly over age 85 reflect the limited educational opportunities of children born and reared during the early 1900s. After World War I, the number of young people graduating from high school began to increase, a change reflected in the education level of today's younger elderly. Tomorrow's elderly will mirror the rapid growth in education that occurred after World War II and will have even higher levels of educational attainment.

In 1998, 73.2 percent of Americans 65 to 69 years old, 68.7 percent of those 70 to 74 years, and 62 percent of those 75 years or older had completed at least four years of high school, compared to 88.1 percent of people in the 25- to 29-year-old age group. Only 18.1 percent of Americans 65 to 69 years of age and 12.5 percent of those 75 years and older had completed four or more years of college, considerably less that the 27.3 percent of the 25- to 29-year-old group. (See Table 5.1.) Figure 5.1 shows the gradual climb in the number of years of education completed by Americans from 1940 to 1997.

Educational attainment levels of the elderly in the twenty-first century will be higher than today's elderly. Today's 50-and-over population will be the elderly population in 2015; 76 percent of them will have completed high school or more. The proportion of the elderly who will have completed college will grow from 13 percent in 1995 to 20 percent in 2015.

TABLE 5.1

Educational Attainment of Persons 15 Years Old and Over, by Age, Sex, Race, and Hispanic Origin: March 1998

[Numbers in thousands. Noninstitutional population]

Age, sex, race, and Hispanic origin	Total	None	Elementary 1st–4th grade	Elementary 5th–6th grade	Elementary 7th–8th grade	High School 9th grade	High School 10th grade	High School 11th grade	High school graduate	Some college, no degree	Associate Degree Occupational	Associate Degree Academic	Bachelor's degree	Master's degree	Professional degree	Doctorate degree	Percent: High school graduate or more	Percent: Bachelor's degree or more
ALL RACES																		
Both Sexes																		
Total, 15 years and over	209 291	887	2 091	3 911	9 039	8 212	9 795	12 993	66 210	38 315	7 296	6 702	30 090	9 295	2 586	1 869	77.8	20.9
15 to 17 years	11 879	10	17	48	2 399	3 746	3 511	1 953	133	57	–	2	3	–	–	–	1.6	.1
18 and 19 years	7 587	9	23	38	116	232	461	2 386	2 185	2 105	19	7	7	–	–	–	57.0	.1
20 to 24 years	17 613	24	61	211	190	333	525	1 078	5 717	6 516	510	591	1 775	63	18	–	86.2	10.5
25 to 29 years	18 998	45	91	296	255	343	432	795	5 754	4 157	841	796	4 196	770	161	64	88.1	27.3
30 to 34 years	20 358	39	144	365	291	376	483	799	6 815	3 629	942	855	4 171	993	314	142	87.7	27.8
35 to 39 years	22 691	76	119	382	368	406	537	984	7 909	4 027	1 170	887	4 098	1 176	315	236	87.3	25.7
40 to 44 years	21 771	85	127	299	300	344	439	880	7 227	4 120	1 023	1 067	4 058	1 201	385	235	88.7	27.0
45 to 49 years	18 634	66	172	264	329	263	357	666	5 899	3 419	904	883	3 338	1 433	367	276	88.6	29.0
50 to 54 years	15 424	88	157	288	383	317	382	609	5 044	2 646	593	528	2 612	1 209	269	300	85.6	28.5
55 to 59 years	12 190	74	147	245	422	263	475	554	4 485	1 909	387	319	1 727	826	183	174	82.1	23.9
60 to 64 years	10 065	75	195	251	539	292	498	528	3 826	1 418	229	228	1 162	519	160	145	76.4	19.7
65 to 69 years	9 361	58	183	308	627	346	458	530	3 460	1 283	211	207	963	429	161	118	73.2	18.1
70 to 74 years	8 512	71	209	285	773	307	439	580	3 038	1 180	188	154	810	315	88	76	68.7	15.1
75 years and over	14 209	168	446	630	2 046	645	799	672	4 717	1 850	280	180	1 152	380	164	102	62.0	12.5
18 years and over	197 412	877	2 074	3 863	6 640	4 467	6 284	11 041	66 078	38 258	7 296	6 700	30 067	9 295	2 586	1 869	82.1	22.2
25 years and over	172 211	844	1 990	3 614	6 334	3 902	5 297	7 577	58 174	29 638	6 767	6 101	28 305	9 232	2 568	1 868	82.8	24.4
65 years and over	32 082	296	837	1 223	3 446	1 298	1 695	1 782	11 215	4 314	678	540	2 945	1 104	413	296	67.0	14.8

Source: *Educational Attainment in the United States: 1998*, U.S. Bureau of the Census, Washington, DC, 1999

Increases in educational attainment will be slower among Blacks and Hispanics than for Whites. In 1995, about 88 percent of Whites ages 45 to 54 had at least a high school diploma, compared with 75.4 percent of Blacks and 51.5 percent of Hispanics. (See Figure 5.2.) Approximately 29 percent of Whites in that age group had at least a bachelor's degree, while about 15 percent of Blacks and 10 percent of Hispanics had completed college.

Educational attainment is generally correlated with economic and health status in old age. The better educated an elderly person is, the more likely he or she is to be healthier longer and better off financially.

Continuing to Learn

A growing number of elderly are going back to school — a "graying of the campus." Adult education means more than it ever has. Retired people are the major participants in what was once termed "adult education," that is, in courses that do not lead to a formal degree. A number of the elderly now have the time and funds to seek learning for personal and social reasons. Some universities allow the elderly to audit courses without charge. They attend courses sponsored by community, senior citizen, and recreation facilities. Increasingly, the elderly also attend two- and four-year universities for undergraduate and graduate degrees, as well as to audit courses for non-credit.

The reasons for returning for additional schooling have changed as

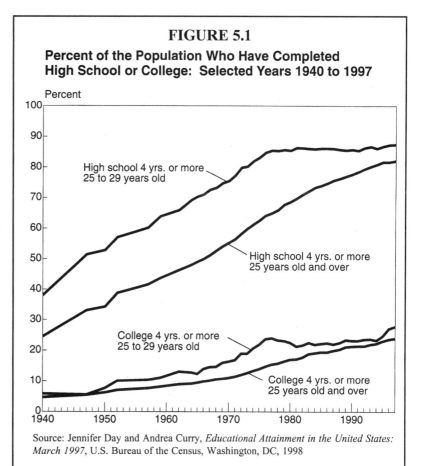

FIGURE 5.1

Percent of the Population Who Have Completed High School or College: Selected Years 1940 to 1997

Source: Jennifer Day and Andrea Curry, *Educational Attainment in the United States: March 1997*, U.S. Bureau of the Census, Washington, DC, 1998

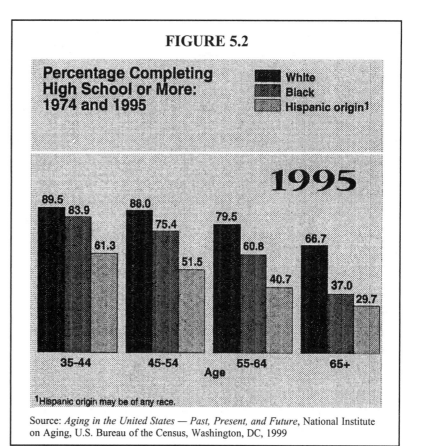

FIGURE 5.2

Source: *Aging in the United States — Past, Present, and Future*, National Institute on Aging, U.S. Bureau of the Census, Washington, DC, 1999

TABLE 5.2

Adult education participation rates in the past 12 months, by age: 1995

Selected characteristics	Total	Type of adult education activity			
		Basic skills	Credential	Work-related	Personal development
		Male and female			
Total	**40.2**	**1.2**	**6.1**	**20.9**	**19.9**
Age					
17–24	47.0	4.6	12.6	14.7	21.5
25–34	48.4	1.2	9.4	25.8	22.2
35–44	49.2	1.1	7.3	30.1	22.8
45–54	45.9	0.6	4.9	29.7	20.5
55–64	28.0	0.2	1.1	14.2	16.3
65 and older	15.2	0.0	0.2	2.3	13.5

TABLE 5.3

Percentage of adults taking one or more work-related courses, by type of provider and age: 1995

Selected characteristics	Type of provider for work-related adult education activities					
	Elementary/ secondary	Post-secondary	Trade organization	Private	Business	Government
Total	**4.3**	**20.4**	**11.1**	**6.6**	**59.6**	**17.3**
Age						
17–24	3.1	24.1	7.8	6.2	54.7	13.4
25–34	2.8	17.1	12.2	6.9	63.2	14.7
35–44	4.3	19.9	11.4	6.2	61.1	18.1
45–54	6.2	23.5	10.5	6.9	57.9	18.7
55–64	4.5	21.3	10.7	5.6	54.4	22.5
65 and older	3.9	16.8	14.1	10.9	49.9	21.5

* Includes adults whose highest education level was grades 9–12 who had not received a high school diploma.

Source of both tables: *The Condition of Education 1998*, National Center for Education Statistics, Washington, DC, 1998

well. While the elderly once might have taken courses primarily for pleasure, today's older students may be in school for more practical reasons as well. Many older people are retraining for new careers or to remain competitive in existing occupations. Some older couples have found they both need to work to afford the activities they enjoy, or they enjoy their work and are not ready to retire. Homemakers "displaced" by divorce or widowhood are often seeking careers. Table 5.2 shows that among persons 65 years of age and older, in 1995, 15.2 percent participated in adult education at some time in the previous year. Most (13.5 percent) of that was for personal development, while 2.3 percent took work-related courses. Table 5.3 shows the types of providers of adult education

courses. Among those 65 and older, in 1995, 49.9 percent of persons participating in adult education did so with business involvement of some kind (offering classes at job sites, paying for courses, requiring training, giving time off for courses). Another 21.5 percent took courses provided by the government.

In addition, some seniors are now moving to retirement communities linked to universities. (For more information, see Chapter XI.)

VOTING BEHAVIOR

Americans are more likely to vote as they get older. Retirement often means more leisure time

TABLE 5.4

Reported Voting and Registration, by Selected Characteristics: November 1996

(Numbers in thousands)

Characteristics	All persons	Total Population				Citizen Population		
		Reported registered		Reported voted		Total Citizens	Percent registered	Percent voted
		Number	Percent	Number	Percent			
Total, 18 years and over	193,651	127,661	65.9	105,017	54.2	179,936	70.9	58.4
Gender								
Male	92,632	59,672	64.4	48,909	52.8	85,753	69.6	57.0
Female	101,020	67,989	67.3	56,108	55.5	94,183	72.2	59.6
Race, Hispanic origin, and Gender[1]								
White, not Hispanic								
Total	145,343	104,101	71.6	86,604	59.6	142,597	73.0	60.7
Male	69,919	49,374	70.6	41,027	58.7	68,663	71.9	59.8
Female	75,424	54,726	72.6	45,577	60.4	73,933	74.0	61.7
Black, not Hispanic								
Total	21,918	13,991	63.8	11,156	50.9	21,040	66.5	53.0
Male	9,733	5,881	60.4	4,554	46.8	9,282	63.4	49.1
Female	12,184	8,110	66.6	6,603	54.2	11,758	69.0	56.2
Hispanic								
Total	18,002	6,435	35.8	4,834	26.9	10,906	59.0	44.3
Male	8,995	2,964	33.0	2,188	24.3	5,265	56.3	41.6
Female	9,007	3,471	38.5	2,645	29.4	5,641	61.5	46.9
Asian and Pacific Islander								
Total	6,775	2,210	32.6	1,741	25.7	3,865	57.2	45.0
Male	3,247	1,048	32.3	838	25.8	1,851	56.6	45.3
Female	3,528	1,161	32.9	902	25.6	2,015	57.7	44.8
Age								
18 and 19 years	7,302	3,167	43.4	2,202	30.2	6,788	46.7	32.4
20 to 24 years	17,348	8,851	51.0	5,794	33.4	15,686	56.4	36.9
25 to 29 years	19,048	10,457	54.9	7,653	40.2	17,050	61.3	44.9
30 to 34 years	21,017	12,321	58.6	9,613	45.7	18,801	65.5	51.1
35 to 44 years	43,327	28,828	66.5	23,785	54.9	39,935	72.2	59.6
45 to 54 years	32,684	23,559	72.1	20,360	62.3	30,828	76.4	66.0
55 to 64 years	21,037	15,930	75.7	14,255	67.8	19,959	79.8	71.4
65 to 74 years	18,176	14,218	78.2	12,748	70.1	17,559	81.0	72.6
75 to 84 years	10,790	8,369	77.6	7,147	66.2	10,533	79.5	67.9
85 years and over	2,922	1,960	67.1	1,461	50.0	2,797	70.1	52.2
Marital Status								
Married – spouse present	111,694	79,349	71.0	68,136	61.0	103,466	76.7	65.9
Married – spouse absent	1,956	949	48.5	732	37.4	1,456	65.2	50.3
Widowed	13,400	9,419	70.3	7,727	57.7	12,814	73.5	60.3
Divorced	18,278	11,576	63.0	8,861	48.5	17,647	65.6	50.2
Separated	4,777	2,657	55.6	1,926	40.3	4,357	61.0	44.2
Never married	43,546	23,712	54.5	17,635	40.5	40,195	59.0	43.9
Educational Attainment								
Less than high school	34,988	15,756	45.0	11,287	32.3	29,078	54.2	38.8
High school graduate or GED equiv.	65,208	40,542	62.2	32,019	49.1	61,931	65.5	51.7
Some college or Associate's degree	50,939	37,160	72.9	30,835	60.5	48,838	76.1	63.1
Bachelor's degree	28,829	22,752	78.9	20,256	70.3	27,339	83.2	74.1
Advanced degree	13,688	11,451	83.7	10,621	77.6	12,750	89.8	83.3

Source: Lynne M. Casper and Loretta E. Bass, *Voting and Registration in the Election of November 1996*, Bureau of the Census, Washington, DC, 1998

to devote to community affairs such as politics. In addition, dependence on Social Security funds by many older people gives them a major personal stake in how the government is run. In 2000, 46 percent of Americans ages 50 and over — 32 million people — are members of the American Association of Retired Persons (AARP), sometimes considered the most powerful lobby on Capitol Hill because of its forceful, non-partisan political activities. The AARP does not endorse any particular candidate but questions candidates on issues such as health care, Social Security and Medicare,

long-term care, pension reform, and age discrimination. A candidate's position on each issue is made available to members of AARP, making these older citizens an informed and potentially formidable force in a candidate's bid for election.

Voting participation increases with age until the age of approximately 75, where it declines slightly. The U.S. Census Bureau found that in the 1996 Presidential election, among those 20 to 24 years old, 51 percent reported registering to vote and 33.4 percent, voting. Among the 35- to 44-

TABLE 5.5

Percent of Persons 65 Years and over Reported Voted,
by Race and Hispanic Origin: November 1964 to Present

(Numbers in thousands)

Year	White Number	White Percent voted	Black Number	Black Percent voted	Hispanic[1] Number	Hispanic[1] Percent voted
1996	28,456	68.1	2,623	63.7	1,488	47.6
1994	27,890	62.8	2,538	51.6	1,356	37.6
1992	27,592	71.5	2,644	64.1	1,184	39.7
1990	26,807	61.7	2,528	51.3	1,072	40.5
1988	25,908	69.8	2,422	63.5	862	45.6
1986	24,982	61.9	2,318	53.3	881	36.5
1984	24,081	68.7	2,203	61.5	674	40.5
1982	23,139	61.1	2,132	50.8	599	29.5
1980	21,748	66.0	2,039	59.4	538	36.8
1978	20,798	57.2	1,943	45.6	511	24.9
1976	19,943	63.2	1,848	54.3	509	29.9
1974	19,058	52.8	1,710	38.5	413	28.1
1972	18,307	64.8	1,613	50.6	412	26.7
1970	17,583	58.6	1,413	39.3	NA	NA
1968	16,989	67.4	1,363	49.9	NA	NA
1966	16,413	57.9	1,316	35.3	NA	NA
1964	15,924	68.1	1,266	45.3	NA	NA

Note: Prior to 1972, data are for persons of voting age, 21
        years old and over, in most states.

NA   Not available.

1/   Persons of Hispanic origin may be of any race.

Source: Current Population Reports, Series P20-466, "Voting and
        Registration in the Election of November 1992," and
        earlier reports.

TABLE 5.6

Reported Reason for Not Voting Among Those Who Reported Registering But Not Voting, by Race, Gender, Age, and Education: November 1996

(Numbers in thousands. Percent distribution)

Characteristics	Number	Total Percent	Reasons Given for Not Voting									
			No trans-portation	No time off/too busy	Out of town	Ill/ disabled/ emergency	Didn't like can-didates	Not inte-rested	Forgot	Lines too long	Other reasons	Don't know/ refused
Total	21,340	100.0	4.3	21.5	11.1	14.9	13.0	16.6	4.4	1.2	10.3	2.7
Race and Hispanic Origin[1]												
White, not Hispanic	16,660	100.0	3.5	21.4	12.0	14.8	14.7	16.5	3.9	1.2	9.7	2.4
Black, not Hispanic	2,579	100.0	7.9	22.3	6.4	17.1	5.9	18.2	6.5	1.2	10.6	3.8
Hispanic	1,459	100.0	6.3	20.4	9.2	13.0	9.2	14.4	7.0	0.3	15.9	4.4
Asian and Pacific Islander	413	100.0	6.8	21.4	15.6	8.7	9.4	14.3	2.8	3.6	12.4	5.0
Gender												
Male	9,948	100.0	3.2	24.5	14.7	9.6	13.2	17.0	3.8	1.3	9.6	3.1
Female	11,392	100.0	5.3	18.8	8.1	19.5	12.9	16.1	4.9	1.1	10.9	2.4
Age												
18 to 24 years	3,587	100.0	4.3	25.8	13.4	3.5	9.4	16.5	6.4	0.5	14.4	5.7
25 to 44 years	9,990	100.0	3.1	27.3	10.5	8.7	13.1	18.0	4.2	1.2	11.3	2.6
45 to 64 years	4,640	100.0	3.7	18.6	12.8	16.7	17.0	15.9	4.0	1.7	7.8	1.9
65 years and over	3,123	100.0	9.5	2.0	8.3	45.1	11.0	13.1	3.3	0.8	5.9	0.9
Education												
Less than high school	4,300	100.0	8.1	11.9	5.8	25.3	11.2	20.4	5.4	0.5	8.9	2.3
High school graduate or GED equivalent	8,045	100.0	4.2	22.7	8.9	13.7	14.8	17.7	4.8	1.2	8.6	3.3
Some college or Associate's degree	5,872	100.0	2.9	25.1	13.3	11.7	13.1	14.4	4.4	1.2	11.6	2.5
Bachelor's degree	2,341	100.0	2.1	23.9	20.4	8.7	10.9	13.2	1.9	2.0	14.2	2.8
Advanced degree	782	100.0	3.2	26.1	19.6	13.1	10.9	9.6	2.4	1.3	12.8	1.1

[1] For selected race categories. Note that the race category used in Tables 3–6 differs from that used in Tables 1 and 2. Because more detailed race and ethnic categories became available in 1996, we are able to include the following categories in Tables 3–6: White, not Hispanic; Black, not Hispanic; Hispanic; and Asian and Pacific Islander. Also, the Hispanic category includes Whites and Blacks, but not Asians and Pacific Islanders, or American Indians, Aleuts, or Eskimos. Instead, the cagetory of Asians and Pacific Islanders includes both Hispanics and non-Hispanics. To keep data comparable for prior years, the former race and Hispanic origin classifications are used in the historical tables (Tables 1 and 2).

Source: Lynne M. Casper and Loretta E. Bass, *Voting and Registration in the Election of November 1996*, Bureau of the Census, Washington, DC, 1998

year-old group, 66.5 percent reported registering, and 54.9 percent voted. Among those 45 to 54 years of age, 72.1 percent registered and 62.3 percent voted. Of those persons 65 to 74, 78.2 percent registered and 70.1 percent voted. Among those 85 years and older, 67.1 percent registered, and 50 percent voted. (See Table 5.4.)

Among persons 65 and older, voting participation has historically been highest among Whites. Table 5.5 shows the rates of voting participation by race from 1964 to 1996. Among those over the age of 65, the primary reason (45.1 percent) for not voting was illness/disability/emergency, a reflection of increasing health problems that often accompany aging (Table 5.6).

Because the elderly vote at such high rates, they are an important voting bloc. Figure 5.3 shows the states where elderly voters are concentrated. With the growing number of elderly and their increasing education and financial resources, voting participation will likely increase. Older Americans are expected to become an even more powerful voting group as the aging population swells.

Party Affiliation

The Center for Political Studies, a political think-tank, has found differences in political party affiliation based on age. Those persons 64 years and older show a firmer identification with the two major American political parties — Democratic

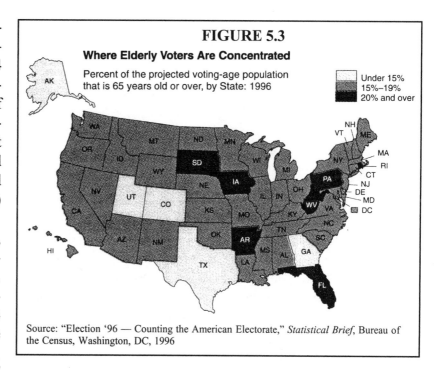

FIGURE 5.3

Where Elderly Voters Are Concentrated

Percent of the projected voting-age population that is 65 years old or over, by State: 1996

Under 15%
15%–19%
20% and over

Source: "Election '96 — Counting the American Electorate," *Statistical Brief*, Bureau of the Census, Washington, DC, 1996

and Republican — than younger Americans. Only half of those younger than 64 years reported attachment to one of those two parties, with a considerable population considering themselves "independent." Among the older citizens, fully three-quarters considered themselves either Democrat or Republican.

This may reflect either a greater flexibility among younger voters or less firmly committed opinions and shorter voting histories. It may also indicate a true shift in attitudes towards political parties among American voters. Voters may become more committed to a particular political party as they age, simply due to maturation. On the other hand, today's younger people may simply have fundamentally different attitudes towards political parties; as they age, they may remain less connected to either of the two major political parties, a trend that could have important political implications.

CHAPTER VI

GENERAL HEALTH AND HEALTH PROBLEMS

One of the fears many people have about growing older is facing the possible loss of mental and physical abilities. Although the human body progressively declines with age, the rate and amount of decline are individual processes. One person may be afflicted with arthritis and senility at age 65, while another is vigorous and active at 90. Nonetheless, overall, older people have more health problems and require more health care than younger ones.

LIFE EXPECTANCY

Americans have longer lives than ever before. Life expectancy has increased dramatically since the turn of the twentieth century. In 1900, the average life expectancy of a baby born in the United States was 40 years, partly because of the high rate of infant mortality. By current estimates, someone born in 1997 will live almost twice that long, 76.5 years, up from 75.8 in 1995 (Table 6.1).

Women Live Longer Than Men

In the twentieth century, women lived longer than men and probably will continue to do so, although the gap is narrowing. The National Center for Health Statistics reported that, in 1997, a man could, on average, expect to live 73.6 years and a woman, 79.4 years. Life expectancy for Whites (77.1 years) continued to exceed that of Blacks (71.1 years). (See Table 6.1.)

Reasons for Increased Life Expectancy

During the first half of the century, increased longevity was a result of reducing or eliminating many diseases that killed infants and children and improved methods of delivering babies, so that more people survived to middle age. In recent years, increased life expectancy is attributed not only to declining infant mortality, but also to decreasing mortality from chronic diseases among the middle-aged and elderly due to new medical knowledge, healthier diet and exercise habits, and life-sustaining technology. In other words, old people are living to be older.

LEADING CAUSES OF DEATH

Seven out of every 10 people die from heart disease, cancer, or stroke. The leading causes of death and the death rate from each cause in 1998 are shown in Table 6.2. (Malignant neoplasms refer to cancer, and cerebrovascular diseases include strokes.)

"Still Number One" — Heart Disease

Cardiovascular disease (CVD)* kills more Americans than any other disease. (Figure 6.1 shows the various types of CVD and the portion of deaths attributed to each in 1997.) The American Heart Association reported that CVD caused 953,110 deaths in the United States in 1997 — 47.2 percent male and 52.8 percent female. Since 1900, CVD has been the number one killer in the United

---

* Note that CVD includes coronary heart disease — CHD — and strokes, as well as other diseases. The Centers for Disease Control and Prevention statistics do not combine them in reporting mortality but figure them separately as "Heart Disease" and "Cerebrovascular diseases."

TABLE 6.1

Life expectancy at birth, at 65 years of age, and at 75 years of age, according to race and sex: United States, selected years 1900–97

[Data are based on the National Vital Statistics System]

Specified age and year	All races			White			Black		
	Both sexes	Male	Female	Both sexes	Male	Female	Both sexes	Male	Female
At birth				Remaining life expectancy in years					
1900[1,2]	47.3	46.3	48.3	47.6	46.6	48.7	[3]33.0	[3]32.5	[3]33.5
1950[2]	68.2	65.6	71.1	69.1	66.5	72.2	60.7	58.9	62.7
1960[2]	69.7	66.6	73.1	70.6	67.4	74.1	63.2	60.7	65.9
1970	70.8	67.1	74.7	71.7	68.0	75.6	64.1	60.0	68.3
1980	73.7	70.0	77.4	74.4	70.7	78.1	68.1	63.8	72.5
1985	74.7	71.1	78.2	75.3	71.8	78.7	69.3	65.0	73.4
1986	74.7	71.2	78.2	75.4	71.9	78.8	69.1	64.8	73.4
1987	74.9	71.4	78.3	75.6	72.1	78.9	69.1	64.7	73.4
1988	74.9	71.4	78.3	75.6	72.2	78.9	68.9	64.4	73.2
1989	75.1	71.7	78.5	75.9	72.5	79.2	68.8	64.3	73.3
1990	75.4	71.8	78.8	76.1	72.7	79.4	69.1	64.5	73.6
1991	75.5	72.0	78.9	76.3	72.9	79.6	69.3	64.6	73.8
1992	75.8	72.3	79.1	76.5	73.2	79.8	69.6	65.0	73.9
1993	75.5	72.2	78.8	76.3	73.1	79.5	69.2	64.6	73.7
1994	75.7	72.4	79.0	76.5	73.3	79.6	69.5	64.9	73.9
1995	75.8	72.5	78.9	76.5	73.4	79.6	69.6	65.2	73.9
1996	76.1	73.1	79.1	76.8	73.9	79.7	70.2	66.1	74.2
1997	76.5	73.6	79.4	77.1	74.3	79.9	71.1	67.2	74.7
At 65 years									
1900–1902[1,2]	11.9	11.5	12.2	- - -	11.5	12.2	- - -	10.4	11.4
1950[2]	13.9	12.8	15.0	- - -	12.8	15.1	13.9	12.9	14.9
1960[2]	14.3	12.8	15.8	14.4	12.9	15.9	13.9	12.7	15.1
1970	15.2	13.1	17.0	15.2	13.1	17.1	14.2	12.5	15.7
1980	16.4	14.1	18.3	16.5	14.2	18.4	15.1	13.0	16.8
1985	16.7	14.5	18.5	16.8	14.5	18.7	15.2	13.0	16.9
1986	16.8	14.6	18.6	16.9	14.7	18.7	15.2	13.0	17.0
1987	16.9	14.7	18.7	17.0	14.8	18.8	15.2	13.0	17.0
1988	16.9	14.7	18.6	17.0	14.8	18.7	15.1	12.9	16.9
1989	17.1	15.0	18.8	17.2	15.1	18.9	15.2	13.0	16.9
1990	17.2	15.1	18.9	17.3	15.2	19.1	15.4	13.2	17.2
1991	17.4	15.3	19.1	17.5	15.4	19.2	15.5	13.4	17.2
1992	17.5	15.4	19.2	17.6	15.5	19.3	15.7	13.5	17.4
1993	17.3	15.3	18.9	17.4	15.4	19.0	15.5	13.4	17.1
1994	17.4	15.5	19.0	17.5	15.6	19.1	15.7	13.6	17.2
1995	17.4	15.6	18.9	17.6	15.7	19.1	15.6	13.6	17.1
1996	17.5	15.7	19.0	17.6	15.8	19.1	15.8	13.9	17.2
1997	17.7	15.9	19.2	17.8	16.0	19.3	16.1	14.2	17.6
At 75 years									
1980	10.4	8.8	11.5	10.4	8.8	11.5	9.7	8.3	10.7
1985	10.6	9.0	11.7	10.6	9.0	11.7	10.1	8.7	11.1
1986	10.7	9.1	11.7	10.7	9.1	11.8	10.1	8.6	11.1
1987	10.7	9.1	11.8	10.7	9.1	11.8	10.1	8.6	11.1
1988	10.6	9.1	11.7	10.7	9.1	11.7	10.0	8.5	11.0
1989	10.9	9.3	11.9	10.9	9.3	11.9	10.1	8.6	11.0
1990	10.9	9.4	12.0	11.0	9.4	12.0	10.2	8.6	11.2
1991	11.1	9.5	12.1	11.1	9.5	12.1	10.2	8.7	11.2
1992	11.2	9.6	12.2	11.2	9.6	12.2	10.4	8.9	11.4
1993	10.9	9.5	11.9	11.0	9.5	12.0	10.2	8.7	11.1
1994	11.0	9.6	12.0	11.1	9.6	12.0	10.3	8.9	11.2
1995	11.0	9.7	11.9	11.1	9.7	12.0	10.2	8.8	11.1
1996	11.1	9.8	12.0	11.1	9.8	12.0	10.3	9.0	11.2
1997	11.2	9.9	12.1	11.2	9.9	12.1	10.7	9.3	11.5

- - - Data not available.

[1]Death registration area only. The death registration area increased from 10 States and the District of Columbia in 1900 to the coterminous United States in 1933.
[2]Includes deaths of persons who were not residents of the 50 States and the District of Columbia.
[3]Figure is for the all other population.

NOTES: Beginning in 1997 life table methodology was revised to construct complete life tables by single years of age that extend to age 100. Previously abridged life tables were constructed for five-year age groups ending with the age group 85 years and over. Data for additional years are available (see Appendix III).

Source: *Health, United States, 1999*, National Center for Health Statistics, Hyattsville, MD, 1999

States every year except 1918, when a worldwide pandemic of influenza swept the nation.

Almost 60 million Americans alive today have a history of CVD. This year, approximately 1.1 million Americans will have heart attacks, and about one-third of them will die. About 85 percent of people who die of heart attacks are age 65 or older. Blacks are more likely to suffer heart-related diseases and deaths than Whites. In 1997, CVD

TABLE 6.2

Deaths and death rates for the 10 leading causes of death in specified age groups: United States, preliminary 1998

[Data are based on a continuous file of records received from the States. Rates per 100,000 population in specified group. For explanation of asterisks preceding cause-of-death categories, see Technical notes. Figures are based on weighted data rounded to the nearest individual, so categories may not add to totals]

Rank [1]	Cause of death and age (Based on Ninth Revision, International Classification of Diseases, 1975)	Number	Rate
	All ages [2]		
...	All causes	2,338,075	865.0
1	Diseases of heart (390-398, 402, 404-429)	724,269	268.0
2	Malignant neoplasms, including neoplasms of lymphatic and hematopoietic tissues (140-208)	538,947	199.4
3	Cerebrovascular diseases (430-438)	158,060	58.5
4	Chronic obstructive pulmonary diseases and allied conditions (490-496)	114,381	42.3
5	Pneumonia and influenza (480-487)	94,828	35.1
6	Accidents and adverse effects (E800-E949)	93,207	34.5
...	Motor vehicle accidents (E810-E825)	41,826	15.5
...	All other accidents and adverse effects (E800-E807, E826-E949)	51,382	19.0
7	Diabetes mellitus (250)	64,574	23.9
8	Suicide (E950-E959)	29,264	10.8
9	Nephritis, nephrotic syndrome, and nephrosis (580-589)	26,295	9.7
10	Chronic liver disease and cirrhosis (571)	24,936	9.2
...	All other causes (Residual)	469,314	173.6
	1-4 years		
...	All causes	5,195	34.2
1	Accidents and adverse effects (E800-E949)	1,881	12.4
...	Motor vehicle accidents (E810-E825)	750	4.9
...	All other accidents and adverse effects (E800-E807, E826-E949)	1,131	7.4
2	Congenital anomalies (740-759)	531	3.5
3	Homicide and legal intervention (E960-E978)	368	2.4
4	Malignant neoplasms, including neoplasms of lymphatic and hematopoietic tissues (140-208)	355	2.3
5	Diseases of heart (390-398, 402, 404-429)	198	1.3
6	Pneumonia and influenza (480-487)	133	0.9
7	Septicemia (038)	81	0.5
8	Certain conditions originating in the perinatal period (760-779)	75	0.5
9	Cerebrovascular diseases (430-438)	54	0.4
10	Benign neoplasms, carcinoma in situ, and neoplasms of uncertain behavior and of unspecified nature (210-239)	50	0.3
...	All other causes (Residual)	1,469	9.7
	5-14 years		
...	All causes	7,700	19.7
1	Accidents and adverse effects (E800-E949)	3,115	8.0
...	Motor vehicle accidents (E810-E825)	1,773	4.5
...	All other accidents and adverse effects (E800-E807, E826-E949)	1,342	3.4
2	Malignant neoplasms, including neoplasms of lymphatic and hematopoietic tissues (140-208)	1,025	2.6
3	Homicide and legal intervention (E960-E978)	423	1.1
4	Congenital anomalies (740-759)	355	0.9
5	Suicide (E950-E959)	318	0.8
6	Diseases of heart (390-398, 402, 404-429)	304	0.8
7	Chronic obstructive pulmonary diseases and allied conditions (490-496)	145	0.4
8	Pneumonia and influenza (480-487)	125	0.3
9	Benign neoplasms, carcinoma in situ, and neoplasms of uncertain behavior and of unspecified nature (210-239)	80	0.2
10	Cerebrovascular diseases (430-438)	76	0.2
...	All other causes (Residual)	1,734	4.4
	15-24 years		
...	All causes	30,211	81.2
1	Accidents and adverse effects (E800-E949)	12,752	34.3
...	Motor vehicle accidents (E810-E825)	9,635	25.9
...	All other accidents and adverse effects (E800-E807, E826-E949)	3,117	8.4
2	Homicide and legal intervention (E960-E978)	5,233	14.1
3	Suicide (E950-E959)	4,003	10.8
4	Malignant neoplasms, including neoplasms of lymphatic and hematopoietic tissues (140-208)	1,670	4.5
5	Diseases of heart (390-398, 402, 404-429)	961	2.6
6	Congenital anomalies (740-759)	429	1.2
7	Chronic obstructive pulmonary diseases and allied conditions (490-496)	224	0.6
8	Pneumonia and influenza (480-487)	211	0.6
9	Human immunodeficiency virus infection (*042-*044)	208	0.6
10	Cerebrovascular diseases (430-438)	182	0.5
...	All other causes (Residual)	4,338	11.7

(continued)

death rates were 438.2 per 100,000 for White males and 542.0 per 100,000 for Black males. White females had a CVD death rate of 301.9 per 100,000 and Black females, 402.8 per 100,000. Studies show that the risk of death from heart disease is much greater among the least-educated than the most-educated people.

Women have less cardiovascular disease than men until they reach menopause, at which point

TABLE 6.2 (Continued)

Deaths and death rates for the 10 leading causes of death in specified age groups: United States, preliminary 1998 - Con.

[Data are based on a continuous file of records received from the States. Rates per 100,000 population in specified group. For explanation of asterisks preceding cause-of-death categories, see Technical notes. Figures are based on weighted data rounded to the nearest individual, so categories may not add to totals]

Rank[1]	Cause of death and age (Based on Ninth Revision, International Classification of Diseases, 1975)	Number	Rate
	25-44 years		
...	All causes	129,309	155.2
1	Accidents and adverse effects (E800-E949)	25,153	30.2
...	Motor vehicle accidents (E810-E825)	13,585	16.3
...	All other accidents and adverse effects (E800-E807, E826-E949)	11,568	13.9
2	Malignant neoplasms, including neoplasms of lymphatic and hematopoietic tissues (140-208)	21,130	25.4
3	Diseases of heart (390-398, 402, 404-429)	16,022	19.2
4	Suicide (E950-E959)	11,602	13.9
5	Human immunodeficiency virus infection (*042-*044)	8,529	10.2
6	Homicide and legal intervention (E960-E978)	7,743	9.3
7	Chronic liver disease and cirrhosis (571)	3,785	4.5
8	Cerebrovascular diseases (430-438)	3,219	3.9
9	Diabetes mellitus (250)	2,432	2.9
10	Pneumonia and influenza (480-487)	1,913	2.3
...	All other causes (Residual)	27,781	33.4
	45-64 years		
...	All causes	378,197	660.5
1	Malignant neoplasms, including neoplasms of lymphatic and hematopoietic tissues (140-208)	132,197	230.9
2	Diseases of heart (390-398, 402, 404-429)	98,700	172.4
3	Accidents and adverse effects (E800-E949)	17,141	29.9
...	Motor vehicle accidents (E810-E825)	8,112	14.2
...	All other accidents and adverse effects (E800-E807, E826-E949)	9,029	15.8
4	Cerebrovascular diseases (430-438)	15,319	26.8
5	Chronic obstructive pulmonary diseases and allied conditions (490-496)	13,102	22.9
6	Diabetes mellitus (250)	13,062	22.8
7	Chronic liver disease and cirrhosis (571)	10,829	18.9
8	Suicide (E950-E959)	7,718	13.5
9	Pneumonia and influenza (480-487)	6,130	10.7
10	Human immunodeficiency virus infection (*042-*044)	3,994	7.0
...	All other causes (Residual)	60,005	104.8
	65 years and over		
...	All causes	1,758,530	5,111.8
1	Diseases of heart (390-398, 402, 404-429)	607,422	1,765.7
2	Malignant neoplasms, including neoplasms of lymphatic and hematopoietic tissues (140-208)	382,468	1,111.8
3	Cerebrovascular diseases (430-438)	138,891	403.7
4	Chronic obstructive pulmonary diseases and allied conditions (490-496)	99,697	289.8
5	Pneumonia and influenza (480-487)	85,909	249.7
6	Diabetes mellitus (250)	48,917	142.2
7	Accidents and adverse effects (E800-E949)	32,343	94.0
...	Motor vehicle accidents (E810-E825)	7,788	22.6
...	All other accidents and adverse effects (E800-E807, E826-E949)	24,555	71.4
8	Nephritis, nephrotic syndrome, and nephrosis (580-589)	22,749	66.1
9	Alzheimer's disease (331.0)	22,510	65.4
10	Septicemia (038)	19,024	55.3
...	All other causes (Residual)	298,600	868.0

... Category not applicable.
[1] Rank based on number of deaths; see Technical notes.
[2] Includes deaths under 1 year of age.

NOTE: Data are subject to sampling and/or random variation. For information on the relative standard errors of the data and further discussion, see Technical notes.

Source: *National Vital Statistics Reports*, vol. 47, no. 25, October 5, 1999

their numbers begin to approach those of men. (See Figure 6.2.) The risk of dying from heart disease increases greatly after age 65, and the death rate more than doubles for each age group between 65 and 85.

Although heart disease is still the number one killer, the past four decades have shown a marked decline in death rates for heart disease. From 1987 to 1997, the death rate for coronary heart disease declined 28 percent. (See Figure 6.3.) Several factors account for the decline, primarily better control of hypertension and cholesterol and changes in exercise and nutrition. Also important is the expanding use of trained mobile emergency personnel (paramedics) in most urban areas. The generalized use of CPR (cardiopulmonary resuscitation) and new emergency medications also increase the likelihood of one's surviving an initial heart attack.

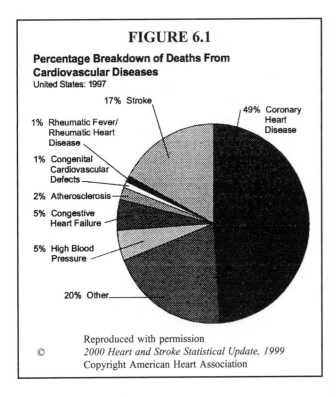

FIGURE 6.1

Percentage Breakdown of Deaths From Cardiovascular Diseases
United States: 1997

17% Stroke

1% Rheumatic Fever/ Rheumatic Heart Disease

1% Congenital Cardiovascular Defects

2% Atherosclerosis

5% Congestive Heart Failure

5% High Blood Pressure

20% Other

49% Coronary Heart Disease

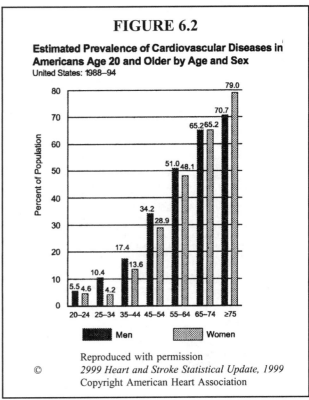

FIGURE 6.2

Estimated Prevalence of Cardiovascular Diseases in Americans Age 20 and Older by Age and Sex
United States: 1988–94

Increased use of procedures such as heart transplant, cardiac catheterization, coronary bypass surgery, pacemakers, and angioplasty have also contributed to extending the lives of those afflicted with heart disease (Figure 6.4). As importantly, these procedures usually improve the quality of life of the individual who typically suffers less pain and inactivity. In 2000, the national cost of cardiovascular disease, including coronary heart disease, congestive heart failure, high blood pressure, and "other" heart diseases, is estimated at $326.6 billion. This includes direct costs, such as the cost of physicians and other professionals, hospital and nursing home services, medications, and home health; and indirect costs, such as lost productivity resulting from illness and death. (See Table 6.3.)

Most recent studies indicate that post-menopausal women not only suffer from heart disease as frequently as their male counterparts, but those with the disease are more than twice as likely to die from an initial heart attack than men. The reasons for this are not known at this time. In general, women do not have heart attacks until later in life — on average, 10 years later — than men and are perhaps in somewhat less good health. Some observers have also suggested that because of the mis-

conception that women do not experience the disease as frequently, their complaints are not taken as seriously as those of men. Also, physiological factors, such as hormone effects and small blood vessel size, may increase difficulty during surgi-

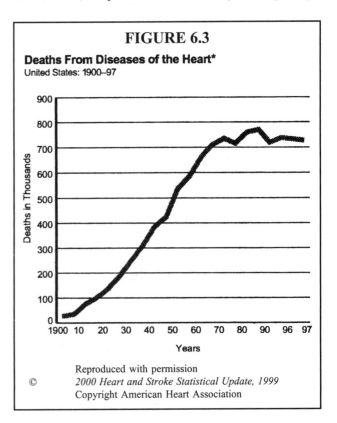

FIGURE 6.3

Deaths From Diseases of the Heart*
United States: 1900–97

cal procedures and play a role in women's succumbing to heart disease. Research on heart disease has historically been done on male subjects, but a growing number of studies include women.

Cancer

The likelihood of developing cancer, the second leading cause of death among the elderly, increases every decade after the age of 30. In 1997, among those 65 to 74, there were 859.1 deaths per 100,000 persons; for those 75 to 84, 1,350.3 per 100,000; and for those 85 and over, 1,808.8 per 100,000 persons (Table 6.4). Success in curing certain tumors (Hodgkin's disease, certain forms of leukemia) has been offset by the rise in rates of other cancers, such as breast and lung cancers. Progress in treating cancer has largely been related to screenings, early diagnoses, and new drug therapies.

Strokes

Strokes ("brain attacks" or cerebrovascular disease) are the third leading cause of death and the primary cause of disability among the elderly. Strokes killed 159,791 people in 1997 — 39.2 percent males and 60.8 percent females. About 4.4 million stroke survivors are alive today. Stroke is the leading cause of serious, long-term disability in the United States. Fifty to 70 percent of stroke survivors regain functional independence, but 15 to 30 percent are permanently disabled.

The incidence of stroke is strongly related to age; after 55 years of age the incidence of stroke more than doubles each successive decade of age (Figure 6.5). The American Heart Association calculated the costs of stroke in 2000 at $51.3 billion, which includes direct costs of physicians, hospitals, nursing services, and medications, as well as indirect costs, such as lost productivity (Table 6.3). Although the actual number of stroke deaths rose 6.6 percent from 1987 to 1997, the stroke death rate fell 13.9 percent.

GENERAL HEALTH OF OLDER AMERICANS

The National Center for Health Statistics (NCHS) reported that, in 1996, 24.4 percent of noninstitutionalized people 65 to 74 years old, 29.4 percent of those 75 to 84, and 36.8 percent of those 85 and older described their health as fair or poor.

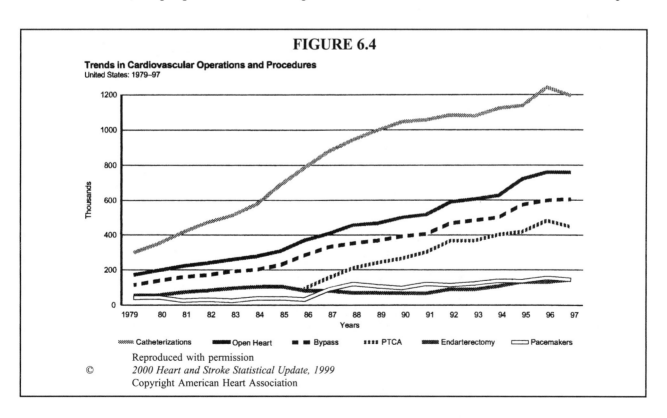

FIGURE 6.4

Trends in Cardiovascular Operations and Procedures
United States: 1979–97

Reproduced with permission
© *2000 Heart and Stroke Statistical Update, 1999*
Copyright American Heart Association

TABLE 6.3

Estimated Direct and Indirect Costs (in Billions of Dollars) of Cardiovascular Diseases and Stroke
United States: 2000

	Heart Disease**	Coronary Heart Disease	Stroke	Hypertensive Disease	Congestive Heart Failure	Total Cardiovascular Disease*
Direct Costs						
Hospital/Nursing Home	$78.9	$42.0	$25.0	$7.4	$15.5	$128.4
Physicians/Other Professionals	14.4	8.1	2.3	8.1	1.5	28.2
Drugs	7.3	3.5	0.4	9.0	1.1	17.7
Home Health/Other Medical Durables	5.2	1.6	2.9	1.6	2.2	11.5
Total Expenditures*	**$105.9**	**$55.2**	**$30.6**	**$26.1**	**$20.3**	**$185.8**
Indirect Costs						
Lost Productivity/Morbidity	17.2	7.2	5.6	5.2	NA	27.6
Lost Productivity/Mortality#	91.6	55.8	15.1	5.9	2.2	113.2
Grand Total*	**$214.7**	**$118.2**	**$51.3**	**$37.2**	**$22.5**	**$326.6**

* Totals may not add up due to rounding and overlap.
** This category includes coronary heart disease, congestive heart failure and part of hypertensive disease as well as other "heart" diseases.
\# Lost future earnings of persons who will die in 2000, discounted at 6 percent.
NA indicates not available.

TABLE 6.4

Death rates for malignant neoplasms, according to sex, detailed race, Hispanic origin, and age: United States, selected years 1950–97

[Data are based on the National Vital Statistics System]

Sex, race, Hispanic origin, and age	1950[1]	1960[1]	1970	1980	1985	1990	1994	1995	1996	1997	1995–97[2]
All persons					Deaths per 100,000 resident population						
All ages, age adjusted	125.4	125.8	129.8	132.8	134.4	135.0	131.5	129.9	127.9	125.6	127.8
All ages, crude	139.8	149.2	162.8	183.9	194.0	203.2	205.2	204.9	203.4	201.6	203.3
Under 1 year	8.7	7.2	4.7	3.2	3.1	2.3	1.5	1.8	2.3	2.4	2.2
1–4 years	11.7	10.9	7.5	4.5	3.8	3.5	3.3	3.1	2.7	2.9	2.9
5–14 years	6.7	6.8	6.0	4.3	3.5	3.1	2.8	2.7	2.7	2.7	2.7
15–24 years	8.6	8.3	8.3	6.3	5.4	4.9	4.8	4.6	4.5	4.5	4.5
25–34 years	20.0	19.5	16.5	13.7	13.2	12.6	12.2	11.9	12.0	11.6	11.9
35–44 years	62.7	59.7	59.5	48.6	45.9	43.3	40.4	40.3	39.3	38.9	39.5
45–54 years	175.1	177.0	182.5	180.0	170.1	158.9	145.9	142.2	137.9	135.1	138.3
55–64 years	390.7	396.8	423.0	436.1	454.6	449.6	424.6	416.0	406.5	395.7	405.9
65–74 years	698.8	713.9	751.2	817.9	845.5	872.3	875.4	868.2	861.6	847.3	859.1
75–84 years	1,153.3	1,127.4	1,169.2	1,232.3	1,271.8	1,348.5	1,367.4	1,364.8	1,351.5	1,335.2	1,350.3
85 years and over	1,451.0	1,450.0	1,320.7	1,594.6	1,615.4	1,752.9	1,789.0	1,823.8	1,798.3	1,805.0	1,808.8
Male											
All ages, age adjusted	130.8	143.0	157.4	165.5	166.1	166.3	159.6	156.8	153.8	150.4	153.6
All ages, crude	142.9	162.5	182.1	205.3	213.4	221.3	220.7	219.5	217.2	214.6	217.0
Under 1 year	9.7	7.7	4.4	3.7	3.0	2.4	1.4	1.8	2.2	2.3	2.1
1–4 years	12.5	12.4	8.3	5.2	4.3	3.7	3.5	3.6	3.1	3.1	3.3
5–14 years	7.4	7.6	6.7	4.9	3.9	3.5	3.1	3.0	3.0	2.8	2.9
15–24 years	9.7	10.2	10.4	7.8	6.4	5.7	5.8	5.5	5.1	5.2	5.3
25–34 years	17.7	18.8	16.3	13.4	13.2	12.6	12.1	11.7	11.5	11.5	11.5
35–44 years	45.6	48.9	53.0	44.0	42.4	38.5	36.7	36.5	35.6	34.5	35.5
45–54 years	156.2	170.8	183.5	188.7	175.2	162.5	148.8	143.7	140.7	138.0	140.7
55–64 years	413.1	459.9	511.8	520.8	536.9	532.9	495.3	480.5	469.1	453.4	467.5
65–74 years	791.5	890.5	1,006.8	1,093.2	1,105.2	1,122.2	1,102.5	1,089.9	1,080.9	1,058.4	1,076.4
75–84 years	1,332.6	1,389.4	1,588.3	1,790.5	1,839.7	1,914.4	1,862.6	1,842.3	1,802.7	1,770.2	1,804.3
85 years and over	1,668.3	1,741.2	1,720.8	2,369.5	2,451.8	2,739.9	2,805.8	2,837.3	2,733.1	2,712.5	2,759.1
Female											
All ages, age adjusted	120.8	111.2	108.8	109.2	111.7	112.7	111.1	110.4	108.8	107.3	108.8
All ages, crude	136.8	136.4	144.4	163.6	175.7	186.0	190.5	191.0	190.2	189.2	190.1
Under 1 year	7.6	6.8	5.0	2.7	3.2	2.2	1.6	1.8	2.4	2.5	2.2
1–4 years	10.8	9.3	6.7	3.7	3.4	3.2	3.0	2.6	2.3	2.6	2.5
5–14 years	6.0	6.0	5.2	3.6	3.1	2.8	2.4	2.4	2.4	2.5	2.4
15–24 years	7.6	6.5	6.2	4.8	4.3	4.1	3.9	3.6	3.8	3.7	3.7
25–34 years	22.2	20.1	16.7	14.0	13.2	12.6	12.3	12.2	12.6	11.7	12.2
35–44 years	79.3	70.0	65.6	53.1	49.2	48.1	44.1	44.0	42.9	43.1	43.4
45–54 years	194.0	183.0	181.5	171.8	165.3	155.5	143.1	140.7	135.2	132.3	136.0
55–64 years	368.2	337.7	343.2	361.7	381.8	375.2	360.7	357.5	349.6	343.2	350.0
65–74 years	612.3	560.2	557.9	607.1	645.3	677.4	694.7	690.7	685.2	676.8	684.3
75–84 years	1,000.7	924.1	891.9	903.1	937.8	1,010.3	1,057.5	1,061.5	1,060.0	1,050.6	1,057.3
85 years and over	1,299.7	1,263.9	1,096.7	1,255.7	1,281.4	1,372.1	1,397.1	1,429.1	1,426.8	1,439.2	1,431.8

Source: *Health, United States, 1999*, National Center for Health Statistics, Hyattsville, MD, 1999.

(See Table 6.5.) The likelihood of being disabled increases with age. In 1996, 31.4 percent of those 65 to 74 had some degree of functional disability. One-tenth of those 65 to 74 had limitations so severe as to make them unable to carry on any major activity. Among those over 75, 43.1 percent suffered limitations due to chronic conditions, and 10.9 percent were limited in their major activities. (See Table 6.6.)

The elderly use professional medical equipment and supplies, dental care, prescription drugs, and vision aids more than people under age 65 and are hospitalized more than younger people. As for all Americans, the average length of hospitalization for a person 65 and older has declined over the years from 12.1 days per stay in 1964 to 8.4 days in 1990 and 6.8 days in 1996, but it is still significantly longer than for younger people (Table 6.7). Shorter stays are partly due to the federal government's introduction of DRGs (Diagnosis Related Groups — categories of illnesses that prescribe/allow for set duration of treatment; see Chapter IX), which encourage hospitals to release patients as quickly as possible, and partly from increasing use of outpatient procedures instead of hospital admission for those procedures.

The aging of the American population increases demand for physician care. In 1996, those over age 65 contacted physicians 11.7 times per year, far more often than for younger people. Those over 75 contacted a doctor 13.7 times that year. In 1990, those 65 and older had 9.2 physician contacts per person with those 75 and older contacting the doctor 10.1 times. (See Table 6.8.)

SOCIOECONOMIC DIFFERENCES

Income or socioeconomic status (SES) is directly related to the onset of chronic illness and disability in later years. The more educated and affluent elderly are more likely to be healthy longer. Americans of the lowest SES experience more chronic illness, such as cancer, heart attacks, strokes, and lung disease. These illnesses are not as common in upper-SES elderly until after the age of 75. The likelihood of experiencing an acute con-

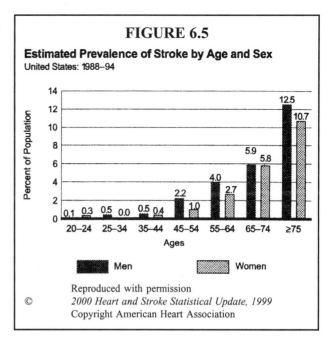

FIGURE 6.5

Estimated Prevalence of Stroke by Age and Sex
United States: 1988–94

dition is also greater at the lower SES levels. Similarly, the number of chronic conditions suffered by an older person varies by SES. Those in the highest SES group generally report fewer simultaneous chronic conditions and less limitation of activity than those in the lowest SES.

As would be expected, therefore, those in the lower SES groups tend to require more contacts with physicians (Table 6.8). Possible explanations for the health differences among elderly of different SES include

- A higher incidence of risk behaviors (smoking, high-fat diet, more sedentary lifestyle) among the lower SES.

- Greater occupational stresses and hazards in the work environments of the lowest SES.

- Acute and chronic stress among the lower SES.

- Decreased access to medical care among the lower SES.

CHRONIC PHYSICAL PROBLEMS OF THE ELDERLY

Chronic conditions (long-lasting or often recurring) are the burden of old age. At the start of

TABLE 6.5

Respondent-assessed health status, according to selected characteristics: United States, 1991–96

[Data are based on household interviews of a sample of the civilian noninstitutionalized population]

	Percent with fair or poor health								
	Both sexes			Male			Female		
Characteristic	1991	1995	1996	1991	1995	1996	1991	1995	1996
Total[1,2]	9.2	9.3	9.2	8.9	8.9	8.7	9.6	9.8	9.7
Age									
Under 18 years	2.6	2.6	2.6	2.7	2.7	2.5	2.6	2.4	2.7
Under 6 years	2.7	2.7	2.6	2.9	3.1	2.6	2.4	2.2	2.5
6–17 years	2.6	2.5	2.6	2.5	2.4	2.4	2.6	2.6	2.8
18–44 years	6.1	6.6	6.7	5.2	5.5	5.6	6.9	7.7	7.7
45–54 years	13.4	13.4	13.1	12.5	12.5	12.3	14.2	14.3	13.9
55–64 years	20.7	21.4	21.2	20.7	20.6	21.4	20.8	22.2	21.1
65 years and over	29.0	28.3	27.0	29.2	28.8	26.6	28.9	28.0	27.4
65–74 years	26.0	25.6	23.8	26.7	26.3	23.2	25.5	25.0	24.4
75–84 years	32.6	31.4	30.2	33.2	31.7	31.3	32.3	31.2	29.4
85 years and over	37.3	35.3	36.2	36.5	38.5	34.9	37.6	33.8	36.8
Race[1,3]									
White	8.5	8.6	8.4	8.3	8.3	8.0	8.7	8.8	8.7
Black	15.0	15.3	15.0	14.0	13.7	13.7	15.9	16.6	16.0
American Indian or Alaska Native	16.8	15.9	18.9	16.1	16.1	19.2	17.0	16.0	17.8
Asian or Pacific Islander	6.7	8.2	8.3	5.9	7.0	6.5	7.3	9.2	10.0
Race and Hispanic origin[1]									
White, non-Hispanic	8.0	8.0	7.9	7.9	7.8	7.6	8.1	8.1	8.1
Black, non-Hispanic	15.0	15.4	14.9	14.1	13.8	13.7	15.9	16.6	15.9
Hispanic[3]	13.7	13.6	12.9	12.3	12.3	11.8	14.9	14.8	14.1
Mexican[3]	14.9	14.9	13.7	13.0	13.9	11.9	16.8	16.0	15.4
Poverty status[1,4]									
Poor	21.8	22.5	22.2	22.4	22.1	21.6	21.5	23.0	22.8
Near poor	13.5	14.2	14.1	13.5	14.9	14.4	13.5	13.8	14.0
Nonpoor	5.5	5.6	5.5	5.4	5.3	5.3	5.7	5.8	5.6
Race and Hispanic origin and poverty status[1,4]									
White, non-Hispanic:									
Poor	21.1	21.4	21.6	22.7	21.6	22.5	20.2	21.5	21.1
Near poor	12.9	13.6	13.8	13.5	15.0	14.7	12.5	12.5	13.2
Nonpoor	5.2	5.2	5.1	5.2	5.1	5.0	5.3	5.3	5.1
Black, non-Hispanic:									
Poor	24.9	26.7	26.9	25.2	26.2	26.0	24.8	27.1	27.8
Near poor	15.5	17.2	16.6	14.6	15.9	15.2	16.3	18.1	17.6
Nonpoor	8.5	8.1	8.5	7.6	7.3	7.6	9.5	8.9	9.3
Hispanic:[3]									
Poor	21.1	21.2	19.9	20.2	20.1	17.7	21.7	22.3	21.8
Near poor	15.8	15.5	14.7	14.3	14.1	14.3	17.4	16.9	15.5
Nonpoor	7.9	7.0	7.7	7.1	6.4	7.6	8.7	7.6	7.5
Geographic region[1]									
Northeast	7.4	8.0	8.2	7.2	7.7	7.7	7.6	8.3	8.7
Midwest	8.0	8.5	8.1	7.7	8.3	7.7	8.3	8.7	8.6
South	11.6	10.9	10.7	11.3	10.3	10.1	11.9	11.4	11.3
West	8.6	8.9	8.7	8.1	8.2	8.4	9.1	9.6	9.2
Location of residence[1]									
Within MSA[5]	8.8	8.9	8.4	8.3	8.4	7.8	9.3	9.4	9.0
Outside MSA[5]	10.6	11.1	11.8	10.9	10.8	11.5	10.4	11.4	12.1

[1]Age adjusted. See Appendix II for age-adjustment procedure.
[2]Includes all other races not shown separately and unknown family income.
[3]The race groups, white, black, American Indian or Alaska Native, and Asian or Pacific Islander, include persons of Hispanic and non-Hispanic origin; persons of Hispanic origin may be of any race.
[4]Poverty status is based on family income and family size using Bureau of the Census poverty thresholds. Poor persons are defined as below the poverty threshold. Near poor persons have incomes of 100 percent to less than 200 percent of poverty threshold. Nonpoor persons have incomes of 200 percent or greater than the poverty threshold. See Appendix II, Poverty level.
[5]Metropolitan statistical area.

Source: *Health, United States, 1999*, National Center for Health Statistics, Hyattsville, MD, 1999.

the century, acute conditions (severe illnesses of limited duration, such as infections) were predominant and often deadly. With the development of antibiotics and cures for many acute infectious diseases, people are living much longer, and chronic conditions are now the prevalent health problem for the elderly. While many chronic conditions are not life-threatening, they pose a substantial burden on the health and financial status of individuals, their families, and the nation as a whole.

TABLE 6.6

Limitation of activity caused by chronic conditions, according to selected characteristics: United States, 1990 and 1996

[Data are based on household interviews of a sample of the civilian noninstitutionalized population]

Characteristic	Total with limitation of activity		Limited but not in major activity		Limited in amount or kind of major activity		Unable to carry on major activity	
	1990	1996	1990	1996	1990	1996	1990	1996
	Percent of population							
Total[1,2]	12.9	13.6	4.1	4.1	5.0	5.2	3.9	4.4
Age								
Under 15 years	4.7	5.7	1.2	1.5	3.1	3.8	0.4	0.5
Under 5 years	2.2	2.6	0.6	0.6	1.0	1.5	0.6	0.5
5–14 years	6.1	7.3	1.6	1.9	4.1	4.9	0.4	0.5
15–44 years	8.5	9.6	2.6	2.7	3.5	3.7	2.4	3.2
45–64 years	21.8	22.0	5.7	5.5	7.5	7.2	8.6	9.4
65 years and over	37.5	36.3	15.4	14.8	11.9	11.0	10.2	10.5
65–74 years	33.7	31.4	13.2	12.0	9.9	9.2	10.6	10.1
75 years and over	43.3	43.1	18.8	18.7	14.9	13.5	9.6	10.9
Sex and age								
Male[1]	12.9	13.7	3.8	4.0	4.7	5.0	4.4	4.7
Under 15 years	5.5	7.0	1.4	1.8	3.6	4.7	0.5	0.6
15–44 years	8.4	9.5	2.3	2.5	3.5	3.6	2.7	3.5
45–64 years	21.4	21.2	4.7	4.5	6.6	6.4	10.1	10.4
65–74 years	34.0	31.1	13.0	12.6	8.4	7.7	12.7	10.8
75 years and over	38.8	41.6	20.3	22.6	10.2	9.5	8.3	9.5
Female[1]	13.0	13.5	4.3	4.2	5.3	5.2	3.4	4.1
Under 15 years	3.9	4.4	1.0	1.2	2.5	2.8	0.4	0.4
15–44 years	8.7	9.6	2.9	2.9	3.6	3.8	2.2	2.9
45–64 years	22.2	22.8	6.6	6.4	8.4	7.9	7.2	8.4
65–74 years	33.5	31.7	13.4	11.6	11.1	10.4	8.9	9.6
75 years and over	46.0	44.0	17.9	16.3	17.7	16.0	10.4	11.7
Race and age								
White[1]	12.8	13.1	4.2	4.1	5.0	5.0	3.6	4.0
Under 15 years	4.7	5.3	1.3	1.4	3.0	3.6	0.4	0.3
15–44 years	8.5	9.3	2.7	2.7	3.6	3.7	2.2	2.9
45–64 years	21.2	21.2	5.8	5.5	7.6	7.0	7.9	8.6
65–74 years	33.2	30.5	13.4	12.1	9.8	9.0	10.0	9.5
75 years and over	42.9	42.7	19.2	19.2	14.7	13.0	9.0	10.4
Black[1]	15.5	17.6	3.8	4.0	5.3	6.5	6.5	7.0
Under 15 years	5.3	8.6	1.2	2.2	3.4	5.3	0.7	1.1
15–44 years	9.4	12.1	2.2	2.7	3.4	4.2	3.9	5.2
45–64 years	28.1	29.3	5.7	5.6	7.7	8.9	14.8	14.7
65–74 years	41.6	39.5	12.4	12.1	11.5	11.7	17.6	15.7
75 years and over	50.9	47.8	16.2	11.5	17.6	19.6	17.0	16.7
Family income[1,3]								
Less than $16,000	22.9	26.4	5.2	5.8	8.1	8.8	9.6	11.8
$16,000–$24,999	14.8	15.7	4.3	4.2	5.7	6.3	4.8	5.2
$25,000–$34,999	11.6	13.2	3.8	4.3	4.7	5.0	3.0	3.8
$35,000–$49,999	10.4	10.6	3.7	3.8	4.4	4.1	2.3	2.6
$50,000 or more	8.4	8.5	3.4	3.5	3.3	3.4	1.7	1.6
Geographic region[1]								
Northeast	11.9	12.8	3.9	4.1	4.5	5.0	3.6	3.8
Midwest	12.9	13.1	3.9	3.8	5.5	5.3	3.4	4.0
South	14.0	14.2	4.1	3.8	5.3	5.5	4.6	4.9
West	12.5	14.0	4.4	4.8	4.5	4.6	3.7	4.5
Location of residence[1]								
Within MSA[4]	12.4	13.1	4.0	4.1	4.7	4.9	3.7	4.0
Outside MSA[4]	14.9	15.5	4.3	4.2	6.1	5.7	4.5	5.5

[1]Age adjusted. See Appendix II for age-adjustment procedure.
[2]Includes all other races not shown separately and unknown family income.
[3]Family income categories for 1996. In 1990 the two lowest income categories are less than $14,000 and $14,000–$24,999; the three higher income categories are as shown.
[4]Metropolitan statistical area.

Source: *Health, United States, 1999*, National Center for Health Statistics, Hyattsville, MD, 1999

In 1995, the majority of persons 70 and over had arthritis, one-third had hypertension, and one-fourth had heart disease. Many have at least one chronic illness, and many have multiple chronic conditions. Leading chronic conditions of people with disabilities are arthritis, hypertension, heart disease, diabetes, lung or respiratory disease, and stroke (Figure 6.6). Older men are more likely than

TABLE 6.7

Discharges, days of care, and average length of stay in short-stay hospitals, according to selected characteristics: United States, 1964, 1990, and 1996

[Data are based on household interviews of a sample of the civilian noninstitutionalized population]

Characteristic	Discharges			Days of care			Average length of stay		
	1964	1990	1996	1964	1990	1996	1964	1990	1996
	Number per 1,000 population						Number of days		
Total[1,2]	109.1	91.0	82.4	970.9	607.1	469.9	8.9	6.7	5.7
Age									
Under 15 years	67.6	46.7	37.3	405.7	271.3	212.3	6.0	5.8	5.7
Under 5 years	94.3	79.9	73.6	731.1	496.4	480.7	7.8	6.2	6.5
5–14 years	53.1	29.0	19.0	229.1	150.8	76.6	4.3	5.2	4.0
15–44 years	100.6	62.6	54.6	760.7	340.5	258.3	7.6	5.4	4.7
45–64 years	146.2	135.7	113.7	1,559.3	911.5	621.4	10.7	6.7	5.5
65 years and over	190.0	248.8	268.7	2,292.7	2,092.4	1,818.0	12.1	8.4	6.8
65–74 years.	181.2	215.4	228.8	2,150.4	1,719.3	1,491.6	11.9	8.0	6.5
75 years and over	206.7	300.6	323.7	2,560.4	2,669.9	2,267.6	12.4	8.9	7.0
Sex[1]									
Male.	103.8	91.0	82.5	1,010.2	622.7	487.6	9.7	6.8	5.9
Female.	113.7	91.7	83.1	933.4	592.9	458.0	8.2	6.5	5.5
Race[1]									
White	112.4	89.5	79.9	961.4	580.9	423.0	8.6	6.5	5.3
Black[3]	84.0	112.0	104.6	1,062.9	875.9	800.3	12.7	7.8	7.7
Family income[1,4]									
Less than $16,000	102.4	142.2	146.0	1,051.2	1,141.2	960.8	10.3	8.0	6.6
$16,000–$24,999.	116.4	98.4	97.7	1,213.9	594.5	572.2	10.4	6.0	5.9
$25,000–$34,999.	110.7	85.1	76.7	939.8	560.6	429.1	8.5	6.6	5.6
$35,000–$49,999.	109.2	73.2	62.3	882.6	380.3	272.0	8.1	5.2	4.4
$50,000 or more	110.7	72.5	54.2	918.9	446.2	257.7	8.3	6.2	4.8
Geographic region[1]									
Northeast	98.5	84.9	67.0	993.8	623.4	405.2	10.1	7.3	6.0
Midwest	109.2	91.5	91.3	944.9	570.8	524.8	8.7	6.2	5.7
South	117.8	106.4	95.3	968.0	713.6	549.5	8.2	6.7	5.8
West	110.5	70.5	66.2	985.9	444.6	339.5	8.9	6.3	5.1
Location of residence[1]									
Within MSA[5]	107.5	85.9	75.7	1,015.4	599.6	444.2	9.4	7.0	5.9
Outside MSA[5]	113.3	109.5	105.7	871.9	636.0	556.3	7.7	5.8	5.3

[1]Age adjusted.
[2]Includes all other races not shown separately and unknown family income.
[3]1964 data include all other races.
[4]Family income categories for 1996. In 1990 the two lowest income categories are less than $14,000 and $14,000–$24,999; the three higher income categories are as shown. Income categories in 1964 are less than $2,000; $2,000–$3,999; $4,000–$6,999; $7,000–$9,999; and $10,000 or more.
[5]Metropolitan statistical area.

NOTES: Estimates of hospital utilization from the National Health Interview Survey (NHIS) and the National Hospital Discharge Survey (NHDS) may differ because NHIS data are based on household interviews of the civilian noninstitutionalized population and exclude deliveries, whereas NHDS data are based on hospital discharge records of all persons. NHDS includes records for persons discharged alive or deceased and institutionalized persons, and excludes newborn infants. Differences in hospital utilization estimated by the two surveys are particularly evident for the elderly and for women.

Source: *Health, United States, 1999*, National Center for Health Statistics, Hyattsville, MD, 1999.

women to have acute illnesses that are life threatening, while older women are more likely to have chronic conditions that cause physical limitation over a long term.

Physical ailments can strike anyone at any age, but some illnesses and conditions are more common among the elderly. Chronic conditions account for most deterioration experienced with aging and are the major cause of high use of medical resources.

Arthritis

Arthritis is an "umbrella term" for a family of more than 100 separate diseases that affect the body's connective tissue. In common usage, it refers to inflammation of the joints. Arthritis is not a disease solely of the elderly, but its prevalence increases with age. Arthritis affects 1 out of 7 people; for those over 65, almost half will experience some form of this joint disease, although impairment ranges from mild occasional stiffness to crippling.

It affects an estimated 42.7 million persons in the United States. As the population ages, that number will likely increase to 60 million by 2020.

The greatest consequence of arthritis is loss of mobility and deformity in the affected tissues or joints. Patients diagnosed with osteoarthritis (a degenerative joint disease) generally experience some loss in ability to perform daily functions, such as household chores, shopping, running errands, and leisure activities. Patients with rheumatoid arthritis (inflammation of primarily the joint lining) often experience a loss in every activity, and the losses are more severe. Arthritis ranks second only to heart disease as a cause of disability payments. In 1997, persons 65 and older accounted for 55.7 of all hospitalizations for arthritis (Table 6.9).

Osteoporosis

Osteoporosis, a bone disorder associated with decrease in bone mass and resulting susceptibility to fracture, has only recently been recognized as a fairly common condition of old age, especially among women. About 25 million Americans, 80 percent of them women, have some form of osteoporosis. According to the National Osteoporosis Foundation, osteoporosis is the leading cause of bone fractures — approximately 1.5 million new fractures each year — in the elderly, with associated medical charges (including rehabilitation and treatment facilities) estimated at $10 billion. As the number of elderly grows, experts estimate these costs will increase to $60 billion by 2000 and $200 billion per year by 2040.

Osteoporosis develops slowly over a person's lifetime. After the mid-20s, bone tissue gradually thins out and is not replaced by new bone as quickly as in earlier years. When osteoporosis advances to the point where 35 to 40 percent of a person's bone density has been destroyed, the vertebrae (bones of the spine) begin to collapse, causing the spine to curve outward in a "dowager's hump." Bone fractures and broken hips become more common, some resulting in permanent damage and even premature death.

The disease is difficult to diagnose in its early stages because X-rays can detect only bone loss of more than 30 percent. The recent introduction of photon densitometry, which can measure very small losses in bone density, enables earlier diagnosis, although such bone scans are not routinely performed.

A person's risk of developing osteoporosis involves heredity. Osteoporosis affects half of all women over age 50. Women are far more susceptible to osteoporosis than men, especially women who are fair-skinned, small-boned, of northern European, Chinese, or Japanese descent, and who have reduced estrogen levels due to menopause or removal of the ovaries. After menopause, women lose bone mass rapidly as loss of estrogen accelerates calcium depletion in the body. At age 65, bone loss rate slows down again.

The most common consequences of osteoporosis are fractures, especially of the hip, spine, and wrist, but hip fractures are considered the most serious. About 20 percent of fractures result in death, and 25 percent cause severe handicaps. (Figure 6.7 shows the outcomes of osteoporosis-related hip fractures.) Two-thirds of those fractures require institutional care. Older women fall more than four times as frequently as older men.

The disease can be prevented or its effects diminished by measures taken earlier in life. Doctors recommend that women over the age of 40 take between 1,000 and 1,500 milligrams of calcium daily by eating calcium-rich food, such as milk, yogurt, cheese, tofu, dark leafy green vegetables, salmon, sardines, and shellfish, or by calcium supplements. It is also important to maintain adequate levels of vitamin D, which helps the body absorb and use calcium and magnesium. Most people get sufficient vitamin D from exposure to sunlight, but the skin loses much of its ability to produce the vitamin as one ages.

Regular exercise, especially walking, jogging, and bicycle riding, also aids in preventing osteoporosis. The risk is increased by smoking, heavy

TABLE 6.8

Physician contacts, according to selected patient characteristics: United States, 1987–96

[Data are based on household interviews of a sample of the civilian noninstitutionalized population]

Characteristic	1987	1988	1989	1990	1991	1992	1993	1994	1995	1996
					Physician contacts per person					
Total[1,2]	5.4	5.3	5.3	5.5	5.6	5.9	6.0	6.0	5.8	5.8
Age										
Under 15 years	4.5	4.6	4.6	4.5	4.7	4.6	4.9	4.6	4.5	4.4
Under 5 years	6.7	7.0	6.7	6.9	7.1	6.9	7.2	6.8	6.5	6.5
5–14 years	3.3	3.3	3.5	3.2	3.4	3.4	3.6	3.4	3.4	3.3
15–44 years	4.6	4.7	4.6	4.8	4.7	5.0	5.0	5.0	4.8	4.6
45–64 years	6.4	6.1	6.1	6.4	6.6	7.2	7.1	7.3	7.1	7.2
65 years and over	8.9	8.7	8.9	9.2	10.4	10.6	10.9	11.3	11.1	11.7
65–74 years	8.4	8.4	8.2	8.5	9.2	9.7	9.9	10.3	9.8	10.2
75 years and over	9.7	9.2	9.9	10.1	12.3	12.1	12.3	12.7	12.9	13.7
Sex and age										
Male[1]	4.6	4.6	4.8	4.7	4.9	5.1	5.2	5.2	4.9	5.0
Under 5 years	6.7	7.3	7.5	7.2	7.6	7.1	7.5	7.0	6.8	7.1
5–14 years	3.4	3.4	3.7	3.3	3.5	3.5	3.8	3.5	3.6	3.6
15–44 years	3.3	3.3	3.4	3.4	3.4	3.7	3.6	3.7	3.3	3.2
45–64 years	5.5	5.2	5.2	5.6	5.8	6.1	6.1	6.3	6.0	6.0
65–74 years	8.1	7.9	8.5	8.0	8.6	9.2	9.3	10.1	9.5	9.4
75 years and over	9.2	9.6	9.9	10.0	11.6	12.2	11.7	11.6	11.9	13.5
Female[1]	6.0	6.0	5.9	6.1	6.3	6.6	6.7	6.7	6.5	6.5
Under 5 years	6.7	6.8	5.9	6.5	6.6	6.7	6.9	6.5	6.3	5.9
5–14 years	3.1	3.3	3.3	3.2	3.2	3.3	3.4	3.3	3.1	3.0
15–44 years	5.8	6.0	5.9	6.0	5.9	6.2	6.4	6.2	6.2	6.0
45–64 years	7.2	6.9	7.0	7.1	7.4	8.2	8.1	8.3	8.1	8.4
65–74 years	8.6	8.8	7.9	9.0	9.7	10.1	10.4	10.5	10.1	10.9
75 years and over	10.0	9.0	9.9	10.2	12.7	12.1	12.8	13.4	13.5	13.7
Race and age										
White[1]	5.5	5.5	5.5	5.6	5.8	6.0	6.0	6.1	5.9	5.8
Under 5 years	7.1	7.6	7.1	7.1	7.4	7.3	7.5	7.1	6.7	6.6
5–14 years	3.5	3.6	3.8	3.5	3.7	3.7	3.9	3.7	3.6	3.5
15–44 years	4.7	4.8	4.8	4.9	4.9	·5.0	5.1	5.1	4.9	4.7
45–64 years	6.4	6.1	6.2	6.4	6.6	7.2	7.0	7.4	7.0	7.2
65–74 years	8.4	8.3	8.0	8.5	9.4	9.6	9.7	10.5	9.9	10.2
75 years and over	9.7	9.3	9.7	10.1	12.1	12.0	12.2	12.4	13.1	13.2
Black[1]	5.1	4.8	4.9	5.1	5.2	5.9	6.0	5.7	5.5	5.7
Under 5 years	5.1	4.6	5.3	5.6	6.0	5.6	6.2	5.2	5.8	5.6
5–14 years	2.3	2.2	2.3	2.2	2.1	2.3	2.4	2.5	2.5	2.7
15–44 years	4.2	4.2	3.9	4.2	4.0	5.3	4.7	4.8	4.3	4.5
45–64 years	7.3	6.6	6.3	7.1	7.5	7.8	8.7	7.7	8.0	7.3
65–74 years	8.6	9.1	10.0	9.2	7.3	10.9	11.5	9.3	9.9	10.2
75 years and over	10.8	8.7	12.7	10.4	15.7	13.7	13.1	16.3	11.5	19.8
Family income[1,3]										
Less than $16,000	6.8	6.2	6.3	6.3	6.8	7.3	7.3	7.6	7.4	7.5
$16,000–$24,999	5.6	5.3	5.2	5.6	5.6	6.0	5.7	5.9	6.1	5.5
$25,000–$34,999	5.2	5.0	5.5	5.2	5.5	5.7	6.0	5.8	5.3	5.6
$35,000–$49,999	5.2	5.5	5.2	5.7	5.8	5.9	6.0	6.2	5.7	5.9
$50,000 or more	5.4	5.5	6.0	5.6	5.8	5.8	5.8	6.0	5.6	5.3
Geographic region[1]										
Northeast	5.2	5.0	5.3	5.2	5.4	5.9	5.9	5.9	5.6	5.7
Midwest	5.6	5.4	5.4	5.3	5.8	5.9	6.2	6.0	5.8	5.7
South	5.1	5.2	5.3	5.6	5.5	5.8	5.7	5.6	5.8	6.1
West	5.5	5.9	5.5	5.6	5.9	6.1	6.0	6.4	5.8	5.3
Location of residence[1]										
Within MSA[4]	5.5	5.5	5.4	5.6	5.8	6.0	6.1	6.0	5.9	5.8
Outside MSA[4]	4.8	4.9	5.2	4.9	5.1	5.6	5.6	5.7	5.3	5.7

[1]Age adjusted.
[2]Includes all other races not shown separately and unknown family income.
[3]Family income categories for 1996. In 1995 the two lowest income categories are less than $15,000 and $15,000–$24,999; the three higher income categories are as shown. In 1989–94 the two lowest income categories are less than $14,000 and $14,000–$24,999; the three higher income categories are as shown. Income categories for 1988 are less than $13,000; $13,000–$18,999; $19,000–$24,999; $25,000–$44,999; and $45,000 or more. Income categories for 1987 are less than $10,000; $10,000–$14,999; $15,000–$19,999; $20,000–$34,999; and $35,000 or more.
[4]Metropolitan statistical area.

Source: *Health, United States, 1999*, National Center for Health Statistics, Hyattsville, MD, 1999.

drinking, high caffeine and protein intake, and lack of regular exercise. The newest experimental therapies involve the intake of sodium fluoride, calcitonin, and various drugs. Estrogen replacement therapy during, after, and sometimes just prior to menopause is now recognized as having the additional side effect of maintaining bone density in women. In 1995, the introduction of a new drug

Fosamax offered hope for improvement to the victims of this disease.

A 1997 study, "The Economic Cost of Hip Fractures in Community-Dwelling Older Adults," *The Journal of the American Geriatrics Society* (vol. 45), found that the cost of a hip fracture, including direct medical care, formal nonmedical care, and informal care provided by family and friends, was between $16,300 and $18,700 during the first year following the injury.

Diabetes

The elderly are quite susceptible to Type II, or non-insulin dependent, diabetes. This form of diabetes, also called adult-onset diabetes, accounts for over 85 percent of all diabetic cases. (Type I diabetes, also known as insulin-dependent diabetes, generally begins in childhood.) In 1998, diabetes killed 64,574 Americans and was the seventh most common cause of death (Table 6.2). In addition, many more people died from heart disease or strokes resulting from diabetes. An estimated 8.7 million Americans have diabetes, although some experts believe that half the victims do not yet know they have the disease.

Frequent complications of diabetes are nerve damage in the legs and feet, sometimes resulting in amputations, and eye problems that can result in blindness. Both forms of the disease require the daily, sometimes even hourly, monitoring of blood sugar and insulin levels and can often be controlled with a diet and weight reduction program. Currently, there are new methods for administering insulin, such as implants and pumps, and home blood sugar self-test kits are now easily available

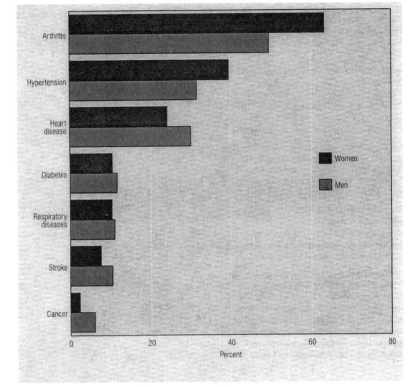

FIGURE 6.6

Percent of persons 70 years of age and over who reported selected chronic conditions by sex: United States, 1995

Notes: Based on interviews conducted between October 1994 and March 1996 with noninstitutionalized persons. Percents are age adjusted.

Source: *Health, United States, 1999*, National Center for Health Statistics, Hyattsville, MD, 1999

for diabetic patients. Oral medications are now widely used.

Diabetes seems to be on the increase. Although much of the increase can be attributed to the growth in the number of older Americans, some experts believe additional factors have contributed to the rise. The Centers for Disease Control and Prevention (CDC) study, *Trends in the Prevalence and Incidence of Self-Reported Diabetes Mellitus — United States, 1980–1994* (1997), found that diabetes increased with age and that the prevalence of the disease has risen 15 percent since 1980 (Table 6.10). Experts suggest several factors, including increased obesity, heredity, and environmental factors, have contributed to this increase.

Prostate Problems

Prostate problems in men increase significantly after age 50. Often the prostate becomes enlarged

TABLE 6.9

Number and percentage distribution of discharges from short-stay hospitals, number and percentage distribution of days of care, and average length of stay for all conditions and for first-listed diagnosis of arthritis and other rheumatic conditions, by age and sex of patients — National Hospital Discharge Survey, United States, 1997

Characteristic	Discharges (thousands) No.	(95% CI*)	% of all arthritis discharges	Days of care (thousands) No.	(95% CI)	% of all arthritis days of care	Average length of stay (days)
All conditions	30,914	(±1,740)	—	157,458	(±10,523)	—	5.1
Arthritis and other rheu-							
matic conditions	744	(± 88)	100.0	3,835	(± 714)	100.0	5.2
Age (yrs)							
<15	21	(± 8)	2.8	63	(± 23)	1.6	3.0
15–44	90	(± 14)	12.1	481	(± 257)	12.6	5.3
45–64	218	(± 27)	29.3	1,023	(± 189)	26.7	4.7
≥65	414	(± 58)	55.7	2,269	(± 586)	59.2	5.5
Sex							
Male	292	(± 19)	39.3	1,307	(± 196)	34.1	4.5
Female	451	(± 57)	60.7	2,529	(± 603)	65.9	5.6

*Confidence interval.

Source: "Impact of Arthritis and Other Rheumatic Conditions on the Health-Care System — United States, 1997," *Morbidity and Mortality Weekly Report*, vol. 48, no. 17, May 7, 1999

with the PSA (prostatic specific antigen) blood test aids in diagnosing cancer in the prostate. Prostate cancer is the third most common cause of death from cancer in men and the most common cause of death from cancer in men 75 and older. The incidence is greatest among Black men over 60.

Urinary Problems

An estimated 15 to 30 percent of noninstitutionalized persons aged 65 and over and at least 50 percent among those in nursing homes have problems controlling urination. The problem increases with age, with an estimated 986,000 persons 65 to 74 years old and 1.2 million persons 75 years and older having some urinary difficulty. The problem is more common in women than men.

and blocks the urethra, the canal through which urine leaves the body, making urination difficult. This condition can often be relieved with surgery.

If found and treated early, cancer of the prostate is generally not life-threatening, since it progresses very slowly and remains localized for a long time. Recent introduction of screening men

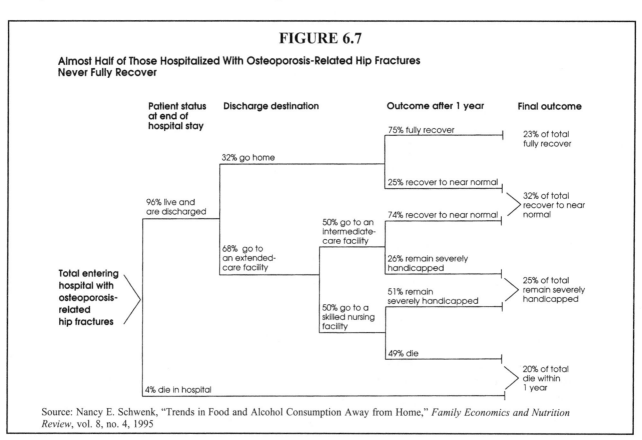

FIGURE 6.7

Almost Half of Those Hospitalized With Osteoporosis-Related Hip Fractures Never Fully Recover

Source: Nancy E. Schwenk, "Trends in Food and Alcohol Consumption Away from Home," *Family Economics and Nutrition Review*, vol. 8, no. 4, 1995

Urinary problems often have a serious emotional impact. People with urinary problems are more likely to report their health as fair to poor and to report deterioration of their health. About three-fourths of those with urinary problems suffer some limitation in at least some activity.

Urinary incontinence, the inability to control bladder function, is not a disease, but rather a symptom of other dysfunctions. Nor is incontinence a necessary consequence of aging. Specialists report that many people do not report their problems with incontinence because they are not aware that help is possible. The aggressive marketing of absorbent undergarments has had the effect of indicating to the elderly that their problem is a normal complication of aging, discouraging many people from seeking help. Doctors estimate that 85 to 90 percent of sufferers could be successfully treated.

Malnutrition

Poor nutritional status is a primary concern for the elderly. Nutritionally inadequate diets can contribute to or exacerbate diseases, hasten the development of degenerative diseases associated with aging, and delay recovery from illness. However, studies seem to suggest that, in general, the elderly are more likely than younger persons to try to eat healthfully.

The CDC's *Surveillance for Five Health Risks Among Older Adults — United States, 1993-1997* (1999) found that the percentage of those who reported eating fruits and vegetables at least five times per day increased with age. Of those 55 to 64, 26.4 percent ate fruits and vegetables at least five times daily; 30.4 percent of persons 65 to 74 and 33.6 percent of those older than 75 ate fruits and vegetables at least five times a day. Women were slightly more likely than men to eat at least five portions of fruits and vegetables, as were Whites more likely to do so than Blacks.

Nonetheless, even with the emphasis in recent years on good nutrition as a major factor contributing to good health, an estimated 30 to 60 percent of all elderly people maintain eating habits that provide them with less than the recommended daily level of nutrients and protein, and a quarter of the elderly suffer from some form of malnutrition. If they are inactive, their bodies become less capable of absorbing and using nutrients in the foods they do eat, and certain medications increase the body's needs for particular nutrients. Many hospital stays are for conditions preventable by proper eating.

The American Dietetic Association believes that few doctors are trained to recognize malnutrition, despite knowing that well-nourished elderly people become ill less often, recover from illness and injury more quickly, and are less expensive to treat.

An individual's eating habits can be affected by many factors — loneli-

TABLE 6.10

Prevalence and incidence of self-reported diabetes mellitus, by year — United States, National Health Interview Survey, 1980–1994

	Prevalence			Incidence		
Year	No. existing cases*	Crude rate[†]	Age-adjusted rate[†]	No. existing cases*	Crude rate[§]	Age-adjusted rate[§]
1980	5528	25.4	25.5	541	2.5	2.5
1981	5645	25.1	25.3	501	2.2	2.2
1982	5729	25.2	25.4	713	3.1	3.2
1983	5613	24.5	24.7	690	3.0	3.0
1984	6004	25.9	26.0	645	2.8	2.8
1985	6134	26.2	26.2	679	2.9	2.9
1986	6563	27.8	27.8	644	2.7	2.7
1987	6609	27.7	27.6	715	3.0	3.0
1988	6162	25.6	25.4	678	2.8	2.8
1989	6467	26.6	26.3	677	2.8	2.8
1990	6212	25.2	24.8	521	2.1	2.1
1991	7206	29.0	28.5	672	2.7	2.7
1992	7365	29.3	28.5	613	2.4	2.4
1993	7783	30.6	29.7	865	3.4	3.3
1994	7744	29.8	29.3	965	3.7	3.7

*In thousands.
[†]The number of persons who reported having diabetes per 1000 population.
[§]The number of persons who reported having had diabetes diagnosed within the previous 12 months per 1000 population.

Source: "Trends in Prevalence and Incidence of Self-Reported Diabetes Mellitus — United States, 1980-1994," *Morbidity and Mortality Weekly Report*, October 31, 1997

ness, depression, poverty, poor appetite, or lack of transportation. Meals provided by community service organizations, whether they are dinners served at a senior center or home-delivered meals, are one of the most important services offered to the elderly. However, experts on nutrition for the elderly increasingly believe the traditional solutions to the problems of hunger and malnutrition, such as Meals on Wheels, may not recognize the whole problem.

Chronic illnesses often depress appetites. In addition, medications can suppress hunger and cause loss of senses that make the older person lose interest in food. In other words, even if one brings food to the elderly, they will not necessarily eat. Sometimes, elderly people are simply too poor to eat properly. In addition, studies show that the protein needs of older people are significantly higher than the daily protein intake recommended by federal agencies.

TABLE 6.11

Nutrient intakes: Women living alone as compared with women living with others

Nutrient	Age (years)					
	All ages	19 - 34	35 - 54	55 - 64	65 - 74	75+
Food energy	L	L	–	–	–	–
Carbohydrate	–	–	–	–	–	–
Protein	L	L	–	L	–	L
Fat	L	L	–	L	–	–
Saturated fat	L	L	L	–	–	–
Vitamin A	H	–	–	H	–	–
Carotenes	–	–	–	–	–	–
Vitamin C	–	–	–	–	–	–
Vitamin E	–	–	–	–	–	–
Thiamin	L	L	–	–	–	–
Riboflavin	–	L	–	–	–	–
Niacin	L	L	–	–	–	–
Vitamin B-6	–	L	–	–	–	–
Vitamin B-12	–	–	–	–	–	–
Folate	–	–	–	–	–	–
Phosphorus	L	L	–	–	–	–
Calcium	L	L	–	–	–	–
Magnesium	–	–	–	–	–	–
Iron	–	L	–	–	–	–
Zinc	L	L	–	L	–	–
Cholesterol	–	–	–	–	–	–
Fiber	–	–	–	–	–	–
Sodium	L	L	–	–	–	L

L = significantly lower; H = significantly higher. From weighted mean 3-day intakes; significant at $p < .05$. Blank cells indicate no statistically significant relation.

Source: "How Does Living Alone Affect Dietary Quality?" *Family Economics and Nutrition Review*, vol.8, no. 4, 1995

Living Alone Affects Dietary Quality

Many elderly people, especially women, live alone. The U.S. Department of Agriculture reported in 1995 that the diets of adults living alone were significantly lower in nutrient intakes than the diets of multi-person households. Of those living alone, younger age groups were as likely, or more than likely, as those over 65 not to get adequate nutrients. Women older than 75 and men older than 65 were deficient in some nutrients (Tables 6.11 and 6.12).

Hearing Loss

Hearing loss is a very common problem among the elderly. The CDC reported, in *Surveillance for Sensory Impairment, Activity Limitation, and Health-Related Quality of Life Among Older Adults—United States, 1993-1997* (December 1999), that 33.2 percent of older adults — approximately 6.7 million persons — experienced hearing impairment. Deafness in one ear was reported in 8.3 percent of older adults, and 7.3 percent were deaf in both ears. Almost 12 percent reported using a hearing aid in the preceding 12 months. (See Table 6.13.) Older men (40 percent) were more likely to suffer hearing loss than women (28.7 percent). Elderly Whites (34.5 percent) were significantly more likely than Blacks (19.3 percent) to have hearing trouble. There are many causes of hearing loss, the most common being age-related changes in the ear's mechanism.

People suffering from hearing loss may withdraw from social contact and are sometimes mislabeled as confused or even senile. They are often reluctant to admit hearing problems, and sometimes hearing loss is so gradual that even the afflicted person may not be aware of it for some time.

Treatment is available for increasing numbers of patients, if they seek help. Many physicians are unaware of the services now available to the hearing impaired, whose options are increasing. Among the solutions now offered are high-tech hearing aids, amplifiers for doorbells and telephones, infrared amplifiers, and even companion dogs trained to respond to sounds for the owner.

Vision Changes

Almost no one escapes changes in vision as he or she grows older. By age 40, a person often notices a change in what may have been perfect vision. It becomes increasingly difficult to read small print or thread a needle at the usual distance. For many, night vision declines. This is often caused by a condition called presbyopia (tired eyes) and is a very common occurrence. People who were previously nearsighted may actually find some improvement in eyesight as they become slightly farsighted.

The CDC (see above) reported that 16.4 percent of elderly men and 19.2 percent of older women — 3.6 million persons — experienced vision impairment. Among older Blacks, 19.6 percent were visually impaired, as were 17.9 percent of older Whites. About 4.4 percent of people 70 and older were blind in one eye, and another 1.7 percent were blind in both eyes. Approximately 91.5 percent of older Americans wore glasses, and 17 percent used a magnifier. (See Table 6.13.)

Eye Diseases

Much more serious than simple loss of visual clarity are cataracts, glaucoma, and problems affecting the retina, which frequently occur in elderly people.

TABLE 6.12

Nutrient intakes: Men living alone as compared with men living with others

Nutrient	All ages	19 - 34	35 - 54	55 - 64	65 - 74	75+
Food energy	L	–	–	–	–	–
Carbohydrate	–	–	–	–	–	–
Protein	L	–	–	–	–	L
Fat	L	–	–	–	–	–
Saturated fat	L	L	–	–	–	–
Vitamin A	–	–	–	–	–	–
Carotenes	–	–	–	–	L	–
Vitamin C	–	–	L	–	–	–
Vitamin E	–	–	L	–	L	–
Thiamin	–	–	L	–	–	–
Riboflavin	–	–	–	–	–	–
Niacin	–	–	–	–	–	–
Vitamin B-6	–	–	–	–	–	–
Vitamin B-12	–	L	–	–	–	–
Folate	–	–	–	–	–	–
Phosphorus	L	–	–	–	–	L
Calcium	L	–	L	–	–	L
Magnesium	–	–	–	–	–	–
Iron	–	–	–	–	–	–
Zinc	–	–	H	–	–	L
Cholesterol	–	–	–	–	–	–
Fiber	–	–	–	–	L	–
Sodium	L	–	L	L	–	–

L = significantly lower; H = significantly higher. From weighted mean 3-day intakes; significant at p < .05. Blank cells indicate no statistically significant relation.

Source: Gerrior, S.A., Guthrie, J.F., Fox, J.J., Lutz, S.M., Keane, T.P., and Basiotis, P.P., 1994, How Does Living Alone Affect Dietary Quality? U.S. Department of Agriculture, Agricultural Research Service, Home Economics Research Report No. 51.

Source: "How Does Living Alone Affect Dietary Quality?" *Family Economics and Nutrition Review*, vol.8, no. 4, 1995

Cataracts

Cataracts occur when the crystalline structure of the eye lens breaks down. The lens becomes clouded, limiting the amount of light reaching the optic nerve and distorting images. Most cataracts develop slowly over time, but they can eventually cause almost total blindness. In recent years there has been a huge increase in lens replacement operations in which the clouded lens is removed and a plastic lens is substituted. The CDC found that among older adults, 24.5 percent had a cataract (Table 6.13).

Glaucoma

Glaucoma is the leading cause of blindness in the United States. Experts estimate that three million Americans have the most common form of the disease, called open-angle glaucoma, and some 80,000 are blind as a result of it. Although glaucoma can affect people of any age, it is most common in people older than 60. Among the elderly, approximately 8 percent have glaucoma (Table 6.13).

Glaucoma is caused by incomplete drainage of fluids out of the eyeball, causing pressure to build up inside the eyeball. It usually presents no early symptoms, but if undetected in its early stages, it can result in irreversible blindness. There is no cure for glaucoma and no way to restore vision lost. Routine glaucoma tests are especially important for older people. Medication (eye drops or pills) can generally manage the condition. At later stages, laser therapy and surgery are effective in stopping further damage.

Problems of the Retina

The retina is a thin lining of nerves on the back of the eye. Over time, it can become torn or detached, jeopardizing vision. If treated in time by laser therapy, tears and separations can almost always be repaired. *Senile macular degeneration* is a condition in which the macula, a specialized part of the retina responsible for sharp central and reading vision, is damaged. Symptoms include blurred vision, a dark spot in the center of the vision field, and vertical line distortion.

Diabetic retinopathy occurs when the small blood vessels that flourish in the retina do not perform properly. Blood vessels can leak fluid that distorts vision, and sometimes blood is released into the center of the eye causing blindness. Diabetic retinopathy is a major cause of blindness.

Vision and Hearing Impairments

The CDC (see above) reported that 8.6 percent of the elderly population — 1.7 million people — suffer both hearing and vision impairment. Older adults who experience both hearing and sight loss are more likely to report difficulty walking, tending their daily needs, and managing their medica-

---

TABLE 6.13

Percentage distribution of selected vision and hearing impairments among adults aged ≥70 years — United States, National Health Interview Second Supplement on Aging, 1994*

Sensory characteristic	Population aged ≥70 yrs	%	(95% CI†)
Vision impairments			
(n = 1,397)	3,652,626	18.1	(±1.1)
Blind in one eye	879,215	4.4	(±0.4)
Blind in both eyes	338,492	1.7	(±0.3)
Any other trouble seeing	2,853,053	14.4	(±0.9)
Glaucoma	1,601,041	7.9	(±0.6)
Cataract	5,125,760	24.5	(±1.1)
Lens implant	3,038,524	15.1	(±1.0)
Used magnifier	3,376,160	17.0	(±1.0)
Wear glasses	18,127,245	91.5	(±0.7)
Hearing impairments			
(n = 2,905)	6,697,497	33.2	(±1.3)
Deaf in one ear	1,542,163	8.3	(±0.7)
Deaf in both ears	1,478,727	7.3	(±0.7)
Any other trouble hearing	4,193,478	22.5	(±1.2)
Used hearing aid during preceding 12 months	2,343,064	11.6	(±0.8)
Cochlear implant	28,018	0.1	(±0.1)

*Total population = 8,767.
†Confidence interval. CIs were calculated by multiplying the standard error by 1.96.

Source: Vincent A. Campbell et al., "Surveillance for Sensory Impairment, Activity Limitation, and Health-Related Quality of Life Among Older Adults — United States, 1993-1997," in "Surveillance for Selected Public Health Indicators Affecting Older Adults — United States," *Morbidity and Mortality Weekly Report*, vol. 48, no. SS-8, December 17, 1999

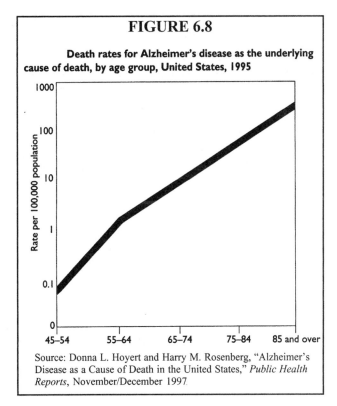

FIGURE 6.8

Death rates for Alzheimer's disease as the underlying cause of death, by age group, United States, 1995

Source: Donna L. Hoyert and Harry M. Rosenberg, "Alzheimer's Disease as a Cause of Death in the United States," *Public Health Reports*, November/December 1997

tions. They also are more likely to fall and suffer fractures and are less often able to socialize.

Parkinson's Disease

Once known as "the shaking palsy" but now named after the physician that first described it — Dr. James Parkinson — in 1817, Parkinson's disease (PD) is a disorder of the central nervous system resulting from a degeneration of nerve cells in the brain. Symptoms may occur at any age, although the first symptoms typically begin in the 60s and 70s. The primary symptoms include tremor, rigidity, impaired gait, and balance and speech problems. Such symptoms also increase the likelihood of falling.

At present, the cause is unknown, although many researchers believe it may have both a genetic and an environmental component. A history of repeated head trauma has been found more common among PD sufferers than in the general population.

There is currently no cure for PD, and treatment is aimed at controlling symptoms. The most effective drug for treating the disease is levodopa,

and many other medications are being investigated. Surgery is sometimes used in advanced cases, although it is not always successful. The American Parkinson Disease Association reports that PD affects approximately 1.5 million people in the United States.

ORGANIC MENTAL DISEASES OF THE ELDERLY — DEMENTIA

As equally devastating as the decline of a once-healthy body is the deterioration of the mind. As with other disorders, mental impairments can occur in persons of any age, but certain types of illnesses are much more prevalent in the elderly. In this area, more than any other, the differences between individuals can vary dramatically. Some people may show no decline in mental ability until far into old age. Others experience occasional forgetfulness. A few are robbed of all their mental faculties before they reach 60. (For information on mental illness among the elderly, see Chapter VII.)

Older people with mental problems were once labeled as "senile." Only in recent years have researchers found that physical disorders can cause progressive deterioration of mental and neurological functions. These disorders produce symptoms that are collectively known as "dementia." Symptoms of dementia include loss of language functions, inability to think abstractly, inability to care for oneself, personality change, emotional instability, and loss of a sense of time or place.

It is important to note that occasional forgetfulness and disorientation are normal signs of the aging process. True dementia is a disease and is not the inevitable result of growing older. Many disorders may cause or simulate dementia. Senile dementia refers to several impairing diseases and disorders, a small proportion of which are potentially reversible. The CDC reported, in *Surveillance for Morbidity and Mortality Among Older Adults— United States, 1995-1996* (December 1999), that the prevalence of dementia increases from 2.8 percent among adults 65 to 74 years to 28 percent among those 85 and older.

Alzheimer's Disease

The most prevalent form of dementia is Alzheimer's disease (AD), named after the German neurologist Alois Alzheimer who, in 1906, discovered the "neurofibrillary tangles" now associated with the disease. Alzheimer's is a degenerative disorder of the brain and nervous system; there is, at present, no known cause, cure, or treatment.

Just a dozen or so years ago, Alzheimer's was still a relatively obscure disease that received little study and still less publicity. Symptoms were generally attributed to aging and the victims diagnosed as senile. Today, Alzheimer's is the subject of intense research and is very much in the public consciousness. Unfortunately, many people have become familiar with the disease because a relative or loved one has been diagnosed with Alzheimer's.

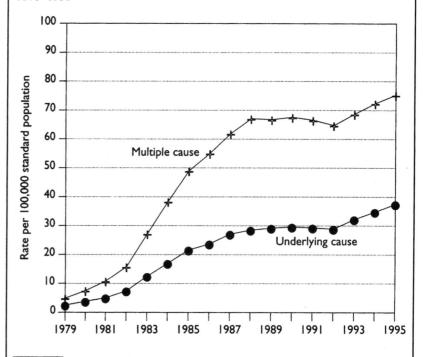

FIGURE 6.9

Age-adjusted death rates per 100,000 standard population for Alzheimer's disease as an underlying cause of death or one of multiple causes of death, decedents ages 65 years and older, United States, 1979–1995

NOTE: Rates for Alzheimer's disease as one of multiple causes includes deaths for which the disease is listed as the underlying cause and deaths for which it is mentioned as one of the causes.

SOURCE: National Center for Health Statistics, National Vital Statistics System

Source: Donna L. Hoyert and Harry M. Rosenberg, "Alzheimer's Disease as a Cause of Death in the United States," *Public Health Reports*, November/December 1997

Almost one-half (48 percent) of those over 85 — the fastest growing segment of society — have AD, and more than 50 percent of nursing home residents are estimated to have some form of dementia. Once considered a rare disorder, AD is now recognized as a major public health problem.

Death Rates

The U.S. Department of Health and Human Services, in *Health, United States, 1999* (1999), reported that Alzheimer's disease was the eighth leading cause of death among women and the tenth leading cause of death in White males and females in 1997. Death rates increase with age — those 85 and older were 19 times more likely to get the disease than those 65 to 74 (Figure 6.8). The death rate for the disease is somewhat greater for the White than for the Black population. Figure 6.9 shows the death rates for Alzheimer's from 1979 to 1995.

Prevalence

The U.S. General Accounting Office (GAO), in *Alzheimer's Disease — Estimates of Prevalence in the United States* (1998), estimated that at least 1.9 million Americans 65 and older suffered from Alzheimer's disease in 1995. (See Table 6.14.) After allowing for the number of cases that are "mixed," that suffer from AD secondary to another form of dementia, and those that were missed in the screening process, the number could approach 2.1 million.

The GAO also projected the number of cases by the year 2015. That year, there will likely be almost 2.9 million cases, 1.6 million of them being severe or moderate. (See Table 6.15.) Allowing for mixed and missed cases, the GAO estimates that could amount to 3.2 million cases, of which 2.1 million will be moderate or severe. However, the National Institute on Aging estimates that 4 million people now suffer from Alzheimer's in the United States, some 3 million of whom live at home and are cared for by family.

TABLE 6.14

Estimates of Any AD and Moderate or Severe AD for Americans 65 Years of Age or Older in 1995

Age	Any AD		Moderate or severe AD	
	Number	Percent	Number	Percent
65-69	104,785	1.1	61,815	0.6
70-74	194,716	2.2	111,111	1.3
75-79	304,399	4.6	169,549	2.5
80-84	411,363	9.2	227,757	5.1
85-89	412,764	17.8	232,726	10.0
90-94	312,509	31.5	185,516	18.7
95+	166,287	52.5	110,595	34.9
Total	**1,906,822**	**5.7**	**1,099,069**	**3.3**

Source: Our integration of prevalence rates from 18 studies in the literature and the U.S. Bureau of the Census population estimates in Statistical Abstract of the United States: 1996 (Washington, D.C.: 1996).

Source: *Alzheimer's Disease — Estimates of Prevalence in the United States*, U.S. General Accounting Office, Washington, DC, 1998

As the population ages, Alzheimer's is becoming more of a concern. As many as 10 percent of people over the age of 65 with memory problems or other mental impairment probably suffer from Alzheimer's. Up to 3 percent of people between 65 and 74, 19 percent of those between 75 and 84, and 47 percent of those over 85 are likely to have the disease. This increase is likely due to the growing number of older persons, improved diagnosis, and increased awareness of the condition. In addition, some research suggests that the prevalence has increased as well.

An accurate count of the number of patients is difficult because of the stigma attached to the disease. Scientists report that when they try to trace the inheritance of Alzheimer's in families, they often meet denial and resistance among family members to admitting the presence of the disease.

Symptoms

The diagnosis of Alzheimer's disease can be positively confirmed only after death. An autopsy of the brain of an Alzheimer's victim reveals abnormal tangles of nerve fibers (neurofibrillary tangles), tips of nerve fibers embedded in plaque, and a significant shortage of the enzymes that produce the neurotransmitter acetylcholine. Researchers are now looking for a diagnostic test for Alzheimer's in living subjects.

The symptoms of living victims usually begin with mild episodes of forgetfulness and disorientation. Most victims develop the disease between the ages of 55 and 80. As the disease progresses, memory loss increases and mood changes are frequent, accompanied by confusion, irritability, restlessness, and speech impairment. Eventually, the victim may lose all control over his or her mental and bodily functions. Table 6.16 shows the behavioral problems that often accompany the physical signs of the disease. Alzheimer's victims survive an average of 8 to 10 years after the first onset of symptoms; some live an additional 25 years.

Suspected Causes

Despite intensified research in recent years, little is known about the cause (or causes) of Alzheimer's. One thing is certain — it is *not* a normal consequence of aging. It is, rather, a disease that either strikes older people almost exclusively, or more likely, its symptoms appear and become more pronounced as a person grows older.

There are several theories on the cause(s) of Alzheimer's. Some theories currently being pursued by researchers are

- A breakdown in the system that produces acetylcholine.

- A slow-acting virus that has already left the body before symptoms appear.

- A genetic (hereditary) origin.

Current research is focusing largely on heredity. Several studies have implicated two specific genes on the chromosomes of Alzheimer's patients. Other studies of twins suggest a strong role of heredity in the development of the disease. Recent research has confirmed a link between Alzheimer's and a high level of certain proteins in cerebrospinal fluid. The protein is not believed to cause the disease but may be a "marker" in diagnosing the disease. Other research suggests that it may be possible to use brain scans to detect mental deterioration years before symptoms become apparent, which would allow the possibility for earlier treatment.

Treatment

Major developments in the treatment of AD include the emergence of human gene therapy to revitalize damaged brain cells and enzyme-blocking therapy. Both of these developments will be tested in 2000. Some researchers contend that the incidence of AD is lower among people who take

TABLE 6.15

Projected Estimates of Any AD and Moderate or Severe AD for Americans 65 Years of Age or Older, 1995-2015

Year	Any AD		Moderate or severe AD	
	Number	% change[a]	Number	% change[a]
1995	1,906,822	[b]	1,099,069	[b]
2000	2,141,772	+12	1,233,932	+12
2005	2,370,615	+24	1,365,085	+24
2010	2,605,231	+37	1,500,727	+37
2015	2,872,420	+51	1,656,046	+51

[a]All percentage changes are relative to the baseline number for 1995.

[b]Zero by definition.

Source: *Alzheimer's Disease — Estimates of Prevalence in the United States*, U.S. General Accounting Office, Washington, DC, 1998

TABLE 6.16

Proportion of the Sample Having Behavioral Problems

Behavioral Problem	Number	Percent with Problem
Forgets what day it is	7,872	93.3
Loses or misplaces things	6,362	75.4
Asks repetitive questions	5,771	68.4
Has trouble recognizing familiar people	4,775	56.6
Leaves tasks uncompleted	4,623	54.8
Is suspicious or accusative	4,379	51.9
Relives situations from the past	4,176	49.5
Hides things	4,033	47.8
Wakes you up at night	3,873	45.9
Has episodes of unreasonable anger	3,889	46.1
Is constantly restless	3,864	45.8
Sees or hears things that are not there	3,628	43.0
Does things that embarrass you	3,350	39.7
Is constantly talkative	2,303	27.3
Wanders or gets lost	2,227	26.4
Has episodes of combativeness	2,168	25.7
Engages in behavior potentially dangerous to self	1,783	21.2
Destroys property	937	11.1
Engages in behavior potentially dangerous to others	911	10.8

NOTE: N = 8,437.

Source: Patrick Fox et al., "Long-Term Care Eligibility Criteria for People with Alzheimer's Disease," *Health Care Financing Review*, vol. 20, no. 4, Summer 1999

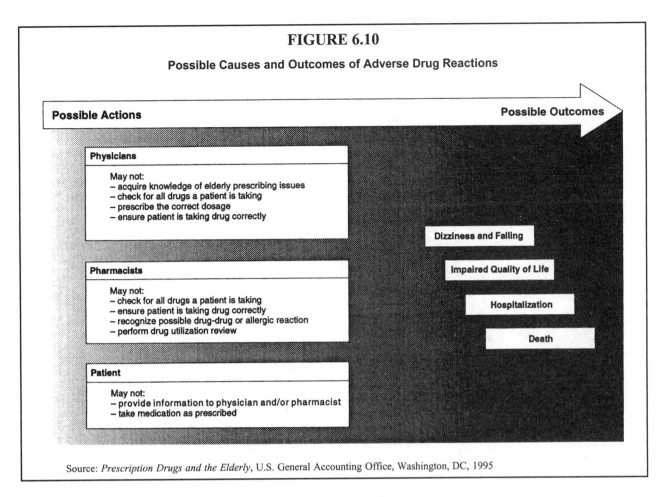

FIGURE 6.10

Possible Causes and Outcomes of Adverse Drug Reactions

Possible Actions

Possible Outcomes

Physicians

May not:
– acquire knowledge of elderly prescribing issues
– check for all drugs a patient is taking
– prescribe the correct dosage
– ensure patient is taking drug correctly

Pharmacists

May not:
– check for all drugs a patient is taking
– ensure patient is taking drug correctly
– recognize possible drug-drug or allergic reaction
– perform drug utilization review

Patient

May not:
– provide information to physician and/or pharmacist
– take medication as prescribed

Dizziness and Falling

Impaired Quality of Life

Hospitalization

Death

Source: *Prescription Drugs and the Elderly*, U.S. General Accounting Office, Washington, DC, 1995

anti-inflammatory medications for arthritis and among post-menopausal women who take estrogen as hormone-replacement therapy, although the exact explanation for this is still unknown. Many doctors recommend vitamin E because that antioxidant seems to delay symptoms in people already known to have AD.

Caring for the Alzheimer's Patient

There are many victims of Alzheimer's besides the person with the disease. While medications such as tranquilizers may reduce some symptoms and occasionally slow the progression of the disease, eventually most Alzheimer's patients need constant care and supervision. Some nursing homes and health care facilities are not equipped to provide this kind of care, and, if they accept Alzheimer's patients at all, they will accept only those in the very earliest stages. A growing number of nursing homes are promoting their institutions as designed to care for Alzheimer's patients,

but they may be beyond the means of many families, and many children of parents with Alzheimer's desire (or feel a moral obligation) to care for them at home as long as possible.

No matter how willing and devoted the caregiver, the time, patience, and resources required to provide care over a long period of time are immense, and the task can become overwhelming. Recent studies show that the stress of caring for an Alzheimer's patient can affect the caregiver's immune system, making him or her more vulnerable than normal to infectious diseases. Most observers believe that the public services that could benefit these patients are underused. Once again, the stigma of the illness may prevent people from seeking available help.

Alzheimer's and Environment

The major challenges to caregivers of Alzheimer's patients are generally the memory loss, disorientation, and wandering. Their crises are usually related to confusion states, not acute medical need. Traditional nursing home care is not designed to deal with such disorientation and wandering; it is rather oriented to immediate physical nursing. Nor do Alzheimer's patients, at least in the early stages of the disease, require nursing care in the classical sense.

Experiments with Alzheimer's patients are currently being done with design and architecture. Some authorities suggest that home and institution design can reduce the confusion of these patients and keep them relaxed, safe, and independent as long as possible. The keeping of mementos and familiar objects from one's past, involvement in household chores, and rooms designed with toilets in sight are parts of the experiments being carried out. Alzheimer's is becoming an enormous public health and social problem with great social and financial costs. Continued research is vital to understanding the management of this disease.

The Government's Role

The prevalence of dementia (especially Alzheimer's disease), the profound emotional and financial burden of caring for its victims, and the predicted increase in the older population are putting pressure on the federal government to provide more assistance in caring for current victims and to increase funding for research to find the causes and a cure.

Millions of dollars are currently being spent for Alzheimer's research. This figure is dwarfed by the estimated billions of dollars the disease costs in terms of care and lost productivity of caregivers as well as patients. The Health Care Financing Ad-

ministration estimates that the annual formal and informal cost of caring for those with AD in the United States is $100 billion, with an average per person lifetime cost of $174,000. As the nation's population ages, federally funded health systems will likely be severely strained.

DRUG USE AMONG THE ELDERLY

A broader view of prescribing for seniors recognizes that problems occur from both the overprescribing and underprescribing of drug therapies. — Paula Rochon, MD, and Jerry Gurwitz, MD, "Prescribing for Seniors: Neither Too Much nor Too Little," *Journal of American Medicine* (July 14, 1999)

In 1997, the National Council on the Aging (NCOA) reported that, in addition to other regular medications they may take, nearly 1 in 5 Americans over age 60 regularly takes medication for chronic pain. According to the NCOA, one senior in 20 suffers from the side effects caused by pain medication. Seniors typically take up to seven medications per day.

TABLE 6.17
Percentage of persons aged ≥55 years who are overweight,* by age group, race,[†] and sex — United States, Behavioral Risk Factor Surveillance System (BRFSS), 1996 and 1997[§]

Age group (yrs)/Sex	White %	White (95% CI[¶])	Black %	Black (95% CI)
55–64				
Men	72.0	(± 1.3)	66.5	(± 5.5)
Women	53.7	(± 1.2)	75.1	(± 3.4)
Total	**62.6**	**(± 0.9)**	**71.3**	**(± 3.1)**
65–74				
Men	65.2	(± 1.4)	66.4	(± 5.5)
Women	52.6	(± 1.2)	73.9	(± 3.5)
Total	**58.1**	**(± 0.9)**	**70.9**	**(± 3.0)**
≥75				
Men	51.0	(± 1.9)	56.2	(± 8.0)
Women	42.5	(± 1.3)	58.4	(± 5.2)
Total	**45.7**	**(± 1.1)**	**57.6**	**(± 4.4)**

*Defined as body mass index ≥25 kg/m².
[†]Race-specific data are presented only for blacks and whites because sample sizes for other racial groups were too small for meaningful analysis.
[§]Multiple years of BRFSS data were combined to obtain stable prevalence estimates. Combined sample size = 81,137.
[¶]Confidence interval. CIs were calculated by multiplying the standard error by 1.96.

Source: Laurie A. Kamimoto et al., "Surveillance for Five Health Risks Among Older Adults — United States, 1993-1997," in "Surveillance for Selected Public Health Indicators Affecting Older Adults — United States," *Morbidity and Mortality Weekly Report*, vol. 48, no. SS-8, December 17, 1999

Unique Effect on Elderly

In recent decades, the pharmaceutical (drug) industry has revolutionized the treatment of disease. New medications are released into the market weekly, many for treatment of conditions common to the elderly. Unfortunately, little is known about the unique physiological response of the older body to many chemicals and medications. As a person ages, the body often responds differently to chemicals than it did at a younger age. Medication taken in incorrect dosages, in combination with other drugs, or on complicated schedules can confuse an elderly person and may result in drug mismanagement. The outcome is often overdose, drug reaction, unsuccessful treatment, or even death.

A major congressional study (*Prescription Drugs and the Elderly*, U.S. General Accounting Office, Washington, DC, 1995) reported that 3 percent of all hospital admissions are caused by adverse drug reactions. However, the percentage is much higher for the elderly, 17 percent, almost six times greater than the general population. This inappropriate use of medications adds about $20 billion to the nation's hospital bills.

The study also reported that less severe reactions to prescribed drugs, including drowsiness, loss of coordination, and confusion, can go unnoticed or be discounted by health professionals or family as normal effects of aging. They can lead to falls or car accidents. An estimated 32,000 elderly people suffer hip fractures every year as a result of falls, and about 16,000 elderly drivers have traffic accidents while suffering from adverse drug reactions. Figure 6.10 shows the possible causes and outcomes of adverse drug reactions.

Indiscriminate Use of Drugs

A second problem for the elderly in drug therapy involves the indiscriminate use of drugs. Patients may be sedated almost routinely when a non-drug therapy may be appropriate. For example, sleep difficulties may be managed not only with medication but by exercise and the elimination of caffeine and naps. The elderly often find it difficult to sleep, and many people think they need sleeping pills. They may be unaware that the pills can cause side effects that resemble psychosis or dementia, especially when taken for long periods of time.

A number of studies show that sleeping pills are not only overused by many old people but are also abused — taken for too long and in alarmingly high doses. Also, many elderly use sleep as an escape from boredom. Dr. Philip Westbrook, director of the Sleep Disorders Center at Cedar Sinai Medical Center in Los Angeles, reported that "the real problem is that they don't have anything to do when they're awake, so they want to be asleep." Some ask their doctors for sleeping pills to prolong the time when they are asleep.

Not Taking Prescribed Drugs

A third medication problem of the elderly is intentional non-compliance. Hospitals report that intentional non-compliance is the second most common factor in drug-related hospitalizations. Elderly persons suffering from depression or resignation, those who have misunderstood their doctor, or those who may be attempting suicide might willfully disregard medication instructions.

Research is now increasing in the study of the elderly. Geriatrics (see below) has become an accepted, although still not widely populated, medical specialty. Research in this field will likely help to develop more effective and safer treatment for the elderly.

GETTING — AND STAYING — HEALTHY

Aging, I came to realize, is not something that begins on one's 65th birthday. Rather, all of the choices we make regarding how we care for ourselves, how we manage our lives, and even how we think about our futures shape who we ultimately become in our later years. It was obvious that many of the painful, punishing challenges of old age could be prevented if informed choices were made earlier in life. — Ken Dychtwald, *Age Power*, 1999

Because of increased educational efforts and general media coverage of health topics, older people, as well as younger, are becoming more aware of personal habits and lifestyles that may contribute to poor health and accelerate the aging process, particularly over a long period of time. Many older people are making a conscious effort to change what may be lifelong bad habits and acquire new ones that can improve their physical and mental conditions.

Among the health practices useful in helping older people to improve and maintain health are keeping mentally and physically active, proper nutrition, proper use of drugs and alcohol, living in a safe environment, eliminating smoking, and participating in screening programs and tests.

Experts believe that the elderly take better care of themselves than younger people do. They are less likely to smoke, drink, or experience stress than younger people. The elderly have better eating habits than their younger counterparts. They are, however, less likely to exercise. Increasing evidence suggests that behavior change, even late in life, is beneficial and can improve disease control and enhanced quality of life.

Weight

Experts estimate that approximately 60 percent of persons over the age of 65 are overweight and that the American public is, in general, more overweight than ever. As the median age goes up, so does the weight. Among the reasons people gain weight as they age are that they tend to exercise less, they may care less about their appearance, and metabolism seems to slow down as people age so that their bodies burn fewer calories.

According to the CDC, in *Surveillance for Five Health Risks Among Older Adults — United States,*

1993-1997 (1999), 62.6 percent of Whites 55 to 64 were overweight in 1997, compared with 58.1 percent of Whites 65 to 74 and 45.7 percent of Whites over 75. Similarly, 71.3 percent of Blacks 55 to 64 were overweight, compared to 70.9 percent of Blacks 65 to 74 and 57.6 percent of Blacks 75 and older. (See Table 6.17. Note: Caution must be used with these statistics, which are affected by survival bias because older adults in the study tended to have healthier lifestyles than older adults who had died. In addition, because data was self-reported, the prevalence of overweight is likely underestimated.)

Cholesterol

Cholesterol is believed to be linked to the risk of heart disease. The Centers for Disease Control and Prevention, in *Health, United States, 1999* (1999), reported that a smaller percentage of Americans have high levels of blood cholesterol and that average serum cholesterol levels have declined. In 1960, 38 percent of men 65 to 74 had high cholesterol levels; in 1994, 21.9 percent of men had high levels. In 1960, 68.5 percent of women 65 to 74 had high cholesterol levels, while, in 1994, 41.3 percent of women did. In 1960, the mean cholesterol levels for men and women 65 to 74 were 230 and 266, respectively. In 1994, the mean cholesterol levels were 212 for men and 233 for women. (See Table 6.18.)

Smoking

Per capita tobacco consumption has declined in the United States in the past decades. In 1995, fewer people over 65 (14.9 percent of males and 11.5 percent for females) smoked than all other age groups. In 1965, 28.5 percent of males over 65 were smokers. A greater percentage of women 65 and older smoked in 1995 (11.5 percent) than in 1965 (9.6 percent). (See Table 6.19.)

A 1999 study by Florida State University Center for Economic Forecasting and Analysis found that smokers entered nursing homes earlier and stayed longer than nonsmokers. Nonsmokers en-

TABLE 6.18

Serum cholesterol levels among persons 20 years of age and over, according to sex, age, race, and Hispanic origin: United States, 1960–62, 1971–74, 1976–80, and 1988–94

[Data are based on physical examinations of a sample of the civilian noninstitutionalized population]

Sex, age, race, and Hispanic origin[1]	Percent of population with high serum cholesterol				Mean serum cholesterol level, mg/dL			
	1960–62	1971–74	1976–80[2]	1988–94	1960–62	1971–74	1976–80[2]	1988–94
20–74 years, age adjusted[3]								
Both sexes	31.8	27.2	26.3	18.9	220	214	213	203
Male	28.7	25.8	24.6	17.5	217	213	211	202
Female	34.5	28.2	27.6	20.0	222	215	214	204
White male	29.4	25.9	24.6	17.8	218	213	211	202
White female	35.1	28.1	28.0	20.2	223	215	214	205
Black male	24.5	25.1	24.1	15.7	210	212	208	199
Black female	30.7	29.2	24.9	19.4	216	217	213	203
White, non-Hispanic male	- - -	- - -	24.7	17.3	- - -	- - -	211	202
White, non-Hispanic female	- - -	- - -	28.3	20.2	- - -	- - -	214	205
Black, non-Hispanic male	- - -	- - -	24.0	15.7	- - -	- - -	208	200
Black, non-Hispanic female	- - -	- - -	24.9	19.8	- - -	- - -	214	203
Mexican male	- - -	- - -	18.8	17.8	- - -	- - -	207	204
Mexican female	- - -	- - -	20.0	17.5	- - -	- - -	207	203
20–74 years, crude								
Both sexes	33.6	28.2	26.8	18.7	222	216	213	203
Male	30.7	26.8	24.9	17.6	220	214	211	202
Female	36.3	29.6	28.5	19.9	225	217	215	204
White male	31.4	26.9	25.0	18.1	221	215	211	203
White female	37.5	29.8	29.2	20.5	227	217	216	205
Black male	26.7	25.1	23.9	14.4	214	212	208	198
Black female	29.9	28.8	23.7	16.8	216	216	212	199
White, non-Hispanic male	- - -	- - -	25.1	17.9	- - -	- - -	211	203
White, non-Hispanic female	- - -	- - -	29.8	20.9	- - -	- - -	216	206
Black, non-Hispanic male	- - -	- - -	23.7	14.5	- - -	- - -	208	198
Black, non-Hispanic female	- - -	- - -	23.7	17.2	- - -	- - -	212	200
Mexican male	- - -	- - -	16.6	15.5	- - -	- - -	203	200
Mexican female	- - -	- - -	16.5	14.0	- - -	- - -	202	197
Male								
20–34 years	15.1	12.4	11.9	8.2	198	194	192	186
35–44 years	33.9	31.8	27.9	19.4	227	221	217	206
45–54 years	39.2	37.5	36.9	26.6	231	229	227	216
55–64 years	41.6	36.2	36.8	28.0	233	229	229	216
65–74 years	38.0	34.7	31.7	21.9	230	226	221	212
75 years and over	- - -	- - -	- - -	20.4	- - -	- - -	- - -	205
Female								
20–34 years	12.4	10.9	9.8	7.3	194	191	189	184
35–44 years	23.1	19.3	20.7	12.3	214	207	207	195
45–54 years	46.9	38.7	40.5	26.7	237	232	232	217
55–64 years	70.1	53.1	52.9	40.9	262	245	249	235
65–74 years	68.5	57.7	51.6	41.3	266	250	246	233
75 years and over	- - -	- - -	- - -	38.2	- - -	- - -	- - -	229

- - - Data not available.

[1]The race groups, white and black, include persons of Hispanic and non-Hispanic origin. Conversely, persons of Hispanic origin may be of any race.
[2]Data for Mexicans are for 1982–84. See Appendix I.
[3]See Appendix II for age-adjustment procedure.

NOTES: High serum cholesterol is defined as greater than or equal to 240 mg/dL (6.20 mmol/L). Risk levels have been defined by the Second report of the National Cholesterol Education Program Expert Panel on Detection, Evaluation and Treatment of High Blood Cholesterol in Adults. National Heart, Lung, and Blood Institute, National Institutes of Health. September 1993. (Summarized in *JAMA* 269 (23): 3015–23. June 16, 1993.)

Source: *Health, United States, 1999*, National Center for Health Statistics, Hyattsville, MD, 1999

tered nursing homes at a later age and lived longer. Smokers ages 60 to 69 spent, on average, 240 days in nursing homes, compared with 110 days for nonsmokers that age. For those 70 to 79, smokers spent 225 days in a home, compared with 175 days for nonsmokers. Smokers 80 to 89 spent 200 days in a nursing home, while nonsmokers that age were in a home 180 days. For those 90 or older, smokers spent 250 days in nursing homes, while nonsmokers were there 340 days. The researchers concluded that smokers became ill sooner.

TABLE 6.19

Current cigarette smoking by persons 18 years of age and over, according to sex, race, and age: United States, selected years 1965–95

[Data are based on household interviews of a sample of the civilian noninstitutionalized population]

Sex, race, and age	1965	1974	1979	1983	1985	1990	1991	1992	1993	1994	1995
18 years and over, age adjusted					Percent of persons						
All persons	42.3	37.2	33.5	32.2	30.0	25.4	25.4	26.4	25.0	25.5	24.7
Male	51.6	42.9	37.2	34.7	32.1	28.0	27.5	28.2	27.5	27.8	26.7
Female	34.0	32.5	30.3	29.9	28.2	23.1	23.6	24.8	22.7	23.3	22.8
White male	50.8	41.7	36.5	34.1	31.3	27.6	27.0	28.0	27.0	27.5	26.4
Black male	59.2	54.0	44.1	41.3	39.9	32.2	34.7	32.0	33.2	33.5	28.5
White female	34.3	32.3	30.6	30.1	28.3	23.9	24.2	25.7	23.7	24.3	23.6
Black female	32.1	35.9	30.8	31.8	30.7	20.4	23.1	23.9	19.8	21.1	22.8
18 years and over, crude											
All persons	42.4	37.1	33.5	32.1	30.1	25.5	25.6	26.5	25.0	25.5	24.7
Male	51.9	43.1	37.5	35.1	32.6	28.4	28.1	28.6	27.7	28.2	27.0
Female	33.9	32.1	29.9	29.5	27.9	22.8	23.5	24.6	22.5	23.1	22.6
White male	51.1	41.9	36.8	34.5	31.7	28.0	27.4	28.2	27.0	27.7	26.6
Black male	60.4	54.3	44.1	40.6	39.9	32.5	35.0	32.2	32.7	33.7	28.5
White female	34.0	31.7	30.1	29.4	27.7	23.4	23.7	25.1	23.1	23.7	23.1
Black female	33.7	36.4	31.1	32.2	31.0	21.2	24.4	24.2	20.8	21.7	23.5
All males											
18–24 years	54.1	42.1	35.0	32.9	28.0	26.6	23.5	28.0	28.8	29.8	27.8
25–34 years	60.7	50.5	43.9	38.8	38.2	31.6	32.8	32.8	30.2	31.4	29.5
35–44 years	58.2	51.0	41.8	41.0	37.6	34.5	33.1	32.9	32.0	33.2	31.5
45–64 years	51.9	42.6	39.3	35.9	33.4	29.3	29.3	28.6	29.2	28.3	27.1
65 years and over	28.5	24.8	20.9	22.0	19.6	14.6	15.1	16.1	13.5	13.2	14.9
White male											
18–24 years	53.0	40.8	34.3	32.5	28.4	27.4	25.1	30.0	30.4	31.8	28.4
25–34 years	60.1	49.5	43.6	38.6	37.3	31.6	32.1	33.5	29.9	32.5	29.9
35–44 years	57.3	50.1	41.3	40.8	36.6	33.5	32.1	30.9	31.2	32.0	31.2
45–64 years	51.3	41.2	38.3	35.0	32.1	28.7	28.0	28.1	27.8	26.9	26.3
65 years and over	27.7	24.3	20.5	20.6	18.9	13.7	14.2	14.9	12.5	11.9	14.1
Black male											
18–24 years	62.8	54.9	40.2	34.2	27.2	21.3	15.0	16.2	19.9	18.7	14.6
25–34 years	68.4	58.5	47.5	39.9	45.6	33.8	39.4	29.5	30.7	29.8	25.1
35–44 years	67.3	61.5	48.6	45.5	45.0	42.0	44.4	47.5	36.9	44.5	36.3
45–64 years	57.9	57.8	50.0	44.8	46.1	36.7	42.0	35.4	42.4	41.2	33.9
65 years and over	36.4	29.7	26.2	38.9	27.7	21.5	24.3	28.3	27.9	25.6	28.5
All females											
18–24 years	38.1	34.1	33.8	35.5	30.4	22.5	22.4	24.9	22.9	25.2	21.8
25–34 years	43.7	38.8	33.7	32.6	32.0	28.2	28.4	30.1	27.3	28.8	26.4
35–44 years	43.7	39.8	37.0	33.8	31.5	24.8	27.6	27.3	27.4	27.1	27.1
45–64 years	32.0	33.4	30.7	31.0	29.9	24.8	24.6	26.1	23.0	22.8	24.0
65 years and over	9.6	12.0	13.2	13.1	13.5	11.5	12.0	12.4	10.5	11.1	11.5
White female											
18–24 years	38.4	34.0	34.5	36.5	31.8	25.4	25.1	28.5	26.8	28.5	24.9
25–34 years	43.4	38.6	34.1	32.2	32.0	28.5	28.4	31.5	28.4	30.2	27.3
35–44 years	43.9	39.3	37.2	34.8	31.0	25.0	27.0	27.6	27.3	27.1	27.0
45–64 years	32.7	33.0	30.6	30.6	29.7	25.4	25.3	25.8	23.4	23.2	24.3
65 years and over	9.8	12.3	13.8	13.2	13.3	11.5	12.1	12.6	10.5	11.1	11.7
Black female											
18–24 years	37.1	35.6	31.8	32.0	23.7	10.0	11.8	10.3	8.2	11.8	8.8
25–34 years	47.8	42.2	35.2	38.0	36.2	29.1	32.4	26.9	24.7	24.8	26.7
35–44 years	42.8	46.4	37.7	32.7	40.2	25.5	35.3	32.4	31.5	28.2	31.9
45–64 years	25.7	38.9	34.2	36.3	33.4	22.6	23.4	30.9	21.3	23.5	27.5
65 years and over	7.1	8.9	8.5	13.1	14.5	11.1	9.6	11.1	10.2	13.6	13.3

NOTES: The definition of current smoker was revised in 1992 and 1993. See discussion of current smoker in Appendix II. See Appendix II for age-adjustment procedure. Data for additional years are available (see Appendix III).

SOURCE: Centers for Disease Control and Prevention, National Center for Health Statistics, Division of Health Interview Statistics: Data from the National Health Interview Survey; data computed by the Division of Health and Utilization Analysis from data compiled by the Division of Health Interview Statistics.

Exercise

Physical activity is at the crux of successful aging, regardless of other factors. — The MacArthur Foundation, 1998

Regular physical activity often comes closer to being a fountain of youth than anything modern medicine can offer. It is almost never too late to start. Researchers have documented many improvements in the health and well-being of older Americans who take up exercise. The major areas of benefit are

- Heart disease and stroke — Exercise can halve the risk of heart disease or stroke by lowering blood pressure, raising the level of protective cholesterol (HDL), reducing clot formation, controlling diabetes, and countering weight gain.

- Cancer — Exercise lowers the risk of cancer of the colon, one of the leading causes of cancer deaths. In animals, exercise protects against breast cancer.

- Osteoporosis — At any age at which exercise is begun, it can increase bone density and reduce fractures. In addition, older people who become active experience improvements in balance, strength, coordination, and flexibility, which all help prevent falls that often result in debilitating fractures.

- Diabetes — Active people are less likely to develop diabetes than sedentary people. Physical activity increases the sensitivity of cells to insulin, which lowers blood sugar and the need for insulin.

- Weight — Exercise helps maintain normal weight or foster weight loss. Most importantly, exercise helps people lose fat and gain muscle. Even in those of normal weight, exercise can counter age-related loss of muscle mass and the deposition of body fat, especially abdominal fat, which has been found to be heart-damaging.

- Immunity — Exercise increases the circulation of immune cells that fight infections and tumors. Physically fit people get fewer respiratory infections and colds than people who are not fit.

- Arthritis — Nearly everyone over 65 has some arthritic symptoms. Studies show that moderate exercise reduces pain and the need for medication.

- Depression — Exercise has long been known to help people overcome clinical depression. With the elderly, the benefits are greatest when they are brought in contact with others in the process.

- Gastrointestinal bleeding — Regular activity significantly reduces gastrointestinal hemorrhage in older people, probably by improving circulation to the digestive tract.

- Memory — Even brief periods of exercise can result in immediate improvements in memory in older adults. Exercise also fosters clearer thinking and faster reaction time by helping to speed the transmission of nerve messages.

- Sleep — In older adults who are sedentary, regular exercise, like walking, improves sleep quality and decreases the time it takes to fall asleep.

Despite these benefits, those over the age of 50 are much less likely than other age groups to exercise. The CDC, in *Surveillance for Five Health Risks Among Older Adults—United States, 1993-1997* (1999), found that physical inactivity increased with age. Thirty-three percent of the elderly 55 to 64, 35 percent of those 65 to 74 , and 46 percent of those 75 or older reported no physical activity. The prevalence of physical inactivity was greater among Blacks than Whites and higher among women than men. Most older people who do exercise engage in low-impact exercises such as walking and swimming.

Drinking and Driving

Drinking and driving is a health risk associated with motor-vehicle-related injury. Little is known about how alcohol affects an older person physiologically. In addition, prescription drugs, more commonly used among the elderly, can worsen the effect of alcohol and impair driving more than alcohol alone. The CDC study found that the prevalence of drinking and then driving was greater among persons 55 to 64 (0.8 percent) than among those 65 to 74 (0.4 percent) or 75 and older (0.2 percent). (For more information on driving, see Chapter XI.)

Use of Preventive Health Services

Use of medical and dental preventive services contributes to the likelihood of healthy aging. The CDC, in *Surveillance for Selected Public Health Indicators Affecting Older Adults — United States* (1999), found that some older Americans underuse preventive procedures and measures.

Most adults — 92 percent of those 55 to 64, 95 percent of those 65 to 74, and 96 percent of those 75 and older — reported having a regular source of medical care. Persons with a source of regular care were much more likely to receive basic medical services, such as routine checkups, which present the opportunity to receive preventive services. Men were slightly less likely to report a regular source of care than women. When asked if they had delayed medical care because of cost, few adults — 8 percent of those 55 to 64, 4 percent of those 65 to 74, and 2.4 percent of those 75 and older — said that had been the case. The CDC concluded that, overall, cost was not a barrier to care for most older adults.

Nevertheless, considerable numbers of elderly did not get preventive screenings in 1997. For breast cancer screenings, the median percentages of women who reported having a mammogram during the preceding two years were 77 percent among those 55 to 64, 75.4 percent among those 65 to 74, and 61.4 percent among those 75 and older. Almost 84 percent of women 55 to 64, 77.4 percent of those women 65 to 74, and 58 percent of women 75 and older reported having a Pap test for cervical cancer during the preceding three years.

Screening for hypertension was high among adults 55 and older — approximately 95 percent. However, rates were lower for blood cholesterol checks, which varied from 85 to 90 percent. Among those 55 to 64, 25.8 percent received a fecal occult blood test for colon cancer in the preceding two years, compared to 32 percent of those 65 to 74 and 27 percent of those 75 and older. Forty percent of Americans 55 to 64 reported they had ever received a proctoscopy or sigmoidoscopy for co-

lon cancer. Forty-eight percent of those 65 to 74 and 46 percent of those 75 and older had had the test at some time.

Among those 55 to 64, 17 percent received a vaccination against pneumonia, compared to 43 percent of those 65 to 74 and 53.3 percent of those 75 and older. Somewhat more received influenza vaccinations — 38 percent of those 55 to 64, 64 percent of those 65 to 74, and 72 percent of those 75 and older. When asked if they had visited a dentist in the preceding year, 67.5 percent of those 55 to 64, 63 percent of those 65 to 74, and 56 percent of those 75 and older said they had done so.

SEXUALITY IN AGING

In 1998, the National Council on the Aging, in *Healthy Sexuality and Vital Aging,* reported that, of a survey of 1,292 people 60 and older, most have active sex lives well into old age. Forty-eight percent said they were sexually active, meaning they had engaged in some type sexual activity at least once a month in the past year. Among those with partners, 80 percent claimed to be active. Since older men are more likely than older women to have partners, they remained more sexually active throughout their lives. But those women with partners were nearly as active as men when in their 60s and 70s and even more active in their 80s.

Older men were twice as likely as older women to want more sex, 56 percent versus 25 percent. Only 18 percent reported sex was more physically satisfying than when they were in their 40s. Of those with partners, 31 percent claimed the physical part of sex was better than it used to be. One in 4 older Americans said sex was more emotionally satisfying than when they were in their 40s. Men (31 percent) were much more likely than women (17 percent) to report that the emotional benefits of sex were greater than they used to be. At the same time, older men were more likely than women to have partners.

Ninety percent of both sexes claimed an honest, moral character and pleasant personality were desirable in a romantic partner. More than 80 percent claimed to value humor, good physical health, and intelligence. Men (78 percent), however, placed substantially more importance on sex than did women (50 percent). They wanted partners who like to have sex. Women (82 percent), on the other hand, valued financial security in a partner far more than men (55 percent) did.

In 1999, the AARP studied 1,384 adults 45 and older on relationships and sexual attitudes. Most men (67 percent) and women (57 percent) said a satisfying sexual relationship was important to the quality of their lives.

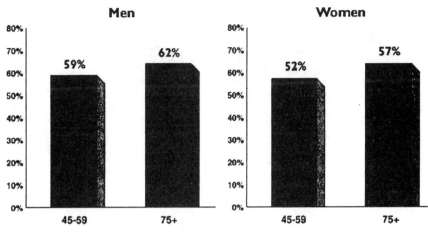

FIGURE 6.11

Attractiveness Over Time

Over half of Americans 45+ find their mates physically attractive, and as time goes on, more attractive.

Source: *AARP/Modern Maturity Sexuality Survey*, American Association of Retired Persons, Washington, DC, 1999. Survey conducted by NFO Research, Inc.

Among those with partners, large majorities (67 percent of men and 57 percent of women) described their partners as "my best friend." Men were slightly more likely to describe their partners as "physically attractive" (59 percent vs. 53 percent), "exciting" (40 percent vs. 33 percent), and "romantic" (39 percent vs. 30 percent). The percent who see their partners as attractive did not decline with age; it actually increased. Among men, 59 percent of those 45 to 74 and 62 percent of those 75 and over said their partner was "physically attractive." Fifty-two percent of women 45 to 59 and 57 percent of those 75 and older found their partners to be attractive. (See Figure 6.11.)

Sexuality seemed to be more important to men than women in the study. Among those 45 to 59, 71 percent of men and 44 percent of women agreed that sexual activity was important to their lives. Among those 75 and older, 35 percent of men and 13 percent of women agreed.

Sexual activity declined with age as health declined and many people lost their partners. Among those with partners, 62 percent of men and 61 percent of women aged 45 to 59 reported they engaged in sex once a week or more, as did 26 percent of men and 24 percent of women 75 and older. Approximately three-fourths of men and women reported engaging in sex at least once a month. Although declining health affects sexual satisfaction and activity, many are not being treated for some ailments that could be affecting their sex lives. Fifty-one percent of those who reported no major illness or depression said they engaged in sex at least once a week, compared to 30 percent of those with either major disease or depression.

Thirty percent of men and 16 percent of women mentioned better health as something that would improve their sex lives, and about 20 percent cited better health for their partner. Men also mentioned less stress (20 percent) and more free time (19 percent) as factors that would help. For women, less stress (20 percent) and finding a partner (15 percent) also made the list. (See Figure 6.12.)

Twenty-six percent of men acknowledged being completely or moderately impotent. Only 41 percent of those said they had sought treatment from a medical professional. Only about 25 per-

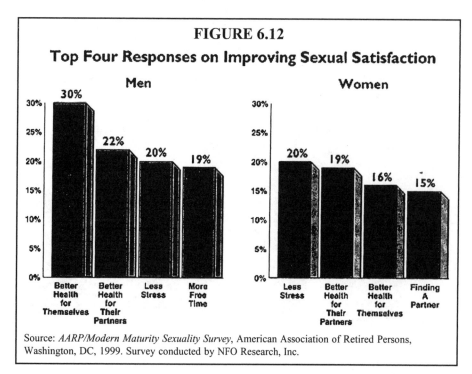

FIGURE 6.12

Top Four Responses on Improving Sexual Satisfaction

Men

30%

Women

Source: *AARP/Modern Maturity Sexuality Survey*, American Association of Retired Persons, Washington, DC, 1999. Survey conducted by NFO Research, Inc.

post-World War II baby boom generation reaches retirement age. Currently, the United States has only one-fifth the number of geriatricians needed.

While the demand for geriatrics data grows and specialists and medical students want training in that area, many medical schools have no qualified staff to train them. The American Geriatrics Society reports that there are 8,800 physicians certified in geriatrics. The United States will need 36,000 physicians with geriatrics training by 2030 to care for about 76 million older Americans.

cent admitted to using any drugs or treatments to enhance sexual performance, including 15 percent who said they had used Viagra.

The researchers found that only a small minority of those with sexual problems were availing themselves of treatments, and large numbers were not even getting treatment for common ailments that can affect sexual performance, such as arthritis. The study concluded, "We can only speculate about what combination of age stereotyping, sexual taboos, lack of access to health care and medications, or other factors, are preventing mid-life and older adults from seeking and/or receiving help."

THE SLOW GROWTH OF GERIATRIC MEDICINE

With frail old people, there's just no margin for error. And with the lack of trained doctors, lots of errors are made. — Dr. David Solomon, UCLA School of Medicine, 1998

The United States faces an acute shortage of doctors trained to treat older patients (geriatricians). This shortage will reach serious proportions as the

Students entering medical school today can expect that at least half the patients they will see as doctors will be over 65. Only doctors who have completed fellowships in geriatrics are eligible for certification, which requires a one-year fellowship in geriatrics and passage of examination by a certifying board. According to a 1996 Alliance for Aging report, only 3 percent of recent medical school graduates have taken elective courses in geriatrics. Only 14 of 128 medical schools require students to take courses in geriatrics, while 86 schools offer geriatrics as an elective course.

Experts believe certain errors are made in treating the elderly by physicians who are untrained in geriatrics. Common errors include prescribing inappropriately high doses of medications or failing to recognize symptoms of severe and acute conditions, which often present with different symptoms in older persons. In addition, some physicians may not know new methods of treating conditions or write them off as inevitable diseases of old age when treatment is available.

CHAPTER VII

MENTAL HEALTH AND ALCOHOL ABUSE

As we grow older, our purpose in life changes. Our task shifts from self-preservation to finding meaning in our lives — and in that search, our character reveals itself. — Dr. James Hillman, *The Force of Character — And the Lasting Life*, 1999

As the nation ages, older Americans — along with their physical and mental well-being — have become topics of increasing interest. Mental illness and alcohol abuse are two major areas of concern that are receiving increased attention from the medical profession.

MENTAL HEALTH IS IMPORTANT

Mental health problems can be as debilitating as physical problems. Mental illness in the elderly may be functional, organic, or a combination of the two. Functional causes can include emotional stress, depression, neuroses, or psychoses. Organic factors may include cerebral arteriosclerosis, chemical imbalances, or tumors. Most functional disorders are curable, while an estimated 15 percent of organic disorders are not. Many conditions are manageable with therapy or medication. (Physical and organic mental illness is discussed in Chapter VI.)

Geriatric medicine, the study of the health problems of older people, is a relatively new field, and research is just beginning in this area. More information is needed on the normal mental ranges and capabilities of older people and the relationship between physiological changes and brain functions, as well as between physical illness and mental confusion. As the number of older people in the United States continues to increase, especially as the population of baby-boomers ages, the demand for geriatric research and resources for physical and mental health care will grow.

PERSPECTIVES OF A LIFETIME MAY CHANGE AS PEOPLE GROW OLDER

Few personal problems disappear with old age, and many become more acute. Marital problems, which may have been controlled because one or both of the spouses were away at work, may erupt when a couple spends more time together in retirement. A possible "identity crisis" and reduced income due to retirement can aggravate a tense situation and put a strain on both husband and wife, especially if one of them becomes ill.

Old age can be a period of regrets, of "if onlies" and "could have beens," which can lead to mutual recriminations. With life expectancy rising, married couples can now expect to spend many years together in retirement. Most elderly couples manage the transition, but some have problems.

Along with psychological adjustments to aging, the physical effects of aging must also be confronted. If good health habits and necessary medical treatment have not been maintained in early life, a person's health may decline more rapidly, and disease may worsen the situation. Hearing loss is common, and close correlations have been found between loss of hearing and depression. Vision loss often occurs, which limits reading, watching television, driving, and mobility. Loss of sight or hearing can cause perceptual disorientation, which, in turn, may lead to depression, paranoia, fear, and alienation.

A constant awareness of death can also become a problem during retirement years. Although most of the elderly in good health resolve their concerns with death, some acknowledge denial and fear. How well one accepts the inevitability of death can be a major factor in shaping that person's aging years.

Satisfaction with Life in General

In 1998, Daniel Mroczek and Christian Kolarz, of Fordham University, surveyed 2,700 adults from 25 to 74 about their life satisfaction. They found that the older the respondents, the more frequently they reported feeling positive emotions, such as cheerfulness, good spirits, and happiness. The age correlation existed even when the researchers took into account education, marital status, stress, personality, and economic status. The link was strongest for men, who showed both an increase in positive emotions and a decline in negative emotions, such as feeling sad, nervous, hopeless, or worthless. Older women also reported increased positive emotions with age, but no difference in negative emotions. The happiest subjects were not only older and male, but also married and extroverted.

The researchers theorized that the results could mean several things. It could mean that older Americans represented a generation less willing to reveal unhappiness or dissatisfaction. Or it could mean that people who survived the Great Depression and World War II are happy because they are aware that life could be much worse. It could also be, however, that happiness actually increases with age.

Marital Satisfaction

Married people seem to remain healthier than those persons who are alone. Research suggests that marriage is correlated with longer and more satisfied lives, especially for men. And in general, marital satisfaction increases with age. For the most

part, frequent disagreements decrease with age. Adults older than 60 are less likely than other age groups to disagree on money, vacation plans, sex, children, and housekeeping, issues that have likely been resolved early in their relationships. In addition, many couples who would be most likely to disagree have divorced. Older couples do, however, disagree on immediate daily concerns, such as which programs to watch on television, just as frequently as younger people.

OLDER AMERICANS CONSIDER THEMSELVES "SURVIVORS"

Because many of today's elderly grew up during the adversity of the Great Depression of 1929 and the early 1930s, most of them do not consider themselves disadvantaged or unable to handle hardship. Instead, many older Americans consider themselves "survivors." This attitude is generally confirmed by studies of older Americans that show that only a small number of the elderly believe they need counseling or consider loneliness to be a very serious problem. The psychological stress of retirement and physical decline may be of concern to some retirees, but not for most.

In fact, the fifties, not the sixties and seventies, are more likely to be reported as the years of confrontation with one's mortality and values. Bernice Neugarten, a psychologist at the University of Chicago, reported that the physical and career shifts that occur when people are in their fifties cause many people to become introspective. By the time they enter their sixties and seventies, many have resolved these conflicts.

Attitudes About Work

The loss of work and the decline in social status that often accompany the loss of employment are two of the major causes of stress during old age. In a work-oriented society, these losses can create feelings of uselessness and lack of self-worth. Such a sense of worthlessness, if not replaced with something meaningful to the individual, can lead to depression, lowered resistance to disease, and lack of motivation. For those living in poverty, these feelings are compounded by poor housing, often in dangerous surroundings, inadequate diets, and financial worries caused by fixed incomes, making the elderly poor more susceptible to mental problems.

In 1994, the National Opinion Research Center of the University of Chicago, in its General Social Survey (GSS), surveyed attitudes of aging Americans. The survey found that work often lost its appeal for workers as they age. Fifty percent of those 55 to 59 reported they would quit working if they could live comfortably the rest of their lives. Among those 60 to 64 years old, 38 percent said they would quit if they could; 15 percent of those over 65 claimed they wanted to quit work. Fifty-one percent of those 50 to 59 said they found life exciting, although their enjoyment seemed to decline after the age of 60. Thirty-four percent of those 60 to 64 and 37 percent of those older than 65 claimed life was exciting.

DEPRESSION

Depression is a common disorder. Although many younger people are willing to admit to themselves that they are depressed and to seek treatment, most elderly, who were raised in an era when mental illness was stigmatized, are generally not. As their numbers and influence grow and as mental illness has become less stigmatized, older Americans and their families have become increasingly unwilling to accept mental health problems as inevitable results of aging. The National Institute of Mental Health estimates that 3 percent of Americans over 65 are clinically depressed, while 7 to 12 percent of the elderly suffer from milder forms of depression that impair their quality of life.

A 1997 study, *Screening for Depression in Elderly Primary Care Patients* (J. M. Lyness et al.), found that 9 percent of elderly patients tested had major depressive disorder (MDD) and another 8 percent suffered minor depression. Neuropsychiatrist Dr. Martiece Carson, of the University of Oklahoma Health Sciences Center, estimates that,

in nursing homes, the situation is far worse, with 20 to 40 percent of patients being very depressed. Experts believe that a large proportion of the elderly population has undiagnosed and untreated depression.

Although many elderly persons are routinely treated by doctors for other conditions, many doctors fail to recognize that their elderly patients are depressed, either because the doctors do not ask or because the elderly do not divulge it. Studies of elderly people who committed suicide as a result of depression have found that three-quarters had visited a doctor within a week of their deaths, but in only one-quarter of those cases did the doctor recognize that the patient was depressed.

Some people have a lifelong tendency toward depression that does not become obvious until later in life when the condition may be triggered by circumstances such as retirement, serious illness, or the loss of a loved one — situations common to aging. Older people face many real-life problems that can compound a biological tendency to depression. While it is natural for a person to feel depressed after a traumatic loss, when it lingers for months or years, it may be due to a physical or emotional disorder.

Often a physical illness itself can cause depression in the elderly by altering the chemicals in the brain. Among the illnesses that can touch off depression are diabetes, hypothyroidism, kidney or liver dysfunction, heart disease, and infections. In people with these ailments, treating the underlying disease usually eliminates the depression. Sometimes medications, including over-the-counter drugs prescribed for other conditions, precipitate depression.

In 1995, scientists reported that depression in the elderly nearly tripled the risk of a stroke, underscoring the need to treat the medical depression, not just to raise their spirits but also to better protect them from other diseases. Other studies have found that elderly people with depression fared worse in recovering from heart attack, hip fractures, and severe infections like pneumonia. They also had more difficulty regaining functions like walking after being stricken by diseases of all kinds.

In some elderly people, depression causes them to willfully disregard medical needs, to take medications incorrectly, and to eat poorly. Experts believe these may be "covert" acts of suicide. In addition, depression interferes with the functioning of the immune system. Treatment works in about 80 percent of cases where patients receive appropriate therapy and take their medications.

TROUBLE WITH COPING — SUICIDE

Loss of a loved one is a major cause of depression and suicide for older people. During the first year after the death of a spouse, the risk of suicide for the remaining partner is 2.5 times greater than the general population; in the second year after a loss, the risk is 1.5 times as great.

Suicide Rates

In 1998, suicide was the third-leading cause of injury-related deaths among older U.S. residents, following deaths from accidental falls and motor vehicle crashes. It was the eighth leading cause of death for those 45 to 64. Among those 65 and older, 16.8 persons of 100,000 died from suicide in 1997. For those 75 and older, the rate increased to about 20 per 100,000, almost twice that of the general population, 10.6 per 100,000. Men older than 65 (33.9 per 100,000 persons) had, by far, the highest suicide rates of all age groups, with those older than 85 most likely to kill themselves (60.3 per 100,000 persons). Women over the age of 65 died from suicide at a rate of 4.9 per 100,000. (See Table 7.1.)

The Centers for Disease Control and Prevention (CDC) reported, in "Surveillance for Injuries and Violence Among Older Adults" (Judy A. Stevens et al., in "Surveillance for Selected Public Health Indicators Affecting Older Adults — United States," *Morbidity and Mortality Weekly Report*,

vol. 48, no. SS-8, December 17, 1999), that approximately 20 percent of the 216,631 suicides that occurred in the United States from 1990 through 1996 involved persons 65 and older. (See Figure 7.1.) Men accounted for 82 percent of suicides in that age group. By race, Whites 65 and older killed themselves more frequently than Blacks or Hispanics (Figure 7.2).

Firearms were the most common method of suicide used by both men (77.3 percent) and women (34.4 percent) over 65. Poisoning was the second most common method among men (12 percent) and women (29 percent). Suicides were highest among divorced/widowed men (76.4 per 100,000) — 2.7 times that of married men.

Why Is There Suicide Among the Elderly?

Suicide figures for the elderly are not always reliable since many suicides are "passive." Persons who are sick, lonely, abandoned, or financially troubled have been known to starve themselves, not take medication, or mix medications dangerously. Also, the deaths counted as suicides are only those where suicide is named on the official death certificate. (Suicides are often attributed to other causes on death certificates.) One in 6 elderly depressives succeed in committing suicide, in contrast to 1 in 100 in the general population.

The upward trend in suicide among the elderly perplexes health care experts, who note that the elderly today are generally more financially secure and healthier than in past generations. Experts suggest that the technological advances being made to extend life (or postpone death) may have resulted in longer but less satisfying lives for many seniors. In particular, older males, who have the highest suicide rates, may become depressed at the loss of job, income, and power status when they retire.

Some mental health professionals have noted that the concept of "rational suicide" is gaining popularity. The elderly, who are faced with the possibility of extending their lives by medical technologies, are weighing the costs, and more of them

TABLE 7.1

Death rates for suicide, according to sex, detailed race, Hispanic origin, and age: United States, selected years 1950–97

[Data are based on the National Vital Statistics System]

Sex, race, Hispanic origin, and age	1950[1]	1960[1]	1970	1980	1985	1990	1994	1995	1996	1997	1995–97[2]
All persons					Deaths per 100,000 resident population						
All ages, age adjusted	11.0	10.6	11.8	11.4	11.5	11.5	11.2	11.2	10.8	10.6	10.8
All ages, crude	11.4	10.6	11.6	11.9	12.4	12.4	12.0	11.9	11.6	11.4	11.7
Under 1 year	...	...	...	...	...	...	...	...	...	...	...
1–4 years	...	...	...	...	...	...	...	...	...	...	...
5–14 years	0.2	0.3	0.3	0.4	0.8	0.8	0.9	0.9	0.8	0.8	0.8
15–24 years	4.5	5.2	8.8	12.3	12.8	13.2	13.8	13.3	12.0	11.4	12.3
25–44 years	11.6	12.2	15.4	15.6	15.0	15.2	15.3	15.3	15.0	14.8	15.1
25–34 years	9.1	10.0	14.1	16.0	15.3	15.2	15.4	15.4	14.5	14.3	14.7
35–44 years	14.3	14.2	16.9	15.4	14.6	15.3	15.3	15.2	15.5	15.3	15.4
45–64 years	23.5	22.0	20.6	15.9	16.3	15.3	14.0	14.1	14.4	14.2	14.2
45–54 years	20.9	20.7	20.0	15.9	15.7	14.8	14.4	14.6	14.9	14.7	14.7
55–64 years	27.0	23.7	21.4	15.9	16.8	16.0	13.4	13.3	13.7	13.5	13.5
65 years and over	30.0	24.5	20.8	17.6	20.4	20.5	18.1	18.1	17.3	16.8	17.4
65–74 years	29.3	23.0	20.8	16.9	18.7	17.9	15.3	15.8	15.0	14.4	15.1
75–84 years	31.1	27.9	21.2	19.1	23.9	24.9	21.3	20.7	20.0	19.3	20.0
85 years and over	28.8	26.0	19.0	19.2	19.4	22.2	23.0	21.6	20.2	20.8	20.9
Male											
All ages, age adjusted	17.3	16.6	17.3	18.0	18.8	19.0	18.7	18.6	18.0	17.4	18.0
All ages, crude	17.8	16.5	16.8	18.6	20.0	20.4	19.8	19.8	19.3	18.7	19.2
Under 1 year	...	...	...	...	...	...	...	...	...	...	...
1–4 years	...	...	...	...	...	...	...	...	...	...	...
5–14 years	0.3	0.4	0.5	0.6	1.2	1.1	1.2	1.3	1.1	1.2	1.2
15–24 years	6.5	8.2	13.5	20.2	21.0	22.0	23.4	22.5	20.0	18.9	20.5
25–44 years	17.2	17.9	20.9	24.0	23.7	24.4	24.8	24.9	24.3	23.8	24.3
25–34 years	13.4	14.7	19.8	25.0	24.7	24.8	25.6	25.6	24.0	23.6	24.4
35–44 years	21.3	21.0	22.1	22.5	22.3	23.9	24.1	24.1	24.6	23.9	24.2
45–64 years	37.1	34.4	30.0	23.7	25.3	24.3	22.1	22.5	23.0	22.5	22.7
45–54 years	32.0	31.6	27.9	22.9	23.6	23.2	22.1	22.8	23.3	22.5	22.8
55–64 years	43.6	38.1	32.7	24.5	27.1	25.7	22.0	22.0	22.7	22.4	22.4
65 years and over	52.8	44.0	38.4	35.0	40.9	41.6	36.6	36.3	35.2	33.9	35.1
65–74 years	50.5	39.6	36.0	30.4	33.9	32.2	27.7	28.7	27.7	26.4	27.6
75–84 years	58.3	52.5	42.8	42.3	53.1	56.1	47.0	44.8	43.4	40.9	43.0
85 years and over	58.3	57.4	42.4	50.6	56.2	65.9	66.6	63.1	59.9	60.3	61.1
Female											
All ages, age adjusted	4.9	5.0	6.8	5.4	4.9	4.5	4.2	4.1	4.0	4.1	4.1
All ages, crude	5.1	4.9	6.6	5.5	5.2	4.8	4.5	4.4	4.4	4.4	4.4
Under 1 year	...	...	...	...	...	...	...	...	...	...	...
1–4 years	...	...	...	...	...	...	...	...	...	...	...
5–14 years	0.1	0.1	0.2	0.2	0.4	0.4	0.5	0.4	0.4	0.4	0.4
15–24 years	2.6	2.2	4.2	4.3	4.3	3.9	3.7	3.7	3.6	3.5	3.6
25–44 years	6.2	6.6	10.2	7.7	6.5	6.2	5.9	5.8	5.8	6.0	5.9
25–34 years	4.9	5.5	8.6	7.1	5.9	5.6	5.1	5.2	5.0	5.0	5.1
35–44 years	7.5	7.7	11.9	8.5	7.1	6.8	6.7	6.5	6.6	6.8	6.6
45–64 years	9.9	10.2	12.0	8.9	8.0	7.1	6.4	6.1	6.4	6.5	6.4
45–54 years	9.9	10.2	12.6	9.4	8.3	6.9	7.0	6.7	7.0	7.3	7.0
55–64 years	9.9	10.2	11.4	8.4	7.8	7.3	5.6	5.3	5.5	5.4	5.4
65 years and over	9.4	8.4	8.1	6.1	6.6	6.4	5.5	5.5	4.8	4.9	5.0
65–74 years	10.1	8.4	9.0	6.5	6.9	6.7	5.4	5.4	4.8	4.7	5.0
75–84 years	8.1	8.9	7.0	5.5	6.7	6.3	5.3	5.5	5.0	5.2	5.2
85 years and over	8.2	6.0	5.9	5.5	4.7	5.4	6.2	5.5	4.4	4.9	4.9

Source: *Health, United States, 1999*, National Center for Health Statistics, Hyattsville, MD, 1999

are rejecting the option to extend life. Recently, as attitudes toward suicide have changed among some people, there has been a rise in the right-to-die movement, living wills, and assisted suicides.

The Centers for Disease Control and Prevention (CDC) suggests that some of the increase in suicide rates is associated with increased firearms use. The CDC also predicts that, because older persons constitute the fastest-growing group in the United States, the number of suicides in this age group will likely continue to increase, especially with the lessening stigma attached to suicide.

Risk Factors

Risk factors for suicide among the elderly differ from those of younger persons. The elderly at risk for suicide often have a higher incidence of alcohol abuse and depression, are socially isolated, and use suicide methods that are more likely to succeed. In addition, older persons make fewer attempts per completed suicide, have a higher male-to-female ratio than other age groups, have often visited a health care provider shortly before their suicide, and have more physical illnesses and affective disorders. (For more information, see *Death and Dying — Who Decides?*, Information Plus, Wylie, Texas, 1998.)

TREATMENT OF MENTAL ILLNESS

While most mental illness among older people can be treated, an estimated 80 percent will never receive treatment. The trend has been to shift the elderly out of the mental health system and into nursing homes, although few nursing homes or intermediate care facilities are equipped to recognize or treat mental illness among the elderly. Consequently, older people placed in nursing homes often receive little or no help with mental health problems.

Mental health experts estimate that 20 to 50 percent of all people labeled "senile" have conditions that are either preventable or reversible if detected and treated early. Today, 50 percent of American medical schools have geriatric courses, but since they are elective courses (not mandatory), only 2 percent of medical students take them.

A Looming Crisis in Mental Health Care for the Aging?

Many experienced doctors find older people more difficult to treat than younger patients because their ailments are often more complicated, and their healing process is slower and therefore less satisfying for the doctor. Furthermore, many elderly have reached the point in their diseases where treatment may be ineffective. This unfamiliarity and discomfort in treating the elderly may help explain why the proportion of mental health services targeted at treating the elderly is only half that of the general population. (See Chapter VI for a discussion of dementia and Alzheimer's disease.)

In 1991, the American Board of Psychiatry and Neurology began certifying geriatric specialists in psychiatry. By 1998, 2,360 psychiatrists were certified as geriatric specialists. Experts warn that an explosion in psychiatric problems among the elderly is imminent. They believe that by the time the baby-boom generation reaches retirement in 2011, 15 million cases involving substance abuse, late-onset schizophrenia, anxiety disorders, and depression will present themselves. They predict a 275 percent jump in psychiatrically ill elderly from 1970 to 2030, compared to a 67 percent increase in comparable cases among those 30 to 44 years of age.

Projections of a large increase in mental illness among the elderly follow recent studies showing a relatively high incidence of men-

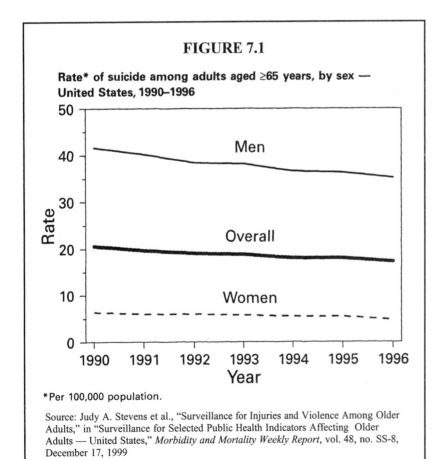

FIGURE 7.1

Rate* of suicide among adults aged ≥65 years, by sex — United States, 1990–1996

*Per 100,000 population.

Source: Judy A. Stevens et al., "Surveillance for Injuries and Violence Among Older Adults," in "Surveillance for Selected Public Health Indicators Affecting Older Adults — United States," *Morbidity and Mortality Weekly Report*, vol. 48, no. SS-8, December 17, 1999

tal health disorders among those born during the post-World War II boom. Factors indicative of that generation include increasing willingness to seek treatment, less family support, and higher incidence of alcoholism and substance abuse. Historically, use of illicit substances among the elderly has been relatively rare. However, the survivors of the drug culture spawned in the 1960s and 1970s are expected to have higher use of recreational drugs and the problems associated with them.

ALCOHOLISM AND ITS EFFECTS

Alcohol is the primary substance of abuse among the older population. Studying the rate of alcoholism among the older population is often more difficult than investigating that of the general population. Because older people are less likely to be employed full-time, job-related problems due to alcohol abuse are infrequent. Since many elderly are widowed, fewer marital conflicts result from alcohol. Older people are less likely to be arrested or brought to hospitals for alcohol abuse

treatment, and once brought in, the proper diagnosis is more likely to be missed.

On the other hand, older Americans are also less likely to drink than younger Americans. Table 7.2 shows that a greater percentage of those over 50 (60 percent) report that they do not drink than do other age groups and that among those elderly who do drink, only 3 percent claim to be heavy drinkers. The percentage of drinkers begins to decline by age 50 and drops sharply after 60. While about 7 out of 10 persons 18 to 29 years old claim to be current drinkers, only 4 out of 10 people over age 65 report being current drinkers.

Several factors may contribute to the overall reduction in alcohol consumption by the elderly. Older people may suffer negative reactions from alcohol, and the expense may also limit their ability to purchase alcohol. Since elderly women outnumber elderly men, and women are less likely to drink than men, the total number of elderly abstainers is greater.

However, the House of Representatives Select Committee on Aging believes that drinking levels are higher among the elderly than reported. The Committee claims that almost 60 percent of older Americans drink daily, and 15 percent of those are heavy drinkers (drink four or more drinks per day). One-third or more of elderly problem drinkers begin drinking heavily with increasing age, when life changes and losses become common. As their metabolism slows, they often become more sensitive to alcohol and get intoxicated more easily. They may also be taking medications that

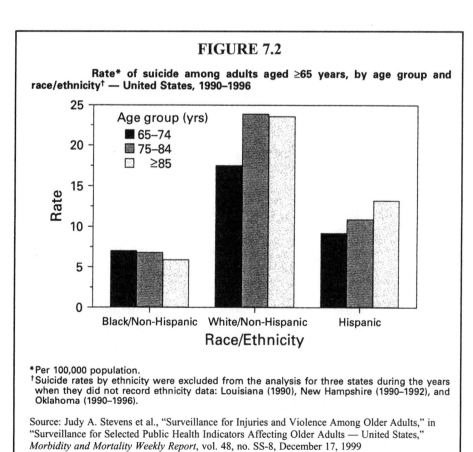

FIGURE 7.2

Rate* of suicide among adults aged ≥65 years, by age group and race/ethnicity[†] — United States, 1990–1996

*Per 100,000 population.
[†]Suicide rates by ethnicity were excluded from the analysis for three states during the years when they did not record ethnicity data: Louisiana (1990), New Hampshire (1990–1992), and Oklahoma (1990–1996).

Source: Judy A. Stevens et al., "Surveillance for Injuries and Violence Among Older Adults," in "Surveillance for Selected Public Health Indicators Affecting Older Adults — United States," *Morbidity and Mortality Weekly Report*, vol. 48, no. SS-8, December 17, 1999

do not mix well with alcohol. Sometimes, children of alcoholics and even health care professionals may interpret their behavior as senility or choose to ignore it.

The National Institute of Alcohol and Alcoholism estimates that 10 to 15 percent of older Americans abuse alcohol, although among those admitted to nursing homes, psychiatric facilities, and hospitals, 20 percent may abuse alcohol.

Dr. Alison A. Moore et al., in "Drinking Habits Among Older Persons: Findings from the NHANESI Epidemiologic Followup Study (1982-84)" (*Journal of the American Geriatrics Society*, vol. 47, no. 4, April 1999), found that 60 percent of those 65 and older who took part in the *National Health and Nutrition Examination Survey I* regularly consumed alcohol at some point in their lives. Seventy-nine percent of those were still regular drinkers, one-fourth of whom drank daily. Sixteen percent of the men and 15 percent of the women were heavy drinkers (two or more drinks a day for men and more than one drink per day for women). Ten percent of those 65 and older could be classified as binge drinkers who consume more than five drinks in one sitting.

Retirement, loss of a spouse, and loneliness can spark drinking. Figure 7.3 shows the stress levels of elderly problem and nonproblem drinkers and the social resources available to help them. As shown, problem drinkers have fewer resources available.

TABLE 7.2
ALCOHOL USE BY KEY DEMOGRAPHIC GROUPS

	Heavy %	Moderate %	Never Drink %	Undesignated %	N #
ALL ADULTS	11	50	37	2	(1257)
GENDER					
Male	18	51	30	1	(620)
Female	6	50	43	1	(637)
RACE/ETHNICITY					
White	11	52	36	1	(1035)
Black	9	42	47	2	(118)
Hispanic	16	43	40	1	(82)
AGE					
18 - 29	23	51	26	1	(260)
30 - 39	11	57	30	2	(553)
40 - 49	7	46	47	*	(212)
50+	3	35	60	2	(215)
EDUCATION					
College graduate	8	66	24	2	(361)
Other college	10	60	29	1	(296)
High school graduate	13	46	40	1	(445)
Less than high school graduate	14	28	57	1	(138)
INCOME					
Over $50,000	12	61	26	1	(305)
$35,001 - $50,000	11	61	28	*	(221)
$25,001 - $35,000	14	52	32	1	(199)
$25,000 or less	12	40	47	1	(369)
REGION					
East	11	52	35	2	(247)
Midwest	14	51	34	1	(332)
South	10	43	46	1	(480)
West	10	59	29	2	(198)
COMMUNITY SIZE					
Urban	10	49	40	1	(365)
Suburban	12	55	32	1	(595)
Rural	12	42	45	1	(296)

Source: *The Prevention Index, 1996 Summary Report*, Rodale Press, Inc., Emmaus, PA, 1996

Characteristics of Alcoholism Among Older People

There are three types of older drinkers, distinguished by the lengths and the patterns of their drinking histories. The first group are those over 60 who have been drinking most of their lives. This group has been termed "survivors" or "early onset problem drinkers." They have beaten the statistical odds by living to an old age despite heavy drinking. These are the persons likely to show numer-

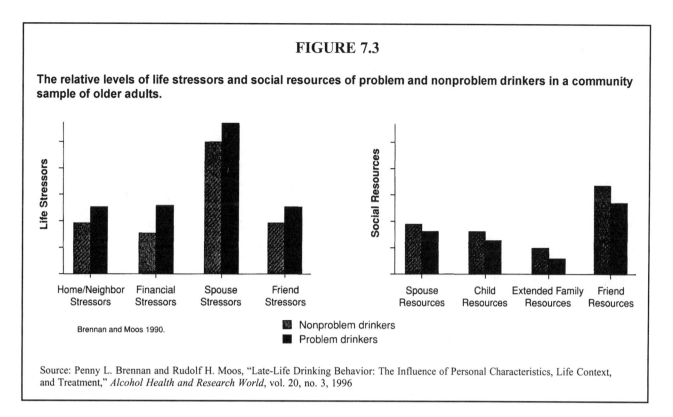

FIGURE 7.3

The relative levels of life stressors and social resources of problem and nonproblem drinkers in a community sample of older adults.

Brennan and Moos 1990.

Nonproblem drinkers
Problem drinkers

Source: Penny L. Brennan and Rudolf H. Moos, "Late-Life Drinking Behavior: The Influence of Personal Characteristics, Life Context, and Treatment," *Alcohol Health and Research World*, vol. 20, no. 3, 1996

ous medical problems, such as cirrhosis of the liver or brain damage, and psychological problems, such as depression.

The second group has histories of "bout" drinking between periods of relative sobriety. These are called "intermittents" because they may revert to heavy alcohol use under the stress and loneliness of aging.

The third group has been characterized as "reactors" or "late-onset problem drinkers." The stress of later years, particularly the loss of work or a spouse, may bring about heavy drinking. These people show few of the physical consequences of prolonged drinking and fewer disruptions of their lives. About two-thirds of those 65 and older who suffer from alcoholism have had long-standing alcohol addictions; in the remaining one-third, alcohol abuse develops late in life.

HEALTH-RELATED CONSEQUENCES OF ALCOHOLISM

Older people generally show a decreased tolerance to alcohol. Consumption of a given amount of alcohol by an elderly person will usually produce a higher blood-alcohol level than it would in a younger individual. Chronic medical problems such as cirrhosis may be present, but the need to detoxify (rid the body of poison) and to treat alcohol-withdrawal problems is less common. One possible explanation may be that those who have heavily abused alcohol do not survive into old age in great numbers.

Alcohol-induced organic brain syndrome (OBS) is characterized by confusion and disorientation. In elderly alcoholics it can be confused with or complicated by a diagnosis of "senility" (infirmity of body and mind associated with old age). A National Institute on Alcohol and Alcoholism (NIAA) program (1992) diagnosed 61 percent of elderly alcoholics as having OBS. Mortality for alcoholics with OBS is higher than those without OBS.

Since elderly people take more medication than other age groups, they are more susceptible to drug/alcohol interactions. Alcohol can reduce the effectiveness and safety of many medications and sometimes result in coma or death. Adverse consequences of alcohol consumption in older people are not restricted to problem drinkers. Older individuals with medical problems, including diabetes, heart disease, liver disease, and central nervous system degeneration, often do not tolerate alcohol well.

Complications in Diagnosis and Treatment

Diagnosis of problem drinking among the aging population is complicated by the fact that many psychological, behavioral, and physical symptoms of problem drinking also occur in people who do not have drinking problems. For example, brain damage, heart disease, and gastrointestinal disorders often develop in older adults but may also occur with drinking. In addition, mood disorders, depression, and changes in employment, economics, or marital status often accompany aging but can also be symptoms of alcoholism. The resulting failure to identify the signs of drinking in an older person may aggravate health, relationship problems, and legal problems associated with alcohol abuse.

Older problem drinkers make up a relatively small proportion of the total number of clients seen by most agencies for treatment of alcohol abuse. Chances for recovery among older drinkers is considered good because older clients tend to complete their therapy more often than younger clients. Problem drinkers with a severe physical disorder or persistent organic brain syndrome (OBS) are often placed in nursing homes, although the staff members generally have limited experience and training in treating alcoholics.

The elderly may have conceptions of alcoholism that prevent them from realizing their abuse. Current theories suggest that alcoholism is a mental or physiological disease. However, only a small segment of the elderly consider it a disease, and a proportionately higher number of elderly than the young claim alcoholism is a lack of willpower or a moral weakness. It is, therefore, more likely that an older person may attach a stigma or moral judgment to alcoholism and not seek treatment out of shame.

CHAPTER VIII

CARING FOR THE ELDERLY — CAREGIVERS

Societies generally recognize a moral obligation to care for their elderly and needy. In earlier, smaller communities, the family usually provided for the elderly. The family often included several generations living in close contact with each other and with other members of the community who could share the responsibility and burden. Family members were the mainstay of the nation's elder care system.

In America today, family units are much smaller, and family members may live great distances from each other. Communities are often made up of commuters and families with two working parents who may lack the time or desire to care for the elderly. Nonetheless, elder care still usually falls to the family, and more specifically, to the wife, daughter, or daughter-in-law.

Women generally live longer than men. The larger numbers of elderly women in American society result in the situation that most elderly men live in family settings (not necessarily with spouses) where they may be more easily assisted, while many elderly women live alone. For the first time in history, a married couple may likely spend more years caring for a parent than for a child. And many of those providing elder care will also be rearing children. With the 65-and-older population projected to increase 15 percent by 2010, their offspring, the "baby boom" generation, can expect to become the most "sandwiched" in history.

DISABILITY AND DEPENDENCY RATES

After the age of 65, the need for assistance increases sharply as the elderly grow older. The Bureau of the Census reported that, in 1995, half of seniors 65 years old and older had a disability, and 33.4 percent had a severe disability. (See Figure 8.1.)

Disability increases with advancing age; by the age of 80, 72 percent had disabilities of some kind, and 54 percent had a severe disability. Blacks were more likely to need assistance than Whites or Hispanics, and females were more likely to require assistance than males. (For more information on disability rates, see Chapter VI.)

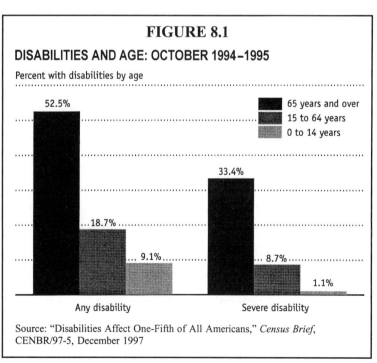

FIGURE 8.1

DISABILITIES AND AGE: OCTOBER 1994–1995

Percent with disabilities by age

- 65 years and over
- 15 to 64 years
- 0 to 14 years

Source: "Disabilities Affect One-Fifth of All Americans," *Census Brief*, CENBR/97-5, December 1997

125

Experts estimate that almost half of the elderly need help with at least one activity, such as getting dressed, going for a walk, or going to the bathroom. Another third need help with two or three activities, and approximately a fifth require assistance with four or more activities. (Activities of daily living — ADLs — consist of getting in or out of bed, bathing, using the toilet, eating, and other personal chores.)

TYPES OF DISABILITY

Older people vary greatly in their health and dependency needs. One measure of health status is an elder's ability to perform activities necessary for day-to-day living, such as personal hygiene and moving about.

Many people have difficulty with "instrumental" activities of daily living (IADLs). These chores also include preparing meals, doing housework and laundry, shopping, getting to medical services, using the telephone, and managing finances. Most caregivers are needed to help with household tasks (meal preparation, housecleaning, and laundry), shopping, and transportation. Table 8.1 shows the definition of disability and the various limitations among the disabled.

In addition, some people have functional disabilities, such as difficulty or inability lifting and carrying weight as heavy as 10 pounds, reading newsprint, hearing normal conversation, or climbing a flight of stairs. These disabilities may vary greatly from person to person. One person may have *difficulty* reading newsprint; another may be *unable* to read it. Other disabilities included in the Bureau of the Census list of disabilities were the necessity of using a wheelchair; use of a cane, crutches, or walker for more than 6 months; Alzheimer's disease or mental retardation; any

TABLE 8.1

Definition of Disability Including Functional Limitations, ADLs, and IADLs

People 15 years old and over were identified as having a disability if they met any of the following criteria:

- Used a wheechair or were a long-term user of a cane, crutches, or a walker
- Had difficulty performing one or more functional activities (seeing, hearing, speaking, lifting/carrying, using stairs, or walking)
- Had difficulty with one or more activities of daily living (the ADLs included getting around inside the home, getting in or out of bed or a chair, bathing, dressing, eating, and toileting)
- Had difficulty with one or more instrumental activities of daily living (the IADLs included going outside the home, keeping track of money and bills, preparing meals, doing light housework, taking prescription medicines in the right amount at the right time, and using the telephone)
- Had one or more specified conditions (a learning disability, mental retardation or another developmental disability, Alzheimer s disease, or some other type of mental or emotional condition)
- Were limited in their ability to do housework
- Were 16 to 67 years old and limited in their ability to work at a job or business
- Were receiving federal benefits based on an inability to work

People age 15 and over were identified as having a severe disability if they were unable to perform one or more functional activities; needed personal assistance with an ADL or IADL; used a wheelchair; were a long-term user of a cane, crutches, or a walker; had a developmental disability or Alzheimer s disease; were unable to do housework; were receiving federal disability benefits; or were 16 to 67 years old and unable to work at a job or business.

Source: John M. McNeil, *Americans with Disabilities: 1994-95*, Bureau of the Census, Washington, DC, August 1997

condition that limits the amount of work an individual is able to perform; and any condition that makes it difficult to do housework.

A GROWING ELDERLY POPULATION — A GROWING NEED

The supply of caregivers is not keeping pace with the growth in the older population. The number of elderly persons for every 100 adults of working age (aged 18 to 64) is called the old-age dependency ratio. In 1990, there were 20 elderly persons for every 100 working-aged adults. When the youngest baby boomers approach retirement age in 2025, there will be 32 elderly persons for every 100 people of working age.

The National Long Term Care Survey

As life expectancy has increased and the number of elderly has grown, some observers have predicted a nation burdened with people living longer who are crippled with disabilities and riddled with pain. Certainly, in some cases, that does occur. However, the predicted pandemic (worldwide epidemic) of pain and disability has not materialized to the extent some have feared. Instead, recent research shows that not only are Americans living longer, but also they are developing fewer chronic diseases and disabilities. America's elderly are defying stereotypes that aging is synonymous with increasing disability and dependence.

Researchers at Duke University, in the *National Long Term Care Survey,** a federal study that surveyed nearly 20,000 people age 65 and older between 1982 and 1994, found that every year there was a smaller and smaller percentage of older people unable to take care of themselves. Although the annual declines were only 1 to 2 percent per year, they were steady. In addition, the percentage of old people with chronic diseases, such as high blood pressure, arthritis, and emphysema, steadily declined.

Dr. Kenneth Manton, Larry Corder, and Eric Stallard, demographers at Duke University who analyzed the survey data, calculated that declining disability rates from 1982 until 1994 saved Medicare $200 million. They explained that if the disability rates of 1982 had held constant into 1994, there would have been nearly 300,000 more disabled people ages 65 to 74 in the population. The researchers found 1.2 million fewer disabled people, a 65-percent reduction, in 1994 than would have been expected had the disability rate remained the same as in 1982.

An important traditional measurement of the extent and severity of disability is the number of people at advanced ages in nursing homes or other institutions. In 1994, there were an estimated 1.7 million elderly people in institutions. If the 1982 rates had prevailed (adjusted for population), 2.1 million persons would have been institutionalized. The net difference of 400,000 persons represents actual improvement in rates of chronic disability. At an annual per capita nursing home cost in 1994 of $43,300, the difference suggests savings of up to $17.3 billion in nursing home expenses. (Some costs may be transferred to other sectors, such as assisted living arrangements or even life sustaining medical technology. Experts believe this cost still represented substantial progress.)

These findings have led researchers on aging to ask why it is that older Americans are less frail than before. One answer is that people either are not developing the diseases that cripple or disable them, or they are developing them later in life. Why? Some explanations include

- Increased education — greater availability of medical knowledge to the public, in general, as well as increasing educational levels among the elderly. Education level has been associated with better health. Higher levels of education are also associated with greater wealth, which often enables a person to live a more healthful life and to get adequate health care.

- Better health habits today, such as exercising more and eating a more healthful diet, which likely improve not only the quality of life but also longevity.

- Improvements in public health (nutrition, water quality, hygiene) that occurred when today's elderly were young.

- Medical advances, like hip replacements, lens replacements for cataract sufferers, and better pain relievers, can delay or prevent the burdens of chronic diseases that afflicted previous generations.

---

*Although the study is somewhat dated, its conclusions remain relevant.

PROFILE OF AMERICA'S CAREGIVERS

Families are the backbone of the long-term care system. — The National Alliance for Caregiving and the Alzheimer's Association, *Who Cares? Families Caring for Persons with Alzheimer's Disease*, 1999

In 1999, the National Alliance for Caregiving and the Alzheimer's Association released *Who Cares? Families Caring for Persons with Alzheimer's Disease* (1999), their study on caregiving in the United States, in general, and special requirements of caregivers of persons with Alzheimer's disease. The report found that families generally take personal responsibility for the needs of family members with disabilities, and they do it willingly, but often at great personal cost. Caregivers of Alzheimer's patients contend with special hardships.

The Majority Are Women

The survey found that 22.4 million U.S. households — nearly 1 in 4 — were involved in family caregiving of elderly relatives or friends. Since 1987, the number of households caring for an older adult has tripled. At least 5 million of those families cared for an Alzheimer's patient.

The typical caregiver is a married woman in her mid-forties who works full time, is a high school graduate, and has an annual household income of $35,000. The average age is 46. Seventy-three percent are female. Among Asians, however, almost equal percentages of men and women are caregivers. Asian caregivers were more highly educated than other racial/ethnic groups. (Table 8.2 shows the characteristics of both Alzheimer's caregivers and non-Alzheimer's caregivers.)

Women who gave care spent more time than men who gave care in caregiving activities — 18.8 hours per week for women and 15.5 hours for men. Women constituted 73 percent of all caregivers and were 79 percent of the constant/40-hour-per-week caregivers. Asians spent significantly less time than other minority groups in providing care — 15.1 hours for Asians, 20.6 hours for Blacks, 19.8 hours for Hispanics, and 17.5 hours for Whites. Thirty-eight percent of caregivers had been caregivers for five years or more; 35 percent, one to 4 years; 24 percent, up to one year, and the remainder had provided care episodically. Forty percent of caregivers were caring for children under 18 at the same time they were caring for elderly relatives or friends.

TABLE 8.2
CHARACTERISTICS OF ALZHEIMER'S AND NON-ALZHEIMER'S CAREGIVERS

		Alzheimer's Caregivers	Non Alzheimer's Caregivers
Caregiving Status	Currently giving care	75%	77%
	Gave care within past 12 months	25	23
Age	18 to 34 years	18%	24%
	35 to 49 years	36	40
	50 to 64 years	30	25
	65 and older	16	11
Race/Ethnicity	White, Non-Hispanic	81%	83%
	Black, Non-Hispanic	13	10
	Asian, Non-Hispanic	1	2
	Hispanic, Black or White	4	5
Gender	Female	76%	71%
	Male	24	29
Marital Status	Married	64%	62%
	Divorced	13	11
	Separated	3	1
	Widowed	7	8
	Single, living with a partner	2	4
	Single, never married	10	13
Employment Status	Working Full-time	46%	53%
	Working Part-time	14	12
	Retired	21	14
	Not Employed	19	20
Children/Grandchildren Under 18 Living at Home	Yes	36%	43%
	No	63	56

Source: *Who Cares? Families Caring for Persons with Alzheimer's Disease*, Alzheimer's Association and National Alliance for Caregiving, Washington, DC, and Bethesda, MD, 1999

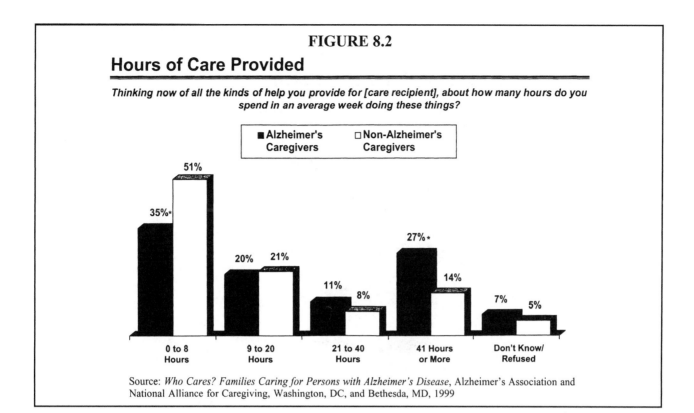

FIGURE 8.2

Hours of Care Provided

Thinking now of all the kinds of help you provide for [care recipient], about how many hours do you spend in an average week doing these things?

■ Alzheimer's Caregivers   □ Non-Alzheimer's Caregivers

- 0 to 8 Hours: 35%* / 51%
- 9 to 20 Hours: 20% / 21%
- 21 to 40 Hours: 11% / 8%
- 41 Hours or More: 27%* / 14%
- Don't Know/Refused: 7% / 5%

Source: *Who Cares? Families Caring for Persons with Alzheimer's Disease*, Alzheimer's Association and National Alliance for Caregiving, Washington, DC, and Bethesda, MD, 1999

Kind of Care

Family caregivers provided anywhere from less than one hour of care per week to "constant care." The average caregiver provided care for 18 hours per week. Figure 8.2 shows the hours per week that caregivers estimated they gave both for Alzheimer's caregivers and non-Alzheimer's caregivers. Alzheimer's patients generally need more hours of care.

Alzheimer's patients required more help with activities of daily living (Figure 8.3) and instrumental activities of daily living (Figure 8.4). Consequently, their caregivers spent more hours assisting their care recipients with such activities in the course of a day. They performed more level 5 care than caregivers of non-Alzheimer's patients, while caregivers of non-Alzheimer's patients performed more level 1 care (Figure 8.5). (Level refers to demand and intensity of care, from level 1 to level 5, with 5 being the highest and most demanding. Level 5 caregivers provided more than 40 hours per week, or "constant care.")

Many caregivers help their patients by giving medicines. Caregivers of Alzheimer's patients re-ported that 51 percent of their patients had trouble taking medications as directed, compared to 15 percent of non-Alzheimer's patients (Figure 8.6). Virtually all the caregivers claimed they knew how to give the medications as prescribed and what each medicine was for. Slightly fewer knew the potential side effects of those medications and how they may interact with other medications. (See Figure 8.7.)

Recipients of Care

Eighty-nine percent of caregivers took care of a relative, and 11 percent, a friend or neighbor. Thirty-one percent of caregivers took care of their own mothers; 11 percent, fathers; 11 percent, grandparents; 10 percent, parents-in-law; 9 percent, aunts or uncles; 9 percent, spouses; and 8 percent, other relatives. (See Figure 8.8.) The average age of care recipients was 77 years.

Among those recipients who did not have Alzheimer's disease, the main illnesses included dementia, heart disease, cancer, stroke, arthritis, diabetes, lung disease, blindness or vision loss, mental or emotional illness, broken bones, neurological problems, and high blood pressure.

FIGURE 8.3

Activities of Daily Living Performed

I'm going to read a list of kinds of help which might be provided to an older person...
For each, just tell me if you provide this kind of help.

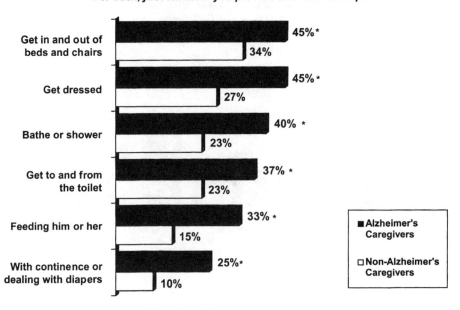

Get in and out of beds and chairs — 45%* / 34%

Get dressed — 45%* / 27%

Bathe or shower — 40%* / 23%

Get to and from the toilet — 37%* / 23%

Feeding him or her — 33%* / 15%

With continence or dealing with diapers — 25%* / 10%

■ Alzheimer's Caregivers

□ Non-Alzheimer's Caregivers

FIGURE 8.4

Instrumental Activities of Daily Living Performed

I'm going to read a list of kinds of help which might be provided to an older person...
For each, just tell me if you provide this kind of help.

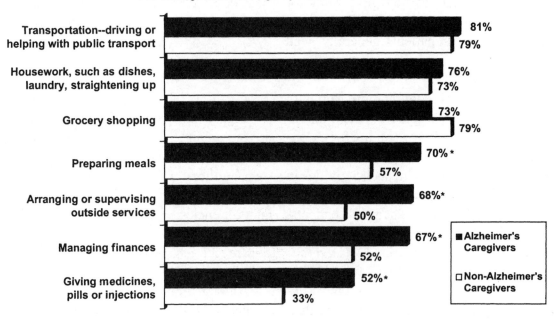

Transportation--driving or helping with public transport — 81% / 79%

Housework, such as dishes, laundry, straightening up — 76% / 73%

Grocery shopping — 73% / 79%

Preparing meals — 70%* / 57%

Arranging or supervising outside services — 68%* / 50%

Managing finances — 67%* / 52%

Giving medicines, pills or injections — 52%* / 33%

■ Alzheimer's Caregivers

□ Non-Alzheimer's Caregivers

Source of both figures: *Who Cares? Families Caring for Persons with Alzheimer's Disease*, Alzheimer's Association and National Alliance for Caregiving, Washington, DC, and Bethesda, MD, 1999

FIGURE 8.5
Level of Care Index

The Level of Care Index takes into account both the number of hours that caregivers spend giving care, as well as the number of Activities of Daily Living and Instrumental Activities of Daily Living performed.

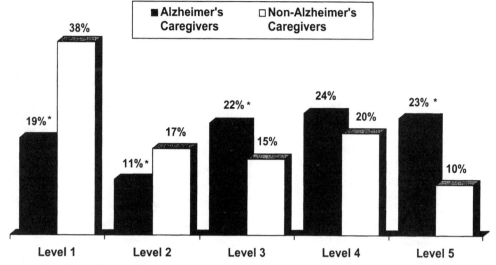

- ■ Alzheimer's Caregivers
- □ Non-Alzheimer's Caregivers

Level 1 — 19% *, 38%
Level 2 — 11% *, 17%
Level 3 — 22% *, 15%
Level 4 — 24%, 20%
Level 5 — 23% *, 10%

Source: *Who Cares? Families Caring for Persons with Alzheimer's Disease*, Alzheimer's Association and National Alliance for Caregiving, Washington, DC, and Bethesda, MD, 1999

One-fourth of care recipients live in the same household as their caregiver. Most (54 percent), however, lived within 20 minutes of the caregiver's home; 11 percent lived within 20 minutes to one hour's drive; 5 percent, one to two hours away; and 5 percent, more than two hours away. Asian care recipients were more likely than Whites to live with their caregivers.

Competing Demands

Taking care of an elderly person changed the lives of many caregivers. Sixty percent of Alzheimer's caregivers and 65 percent of non-Alzheimer's caregivers worked full- or part-time (Table 8.2). Half of them reported making adjustments to their work schedule (rearranging their work schedules, taking time off without pay, working part-time, or quitting their jobs) for caregiving responsibilities. Fifty-seven percent of Alzheimer's caregivers and 47 percent of non-Alzheimer's caregivers went to work late or took time off. Ten percent of Alzheimer's caregivers and 6 percent of non-Alzheimer's caregivers said they gave up work entirely, and 7 percent of Alzheimer's caregivers

FIGURE 8.6
Medication Management

Does your [care recipient] take medications on time, in the right amount, with no problem, or would you say s/he has trouble taking medicine as directed?

Alzheimer's Caregivers

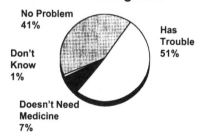

No Problem 41%
Don't Know 1%
Doesn't Need Medicine 7%
Has Trouble 51%

Non-Alzheimer's Caregivers

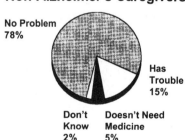

No Problem 78%
Don't Know 2%
Doesn't Need Medicine 5%
Has Trouble 15%

Source: *Who Cares? Families Caring for Persons with Alzheimer's Disease*, Alzheimer's Association and National Alliance for Caregiving, Washington, DC, and Bethesda, MD, 1999

and 3 percent of non-Alzheimer's caregivers took early retirement. Thirteen percent of Alzheimer's caregivers and 6 percent of non-Alzheimer's caregivers took a less demanding job. (See Figure 8.9.) Although working men also reported these conflicts, fewer of them rearranged their work lives to accommodate caregiving than did women.

Caregivers Need Care Too

Caregivers have become the casualties of our ability to live longer. — Jack Nottingham, executive director, Rosalyn Carter Institute for Human Development, Georgia Southwestern College

For many people, caring for an ill or disabled elderly person can, over time, become an enormous burden. Elder caretakers may neglect their own health and needs because no one else is available to care for their elderly spouse or parent.

The National Alliance for Caregiving and the Alzheimer's Association survey reported that 56 percent of Alzheimer's caregivers and 40 percent of non-Alzheimer's caregivers said their caregiving duties caused them to give up time with other family members; 53 percent of Alzheimer's caregivers and 40 percent of non-Alzheimer's caregivers gave up vacations, hobbies, or other activities. Twenty-three percent of Alzheimer's caregivers and 12 percent of non-Alzheimer's caregivers reported experiencing physical or mental health problems due to caregiving. Forty-three percent of Alzheimer's caregivers and 20 percent of non-Alzheimer's caregivers reported "much stress."

The number one mechanism mentioned to cope with stress

was prayer. Talking with friends, hobbies, and exercise were also indicated. Some mentioned help from professionals or other counselors, use of medications, or use of alcohol. (See Figure 8.10; the sampling error for the study, at the 95 percent confidence level, is plus or minus 5.5 percentage

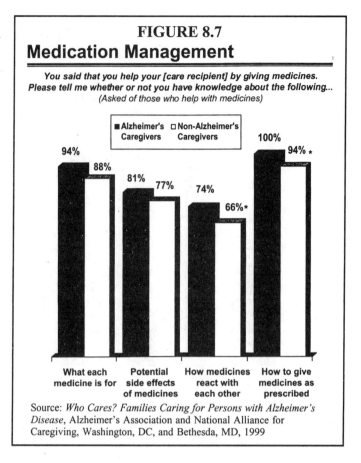

FIGURE 8.7
Medication Management

You said that you help your [care recipient] by giving medicines. Please tell me whether or not you have knowledge about the following... (Asked of those who help with medicines)

Source: *Who Cares? Families Caring for Persons with Alzheimer's Disease*, Alzheimer's Association and National Alliance for Caregiving, Washington, DC, and Bethesda, MD, 1999

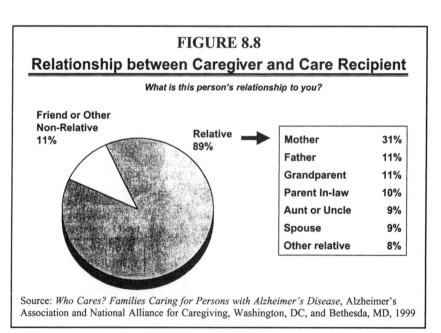

FIGURE 8.8
Relationship between Caregiver and Care Recipient

What is this person's relationship to you?

Mother	31%
Father	11%
Grandparent	11%
Parent In-law	10%
Aunt or Uncle	9%
Spouse	9%
Other relative	8%

Source: *Who Cares? Families Caring for Persons with Alzheimer's Disease*, Alzheimer's Association and National Alliance for Caregiving, Washington, DC, and Bethesda, MD, 1999

points for Alzheimer's caregivers and 2.8 percentage points for non-Alzheimer's caregivers. Statistically significant differences between the two groups are shown with an asterisk.)

The Caregiver Health Effects Study

In 1999, the American Medical Association, in "Caregiving as a Risk Factor for Mortality" (*Journal of American Medicine*, December 15, vol. 282, no, 23), published the results of a study performed by Richard Schulz, Ph.D., and Scott R. Beach, Ph.D. The study found that after four years of follow-up of caregivers ages 66 to 96 (51 percent were women, and 49 percent were men), 103 caregivers had died. After adjusting for socioeconomic factors, existing medical conditions, and subclinical cardiovascular disease, participants who were caregivers and who were experiencing stress (56 percent) had mortality risks 63 percent higher than the noncaregiving control group. Participants who were caregivers but not experienc-

ing strain and those who had disabled spouses but were not providing care for them did not have elevated mortality rates relative to the noncaregiving control group.

Researchers found that strained caregivers experienced more depression and anxiety and a reduced level of health. They also were less likely to get adequate rest, to have time to rest when they were sick, or to have time to exercise.

Biggest Difficulty and Greatest Rewards of Caregiving

The leading difficulty reported by caregivers was seeing the deterioration of their loved one. One in 5 caregivers mentioned the demands on their time and not being able to do what they wanted; 12 percent said a major problem was the recipient's attitude (uncooperative, demanding).

When asked what were the greatest rewards of care-giving, caregivers cited knowing their recipient was well cared for, the satisfaction of doing a good deed, and the recipient's appreciation. Also mentioned were watching the recipient's health improve, family loyalty, "giving back," fulfilling family obligations, and spending time together.

When asked to describe their caregiving experience in one word, 57 percent chose positive words, such as "rewarding," "thankful," "loving," and "OK." Just over one-third used negative words — "stressful," "burdened," "exhausting" — to describe their caregiving. Eight percent said they did not know how they felt about caregiving.

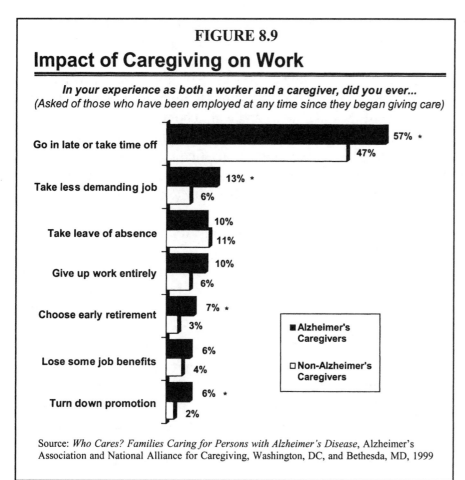

FIGURE 8.9

Impact of Caregiving on Work

In your experience as both a worker and a caregiver, did you ever...
(Asked of those who have been employed at any time since they began giving care)

Go in late or take time off — 57% *, 47%

Take less demanding job — 13% *, 6%

Take leave of absence — 10%, 11%

Give up work entirely — 10%, 6%

Choose early retirement — 7% *, 3%

Lose some job benefits — 6%, 4%

Turn down promotion — 6% *, 2%

■ Alzheimer's Caregivers
□ Non-Alzheimer's Caregivers

Source: *Who Cares? Families Caring for Persons with Alzheimer's Disease*, Alzheimer's Association and National Alliance for Caregiving, Washington, DC, and Bethesda, MD, 1999

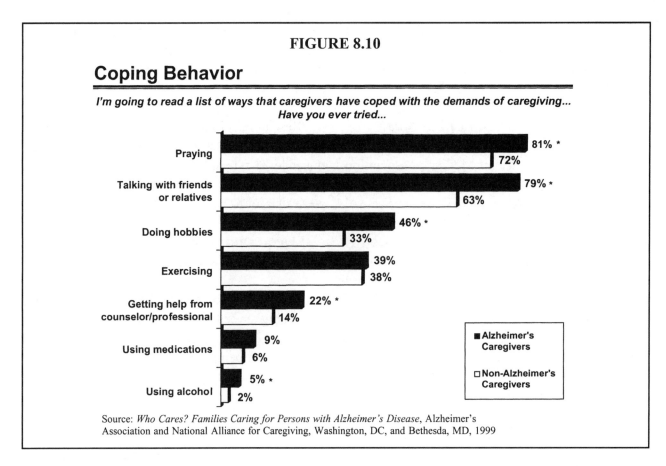

FIGURE 8.10

Coping Behavior

I'm going to read a list of ways that caregivers have coped with the demands of caregiving...
Have you ever tried...

Praying — 81% * / 72%

Talking with friends or relatives — 79% * / 63%

Doing hobbies — 46% * / 33%

Exercising — 39% / 38%

Getting help from counselor/professional — 22% * / 14%

Using medications — 9% / 6%

Using alcohol — 5% * / 2%

■ Alzheimer's Caregivers
□ Non-Alzheimer's Caregivers

Source: *Who Cares? Families Caring for Persons with Alzheimer's Disease*, Alzheimer's Association and National Alliance for Caregiving, Washington, DC, and Bethesda, MD, 1999

Experts agree that even a small break from the responsibilities of elder care can be of enormous benefit to a caregiver, and many believe that it can prevent older people from being placed in nursing homes prematurely. In fact, elderly people are more likely to be placed in institutions because of the caregiver's burnout than because of a decline in their own conditions. Recent attention to the special needs of caretakers has resulted in a variety of formal and informal programs designed to provide some relief. While these programs generally provide services to the dependent elderly, their purpose is primarily to assist the caregiver. With hospitals discharging patients sooner and sicker than in previous years, the role of caregiver has taken on added importance.

The Need for Training

In 1998, the National Alliance for Caregiving, with funding from the Equitable Foundation, in *The Caregiving Boom: Baby Boomer Women Giving Care*, found that women caregivers felt the need for information on a variety of topics. Approxi-

mately three-fourths of caregivers reported they would have found it helpful to know how to deal with the stresses of giving care and with finding in-home services. Seventy-one percent felt they needed "hands-on" training and training in balancing home and work chores with caregiving. Also helpful would have been information on the use of prescription drugs, finding assisted living or nursing homes, managing finances, buying insurance, and veteran's benefits. (See Figure 8.11.)

Thinking About the Future

The Caregiving Boom: Baby Boomer Women Giving Care (see above) found that their caregiving experiences caused women to think differently about their own lives. As a result of caring for others, 21 percent said they thought more about the savings needed for their own elder care. Some said they worried about the adequacy of insurance (12 percent), the need to plan (11 percent), and the possibility of being a burden to others (7 percent). Others became more conscious of their own physical health, and a few said they were concerned

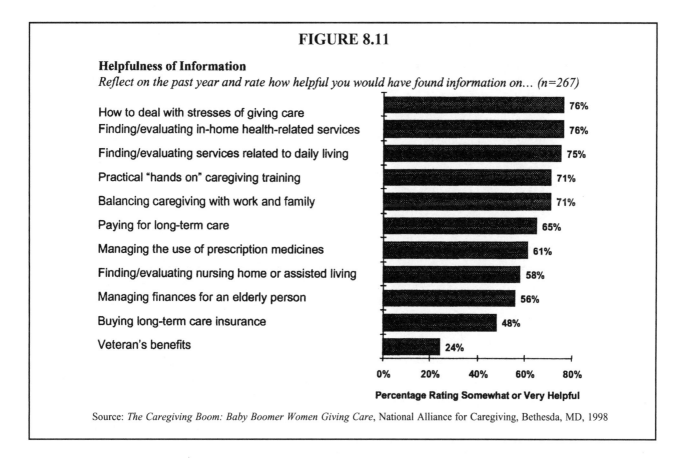

FIGURE 8.11

Helpfulness of Information
Reflect on the past year and rate how helpful you would have found information on... (n=267)

How to deal with stresses of giving care — 76%
Finding/evaluating in-home health-related services — 76%
Finding/evaluating services related to daily living — 75%
Practical "hands on" caregiving training — 71%
Balancing caregiving with work and family — 71%
Paying for long-term care — 65%
Managing the use of prescription medicines — 61%
Finding/evaluating nursing home or assisted living — 58%
Managing finances for an elderly person — 56%
Buying long-term care insurance — 48%
Veteran's benefits — 24%

0%   20%   40%   60%   80%

Percentage Rating Somewhat or Very Helpful

Source: *The Caregiving Boom: Baby Boomer Women Giving Care*, National Alliance for Caregiving, Bethesda, MD, 1998

about who would take care of them and the future, in general. (See Table 8.3.) As a result, most took action to improve their future, such as saving more money, obtaining more insurance, writing a will, and taking better care of their physical health (Figure 8.12).

The Cost to Caregivers

One of America's great assets is the number of family members who provide care for ill or disabled relatives. The millions of informal caregivers save the formal health care system billions of dollars annually. One major reason this situation exists is the vast discrepancy between government funding allocated to family caregivers and that going to institutions. Of the billions of dollars spent in the field, only a fraction is targeted toward family support services. Most goes to large public and private institutions and group homes.

In a 1997 study, *Family Caregiving in the United States: Findings from a National Survey*, conducted by the National Alliance for Caregivers

and the National Center for Women and Aging for Metropolitan Life Insurance Company, caregivers reported that taking care of an elderly relative or friend had cut into their earnings. The financial effect was estimated at an average of $659,139 in lost wages, Social Security, and pension benefits over their lifetimes. (For data from that study on costs to business, see below.)

The Caregiving Boom: Baby Boomer Women Giving Care (see above) found that 49 percent of women reported that they had suffered a great deal of financial hardship as a result of their caregiver responsibilities.

In 1999, the Clinton Administration proposed a $6 billion five-year package to address the long-term needs of Americans with chronic illness or disabilities and their family caregivers. In directly recognizing that family members are the core of long-term health care in the United States, the president opened debate on the issue. Because "informal" caregiving is outside the market economy, its economic value is not generally recognized.

135

While some features of family contributions to caregiving are impossible to measure, such as the comfort of being cared for at home by familiar people, a price can be put on other aspects.

In 1999, Peter Arno, Carol Levine, and Margaret Memmott, in the "Economic Value of Informal Caregiving" (*Health Affairs*, March/April 1999, vol. 18, no. 2), studied the market value of the care provided by unpaid family and friends to ill and disabled adults. They estimated that the national economic value of caregiving was $196 billion in 1997. (They used a mid-range estimate of 25.8 million caregivers in 1997, an average weekly figure of 17.9 hours of care per caregiver — 24 billion hours, and a midrange rate of $8.18 per hour.) (See Figure 8.13.) That equals approximately 18 percent of total national health care spending of $1,092 billion (Figure 8.14). (Informal caregiving is not counted in national health care costs; if it were, total health care would amount to nearly $200 billion.)

That amount dwarfs national spending for formal caregiving in homes ($32 billion) or nursing homes ($83 billion) (Figure 8.14). Note that this amount does not include the direct costs families pay in unreimbursed health care expenses, loss of income and other benefits, such as Social Security, when a caregiver gives up a job or reduces work hours.

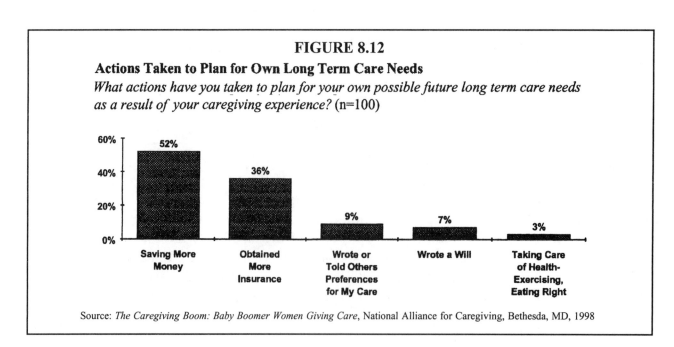

FIGURE 8.12

Actions Taken to Plan for Own Long Term Care Needs

What actions have you taken to plan for your own possible future long term care needs as a result of your caregiving experience? (n=100)

Source: *The Caregiving Boom: Baby Boomer Women Giving Care*, National Alliance for Caregiving, Bethesda, MD, 1998

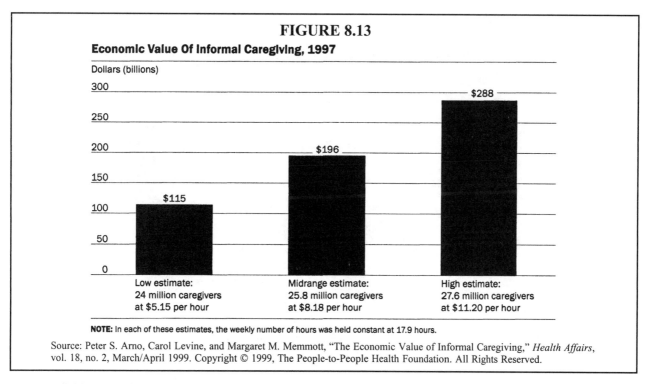

FIGURE 8.13

Economic Value Of Informal Caregiving, 1997

Dollars (billions)

Low estimate: 24 million caregivers at $5.15 per hour	Midrange estimate: 25.8 million caregivers at $8.18 per hour	High estimate: 27.6 million caregivers at $11.20 per hour
$115	$196	$288

NOTE: In each of these estimates, the weekly number of hours was held constant at 17.9 hours.

Source: Peter S. Arno, Carol Levine, and Margaret M. Memmott, "The Economic Value of Informal Caregiving," *Health Affairs*, vol. 18, no. 2, March/April 1999. Copyright © 1999, The People-to-People Health Foundation. All Rights Reserved.

Differing Perceptions of Generations

In 1998, ICR Research, Inc., a research organization, and the American Association of Retired Persons (AARP) surveyed people 65 and older who had adult children 35 or older. The survey assessed how older parents defined independent living, the extent to which the generations have communicated about living independently, and the types of assistance received or needed. The data produced companion studies, *Independent Living: Do Older Parents and Adult Children See It the Same Way?* and *Independent Living: Adult Children's Perceptions of Their Parents' Needs,* from the two different perspectives.

The survey found, in general, a picture of healthy older parents who were able to take care of themselves. It found that adult children do not begin to be concerned about their parents' ability to live independently until their parents begin to experience problems that affect this capacity. Other findings include

- Adult children and older parents *agreed* about the meaning of independent living. About half the time definitions focused on being able to take care of oneself.

- Adult children and older parents *disagreed* about the assistance adult children provided older parents when he or she had a problem in the past five years. Older parents were more than twice as likely (36 percent) as the younger generation (16 percent) to say their adult child(ren) did not provide them with any help when they had a problem. Adult children were more likely than older parents to identify specific types of help they provided, such as being there, housekeeping, or money.

- Older parents were generally less concerned than adult children about their own ability to live independently. Older parents (60 percent) were more likely than adult children (41 percent) to say they (older parents) do not currently receive help from any source to live independently. Older parents (67 percent) were also more likely than adult children (51 percent) to say they (older parent) do not currently need help to live independently.

- Adult children (52 percent) were more likely to consider giving older parents information than older parents (34 percent) were to consider asking adult children for information regarding assistance to live independently.

137

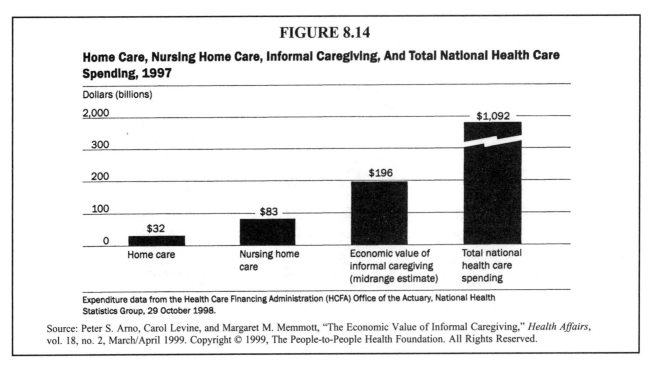

FIGURE 8.14

Home Care, Nursing Home Care, Informal Caregiving, And Total National Health Care Spending, 1997

Dollars (billions)

- Home care: $32
- Nursing home care: $83
- Economic value of informal caregiving (midrange estimate): $196
- Total national health care spending: $1,092

Expenditure data from the Health Care Financing Administration (HCFA) Office of the Actuary, National Health Statistics Group, 29 October 1998.

Source: Peter S. Arno, Carol Levine, and Margaret M. Memmott, "The Economic Value of Informal Caregiving," *Health Affairs*, vol. 18, no. 2, March/April 1999. Copyright © 1999, The People-to-People Health Foundation. All Rights Reserved.

- Most younger respondents (68 percent) said they had not talked with their parents about what it would take for them to live independently. Not surprisingly, 71 percent of respondents said their parents had not experienced a problem in the past five years that affected their ability to live independently.

- Forty-one percent of the younger generation said their parents did not receive help. Among those who did receive help, 49 percent said financial help was the most frequent help. Transportation (11 percent) was the second most frequent type of assistance.

Interestingly, a 1997 study done by Princeton Survey Research Associates, a group funded by Pew Charitable Trusts, surveyed adults with at least one living parent and then surveyed those older parents. The survey found that many adults also depend on their older parents in many ways. Among adult children 65 and older, 4 percent of them said they were dependent on their parents, 57 percent reported their parents were more dependent on them, and 29 percent claimed they were equally dependent on their older parents as their parents were on them. Among those 55 to 64, 13 percent said they depended on their older parents, while 50 percents said their parents depended on them more. Thirty-five percent said they were as dependent on their parents as their parents were on them.

RESPITE CARE

Families caring for elderly relatives often do not think of themselves as caregivers. Although they may know they need a break, they may not be aware of the concept of respite care, nor do they know how to arrange for it. The dictionary definition of respite is "an interval of temporary relief or rest, as from pain, work, duty, etc." The Foundation of Long Term Care (FLTC) has formulated a working definition of geriatric respite care as, "the temporary supportive care of an elder who normally lives in the community with a caregiver, by a substitute caregiver, in order to strengthen and maintain the regular caregiver's well-being and ability to maintain care at home."

Respite care takes many forms. In some cases, the respite worker comes to the home to take care of the elderly person so that the caregiver can take a few hours for personal needs, relaxation, or rest. Respite care is also available for longer periods so that caregivers can recuperate from their own illnesses or even take a vacation.

Adult day-care programs around the country provide structured daytime programs through which functionally impaired adults can receive the social, health, and supportive services needed to restore or maintain optimal functioning. While not designed specifically to aid caregivers, adult day-care programs serve a similar purpose as formal respite programs by temporarily giving the caregiver physical and psychological relief from the burden of elder care.

FROM INFORMAL TO
FORMAL SERVICES

At the same time that the elderly population is increasing, the segment of the general public available to provide unpaid care, generally family members, is decreasing. The once familiar extended family has become less common in the United States. In addition, several other trends continue to decrease the availability of caregivers, including more women employed outside the home, greater geographical separation of families, high divorce rates, and smaller families. Fewer caregivers will be available for the increasing number of elderly needing support. As a result, the elderly will likely have to pay for a higher proportion of professional services. (See Chapter IX for information on health care.)

Foster Care

Although many elderly do not need intensive nursing home care, some of those who need limited assistance are increasingly being cared for in foster homes. It is an alternative that gives an older person safe and comfortable care at approximately one-third the cost of nursing home care.

Foster care for adults is like foster care for children; a person or a family is paid to take in other people and provide them a home — meals, laundry, a place to sleep, and someone to talk to and watch over them. In some programs, the residents pay for the care with their own money, although often a government agency or non-profit agency brings the family and the participant together. Some elderly pay for their care with their Social Security or pension income, some from Supplemental Security Income (SSI). In some cases, states have received Medicaid waivers that allow them to spend federal long-term nursing funds for community-based care programs like adult foster homes. Licensing regulations vary from state to state.

There are no overall figures on how many older people are living in foster homes since no single agency monitors the dozens of programs nationwide. Experts estimate that tens of thousands are in foster care, and they see those numbers increasing.

The benefits of foster care, in addition to cost, are considerable. Residents report enjoying family life and personal relationships with their foster care families, they tend to focus less on their infirmities and be more independent, and their families are happier not to have to admit them to nursing homes.

Cluster Care

Cluster care is another alternative form of personal care for those elderly who do not need full-time, trained nursing care. Begun as an experiment in New York State in the mid-1980s, in cluster care, a team of workers employed by one home attendant agency is responsible for the care of a group of clients who live in close proximity. With the supervision of a nurse and a case manager, the clients' schedules are set by evaluating which activities of daily living they need help with and how long it takes to perform those tasks. One worker (a "shared aide") can coordinate visits to several clients in a day. Said one family member, "Cluster care approximates the kind of care we are used to giving those we love in extended families."

Experts predict the program will become increasingly popular across the country as states strapped for money face a population growing older and in greater need of care. However, some elderly and disabled cannot be served by such a program — those so frail they need constant monitoring during their waking, and often sleeping, hours, and those living far from other personal-care clients.

The On Lok Program

One comprehensive-care program for frail elderly people that is winning support across the country is based on a San Francisco model. The On Lok center in San Francisco's Chinatown weaves medical care, home care, social services, and case management into a single web of care. Founded 20 years ago, the On Lok center was named from the Chinese words for "peaceful" and "happy."

"It's not for everyone," said Don Sherwood, who tracks the On Lok program for the Office of Research and Demonstration at the Health Care Financing Administration, the federal agency that manages Medicare and Medicaid. "Only 5 percent of those over 65 are frail enough to be eligible, and many don't want to change doctors and go to a day health center. But for those who want comprehensive care, it's very good."

Clients sign over their Medicaid and Medicare policies. In return, they receive housing and total care, as long as they use the program's doctors and nurses. Central to the On Lok model is the day health center, a vastly expanded version of the social day programs that proliferated in the 1970s. In addition to recreational activities, the centers have added health services with on-site geriatricians, rehabilitation therapists, nurse-practitioners, and other health professionals. When needed, clients are hospitalized. They may also receive, if necessary, intravenous antibiotic or hydration therapy at the center.

Most participants like the program because they are guaranteed health care, including hospitalization or nursing home care, until they die or leave the program. Despite the support services, which are more extensive than would be generally supplied under Medicaid, the program is less expensive than nursing home care. Because the participants' health is constantly monitored, their use of hospitals is so sharply reduced that On Lok facilities cost less than regular care under Medicaid or Medicare, despite all the extra services that the model provides.

CORPORATE INVOLVEMENT

Corporations are not welfare agencies. Their focus is on a profitable balance sheet. Nevertheless, many companies are exploring elder care issues because, for many reasons, it may be in their best interest.

Labor Costs

Companies with a high average age among employees, or with more female workers, are more likely to have a higher number of caregivers and, hence, more work time lost to elder care tasks. Tardiness and increased use of the telephone frequently occur among some caregivers; work disruptions that can affect the morale of other employees, who may feel they must work harder to compensate for co-workers who assume the duties of caregivers. Employees distracted on the job are more likely to make mistakes and have higher accident rates, as well as increased conflict with fellow employees.

Caregiving problems can also remain hidden from the employer because employees may "cover up" their activities when late or absent. Caregivers may work fewer hours, change schedules, and take time off without pay, which lead to increased hiring and training by the employer. However, until recently, the additional labor losses attributable to caregiving had not been quantified.

The MetLife Study of Employer Costs for Working Caregivers

Employers, as well as employees, bear a financial burden from personal caregiving. In response to the growing evidence that caregiving for older family members is exacting a cost on U.S. business, the National Alliance for Caregiving and Metropolitan Life Insurance Company conducted a 1997 study, *Family Caregiving in the United States: Findings from a National Survey*, to collect new data on the cost of caregiving. The study included only full-time employees and only those identified as Levels III, IV, and V caregivers. These caregivers provided assistance with at least two Activities of Daily Living (ADLs; bathing, toileting, feeding, transferring, or walking) and at least four Instrumental Activities of Daily Living (IADLs; financial management, transportation, help with medications, shopping, preparing meals, etc.). They provided between 9 (Level III) and 56 hours (Level V) of care each week.

According to the study, 23.2 percent of all households, or 22.4 million households, were involved in caregiving. The majority (64.2 percent) of caregivers were employed, most (52 percent) full-time. Based on these findings, 14.4 million employed caregivers were balancing work with their caregiving roles.

Replacing Employees Who Quit

Over 17 percent of caregivers said they had to quit their jobs or take early retirement because of caregiving tasks. These people provided care an average of four years. Table 8.4 shows the replacement costs — a total of almost $5 billion — for employees who quit.

Absenteeism

The study found that 10.5 percent of employed caregivers were absent a minimum of three or more days in the previous six months due to caregiving chores. The total cost to employers was almost $400 million (Table 8.5). Most (59 percent) employed caregivers arrived late for work, left early, took extended lunch breaks, or in some other way altered their work schedule. These caregivers lost an estimated one hour per week that could not be made up, for a total cost to employers of $488 million (Table 8.6).

Interruptions at Work

Many caregivers were interrupted during their workdays by phone calls to the care recipient or service providers or by other caregiving chores. These breaks in work were estimated at one hour per week, a total cost to employers of $3.7 billion (Table 8.7). Sixty percent of caregivers reported experiencing an elder care crisis in the previous months that caused additional phone calls, loss of concentration, and partial absenteeism that caused a loss of three days per year and a total cost of more than $1 billion (Table 8.8).

Supervising Caregivers

Eighty-one percent of employed caregivers said their supervisors were sympathetic regarding their caregiving burdens. However, the cost to employers in providing emotional support, arranging coverage for caregivers to be absent, counseling about benefits, and dealing with work disruptions was estimated to be one hour per month and $805 million (Table 8.9).

Total Cost to Business

The MetLife study estimated that the total cost of caregiving in lost productivity to U.S. business was $11.5 billion per year (Table 8.10), a conservative figure because it is based on median wages and do not include those giving Level I and Level II care or those working part-time. If those caregivers were also included in the calculations, the study concluded that the total costs to U.S. business would exceed $29 billion per year.

Physical and Mental Costs to Caregiver

Working caregivers are subject to more frequent headaches, weight loss or gain, anxiety or depression, and are slightly more likely to be under a physician's care. Twenty percent of caregivers reported being under a doctor's care, compared to 16 percent of employees who were not caregivers. Twenty-two percent of caregivers compared to 8 percent of non-caregivers reported anxiety and depression. (It should be noted that caregivers to the elderly may be older than many other workers and perhaps under care for reasons not associated with their caregiving status.)

TABLE 8.4

	Replacement Costs for Employees Who Quit		
Full-Time Employed Caregivers by Gender (Levels III, IV, and V)	Number who quit in a given year (4.2%)	Median Weekly Wage	Cost to Employers (75% of annual wage)
Men	59,642	$ 701	$ 1,630,553,866
Women	180,981	$ 468	$ 3,303,262,439
Total	240,623		$ 4,933,816,305

TABLE 8.5

	Costs Due to Absenteeism		
Full-Time Employed Caregivers by Gender (Levels III, IV, and V)	Number absent average 6 days per year (10.5%)	Median Weekly Wage	Cost to Employers
Men	156,205	$ 701	$ 131,399,945
Women	473,997	$ 468	$ 266,196,973
Total	630,203		$ 397,596,918

TABLE 8.6

	Costs Due to Partial Absenteeism			
Full-Time Employed Caregivers by Gender (Levels III, IV, and V)	Number experiencing partial absenteeism (59%)	Number unable to make up 50 hours/year (22%)	Median Weekly Wage	Cost to Employers
Men	837,082	184,166	$ 701	$ 161,375,558
Women	2,540,085	558,843	$ 468	$ 326,923,158
Total	3,377,168	743,009		$ 488,298,715

Source of above tables: *The MetLife Study of Employer Costs for Working Caregivers*, Metropolitan Life Insurance Company, Westport, CT, 1997

Unless the workplace offers some kind of support for the caregiver through assistance programs or other benefits, the employee may not seek help until physical symptoms occur. Thus, health care benefits may end up becoming the major source of corporate support available to most caregivers — a very expensive program for such a purpose.

Caregivers often use their "sick days" or vacation days for caregiving responsibilities. This places the employee in need of such time for his or her own recuperation or recreation, but having it already used up for caregiving. Caregivers are one-third more likely to report their health as "poor."

"Trailing Parents"

Just when corporations were getting used to the "trailing spouse" — the wife or husband whose career puts obstacles in the way of business moves — a new problem has appeared. The graying of America is creating "trailing parents," who pose even greater relocation problems for employees and corporations in an economy that has always depended on a high degree of mobility.

Nobody knows the exact extent of the problem, but already an estimated 20 percent of the work force is responsible for an aging relative, and

TABLE 8.7

	Costs Due to Workday Interruption			
Full-Time Employed Caregivers by Gender (Levels III, IV, and V)	Number experiencing workday interruptions	Hours lost due to interruptions (avg. 50 hr/yr)	Median Weekly Wage	Cost to Employers
Men	1,420,049	71,002,434	$ 701	$ 1,244,317,663
Women	4,309,068	215,453,391	$ 468	$ 2,520,804,670
Total	5,729,117	286,455,825		$ 3,765,122,333

TABLE 8.8

	Costs Due to Eldercare Crises			
Full-Time Employed Caregivers by Gender (Levels III, IV, and V)	Number affected by crises (60%)	Days lost to crises (3 per year)	Median Weekly Wage	Cost to Employers
Men	852,029	2,556,088	$ 701	$ 358,363,487
Women	2,585,441	7,756,322	$ 468	$ 725,991,745
Total	3,437,470	10,312,410		$ 1,084,355,232

TABLE 8.9

	Costs Associated with Supervising Personal Caregivers			
Full-Time Employed Caregivers by Gender (Levels III, IV, and V)	Number with supportive supervisors (81%)	Supervisor's time (12 hours per year)	Median Weekly Wage	Cost to Employers
Men	1,150,239	13,802,873	$ 771	$ 266,084,889
Women	3,490,345	41,884,139	$ 515	$ 539,048,871
Total	4,640,584	55,687,012		$ 805,133,760

Source of above tables: *The MetLife Study of Employer Costs for Working Caregivers*, Metropolitan Life Insurance Company, Westport, CT, 1997

that figure will rise. Companies are beginning to deal with the implications of trailing parents. A few, like Apple Computer, have sometimes agreed to foot the bill for moving elderly relatives rather than settle for a second choice in important personnel appointments.

Meanwhile, corporations are eager for a mobile work force. Companies move ever more people each year. And that does not include the outside talent that companies seek to fill crucial slots. With larger numbers of people looking after elderly relatives, corporations are likely to see some of their choices turn down an offer — even at top levels.

Recruiters report that applicants who are caregivers often drop out of the job-changing market, at least temporarily, or restrict how far they will move, or both. Relocation specialists claim that people often do not volunteer the information that they are caregivers, lest they be left out of the running for promotions. In a 1995 Atlas Van Lines questionnaire, "family ties," cited by 64 percent of respondents, edged out "spousal employment" for two consecutive years as the primary reason employees turned down relocations.

Many companies have not decided how to respond to the elder care problem. IBM, for example, has no formal policy on moving elderly parents

TABLE 8.10

All Costs to Employers		
	Cost per Employee	Total US Employer Costs
Replacing Employees		$ 4,933,816,305
Absenteeism	$ 69	$ 397,596,918
Partial Absenteeism	$ 85	$ 488,298,715
Workday Interruptions	$ 657	$ 3,765,122,333
Eldercare Crises	$ 189	$ 1,084,355,232
Supervisor's Time	$ 141	$ 805,133,760
Total	$ 1,142	$ 11,474,323,263

Source: *The MetLife Study of Employer Costs for Working Caregivers*, Metropolitan Life Insurance Company, Westport, CT, 1997

unless they live with an employee. Then they move with the household. In the Atlas questionnaire, only 3 percent of the companies said they would pay to move an elderly relative of a newly hired employee.

However, sometimes companies disregard the rules and make decisions on an individual basis. When a manager wants a particular employee, a company often makes an exception and pays for a relocation of any family members. They may also arrange for referrals to nursing homes and research doctors, hospitals, and home health aides. This is especially true at the upper management level of companies. That fact alone may explain growing corporate interest in elder care — it affects an increasing number of older, upper-level employees.

Looking for Answers

We don't all have kids, but we all have parents, and at one time or other we'll all get touched by it. — Marie, human resources manager, Bank of America in Texas, 1998

Employers are beginning to understand they are incurring elder care-related costs in terms of lost work time, impaired productivity, higher use of health benefits, higher turnover rates, and size of applicant pools. (Some job seekers do not even apply for some jobs because they know in advance that their caregiving responsibilities will interfere.) Just as employers now recognize the value of addressing child care issues in the workplace, many of them are also looking for ways to deal with the care of elders, as greater numbers of employees become caregivers over the next few years.

In 1995, 21 companies nationwide formed the American Business Collaboration for Quality Dependent Care. The group pledged to spend at least $100 million over six years, in addition to each firm's internal programs, to address child- and elder-care needs. About 20 percent of the funds are being spent on elder care. IBM, one of the member companies, found, from a 1997 survey of its workers, that 28 percent expected to be responsible for care of an older relative in the near future. The objective is to help elderly people live independently as long as possible — and to give working adult children a break. Among the types of services funded are home repair and escorted transportation services.

CHAPTER IX

PROVIDING HEALTH CARE FOR THE ELDERLY

While providing health care for the elderly is an important issue today, it will become a concern of gigantic proportion as the elderly population of the United States increases. The elderly are the biggest group of users of health services, accounting for more than one-third of the nation's total personal health expenditures. Rising costs, demands for additional services, the further development of life-sustaining technologies, and the role of government are, and will continue to be, subjects of intense debate. In this chapter, health care facilities, costs, and private and government health programs are discussed separately, although there is considerable overlap among the areas.

WHERE DO THE ELDERLY GET HEALTH CARE?

Getting proper health care is difficult for many elderly people. Even if they can afford to pay for the best care, and many cannot, they may not be able to find a facility or the skilled health care professionals to provide the services they need. As with living arrangements, there is no single answer as to the best way to deliver health care to the elderly; there are advantages and disadvantages to all the programs.

Home Care

In Their Own Homes

Most Americans prefer to live independently as long as possible. Many elderly people with moderate and even severe health problems manage to remain in their own homes for many years by adjusting their lifestyles, modifying their environments, taking the proper medication, and using outside resources, such as relatives, friends, or paid nurses or caregivers, to assist them.

At some point, most elderly people with health problems will need outside assistance. If family members do not have the time or knowledge to provide the needed care, they must find someone who can. Finding a dependable, skilled caregiver is often very difficult. Paid providers may work directly for clients or for private agencies who contract with the state to serve clients.

Home health care is a rapidly growing industry in today's U.S. health care system. In 1996, almost 1.8 million elderly persons were served by home health care agencies, up from 1.2 million in 1992. Elderly patients were predominantly female (70 percent), in the age group 75 to 84 (47 percent), White (69 percent), widowed (47 percent), living in private residences (92 percent), and living with family members (50 percent). (See Table 9.1.)

The most frequent services rendered were bathing or showering (53 percent), dressing (46 percent), transferring to or from a bed or chair (30 percent), and using the toilet (23 percent) (Table 9.2). The most common instrumental services provided were shopping for groceries or clothes (84 percent), light housework (39 percent), administering medications (23 percent), and preparing meals (23 percent). A few also helped with placing telephone calls and managing money.

TABLE 9.1

Number and percent distribution of elderly home health care current patients 65 years and over by selected demographic characteristics, according to sex: United States, 1996

Demographic characteristic	Both sexes[1]		Male		Female	
	Number	Percent distribution	Number	Percent distribution	Number	Percent distribution
Total	1,753,400	100.0	528,300	100.0	1,224,800	100.0
Age						
65–74 years	527,900	30.1	180,400	34.2	347,500	28.4
75–84 years	820,500	46.8	253,500	48.0	566,800	46.3
85 years and over	404,900	23.1	94,400	17.9	310,600	25.4
Race						
White	1,215,300	69.3	353,900	67.0	861,400	70.3
Black and other	214,000	12.2	65,000	12.3	149,100	12.2
Black	190,900	10.9	56,200	10.7	134,700	11.0
Unknown	324,000	18.5	109,400	20.7	214,400	17.5
Hispanic origin						
Hispanic	47,300	2.7	*17,200	*3.27	*30,100	*2.5
Non-Hispanic	1,134,800	64.7	320,000	60.6	814,800	66.5
Unknown	571,200	32.6	191,000	36.2	379,900	31.0
Marital status						
Married	510,600	29.1	268,200	50.8	242,200	19.8
Widowed	820,200	46.8	102,600	19.4	717,700	58.6
Divorced or separated	49,700	2.8	*18,800	*3.6	*31,000	*2.5
Never married/single	144,100	8.2	*49,000	*9.3	95,100	7.8
Unknown	228,700	13.0	89,800	17.0	138,900	11.3
Living quarters						
Private residence	1,616,600	92.2	496,800	94.1	1,119,500	91.4
Rented room and board	*	*	*	*	*	*
Retirement home	37,700	2.2	*	*	*32,300	*2.6
Board and care or residential care facility	62,900	3.6	*	*	49,800	4.1
Health facility	*	*	*	*	*	*
Other or unknown	*15,900	*0.9	*	*	*	*
Living arrangement						
Family members	881,700	50.3	317,100	60.0	564,400	46.1
Nonfamily members	92,700	5.3	*24,100	*4.0	68,700	5.6
Alone	685,600	39.1	143,100	27.1	542,400	44.3
Other or unknown	*93,400	*5.3	*	4.0	*49,300	*4.0

*Figure does not meet standard of reliability or precision (sample size is less than 30) and therefore not reported. If shown with a number, it should not be assumed reliable because the sample size is between 30–59 or the sample size is greater than 59 but has a relative standard error over 30 percent.

[1]Includes a small number of patients with unknown sex.

NOTES: Numbers may not add to totals because of rounding. Percents are based on the unrounded figures.

Source: "Characteristics of Elderly Home Health Cares Users: Data from the 1996 National Home and Hospice Care Survey," *Advance Data*, no. 309, December 22, 1999

Of those discharged from home health care, most no longer needed the services. Some were stabilized or recovered, some were admitted to hospitals, and others had met their goals (recovered or stabilized to the point that they or another person could resume the activities). Some went on to be transferred to nursing homes, and some died.

Medicare pays only for medically related care. Medicaid or state financed programs, which are means-tested (available only to those with low incomes), finance some non-medical home care, such as bathing, meal preparation, dressing, and toileting — the services that people with chronic conditions like Alzheimer's disease require.

Dramatically rising expenditures caused home health care to consume about $1 of every $12 of Medicare expense in 1997, up dramatically from $1 of every $40 in 1989. Concerns about rising cost and fraud led Congress to pass the Balanced Budget Act of 1997 (PL 105-33). Title IV of that act controls home health care expense by limiting costs and the number of visits allowed. Subsequently, 14 percent of home health care agencies closed, leaving approximately 9,000 agencies,

TABLE 9.2

Number and percent of elderly men and women home health care current patients 65 years and over receiving help with activities of daily living, walking, and instrumental activities of daily living, percent distribution of number of functional activities for which help was received, and percent with continence problem, according to sex: United States, 1996

Functional status	Both sexes[1]	Male	Female
		Number	
Total	1,753,400	528,300	1,224,800
Received personal help with the following ADL's		Percent	
Bathing or showering	53.2	50.9	54.2
Dressing	45.8	43.0	47.1
Eating	9.3	9.4	9.2
Transferring in or out of bed or chair	29.6	30.2	29.3
Using toilet room	22.6	19.7	23.9
Help with walking	30.6	28.4	31.6
Functional status in ADL's		Percent distribution	
Receives no help from agency in ADL's	43.8	45.9	42.9
Receives help from agency in 1 ADL	4.9	*4.8	5.0
Receives help from agency in 2 ADL's	13.8	13.2	14.1
Receives help from agency in 3 ADL's	12.5	12.7	12.4
Receives help from agency in 4 ADL's	9.2	9.1	9.2
Receives help from agency in 5 ADL's	10.6	10.0	10.9
Receives help from agency in 6 ADL's	5.2	*4.4	5.6
Received personal help with the following IADL's		Percent	
Doing light housework	38.9	34.1	41.0
Managing money	2.8	*	*2.8
Shopping for groceries or clothes	84.3	79.5	85.8
Using telephone	2.7	*	*3.1
Preparing meals	23.0	20.1	24.3
Taking medications	23.4	20.7	24.6
Functional status in IADL's		Percent distribution	
Receives no help from agency in IADL's	50.5	54.9	48.6
Receives help from agency in 1 IADL	21.4	20.9	21.6
Receives help from agency in 2 IADL's	11.1	11.3	11.0
Receives help from agency in 3 IADL's	9.9	8.1	10.7
Receives help from agency in 4 IADL's	4.7	*2.8	5.6
Receives help from agency in 5 IADL's	1.6	*	*
Receives help from agency in 6 IADL's	0.8	*	*
Continence status		Percent	
Difficulty controlling bowels	15.0	14.6	15.1
Difficulty controlling bladder	27.4	23.5	29.1
Difficulty controlling both bowels and bladder	11.8	10.7	12.3
Have an ostomy or an indwelling catheter	5.9	*7.8	5.1
Received help in caring for this device	5.8	*7.8	4.9

*Figure does not meet standard of reliability or precision (sample size is less than 30) and therefore not reported. If shown with a number, it should not be assumed reliable because the sample size is between 30–59 or the sample size is greater than 59 but has a relative standard error over 30 percent.

[1] Includes a small number of patients with unknown sex.

NOTE: ADL is activities of daily living and IADL is instrumental activities of daily living.

Source: "Characteristics of Elderly Home Health Cares Users: Data from the 1996 National Home and Hospice Care Survey," *Advance Data*, no. 309, December 22, 1999

about the same as were operating in 1996 (Figure 9.1). The U.S. General Accounting Office, in *Medicare Home Health Agencies: Closures Continue, with Little Evidence Beneficiary Access Is Impaired* (1999), reported, however, that it found no reason to believe that reductions in the numbers of home health care agencies had compromised care. Figure 9.2 shows that home health agencies are generally available throughout the United States, except for a significant number of rural areas.

Paid home health care will become more important in the years ahead. Three factors account for the growth in home health care:

- Advancements in medical technology that allow for care at home at a lower cost than in an institution.

- The enactment of Medicare in 1965, which allowed for payment for certain home services.

• The increase in the number of elderly.

In 1999, the Park Ridge Center, a private research organization, reported that among the more than 500,000 home care workers, most are women, mostly poor, and predominantly Blacks or immigrants. They typically earn the minimum wage and receive no benefits, though unionization and a shortage of workers are changing that in many areas.

The elderly often do not want to burden their families and may ask for less help than they need, even at their own peril. Some home care recipients experience discomfort with the presence of a "stranger" in their house. With paid caregivers, they may feel uneasy with the forced intimacy of sharing their private lives. Others become close to their caregivers.

In the Homes of Others

When chronic health problems prevent elderly people from living alone or with spouses, they may move in with their children or other relatives. Families take ill relatives into their homes because they want to care for them as long as possible or because they cannot find suitable or affordable long-term care facilities. Having an elderly, ill parent or relative in the home can place an emotional and/or financial strain on any family, depending on the type and degree of the health problem. In Alzheimer's cases, for example, the burden can be especially severe and prolonged. (See Chapter VI.)

Younger caregivers, most often daughters and daugh-

ters-in-law, may struggle with divided loyalties, with unequal contributions among siblings, or a history of a poor relationship with the very parent they must care for. On the other hand, caregivers may view these responsibilities as a last gift to the parent who raised them. Many caregivers experience both conflicting sentiments.

Hospitals

While most elderly people receive medical treatment in doctors' offices or health clinics, the incidence of hospitalization rises with age. In 1996, those ages 65 to 74 were hospitalized at a rate of 257.3 per 1,000 people; those 75 and older were hospitalized at the rate of 455.2 per 1,000. These rates compared to 87 per 1,000 for those 15 to 44

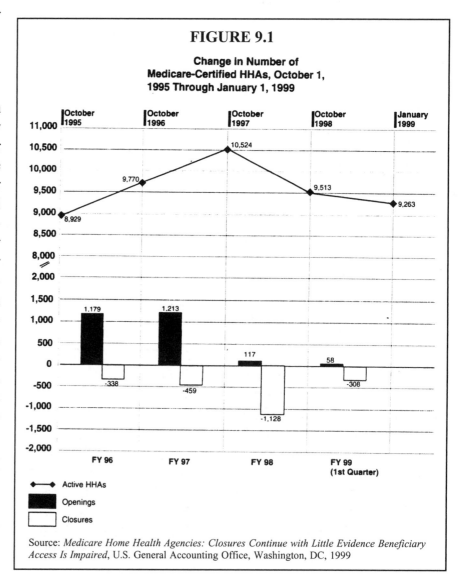

FIGURE 9.1

Change in Number of Medicare-Certified HHAs, October 1, 1995 Through January 1, 1999

Source: *Medicare Home Health Agencies: Closures Continue with Little Evidence Beneficiary Access Is Impaired*, U.S. General Accounting Office, Washington, DC, 1999

148

FIGURE 9.2

Counties With No HHAs on January 1, 1999

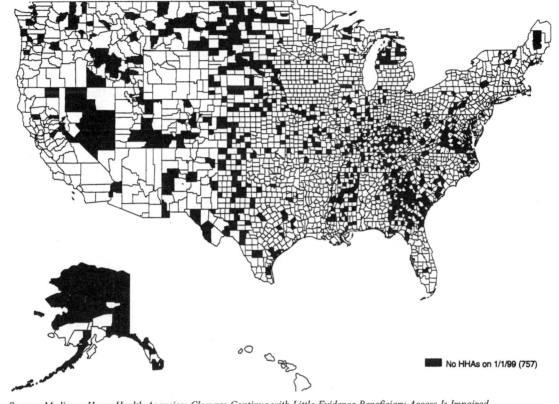

No HHAs on 1/1/99 (757)

Source: *Medicare Home Health Agencies: Closures Continue with Little Evidence Beneficiary Access Is Impaired*, U.S. General Accounting Office, Washington, DC, 1999

years of age and 117.2 per 1,000 for those 45 to 64. The average length of stay in 1996 was 6.2 days for those 65 to 74 years old and 6.8 days for those older than 75 years. As with the general population, the average stay of those over 65 has been shortening over the past decade and a half — from 10.7 days in 1980 to 6.5 days in 1996. (See Table 9.3.)

Part of the cost of hospitalization for most elderly patients is covered under Medicare. After the enactment of the Diagnosis Related Groups (DRG) system (see *How Medicare Pays*, below), Medicare payments to hospitals fell below many of the hospitals' own expenses. This led hospitals to make the patient's stay as short as possible in order to make treatment more profitable. It also forced some community hospitals to close. Most of the closures have been in rural communities.

Hospices

Hospice care is a program of care involving physical, psychological, social, and spiritual care for dying persons, their families, and other loved ones. Hospice services are available in both home and inpatient settings. Those persons in hospice care are generally there for relatively short periods of time. Hospices provide skilled nursing care and pain relief for those who are terminally ill (less than six months to live). Hospice is not intended to treat the illness.

The Centers for Disease Control and Prevention (CDC) reported that, in 1996, almost 60,000 patients were treated in hospices in the United States. About 78 percent of those were 65 and older. Somewhat more women (55.1 percent) than men (44.9 percent) were treated in hospices. The great-

TABLE 9.3

Discharges, days of care, and average length of stay in non-Federal short-stay hospitals, according to selected characteristics: United States, selected years 1980–96

[Data are based on a sample of hospital records]

Characteristic	1980[1]	1985[1]	1990	1992	1993[2]	1994	1995	1996
	Discharges per 1,000 population							
Total[3]	158.5	137.7	113.0	110.5	107.6	106.5	104.7	102.3
Sex[3]								
Male	140.3	124.4	100.9	98.6	95.2	94.2	92.3	89.7
Female	177.0	151.8	126.0	123.2	120.5	119.1	117.4	115.3
Age								
Under 15 years	71.6	57.7	44.6	45.2	37.7	39.2	41.7	38.2
15–44 years	150.1	125.0	101.6	96.0	95.4	93.2	89.8	87.0
45–64 years	194.8	170.8	135.0	131.0	126.8	124.1	118.2	117.2
65 years and over	383.7	369.8	330.9	336.5	341.6	341.6	344.6	346.1
65–74 years	315.8	297.2	259.1	264.5	262.2	261.6	257.6	257.3
75 years and over	489.3	475.6	429.9	432.7	446.3	445.3	455.2	455.2
Geographic region[3]								
Northeast	147.6	129.1	121.0	123.9	118.3	121.3	120.0	112.6
Midwest	175.4	143.4	115.1	105.3	102.2	102.6	99.5	99.6
South	165.1	143.5	119.2	116.3	116.9	111.8	110.9	105.7
West	136.9	130.3	92.1	93.7	87.6	87.6	86.0	90.3
	Days of care per 1,000 population							
Total[3]	1,129.0	872.1	705.0	659.3	626.9	594.0	544.3	520.6
Sex[3]								
Male	1,076.0	848.2	690.4	656.3	616.3	580.8	533.1	511.8
Female	1,187.1	902.0	725.3	667.5	640.5	609.5	556.7	531.6
Age								
Under 15 years	315.7	263.0	215.4	219.6	195.5	189.2	185.6	174.4
15–44 years	786.8	603.3	465.3	416.1	399.3	390.4	346.0	333.9
45–64 years	1,596.9	1,201.6	911.5	827.1	785.0	727.5	655.6	624.3
65 years and over	4,098.4	3,228.0	2,867.7	2,771.7	2,676:2	2,516.3	2,352.4	2,263.7
65–74 years	3,147.0	2,437.3	2,067.7	2,040.8	1,927.1	1,798.8	1,669.0	1,603.8
75 years and over	5,578.7	4,381.4	3,970.7	3,747.8	3,664.6	3,445.7	3,220.1	3,074.7
Geographic region[3]								
Northeast	1,204.7	953.5	878.0	838.6	787.2	774.9	722.1	666.9
Midwest	1,296.2	952.0	713.4	626.2	600.5	553.9	502.9	484.4
South	1,105.5	848.9	704.1	676.2	655.1	618.0	564.9	532.2
West	836.2	713.2	509.9	483.1	445.2	420.3	385.2	402.5
	Average length of stay in days							
Total[3]	7.1	6.3	6.2	6.0	5.8	5.6	5.2	5.1
Sex[3]								
Male	7.7	6.8	6.8	6.7	6.5	6.2	5.8	5.7
Female	6.7	5.9	5.8	5.4	5.3	5.1	4.7	4.6
Age								
Under 15 years	4.4	4.6	4.8	4.9	5.2	4.8	4.5	4.6
15–44 years	5.2	4.8	4.6	4.3	4.2	4.2	3.9	3.8
45–64 years	8.2	7.0	6.8	6.3	6.2	5.9	5.5	5.3
65 years and over	10.7	8.7	8.7	8.2	7.8	7.4	6.8	6.5
65–74 years	10.0	8.2	8.0	7.7	7.3	6.9	6.5	6.2
75 years and over	11.4	9.2	9.2	8.7	8.2	7.7	7.1	6.8
Geographic region[3]								
Northeast	8.2	7.4	7.3	6.8	6.7	6.4	6.0	5.9
Midwest	7.4	6.6	6.2	5.9	5.9	5.4	5.1	4.9
South	6.7	5.9	5.9	5.8	5.6	5.5	5.1	5.0
West	6.1	5.5	5.5	5.2	5.1	4.8	4.5	4.5

[1]Comparisons of data from 1980–85 with data from later years should be made with caution as estimates of change may reflect improvements in the design rather than true changes in hospital use.
[2]In 1993 children's hospitals had a high rate of nonresponse that may have resulted in underestimates of hospital utilization by children.
[3]Age adjusted.

NOTES: Rates are based on the civilian population as of July 1. Estimates of hospital utilization from the National Health Interview Survey (NHIS) and the National Hospital Discharge Survey (NHDS) may differ because NHIS data are based on household interviews of the civilian noninstitutionalized population and exclude deliveries, whereas NHDS data are based on hospital discharge records of all persons. NHDS includes records for persons discharged alive or deceased and institutionalized persons, and excludes newborn infants. Differences in hospital utilization estimated by the two surveys are particularly evident for the elderly and for women.

Source: *Health, United States, 1998*, National Center for Health Statistics, Hyattsville, MD, 1999

est proportion of cases (58.3 percent) were being treated for cancer (malignant neoplasms). (See Table 9.4.)

In 1997, most of the hospices (88 percent) were nonprofit, only 5 percent were proprietary (for-profit), and 6.7 percent were owned by government

TABLE 9.4

Home health care and hospice patients, according to selected characteristics: United States, 1992–96

[Data are based on a survey of current home health care and hospice patients]

Type of patient and characteristic	1992	1994	1996
Home health care patients	Number of current patients		
Total.	1,232,200	1,879,510	2,427,483
Age at admission[1]:	Percent distribution		
Under 65 years	24.1	27.2	27.5
65 years and over	75.9	72.8	72.5
65–74 years.	24.5	22.0	21.8
75–84 years.	34.0	31.1	33.9
85 years and over	17.5	19.7	16.7
Sex:			
Male.	33.2	32.5	32.9
Female.	66.8	67.5	67.1
Primary admission diagnosis[2]:			
Malignant neoplasms.	5.7	5.7	4.8
Diabetes.	7.7	8.1	8.5
Diseases of the nervous system and sense organs.	6.3	8.0	5.8
Diseases of the circulatory system	25.9	27.2	25.6
Diseases of heart.	12.6	14.3	10.9
Cerebrovascular diseases	5.8	6.1	7.8
Diseases of the respiratory system	6.6	6.1	7.7
Decubitus ulcers	1.9	1.1	1.0
Diseases of the musculoskeletal system and connective tissue	9.4	8.3	8.8
Osteoarthritis	2.5	2.8	3.2
Fractures, all sites.	3.8	3.7	3.3
Fracture of neck of femur (hip).	1.4	1.7	1.3
Other	32.7	31.8	34.6
Hospice patients	Number of current patients		
Total.	52,100	60,783	59,363
Age at admission[1]:	Percent distribution		
Under 65 years	20.4	31.2	22.1
65 years and over	79.6	68.8	77.9
65–74 years.	27.4	23.1	24.6
75–84 years.	39.1	29.0	31.9
85 years and over	13.0	16.7	21.4
Sex:			
Male.	46.1	44.7	44.9
Female.	53.9	55.3	55.1
Primary admission diagnosis[2]:			
Malignant neoplasms.	65.7	57.2	58.3
Malignant neoplasms of large intestine and rectum	9.0	8.0	4.0
Malignant neoplasms of trachea, bronchus, and lung	21.1	12.5	15.8
Malignant neoplasm of breast	3.9	4.8	6.2
Malignant neoplasm of prostate	6.0	5.9	6.6
Diseases of heart	10.2	9.3	8.3
Diseases of the respiratory system	4.3	6.6	7.3
Other	19.8	27.0	26.1

[1]Denominator excludes persons with unknown age.
[2]Denominator excludes persons with unknown diagnosis.

NOTES: Current home health care and hospice patients are those who were under the care of their agency on any given day during the survey period. Diagnostic categories are based on the *International Classification of Diseases, 9th Revision, Clinical Modification*. For a listing of the code numbers, see Appendix II, table VII.

Source: *Health, United States, 1998*, National Center for Health Statistics, Hyattsville, MD, 1999

agencies. Most (66 percent) of the hospices were certified by Medicare; Medicaid had certified 57 percent. (Medicaid/ Medicare had approved the hospices for payment by their programs.)

NURSING HOMES — A REVOLUTION IN PROGRESS

Nursing homes provide long-term care for those with health problems so severe that they re-quire specialized, intensive, or prolonged medical treatment.

The Declining Nursing Home Population

Approximately 5 percent of the population 65 years and older reside in nursing homes at any one time, but more may have lived in nursing homes at some period during their lifetimes. In 1999, approximately 17,000 nursing homes provided care for 1.6 million residents. The majority of elderly nursing home residents were female, over age 75, White, and widowed. About 60 percent were 65 to 84 years of age, and 40 percent were over the age of 85.

In the 1980s, many investors assumed that growing numbers of elderly would lead to rapid increases in nursing home populations. As a result, they added 147,000 nursing home beds between 1985 and 1995 to accommodate an expected 2.1 million elderly. The occupancy rate, however, fell from 92 percent to 87 percent over that time because many of the elderly suffered less disability and were able to live elsewhere, and many nursing homes turned out to be poor investments.

Many experts, however, believe that nursing home use has declined for another reason — there are better options. With disability rates declining, the elderly are able to be treated in assisted living centers or, with home health care, in their own homes.

Length of Stay

Contrary to popular belief, people do not necessarily go to nursing homes to die. In fact, in 1995, residents were discharged after an average stay of 838 days, compared to 1,026 days in 1985. This decline in nursing home use is likely due to the increases in availability of home care services. While most nursing home residents are there because they suffer from serious health problems, some have problems that would not normally require institutionalization. Their needs may not be primarily medical, but they have nowhere else to go. They are usually poor and/or have no one in the community who is able or willing to care for them. Many of these can now be cared for by home health care providers.

The Cost of Nursing Home Care

Nursing home care is expensive. An average one-year stay in a nursing home costs more than $43,300. Most nursing home residents rely on Medicaid. The second most common source of payment at admission is private insurance, own income, or family support, followed by Medicare. The primary source of payment changes as a stay lengthens. After their funds are "spent down," many of those on Medicare shift to Medicaid, until more than half are Medicaid-funded.

Conditions Have Improved . . . Somewhat

For some people, the prospect of living in a nursing home is terrifying. The unsavory reputation of some nursing homes is not entirely undeserved. However, living conditions in these facilities have improved over the past few years. Both physical conditions and workers' attitudes towards residents have improved as a result of media attention, government regulation, demands by families, and the concern of the nursing home industry itself.

The industry recognizes the potential market of an aging population and is anxious to convey a positive image. A major problem is retaining good employees. Next to child-care facilities, nursing homes have the highest employee turnover rate of any occupation, especially among unskilled and semi-skilled workers. Nursing home aides, the people who provide most of the direct patient care, are very poorly paid. In most areas of the country, a person can earn a higher hourly wage at a fast-food restaurant than in a nursing home.

Competition in the Industry

In order to stay competitive with the growing home care industry and the increasing array of services available for the elderly, nursing homes have tried to reinvent themselves, offering additional programs and services along with traditional institutional care. Among those services are adult day care, visiting nurses, respite care (short-term stays when primary caregivers are not available, as on a vacation), transportation, and minimal care apartment units. Craig Duncan, executive director of the Eddy Nursing Home in Troy, New York, explained,

We are moving away from an institutional base except for the frailest population, and that's because we have better-educated older consumers telling us what they want, and that is to stay out of a nursing home. If we want to maintain and gain a share of that market — and let's face it, all of us are revenue-driven — we had better respond.

Sub-Acute Care

In order to make nursing homes more profitable, nursing home operators have begun to compete with hospitals for sub-acute care patients. Patients recovering from cancer, heart bypass operations, joint replacement surgery, or serious accidents are increasingly receiving post-operative therapy in nursing homes rather than in hospitals because nursing home care is less expensive. The average daily charges for sub-acute care in nursing homes range from $300 to $550; the same treatment in hospitals costs between $700 and $1,000. Health care analysts estimate that 10 to 20 percent of general acute-care hospital patients could be cared for in sub-acute units of nursing homes. Thousands of nursing home beds are being shifted from caring for lower-profit traditional patients to providing for people who no longer need the services of acute-care hospitals but who are still too sick to go home.

The Crisis in Nursing Home Care

Most industry analysts believe progress has been made in meeting the health care demands of an aging population. Nonetheless, governmental budget cuts to Medicare, Medicaid, and Social Security, along with attempts in Congress to lessen regulation, may threaten the quality of long-term care. The American Association of Retired Persons (AARP), the nation's largest organization of older people, predicted that more than two million people could lose coverage for long-term care — including nursing home coverage and assistance at home — if budget cuts occur. The supporters of less regulation counter that strict regulation is no longer necessary and that free-market conditions will both improve the quality of care and decrease the cost of nursing home care.

THE HIGH COST OF HEALTH CARE FOR THE ELDERLY

The elderly make up 12 percent of the U.S. population, but account for one-third of total personal health care expenditures (money spent for the direct consumption of health care goods and services). In 1998, health care spending — more than $1,149 billion — was approximately 13.5 percent of gross domestic product (GDP), a proportion that has remained relatively stable since 1993 (Table 9.5).

An Especially Severe Burden on the Elderly

The cost of health care in the United States is a serious problem for the elderly. Health care is the only budget expense for the elderly that is both a higher percentage of their income and a greater dollar amount than for the nonelderly. Many elderly Americans are forced into poverty paying for health care for themselves or for loved ones. Before a family can qualify for some forms of assistance, such as Medicaid, it must often "spend down," that is, spend its assets to the poverty level. This often leaves the surviving spouse and families in financial ruin. In 1995, Robert M. Ball, chairman of the National Academy of Social Insurance, a non-profit research organization in Washington, DC, stated,

Sometime in the not-too-distant future, we will get a major national program protecting families against the cost of long term care.... I expect it to come, not primarily because of the potential power of the elderly ... but because of pressure from those middle-aged, the sons and daughters of the elderly. They are the ones most at risk.

Where Does the Money Go?

The typical person 65 to 74 years of age spends 10.5 percent of his/her expenditures on health care,

TABLE 9.5

National Health Expenditures, Aggregate And Per Capita Amounts, And Share Of Gross Domestic Product (GDP), Selected Calendar Years 1980–1998

Spending category	1980	1990	1993	1994	1995	1996	1997	1998
National health expenditures								
(NHE, billions)	$247.3	$699.4	$898.5	$947.7	$993.3	$1,039.4	$1,088.2	$1,149.1
Real NHE[a]	409.6	747.2	875.7	901.8	923.9	948.9	975.4	1,019.5
Health services and								
supplies	235.6	674.8	869.5	917.3	962.5	1,007.5	1,053.5	1,113.7
Personal health care	217.0	614.7	790.5	834.0	879.1	924.0	968.6	1,019.3
Hospital care	102.7	256.4	323.0	335.7	347.0	359.4	370.2	382.8
Physician services	45.2	146.3	185.9	193.0	201.9	208.5	217.8	229.5
Dental services	13.3	31.6	39.5	42.4	45.0	47.5	51.1	53.8
Other professional								
services	6.4	34.7	46.1	49.6	53.6	57.4	61.5	66.6
Home health care[b]	2.4	13.1	23.0	26.2	29.1	31.2	30.5	29.3
Drugs and other								
medical nondurables	21.6	59.9	76.2	81.5	88.6	98.0	108.6	121.9
Prescription drugs	12.0	37.7	50.6	55.2	61.0	68.9	78.5	90.6
Vision products and								
other medical								
durables	3.8	10.5	12.3	12.6	13.3	14.1	15.1	15.5
Nursing home care[b]	17.6	50.9	66.4	71.1	75.5	80.2	84.7	87.8
Other personal health								
care	4.0	11.2	18.0	21.9	25.1	27.6	29.2	32.1
Program administration								
and net cost of private								
health insurance	11.9	40.5	53.7	55.2	53.6	52.1	50.3	57.7
Government public								
health activities	6.7	19.6	25.3	28.2	29.8	31.3	34.6	36.6
Research and								
construction	11.6	24.5	29.0	30.4	30.8	32.0	34.8	35.3
Research[c]	5.5	12.2	14.5	15.9	16.7	17.2	17.9	19.9
Construction	6.2	12.3	14.5	14.6	14.0	14.8	16.9	15.5
NHE per capita	$1,052	$2,689	$3,350	$3,501	$3,637	$3,772	$3,912	$4,094
Population (millions)	235	260	268	271	273	276	278	281
GDP, billions	$2,784	$5,744	$6,558	$6,947	$7,270	$7,662	$8,111	$8,511
Chain-weighted GDP index	60.4	93.6	102.6	105.1	107.5	109.5	111.6	112.7
NHE as percent of GDP	8.9%	12.2%	13.7%	13.6%	13.7%	13.6%	13.4%	13.5%

SOURCES: Health Care Financing Administration, Office of the Actuary, National Health Statistics Group; U.S. Department of Commerce, Bureau of Economic Analysis; and Social Security Administration.

NOTE: Numbers may not add to totals because of rounding.

[a] Deflated using the GDP chain-type price index (1992 = 100.0).

[b] Freestanding facilities only. Additional services of this type are provided in hospital-based facilities and counted as hospital care.

[c] Research and development expenditures of drug companies and other manufacturers and providers of medical equipment and supplies are excluded from research expenditures but are included in the expenditure class in which the product falls.

Source: Health Care Financing Administration, Baltimore, MD, 1999

while the average person 75 years of age and over spends 14 percent. Of this expenditure, health insurance accounts for 47 percent; medical services, 31.4 percent; physicians' services, 10.8 percent; and prescription drugs, 18.7 percent. Costs increase with age in all categories of service. People over 85 spend, by far, the greatest amount per capita on health care.

Where Does the Money Come From?

Almost all Americans 65 years and older receive some help with medical expenses from government programs, such as Medicare and Medicaid (see below), and/or are covered by private medical insurance. Many elderly people mistakenly believe that Medicare will pay for all their health costs.

No single government or private program covers all health costs. It is possible, however, to obtain total, or almost total, financial coverage for medical costs with a combination of government programs, private health insurance, and out-of-pocket payments by the patient. The cost of such a package, though, can be prohibitive for many elderly people, and qualifications for enrollment in some programs may be difficult or impossible to meet. Figure 9.3 shows the sources of health care coverage in 1998.

In 1997, about one-fifth of those 65 and older had Medicare only, around 70 percent had private insurance, and 7.5 percent of those 65 to 74 and 8.4 percent of those 75 and over had Medicaid. (See Table 9.6.) Those over 65 who qualify for Medicaid also receive Medicare, and most over 65 who have private insurance also have Medicare. In 1998, only 1.1 percent of all people over 65 and 3.2 percent of poor older Americans had no health insurance (Figure 9.4). In addition, the family of an elderly person often pays for nursing home care out of their pockets.

GOVERNMENT HEALTH CARE PROGRAMS

The United States is one of the few industrialized nations that does not have a national health care program. In most other developed countries, government programs cover almost all health-related costs, from maternity care to long-term care.

In the United States, the two major government health care programs are Medicare and Medicaid. They provide financial assistance for the elderly, the poor, and the disabled. Before the existence of these programs, a large number of older Americans could not afford adequate medical care.

Medicare

The spirit in which this law is written draws deeply upon the ancient dreams of all mankind. In Leviticus, it is written, "Thou shall rise up before the hoary head, and honor the face of an old man." — Russell B.

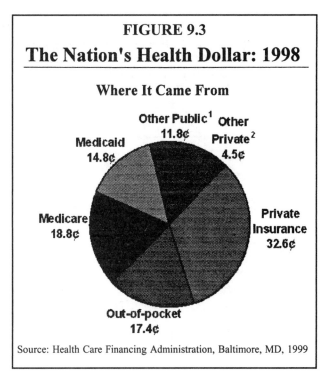

FIGURE 9.3

The Nation's Health Dollar: 1998

Where It Came From

Source: Health Care Financing Administration, Baltimore, MD, 1999

Long, Democratic Senator, Louisiana, at the original vote for Medicare in 1965

The Medicare program, enacted under Title XVIII ("Health Insurance for the Aged") of the Social Security Act, was signed into law by President Lyndon Johnson and went into effect on July 1, 1966. That year, 19 million elderly entered the program. Today, Medicare provides insurance coverage for about 39 million persons 65 and older. The Health Care Financing Administration forecasts that, by 2017, more than 56 million elderly will be enrolled in Medicare. (See Figure 9.5.)

The program is composed of two parts.

- Part A provides hospital insurance. Coverage includes doctors' fees, nursing services, meals, a semiprivate room, special care units, operating room costs, laboratory tests, and some drugs and supplies. Part A also covers rehabilitation services, limited post-hospital skilled nursing facility care, home health care, and hospice care for the terminally ill.

- Part B (Supplemental Medical Insurance or SMI) is elective medical insurance; enrollees must pay premiums to get coverage. It covers

TABLE 9.6

TABLE 9.6

(page 1 of 2). Health care coverage for persons 65 years of age and over, according to type of coverage and selected characteristics: United States, selected years 1984–97

[Data are based on household interviews of a sample of the civilian noninstitutionalized population]

Characteristic	Private insurance[1]						Private insurance obtained through workplace[1,2]					
	1984	1989	1994[3]	1995	1996	1997[3,4]	1984	1989	1994[3]	1995	1996	1997[3,4]
	Number in millions											
Total[5]	19.4	22.4	24.0	23.5	22.9	22.3	10.2	11.2	12.5	12.5	12.1	12.0
	Percent of population											
Total, age adjusted[5]	73.5	76.6	77.5	74.9	72.0	69.6	39.1	38.8	41.0	40.1	38.6	38.2
Total, crude[5]	73.3	76.5	77.3	74.8	72.0	69.5	38.8	38.4	40.4	39.6	38.1	37.5
Age												
65–74 years	76.5	78.2	78.4	75.3	72.4	69.9	45.1	43.7	45.6	43.3	41.5	42.0
75 years and over	68.1	73.9	75.8	74.2	71.3	69.1	28.6	30.2	33.0	34.3	33.3	31.6
75–84 years	70.8	75.9	77.9	76.0	73.3	70.2	30.8	32.0	35.0	36.1	35.5	33.2
85 years and over	56.8	65.5	67.9	67.8	63.9	64.7	18.9	22.8	25.1	27.5	25.3	25.6
Sex[6]												
Male	74.3	77.5	78.9	76.5	73.6	72.0	44.2	43.4	45.1	44.3	42.7	42.9
Female	72.9	76.2	76.5	73.9	71.0	67.8	35.7	35.6	38.1	37.0	35.5	34.9
Race[6,7]												
White	76.8	80.3	81.2	78.6	75.3	72.9	40.9	40.3	42.7	41.6	39.8	39.1
Black	42.3	43.0	44.7	41.9	44.0	43.5	24.0	24.9	26.5	26.4	30.1	32.1
Hispanic origin and race[6,7]												
All Hispanic	40.5	44.6	51.2	40.9	38.6	31.9	25.4	24.3	22.1	20.1	19.4	19.0
Mexican	41.4	36.6	44.6	33.0	35.6	32.4	25.5	22.4	23.1	17.4	18.7	19.0
White, non-Hispanic	77.9	81.5	82.6	80.7	77.2	75.0	41.4	40.9	43.8	42.9	40.8	40.2
Black, non-Hispanic	42.0	43.1	45.2	41.7	44.8	43.7	23.8	24.9	26.8	26.1	30.7	32.1
Percent of poverty level[6,8]												
Below 100 percent	43.0	45.3	40.1	36.8	32.7	31.0	13.4	11.5	10.6	11.3	10.2	7.3
100–149 percent	67.3	66.7	68.0	67.4	58.8	53.2	27.8	22.4	25.2	25.3	22.3	17.2
150–199 percent	78.6	81.1	81.3	77.4	75.0	69.0	41.4	39.8	37.3	39.9	37.3	32.9
200 percent or more	85.7	86.2	88.9	86.6	84.0	81.4	52.8	51.5	54.0	51.7	49.9	49.4
Geographic region[6]												
Northeast	76.8	76.7	78.3	76.0	72.9	73.0	43.9	44.2	45.2	45.3	42.5	43.8
Midwest	79.6	82.3	84.6	82.5	80.8	78.5	40.6	41.4	43.6	46.0	42.3	41.9
South	68.0	73.5	71.2	71.6	67.2	66.3	35.3	33.5	36.8	35.1	34.7	34.2
West	70.8	75.1	78.2	69.3	69.0	59.5	38.2	38.5	40.1	34.9	36.2	34.4
Location of residence[6]												
Within MSA[9]	74.5	77.2	78.0	75.1	72.2	68.4	42.3	41.6	42.6	42.0	40.5	39.8
Outside MSA[9]	71.8	75.1	76.0	74.4	71.3	73.6	33.7	31.3	36.5	33.5	32.2	33.0

See footnotes at end of table.

(continued)

private physicians' services, diagnostic tests, outpatient hospital services, outpatient physical therapy, speech pathology services, home health services, and medical equipment and supplies.

In 1996, the average enrollee received $3,759 in benefits, although, in a typical year, approximately 17 percent of the elderly covered by Medicare do not file a single claim. The fastest growing segment of Medicare enrollees is the over-85 age group. The impact of an aging Medicare population on health care expenditures is significant since, on the average, the aged tend to be sicker and incur much greater expense per capita.

How Medicare Pays

Doctors are reimbursed on a fee-for-service basis. This system presents a number of problems. Because of paperwork, inadequate compensation, and delays in reimbursements, some doctors will not provide service under the Medicare program. The (George) Bush Administration initiated a fee schedule that went into effect in 1992 that substantially cut payments to doctors. Critics claim such reductions have made it harder for elderly people to gain access to health care because fewer doctors will participate in the program. However, as of January 1998, the law allowed doctors to contract privately with Medicare enrollees for ser-

TABLE 9.6 (Continued)

(page 2 of 2). Health care coverage for persons 65 years of age and over, according to type of coverage and selected characteristics: United States, selected years 1984–97

[Data are based on household interviews of a sample of the civilian noninstitutionalized population]

Characteristic	Medicaid[1,10]						Medicare only[11]					
	1984	1989	1994[3]	1995	1996	1997[3,4]	1984	1989	1994[3]	1995	1996	1997[3,4]
	Number in millions											
Total[5]	1.8	2.0	2.5	2.9	2.7	2.5	4.7	4.5	4.1	4.6	5.7	6.7
	Percent of population											
Total, age adjusted[5]	6.9	7.0	7.8	9.0	8.3	7.8	17.7	15.3	13.1	14.7	18.1	20.7
Total, crude[5]	7.0	7.0	7.9	9.2	8.5	7.9	17.9	15.4	13.2	14.8	18.1	20.8
Age												
65–74 years	6.0	6.3	6.8	8.3	7.5	7.5	15.2	13.8	12.3	14.4	18.0	20.3
75 years and over	8.5	8.2	9.6	10.4	9.9	8.4	22.3	17.8	14.5	15.2	18.2	21.5
75–84 years.............	7.7	7.9	8.4	9.5	9.0	7.9	20.6	16.2	13.3	14.1	16.8	20.5
85 years and over	11.7	9.7	14.2	13.7	13.0	10.2	29.8	24.9	19.1	19.3	23.4	25.2
Sex[6]												
Male.....................	4.5	5.0	4.7	5.6	5.5	5.2	17.4	14.6	12.9	14.4	17.1	19.6
Female..................	8.6	8.4	10.0	11.5	10.4	9.7	18.1	15.6	13.3	14.9	18.7	21.5
Race[6,7]												
White	5.0	5.4	6.0	6.9	6.6	6.4	16.5	13.4	11.6	13.4	16.9	19.2
Black	24.9	20.4	21.7	26.8	21.8	19.3	30.7	34.5	28.7	28.6	30.1	33.9
Hispanic origin and race[6,7]												
All Hispanic................	24.9	25.6	26.5	31.1	28.9	27.6	28.5	21.6	18.7	24.5	29.0	34.9
White, non-Hispanic..........	4.4	4.7	5.1	5.6	5.4	5.4	16.1	13.1	11.3	12.8	16.3	18.3
Black, non-Hispanic..........	25.2	20.4	21.2	27.0	21.7	19.0	30.8	34.5	28.8	28.7	29.3	34.0
Percent of poverty level[6,8]												
Below 100 percent...........	28.0	29.0	37.4	40.6	39.9	41.0	27.5	26.0	23.0	22.1	25.6	26.9
100–149 percent............	6.9	9.2	10.8	13.3	12.5	14.6	22.5	21.1	19.0	18.3	26.6	28.6
150–199 percent............	3.3	4.7	3.8	5.2	4.6	5.1	16.2	13.5	12.8	16.2	19.6	23.1
200 percent or more	1.8	2.3	1.8	1.8	1.9	2.5	11.0	10.4	7.8	9.9	12.4	15.0
Geographic region[6]												
Northeast	5.3	5.4	7.3	8.9	7.3	6.4	17.1	16.8	14.0	15.4	20.3	19.5
Midwest	4.2	3.6	3.7	5.6	5.1	5.0	15.2	13.4	10.7	10.9	12.8	15.2
South....................	9.5	9.1	10.3	10.8	9.9	9.7	19.8	16.3	16.0	15.8	19.7	21.3
West	7.9	9.3	9.4	10.8	10.8	9.9	18.4	13.8	10.3	17.3	18.6	28.5
Location of residence[6]												
Within MSA[9]	6.2	6.4	7.3	8.4	7.7	7.4	17.6	15.3	12.9	14.9	18.7	22.2
Outside MSA[9]	8.1	8.4	9.2	11.1	10.4	9.2	17.9	15.2	13.9	14.1	15.9	15.6

[1]Almost all persons 65 years of age and over are covered by Medicare also. In 1997, 92 percent of older persons with private insurance also had Medicare.
[2]Private insurance originally obtained through a present or former employer or union.
[3]The questionnaire changed compared with previous years. See Appendix II, Health insurance coverage.
[4]Preliminary data.
[5]Includes all other races not shown separately and unknown poverty level.
[6]Age adjusted. See Appendix II for age-adjustment procedure.
[7]The race groups white and black include persons of Hispanic and non-Hispanic origin; persons of Hispanic origin may be of any race.
[8]Poverty level is based on family income and family size using Bureau of the Census poverty thresholds. See Appendix II.
[9]Metropolitan statistical area.
[10]Includes public assistance through 1996. In 1997 includes state-sponsored health plans. In 1997 the age-adjusted percent of the population 65 years of age and over covered by Medicaid was 7.4 percent, and 0.4 percent were covered by state-sponsored health plans.
[11]Persons covered by Medicare but not covered by private health insurance, Medicaid, public assistance (through 1996), state-sponsored or other government-sponsored health plans (1997), or military plans. See Appendix II, Health insurance coverage.

NOTE: Percents do not add to 100 because persons with both private health insurance and Medicaid appear in more than one column, and because the percent of persons without health insurance (1.1 percent in 1997) is not shown.

Source: *Health, United States, 1998*, National Center for Health Statistics, Hyattsville, MD, 1999

vices covered by Medicare (patients agree to pay the doctor out of their own pocket).

Since 1983, hospitals have received reimbursement under the prospective payment system (PPS), in which a Medicare patient is classified into one of 477 diagnosis-related groups (DRGs) for which there is a fixed, pre-determined payment. Hospitals that can provide care for less than the payment keep the difference; those whose costs run over the payment must absorb the loss.

Many health care and elderly advocacy organizations and members of Congress are concerned that PPS may be affecting the care Medicare patients receive. Since hospitals are paid a fixed reimbursement for a DRG regardless of their expenses, they may find it expedient to provide less service than necessary, to discharge a patient sooner than usual, or not to admit certain patients. Several studies have found that such cost control measures have not resulted in reduced quality of care while an elderly patient was hospitalized but did increase the likelihood that the elderly patient would be discharged in a medically unstable condition.

Providing Only Limited Protection

Medicare has been an extremely successful program. In 1965, when President Johnson signed the bill creating it into law, only half of America's elderly had any health insurance. Today, Medicare pays hospital and doctor bills for more than 38.6 million Americans over 65 — approximately 97 percent of the elderly — making this age group the only one in America with virtually universal coverage. Medicare, along with increased Social Security benefits, has helped transform a group that has suffered from high rates of poverty into a more economically secure group.

Medicare, however, does not provide complete health care coverage. The basic plan does not pay for basic medical expenses such as

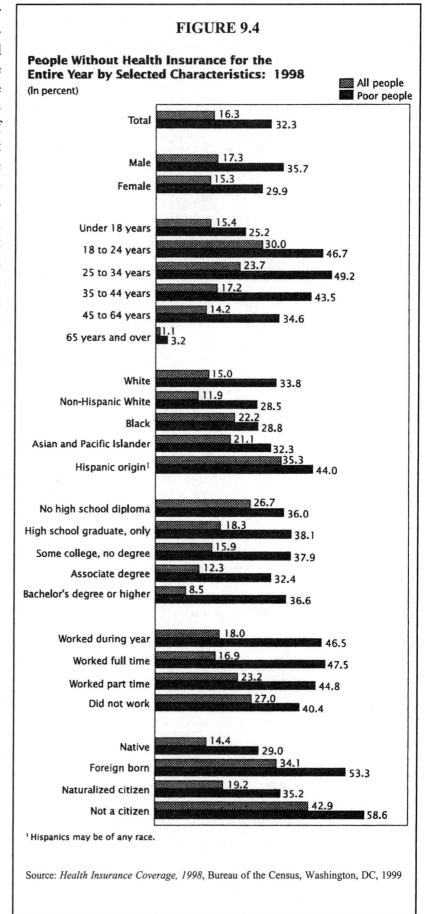

FIGURE 9.4

People Without Health Insurance for the Entire Year by Selected Characteristics: 1998
(In percent)

■ All people
■ Poor people

	All people	Poor people
Total	16.3	32.3
Male	17.3	35.7
Female	15.3	29.9
Under 18 years	15.4	25.2
18 to 24 years	30.0	46.7
25 to 34 years	23.7	49.2
35 to 44 years	17.2	43.5
45 to 64 years	14.2	34.6
65 years and over	1.1	3.2
White	15.0	33.8
Non-Hispanic White	11.9	28.5
Black	22.2	28.8
Asian and Pacific Islander	21.1	32.3
Hispanic origin[1]	35.3	44.0
No high school diploma	26.7	36.0
High school graduate, only	18.3	38.1
Some college, no degree	15.9	37.9
Associate degree	12.3	32.4
Bachelor's degree or higher	8.5	36.6
Worked during year	18.0	46.5
Worked full time	16.9	47.5
Worked part time	23.2	44.8
Did not work	27.0	40.4
Native	14.4	29.0
Foreign born	34.1	53.3
Naturalized citizen	19.2	35.2
Not a citizen	42.9	58.6

[1] Hispanics may be of any race.

Source: *Health Insurance Coverage, 1998*, Bureau of the Census, Washington, DC, 1999

routine physical examinations, prescription drugs, eyeglasses, prostheses (artificial body parts), and, perhaps most importantly, long-term at-home or nursing-home care. Older Americans are, in fact, spending a higher proportion of their incomes on health care now than they were in 1965 before Medicare and Medicaid were enacted.

The House Select Committee on Aging reported that Medicare pays less than half (48 percent) of older persons' health care cost. Contributing to high health costs are the skyrocketing price of health care in general and the rapid escalation of Medicare premiums, deductibles, and co-insurance. Figure 9.6 shows the additional forms of coverage that 90 percent of Medicare recipients must carry. (Qualified Medicare Beneficiaries [QMB] and Specified Low-Income Medicare Beneficiaries [SLMB] receive some assistance but do not qualify for Medicaid.)

Out-of-pocket spending on health varies greatly depending on the type of supplemental coverage. People who have Medigap policies spend the most — $3,250 versus $2,430 for all beneficiaries — out-of-pocket for health care than others. Enrollees in Medicare + Choice pay the least among non-Medicaid beneficiaries, $1,630. Persons receiving Medicaid pay the least, $280. (See Figure 9.7.)

Of their out-of-pocket spending on health care, in 1999, Medicare beneficiaries spent an average of 27 percent on private insurance premiums, including Medicare + Choice. The second highest cost (19 percent) was for Part B premiums, followed by prescription drugs and physician/supplier/vision items (17 percent each), dental and nursing home care (8 percent each), and outpatient and inpatient hospital (3 percent each). (See Figure 9.8.)

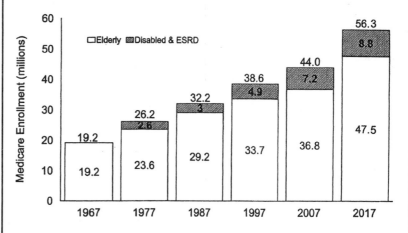

FIGURE 9.5
NUMBER OF MEDICARE BENEFICIARIES, FY 1967-2017

In Fiscal Year 1997, 87 percent of Medicare beneficiaries were elderly and about 13 percent were disabled (including ESRD). Medicare beneficiaries with disabilities are expected to grow to almost 16 percent of beneficiaries in 2017.

Source: *A Profile of Medicare, 1998*, Health Care Financing Administration, Baltimore, MD, no date

A Program in Crisis

Policy makers generally agree that Medicare cannot be sustained in its current form. Its costs are rising and must be controlled before the wave of baby boomers begin receiving benefits around 2010. The costs for medical procedures often used by the elderly, such as angioplasty and coronary bypass surgery, have increased. In addition, people are living longer. In 1995, for the first time since 1972, Medicare's trust fund lost money, a sign that the financial condition of Medicare was worse than assumed. The Health Care Financing Administration (HCFA), which runs Medicare, had not expected a deficit until 1997. Income to the trust fund, primarily from payroll taxes, was less than expected, and spending was higher.

The deficit is significant because the losses are expected to grow from year to year. No tax increases are scheduled under current law, and federal officials do not expect a reduction in the rate of spending unless a budget deal is reached between President Clinton and the Congress. No such solution seems likely. There are enough assets to cover the shortfall over the next few years, but once

159

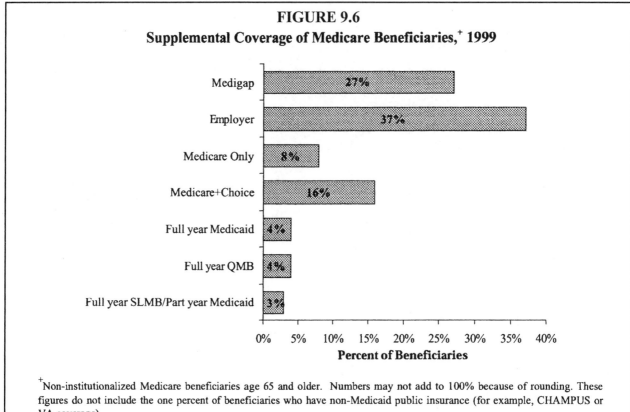

FIGURE 9.6
Supplemental Coverage of Medicare Beneficiaries,[+] 1999

[+]Non-institutionalized Medicare beneficiaries age 65 and older. Numbers may not add to 100% because of rounding. These figures do not include the one percent of beneficiaries who have non-Medicaid public insurance (for example, CHAMPUS or VA coverage).

Source: *Out-of-Pocket Spending on Health Care by Medicare Beneficiaries Age 65 and Older: 1999 Projections*, Public Policy Institute, American Association of Retired People, Washington, DC, 1999

the assets of the trust fund are depleted, there is no way to pay all the benefits that are due.

Politicians and policy-makers are bitterly divided over how Medicare should be changed, and how quickly. The Medicare payroll tax has not been increased since 1986. Medicare remains essentially unchanged since its beginning, a promise by the government to give the elderly free choice of doctors and specialists and to reimburse those doctors on the basis of each service they perform. Beneficiaries are responsible for deductibles, copayments, and many other costs not covered by Medicare. Most (70 percent) elderly people buy "Medigap" insurance (see below) with private agencies to help cover these costs.

Some Democrats have argued that only a true social insurance program, financed by payroll taxes and covering everyone, would spread the risk sufficiently and insure that all the elderly, rich and poor, could receive complete medical coverage. Republicans, by and large, have argued for a vol-

untary system. Both Democrats and Republicans, in general, believe that recipients should have more choices and more financial responsibility for what they choose.

While almost no one advocates an abrupt withdrawal of benefits from today's retirees, the benefits cannot last forever in their current form. Recipients will likely have to contribute more, benefits will have to decline, or Medicare payments to doctors and hospitals, already very low, will have to be cut even more. None of these options are politically appealing to a congressperson running for re-election.

In 1997, Congress passed the Balanced Budget Act (BBA; PL 105-33), which expanded health plan options and lower program spending. The act encouraged wider availability of HMOs (see below) and permitted other types of plans, such as preferred provider organizations, to participate in Medicare. It modified the way plan payments are figured and created the Medicare + Choice program. Under the Medicare + Choice plan, a member receives not only the required package of benefits available under Medicare, but also coverage for prescription drugs, routine physical exams, and dental care.

However, Congress underestimated the savings that would be produced when they passed the BBA. The budget cuts of payments for many services has hurt many health care providers. Some providers, faced with drastic declines in revenues, have lobbied Congress to restore money cut from their payments. They claim some nursing homes will be forced to close.

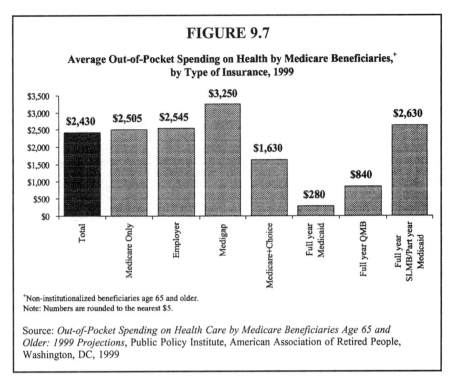

FIGURE 9.7

Average Out-of-Pocket Spending on Health by Medicare Beneficiaries,[+] by Type of Insurance, 1999

[+]Non-institutionalized beneficiaries age 65 and older.
Note: Numbers are rounded to the nearest $5.

Source: *Out-of-Pocket Spending on Health Care by Medicare Beneficiaries Age 65 and Older: 1999 Projections*, Public Policy Institute, American Association of Retired People, Washington, DC, 1999

Medicare Health Maintenance Organizations

Medicare's fee-for-service system was the method of payment for medicine in 1965, but it is no longer. In the past two decades, the elderly have had the option of receiving managed care through health maintenance organizations (HMOs). HMOs provide health care services for a fixed prepayment. For monthly pre-paid premiums, HMO enrollees received benefits not available under Medicare alone, such as free prescription drugs, dental care, eyeglasses, hearing aids, and hospitalization. The HMOs, in turn, received fixed payments from the HCFA. This managed care system was supposedly intended to control costs while maintaining quality medical care.

Initially, observers saw HMOs as the way to control rising Medicare costs. In 1997, approximately 12 percent (4 million) of Medicare recipients had enrolled in an HMO, almost triple the number enrolled in 1987. Medicare HMO coverage is not evenly spread among the states and, in fact, there is a strong concentration in a handful of states. The highest levels of participation were in the West (Figure 9.9). Ten states had no enrollees.

Effective in 1998, following the Balanced Budget Act (BBA; see above), many HMOs cut back popular benefits, such as free prescription drugs, eyeglasses, and dental care, and/or raised fees for their services. Many private insurers, such as employers, have eliminated drug benefits for retired persons as well. Some people are turning to Medicare + Choice to replace some of those benefits. Some health care providers claim their patients are sometimes unable to afford needed medications, and their health suffers. Furthermore, many HMOs who are no longer able to make a profit insuring older Americans no longer insure the elderly.

Public Opinion

A 1997 nationwide poll by the *Los Angeles Times*, of 1,258 Americans, found 59 percent of those over 65 willing to pay more for health care, including higher premiums. Thirty-two percent opposed such proposals, predominantly those 18 to 44. Sixty-eight percent of all ages opposed increasing the age of eligibility for benefits from 65 to 67.

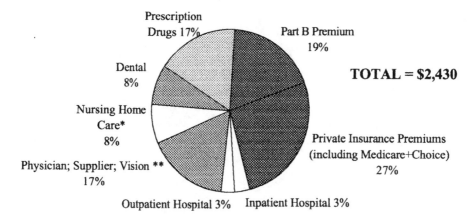

FIGURE 9.8

**Average Out-of-Pocket Spending on Health Care by Medicare Beneficiaries,[+]
by Type of Service, 1999**

Prescription Drugs 17%

Part B Premium 19%

Dental 8%

TOTAL = $2,430

Nursing Home Care* 8%

Private Insurance Premiums (including Medicare+Choice) 27%

Physician; Supplier; Vision ** 17%

Outpatient Hospital 3%   Inpatient Hospital 3%

[+]Non-institutionalized Medicare beneficiaries age 65 and older.
*Includes costs for short-term nursing facility care only.
**The Medicare Benefits Model does not separate spending on physician services, supplier, and vision items. Prior studies suggest that out-of-pocket spending for physician services account for about 85 percent of the combined physician/supplier/vision spending. See Gross, et al., 1997.
Note: Figures may not sum to 100% due to rounding.

Source: *Out-of-Pocket Spending on Health Care by Medicare Beneficiaries Age 65 and Older: 1999 Projections*, Public Policy Institute, American Association of Retired People, Washington, DC, 1999

A 1997 Gallup poll also found that the American public has mixed feelings about Medicare reform. Seventy percent believed that senior citizens with higher incomes should pay more for Medicare, while 28 percent favored equal costs for all Medicare recipients. They were staunchly against (64 percent) raising the minimum age for eligibility to 67 instead of 65. (See Table 9.7.)

Some people have predicted a "generational war" over benefit programs for the elderly, with baby boomers at odds with their children, who may be increasingly resentful over the heavy financial burden they are expected to bear for the programs. Many policy analysts see the young and the old locked in an ugly struggle, epitomized in a *Newsweek* cover showing a weary young man with an old woman in a wheelchair on his back.

This does not seem to be the case. Younger voters seem to be just as concerned about protecting Medicare and Social Security as their parents. Scholars believe the reason for this is that, despite the talk about the breakdown of the extended fam-

ily, the bonds between generations remain surprisingly strong. Senator Bob Kerrey (D-NE), a leader in the effort to overhaul benefit programs, believes the young want the elderly to be secure. "They want them to have quality health care. And they don't want them to be dependent on them [the young]." This is a matter of self-interest — curtailing benefits for the elderly will likely translate into additional burdens and/or worries for their families.

Problems with Medicare and the trimming of benefits of many older Americans will undoubtedly be a major campaign issue in the 2000 Presidential elections. In addition, some powerful lobbies, such as pharmaceutical researchers, fiercely oppose government price controls, claiming such cuts hinder research.

Medicaid

Medicaid ("Grants to States for Medical Assistance Programs," Title XIX of the Social Security Act) is a program established in 1966 to provide medical assistance to certain categories of low-

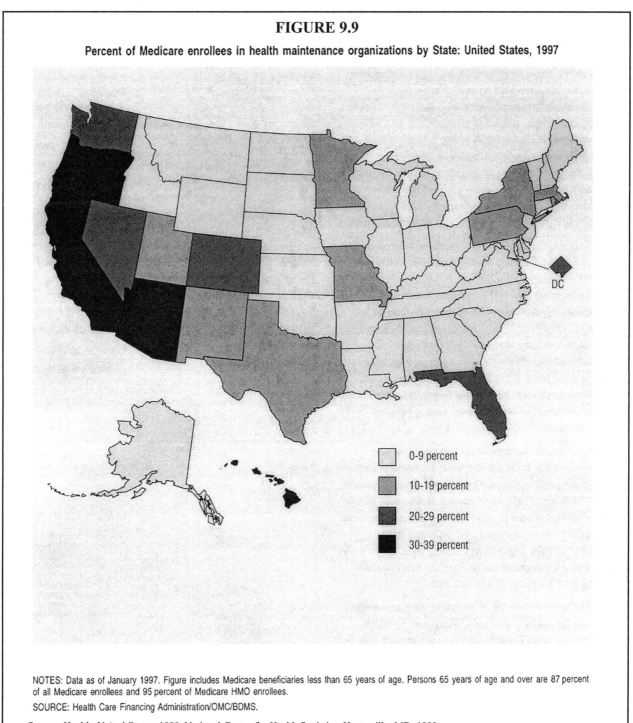

FIGURE 9.9

Percent of Medicare enrollees in health maintenance organizations by State: United States, 1997

0-9 percent

10-19 percent

20-29 percent

30-39 percent

NOTES: Data as of January 1997. Figure includes Medicare beneficiaries less than 65 years of age. Persons 65 years of age and over are 87 percent of all Medicare enrollees and 95 percent of Medicare HMO enrollees.

SOURCE: Health Care Financing Administration/OMC/BDMS.

Source: *Health, United States, 1999*, National Center for Health Statistics, Hyattsville, MD, 1999

income Americans: the aged, blind, disabled, or members of families with dependent children. The costs of the Medicaid program are financed jointly by the federal government and the states. Medicaid covers hospitalization, doctors' fees, laboratory fees, X-rays, and long-term nursing home care. It is the largest source of funds for medical and health-related services to America's poorest people and the second largest public payer of health care costs after Medicare.

In 1998, Medicaid spent $170.6 billion on health care costs. Medicaid is the principal source (52 percent) of public financing for nursing home care, and nursing homes account for almost one-quarter of Medicaid expenses. Two-thirds of the

TABLE 9.7

Proposed Medicare Changes

June 26-29, 1997; GP 9706016 [GO 118604], Q. 15.

QUESTION: (Asked of half-sample B, 505 respondents, ±5%) As you may know, the U.S. Senate recently passed a bill making several changes to the Medicare system. For each of the changes, please indicate if you favor or oppose it:

Senior citizens who are single and make more than $50,000 a year, or those who are married and earn more than $75,000 a year, would have to pay more for Medicare than senior citizens with lower incomes. Do you favor or oppose this change?

Beginning in the year 2003, the age of eligibility for Medicare would gradually be extended from age 65 to age 67. Do you favor or oppose this change? (ROTATED)

	Wealthier pay more			Eligibility age raised			
	Favor	Oppose	No opinion	Favor	Oppose	No opinion	No. of interviews
National	70%	28	2	35%	64	1	505
Sex							
Male	68%	31	1	36%	64	•	247
Female	73%	25	2	35%	64	1	258
Age							
18-29 years	70%	29	1	36%	63	1	113
30-49 years	69%	31	•	32%	68	•	211
50 and older	73%	23	4	39%	60	1	176
Region							
East	76%	19	5	30%	69	1	109
Midwest	68%	32	0	40%	60	•	103
South	66%	33	1	37%	62	1	192
West	75%	23	2	33%	66	1	101
Community							
Urban	67%	30	3	37%	61	2	154
Suburban	72%	26	2	36%	64	0	254
Rural	71%	29	0	32%	67	1	97
Race							
White	71%	27	2	35%	64	1	420
Non-white	69%	30	1	31%	67	2	83
Education							
College graduate	73%	26	1	49%	49	2	167
Some college	75%	23	2	36%	64	•	142
High school or less	67%	31	2	28%	71	1	194
Politics							
Republicans	61%	38	1	45%	55	•	138
Democrats	74%	23	3	36%	63	1	166
Independents	73%	26	1	28%	71	1	201
Ideology							
Liberal	67%	29	4	28%	69	3	99
Moderate	74%	25	1	39%	61	•	201
Conservative	78%	21	1	35%	65	•	161
Clinton approval							
Approve	74%	24	2	36%	63	1	277
Disapprove	63%	36	1	38%	62	0	186
Income							
$50,000 & over	74%	25	1	44%	56	•	167
$30,000-49,999	76%	23	1	28%	72	•	140
Under $30,000	64%	32	4	32%	66	2	174

• Less than one percent

Source: *The Gallup Poll Monthly*, July 1997

people in nursing homes get assistance from Medicaid. With the average cost of a year's nursing home service exceeding $43,000, it generally does not take long for most Americans to deplete their savings and qualify for Medicaid coverage; half of them do so within six months. "The fact is," said Jeff Eagan, executive director of the Long-Term Care Campaign, a coalition representing the disabled, "Right now, Medicaid is the long-term care safety net." In addition, it is the primary source of prescription drug coverage for a large number of the poor elderly. Although home health services presently account for a small share of Medicaid expenditures for the aged, it is the fastest growing sector. (See Table 9.8.)

TABLE 9.8

Medicaid recipients and medical vendor payments, according to type of service: United States, selected fiscal years 1972–97

[Data are compiled by the Health Care Financing Administration]

Type of service	1972	1975	1980	1985	1990	1994	1995	1996	1997
Recipients					Number in millions				
All recipients.	17.6	22.0	21.6	21.8	25.3	35.1	36.3	36.1	33.6
					Percent of recipients				
Inpatient general hospitals.	16.1	15.6	17.0	15.7	18.2	16.7	15.3	14.8	14.1
Inpatient mental hospitals	0.2	0.3	0.3	0.3	0.4	0.2	0.2	0.3	0.3
Mentally retarded intermediate care facilities . .	- - -	0.3	0.6	0.7	0.6	0.5	0.4	0.4	0.4
Nursing facilities	- - -	- - -	- - -	- - -	- - -	4.7	4.6	4.4	4.8
Skilled	3.1	2.9	2.8	2.5	2.4	- - -	- - -	- - -	- - -
Intermediate care.	- - -	3.1	3.7	3.8	3.4	- - -	- - -	- - -	- - -
Physician.	69.8	69.1	63.7	66.0	67.6	69.2	65.6	63.3	63.0
Dental	13.6	17.9	21.5	21.4	18.0	18.1	17.6	17.2	17.7
Other practitioner	9.1	12.1	15.0	15.4	15.3	15.4	15.2	14.8	15.3
Outpatient hospital	29.6	33.8	44.9	46.2	49.0	47.2	46.1	44.0	40.6
Clinic.	2.8	4.9	7.1	9.7	11.1	15.0	14.7	14.0	14.0
Laboratory and radiological	20.0	21.5	14.9	29.1	35.5	38.3	36.0	34.9	33.0
Home health.	0.6	1.6	1.8	2.5	2.8	3.9	4.5	4.8	5.5
Prescribed drugs	63.3	64.3	63.4	63.8	68.5	69.8	65.4	62.5	62.4
Family planning	. . .	5.5	5.2	7.5	6.9	7.3	6.9	6.6	6.2
Early and periodic screening	. . .	. . .	. . .	8.7	11.7	18.4	18.2	18.2	19.2
Rural health clinic.	. . .	. . .	. . .	0.4	0.9	2.7	3.4	3.9	4.3
Other care	14.4	13.2	11.9	15.5	20.3	28.4	31.5	36.3	36.9
Vendor payments[1]					Amount in billions				
All payments	$ 6.3	$ 12.2	$ 23.3	$ 37.5	$ 64.9	$ 107.9	$ 120.1	$ 121.7	$ 123.6
					Percent distribution				
Total	100.0	100.0	100.0	100.0	100.0	100.0	100.0	100.0	100.0
Inpatient general hospitals.	40.6	27.6	27.5	25.2	25.7	24.2	21.9	20.7	18.7
Inpatient mental hospitals	1.8	3.3	3.3	3.2	2.6	1.9	2.1	1.7	1.6
Mentally retarded intermediate care facilities . .	- - -	3.1	8.5	12.6	11.3	7.7	8.6	7.9	7.9
Nursing facilities	- - -	- - -	- - -	- - -	- - -	24.9	24.2	24.3	24.7
Skilled	23.3	19.9	15.8	13.5	12.4	- - -	- - -	- - -	- - -
Intermediate care.	- - -	15.4	18.0	17.4	14.9	- - -	- - -	- - -	- - -
Physician.	12.6	10.0	8.0	6.3	6.2	6.7	6.1	5.9	5.7
Dental	2.7	2.8	2.0	1.2	0.9	0.9	0.8	0.8	0.8
Other practitioner	0.9	1.0	0.8	0.7	0.6	1.0	0.8	0.9	0.8
Outpatient hospital	5.8	3.0	4.7	4.8	5.1	5.9	5.5	5.3	5.0
Clinic.	0.7	3.2	1.4	1.9	2.6	3.5	3.6	3.5	3.4
Laboratory and radiological	1.3	1.0	0.5	0.9	1.1	1.1	1.0	1.0	0.8
Home health.	0.4	0.6	1.4	3.0	5.2	6.5	7.8	8.9	9.9
Prescribed drugs	8.1	6.7	5.7	6.2	6.8	8.2	8.1	8.8	9.7
Family planning	. . .	0.5	0.3	0.5	0.4	0.5	0.4	0.4	0.3
Early and periodic screening	. . .	. . .	. . .	0.2	0.3	0.9	1.0	1.1	1.3
Rural health clinic.	. . .	. . .	. . .	0.0	0.1	0.2	0.2	0.2	0.2
Other care	1.8	1.9	1.9	2.5	3.7	6.0	7.7	8.4	8.9
Vendor payments per recipient[1]					Amount				
Total payment per recipient	$ 358	$ 556	$ 1,079	$ 1,719	$ 2,568	$ 3,080	$ 3,311	$ 3,369	$ 3,679
Inpatient general hospitals.	903	983	1,742	2,753	3,630	4,462	4,735	4,696	4,878
Inpatient mental hospitals	2,825	6,045	11,742	19,867	18,548	24,024	29,847	21,873	23,026
Mentally retarded intermediate care facilities . .	- - -	5,507	16,438	32,102	50,048	52,269	68,613	68,232	72,033
Nursing facilities	- - -	- - -	- - -	- - -	- - -	16,424	17,424	18,589	19,029
Skilled	2,665	3,864	6,081	9,274	13,356	- - -	- - -	- - -	- - -
Intermediate care.	- - -	2,764	5,326	7,882	11,236	- - -	- - -	- - -	- - -
Physician.	65	81	136	163	235	296	309	317	333
Dental	71	86	99	98	130	153	160	166	175
Other practitioner	37	48	61	75	96	192	178	205	190
Outpatient hospital	70	50	113	178	269	383	397	409	453
Clinic.	82	358	209	337	602	714	804	833	902
Laboratory and radiological	23	27	38	53	80	88	90	96	93
Home health.	229	204	847	2,094	4,733	5,124	5,740	6,293	6,575
Prescribed drugs	46	58	96	166	256	363	413	474	571
Family planning	. . .	55	72	119	151	201	206	200	200
Early and periodic screening	. . .	. . .	. . .	45	67	152	177	212	251
Rural health clinic.	. . .	. . .	. . .	81	154	199	174	215	213
Other care	44	80	172	274	465	656	807	782	891

- - - Data not available.
. . . Category not applicable.
[1]Excludes disproportionate share hospital payments ($16 billion in 1997) and payments to health maintenance organizations ($18 billion in 1997).

Source: *Health, United States, 1998*, National Center for Health Statistics, Hyattsville, MD, 1999

TABLE 9.9

Medicaid recipients and medical vendor payments, according to basis of eligibility: United States, selected fiscal years 1972–97

[Data are compiled by the Health Care Financing Administration]

Basis of eligibility	1972	1975	1980	1985	1990	1994	1995	1996	1997
Recipients					Number in millions				
All recipients	17.6	22.0	21.6	21.8	25.3	35.1	36.3	36.1	33.6
					Percent of recipients[1]				
Aged (65 years and over)	18.8	16.4	15.9	14.0	12.7	11.5	11.4	11.9	11.8
Blind and disabled	9.8	11.2	13.5	13.8	14.7	15.6	16.1	17.2	18.3
Adults in families with dependent children[2] .	17.8	20.6	22.6	25.3	23.8	21.6	21.0	19.7	20.2
Children under age 21[3]	44.5	43.6	43.2	44.7	44.4	49.0	47.3	46.3	45.5
Other Title XIX[4]	9.0	8.2	6.9	5.6	3.9	1.7	1.7	1.8	4.3
Vendor payments[5]					Amount in billions				
All payments	$ 6.3	$ 12.2	$ 23.3	$ 37.5	$ 64.9	$107.9	$120.1	$121.7	$123.6
					Percent distribution				
Total	100.0	100.0	100.0	100.0	100.0	100.0	100.0	100.0	100.0
Aged (65 years and over)	30.6	35.6	37.5	37.6	33.2	30.9	30.4	30.4	30.5
Blind and disabled	22.2	25.7	32.7	35.9	37.6	39.1	41.1	42.8	43.8
Adults in families with dependent children[2] .	15.3	16.8	13.9	12.7	13.2	12.6	11.2	10.1	10.0
Children under age 21[3]	18.1	17.9	13.4	11.8	14.0	16.0	15.0	14.4	12.7
Other Title XIX[4]	13.9	4.0	2.6	2.1	1.6	1.2	1.2	1.2	3.0
Vendor payments per recipient[5]					Amount				
All recipients	$ 358	$ 556	$1,079	$1,719	$2,568	$3,080	$3,311	$3,369	$3,679
Aged (65 years and over)	580	1,206	2,540	4,605	6,717	8,264	8,868	8,622	9,539
Blind and disabled	807	1,276	2,618	4,459	6,564	7,735	8,435	8,369	8,832
Adults in families with dependent children[2] .	307	455	662	860	1,429	1,791	1,777	1,722	1,810
Children under age 21[3]	145	228	335	452	811	1,007	1,047	1,048	1,027
Other Title XIX[4]	555	273	398	657	1,062	2,165	2,380	2,152	2,599

[1]Recipients included in more than one category for 1980 and 1985. From 1990 to 1996 between 0.2 and 2.5 percent of recipients have unknown basis of eligibility. In 1997 unknowns are included in Other Title XIX.
[2]Includes adults in the Aid to Families with Dependent Children (AFDC) program.
[3]Includes children in the AFDC program.
[4]Includes some participants in the Supplemental Security Income program and other people deemed medically needy in participating States.
[5]Payments exclude disproportionate share hospital payments ($16 billion in 1997) and payments to health maintenance organizations ($18 billion in 1997).

NOTES: 1972 and 1975 data are for fiscal year ending June 30. All other years are for fiscal year ending September 30. Data for additional years are available (see Appendix III). 1997 data for Hawaii not reported.

Source: *Health, United States, 1998*, National Center for Health Statistics, Hyattsville, MD, 1999

In 1997, while the elderly accounted for 11.8 percent of the 33.6 million Americans receiving Medicaid (down from 17.6 percent in 1972), the elderly received 30.5 percent of Medicaid benefits, an average of $9,539 per person. (See Table 9.9.)

Veterans' Benefits

Those who have served in the U.S. military — an estimated 25.6 million people, with 36 percent of them 65 and older — are entitled to medical treatment at any of the many veterans facilities around the nation. In 1997, the Department of Veterans Affairs spent more than $17 billion on health care for veterans. Forty-three percent of the total spent was for inpatient hospital care, 37 percent for outpatient care, and 10 percent for nursing home care. Almost 40 percent of that was for veterans with service-related disabilities. (See Table 9.10.)

PRIVATE HEALTH CARE PROGRAMS

Recognizing that Medicare (or Medicaid) will not cover all of their health care costs, many people seek other types of coverage to cover the gap between Medicare benefits and actual expenses. Additional coverage, however, can be costly and beyond the reach of some elderly persons. In 1997, 22.3 million Americans 65 and older had private insurance (Table 9.6).

Employer Health Insurance

Persons over 65 who are actively employed may be covered under a company health care policy. Coverage may not be denied or reduced just because of age or because a person is eligible for benefits under a federal program. Even after retirement, a person may be able to receive contin-

TABLE 9.10

Department of Veterans Affairs health care expenditures and use, and persons treated according to selected characteristics: United States, selected fiscal years 1970–97

[Data are compiled by Department of Veterans Affairs]

	1970	1980	1990	1992	1993	1994	1995	1996	1997
Health care expenditures					Amount in millions				
All expenditures[1]	$1,689	$ 5,981	$11,500	$13,682	$14,612	$15,401	$16,126	$16,373	$17,149
					Percent distribution				
All services	100.0	100.0	100.0	100.0	100.0	100.0	100.0	100.0	100.0
Inpatient hospital	71.3	64.3	57.5	55.8	54.8	53.8	49.0	46.3	43.1
Outpatient care	14.0	19.1	25.3	27.1	28.0	28.4	30.2	33.6	37.1
Nursing home care	5.5	7.1	9.5	10.0	10.4	10.5	10.0	10.1	10.2
All other[2]	9.1	9.6	7.7	7.1	6.8	7.3	10.8	10.0	9.6
Health care use					Number in thousands				
Inpatient hospital stays[3]	787	1,248	1,029	935	920	907	879	807	671
Outpatient visits	7,312	17,971	22,602	23,902	24,236	25,158	27,527	29,295	31,919
Nursing home stays[4]	47	57	75	75	78	78	79	79	87
Inpatients[5]									
Total	- - -	- - -	598	564	556	547	527	491	417
					Percent distribution				
Total	- - -	- - -	100.0	100.0	100.0	100.0	100.0	100.0	100.0
Veterans with service-connected disability	- - -	- - -	38.9	39.0	39.4	39.1	39.3	39.5	39.2
Veterans without service-connected disability	- - -	- - -	60.3	60.1	59.6	60.0	59.9	59.6	59.7
Low income	- - -	- - -	54.8	55.7	55.2	56.6	56.2	55.7	55.5
Exempt[6]	- - -	- - -	2.5	2.7	2.4	0.9	0.8	0.8	0.9
Other[7]	- - -	- - -	2.8	1.6	1.9	2.4	2.8	3.0	3.2
Unknown	- - -	- - -	0.2	0.1	0.1	0.1	0.1	0.1	0.1
Nonveterans	- - -	- - -	0.8	0.9	1.0	0.9	0.8	0.8	1.0
Outpatients[5]					Number in thousands				
Total	- - -	- - -	2,564	2,639	2,684	2,714	2,790	2,846	2,958
					Percent distribution				
Total	- - -	- - -	100.0	100.0	100.0	100.0	100.0	100.0	100.0
Veterans with service-connected disability	- - -	- - -	38.3	37.8	37.4	37.4	37.5	37.8	37.9
Veterans without service-connected disability	- - -	- - -	49.8	50.9	50.6	50.5	50.5	50.2	51.5
Low income	- - -	- - -	41.1	42.4	41.5	42.6	42.2	41.9	41.9
Exempt[6]	- - -	- - -	2.9	2.8	2.6	1.0	0.9	0.9	0.7
Other[7]	- - -	- - -	3.6	2.6	2.9	3.6	4.2	4.7	5.9
Unknown	- - -	- - -	2.2	3.1	3.6	3.3	3.2	2.8	3.0
Nonveterans	- - -	- - -	11.8	11.3	12.0	12.1	12.0	12.1	10.6

- - - Data not available.

[1]Health care expenditures exclude construction, medical administration, and miscellaneous operating expenses.
[2]Includes miscellaneous benefits and services, contract hospitals, education and training, subsidies to State veterans hospitals, nursing homes, and domiciliaries, and the Civilian Health and Medical Program of the Department of Veterans Affairs.
[3]One-day dialysis patients were included in fiscal year 1980. Interfacility transfers were included beginning in fiscal year 1990.
[4]Includes Department of Veterans Affairs nursing home and domiciliary stays, and community nursing home stays.
[5]Individuals.
[6]Prisoner of war, exposed to Agent Orange, and so forth. Prior to fiscal year 1994, veterans who reported exposure to Agent Orange were classified as Exempt. Beginning in fiscal year 1994 those veterans reporting Agent Orange exposure but not treated for it were means tested and placed in the low income or other group depending on income.
[7]Financial means-tested veterans who receive medical care subject to copayments according to income level.

NOTES: Figures may not add to totals due to rounding. In 1970 and 1980, the fiscal year ended June 30; for all other years the fiscal year ends September 30. The veteran population was estimated at 25.6 million in 1997 with 36 percent age 65 or over, compared with 11 percent in 1980. Twenty-six percent had served during World War II, 17 percent during the Korean conflict, 32 percent during the Vietnam era, 7 percent during the Persian Gulf War, and 23 percent during peacetime. Beginning in fiscal year 1995 categories for health care expenditures and health care use were revised. Data for additional years are available (see Appendix III).

Source: *Health, United States, 1998*, National Center for Health Statistics, Hyattsville, MD, 1999

---

ued coverage under a company policy. In 1997, 12 million people 65 and older carried insurance through a present or previous employer. (See Table 9.6.)

Medigap

An increasing number of private insurance companies are offering policies (often called co-insurance or "Medigap" insurance) that pay for services not included in Medicare. These policies can be expensive and, in some cases, do not provide complete coverage. Abuses in the Medigap insurance field have included overlapping coverage, selling clients more coverage than they need, and deceptive advertising. Because federal and state laws set a minimum level of benefits for a supplemental policy, one such policy is enough in virtually every case, although some policyholders have more than one policy.

The Omnibus Budget Reconciliation Act of 1990 (PL 101-508) allowed people reaching the age of 65 to buy Medigap policies regardless of the condition of their health, provided they do so within six months after enrolling in Medicare. These protections apply to new beneficiaries, approximately 2 million people a year. Nearly 68 percent of the elderly have some form of private insurance in addition to Medicare. Blacks are only half as likely to have supplemental coverage as their White counterparts.

Having No Health Insurance

The Bureau of the Census reported, in 1998, that only 1.1 percent of all Americans over 65, or 3.2 percent of poor people over 65, had no health insurance. The remainder were covered by Medicare (Figure 9.4).

LONG-TERM HEALTH CARE

The senior boom is one of the central challenges of the coming century. If we face these challenges together and make them our top priorities, if we make the efforts I have addressed today, then we can prove what no generation in history has had the opportunity to prove — that the infirmities of age need not be the indignities of age.
— President Bill Clinton, 1999

Perhaps the most pressing and most difficult health care problem facing America today is long-term care. Long-term care refers to services needed by individuals with chronic illnesses or mental or physical conditions so severe that they cannot care for themselves over long periods of time. Longer life spans and improved life-sustaining technologies are increasing the possibility that an individual may eventually require long-term care.

In the United States, long-term health care originated in "welfare" policy. Only recently has care for the disabled elderly been viewed distinct from the needs of "the poor." Elderly people without families to care for them were handled in institutional settings as a form of charity — almshouses or "homes for the aged and infirm."

Because of the stigma attached to public institutions, some religious and charitable organizations stepped in to establish their own "old-age" homes. The rise of the modern concept of hospitals being for the acutely ill accelerated this trend. Hospitals increasingly refused to accommodate chronic, incurable patients, but their sponsoring charitable organizations often built attached or affiliated old-age homes.

In 1996, the John Hancock Mutual Life Insurance Company, in conjunction with the National Council on Aging, surveyed Americans about their plans for future long-term medical need. The study found that less than half of all adults had planned for the possibility of debilitating illness. Among the reasons given for lack of planning were "the issue is difficult to face," having more immediate needs, procrastination, lack of affordability, and unwillingness to take financial risks.

Predominating reasons varied depending upon age group. Baby boomers most often (75 percent) cited being too busy, although the youngest boomers claimed to have more pressing needs associated with child rearing. Those 51 to 75 said the issue is better dealt with when it arises, and two-thirds of that group said the issue is too hard to face. The oldest Americans, born before 1925, believed it was too late to save meaningfully toward the possibility of need. Three-fourths of respondents of working age claimed they would take advantage of long-term insurance if it were offered by their employers.

Options Are Limited and Expensive

The options for good, affordable long-term care in the United States are few. One year's stay in a nursing home currently costs, on average, between $40,000 and $50,000 depending on the amount of care required. Even hiring an unskilled caregiver who makes home visits can cost more than $25,000 a year; skilled care costs much more. Most elderly people and young families cannot afford this expense. Lifetime savings can be consumed before the need for care ends.

A Dilemma for the Entire Family

The inability to care for oneself affects not only the patient, but the entire family. Most people prefer to care for disabled parents or relatives at home as long as they can, but the emotional and financial strain on all family members can be great. As a loved one's condition deteriorates, there may come a time when home care is impossible, and the family has no alternative but to find an outside source of help.

Families who provide long-term care often sacrifice their own needs and wishes to meet the physical and financial obligations inherent in long-term care. They may delay sending a child to college, quit jobs, or reduce hours, or they may exhaust their savings or go deeply into debt to pay for nursing home or specialized care.

Little Relief from Government Programs

Most government or "social" programs are funded with taxpayer dollars. Yet the elderly, most of whom have paid taxes over long, productive lifetimes, are often on their own when the time comes to need long-term care.

The only government program that provides any substantial assistance for long-term health care is Medicaid, the federal-state health program designed to aid the poor. In order for elderly persons to qualify for nursing home care under Medicaid, they usually must reduce their personal financial status to the poverty level. Often they reach the poverty level by spending most of their hard-earned assets and income on their nursing home care. If the person is married, his or her spouse is now not only alone, but also poor.

Although advocates for the elderly have long campaigned for a more comprehensive system —

particularly a broad-based insurance system like Social Security or Medicare — the political climate of the past 15 years has not been conducive to expansion of the social welfare system. In 1999, more than 5 million Americans had significant limitations due to illness or disability and required long-term care; about two-thirds of them were 65 or older.

... or Private Insurance Policies

For older Americans who can afford private policies, long-term care insurance is another way to pay for long-term care. Long-term care insurance is a relatively new type of insurance. It was introduced in the 1980s as nursing home insurance but covers more than that today. In 1996, Congress passed the Health Insurance Portability and Accountability Act (HIPAA; PL 104-191) to give some federal income tax advantages to people who buy certain long-term insurance policies. Those polices are called Tax-Qualified Long-term Care Insurance Contracts. Policies vary depending upon the insurer.

FALLING THROUGH THE CRACKS

A 1997 Public Health Service study found that 6 percent — 3.3 million — of the elderly reported that they did not have a regular source of medical care. Older persons with Medicare and private health insurance or Medicare and public insurance coverage were more likely to have a regular source of care than those who had Medicare only or who were uninsured. Among the reasons cited for their lack of care were "does not need a doctor" (47 percent), inconvenience (23 percent), "does not trust doctor" (7 percent), cannot afford (7 percent), and other (10 percent).

Unmet needs were most likely to include dental care (1.4 million elderly), glasses (1 million), medical care (500,000), and prescription medications (600,000). Although the majority of elderly people had a regular source of care, many did not get routine preventive services such as immunizations, Pap smears, or mammograms. Almost 41 percent did not get influenza immunization, 62.7

TABLE 9.11

Estimated Prevalences of Failure to Receive Selected Preventive Care Services
Among Behavioral Risk Factor Surveillance System Respondents with Health Insurance
Who Were 65 Years of Age or Over, by Region[1], Sex, and Race/Ethnicity: United States, 1995

Region and Characteristic	Percent Not Receiving an Influenza Immunization in Past 12 Months	95-Percent Confidence Interval	Percent Never Receiving a Pneumonia Vaccination	95-Percent Confidence Interval	Percent Not Receiving a Mammogram in Past 2 Years[2]	95-Percent Confidence Interval	Percent Not Receiving a Digital Rectal Examination in Past Year	95-Percent Confidence Interval
United States Total	40.9	39.9, 41.9	62.7	61.7, 63.7	--	--	49.6	48.4, 50.8
Male	40.4	38.6, 42.2	63.6	61.8, 65.4	--	--	41.2	39.4, 43.0
Female	41.2	39.8, 42.6	62.1	60.7, 63.5	32.1	30.9, 33.3	55.5	54.1, 56.9
White, not Hispanic	39.1	37.9, 40.3	61.0	59.8, 62.2	32.0	30.6, 33.4	48.9	47.7, 50.1
Black, not Hispanic	59.4	55.5, 63.3	78.9	75.6, 82.2	36.4	31.7, 41.1	53.1	49.0, 57.2
Hispanic	47.2	40.7, 53.7	72.8	66.9, 78.7	25.9	19.4, 32.4	56.5	50.0, 63.0
Other	41.6	31.4, 51.8	63.6	53.0, 74.2	23.0	14.6, 31.4	59.7	49.1, 70.3

Source: "Behavioral Risk Factor Surveillance of Aged Medicare Beneficiaries, 1995," *Health Care Financing Review*, Health Care Financing Administration, Washington, DC, Summer 1997

percent did not get pneumonia immunizations, 32.1 percent of women did not get mammograms, and 49.6 percent did not receive digital rectal examinations for colon or prostate cancer (Table 9.11). For whatever reasons, many elderly are not taking the time to get preventive care services.

PROVIDING HEALTH CARE — ALSO AN ETHICAL CONCERN

Health care costs continue to rise mainly because of increased prices for services, higher technology, rising demand for services, and inflation. How much and what kind of health care protection should be available are on-going questions with no easy answers. The problems have not gone unnoticed by Congress. A wide array of bills have been introduced with proposals ranging from almost total protection under federal programs to almost complete dependence on the private sec-

tors. There is little consensus on a solution. Faced with an aging population and ever-rising medical costs, the government's and the nation's health care predicament will likely worsen.

To some extent, rationing of health care has already occurred and is perhaps already widespread. Some policy makers have suggested limiting the use of intensive care for the elderly as an approach to reducing health care expenditures. For example, is it advantageous to allocate scarce organs for transplant to younger patients who would generally be in better health and who likely have more years of life remaining? Is it "worthwhile" to maintain an older person on life-support when he or she likely will not live much longer anyway? Would the expense of continuing his or her life be "worth it"? Should people who might benefit from inheritances and other financial assets at death be able to make decisions about their ailing elders?

CHAPTER X

ELDERLY VICTIMS

CRIMES AGAINST THE ELDERLY

The U.S. Department of Justice, Bureau of Justice Statistics, in *Crimes Against Persons Age 65 or Older, 1992-97* (Washington, DC, January 2000), reported that Americans 65 years and older were considerably less likely to be crime victims than younger people. The elderly made up 15 percent of the population age 12 and older, but accounted for 7 percent of crime victims. Between 1992 and 1997, the elderly were victims of almost 2.7 million property and violent crimes (Table 10.1).

People over 65 experienced violent crime at the rate of about 5 per 1,000 persons, compared to a rate of more than 100 per 1,000 people for those under 25, a rate of 48 per 1,000 in those 25 to 49, and 15 per 1,000 among those 50 to 64. (See Figure 10.1.) For property crimes, the elderly were victimized at a rate of 117.3 per 1,000, compared to almost 500 per 1,000 for those 12 to 24, 350 per 1,000 among those 25 to 49, and almost 250 per 1,000 for those 50 to 64 (Figure 10.2).

Crime victimization rates among the elderly have generally declined by half since 1973. Murders of those over 65 dropped by half from 1976 to 1997, nonfatal violence fell from 9 incidents per 1,000 in 1973 to 4.5 incidents in 1997, and property crimes decreased from 205 per 1,000 in 1973 to 96 per 1,000 incidents in 1997. (See Figures 10.3–10.5.)

Experts believe that some economic crimes, such as fraud and confidence schemes, disproportionately affect persons 65 and older, although statistics on these crimes are not collected by the major crime reporting agencies. The elderly often live on fixed incomes and limited savings. "Get rich" schemes can appear very attractive to the elderly because they offer the promise of economic security.

The Emotional Impact of Crime

Virtually every major type of crime measured decreased significantly between 1993 and 1998.

TABLE 10.1

Victimizations of persons age 65 or older or of households with a head of household age 65 or older

	Average number per year, 1992-97	Percent
Total crimes	2,694,290	100.0%
Personal crimes	212,420	7.9%
Crimes of violence	166,330	6.2
Murder	1,000	0.04
Nonfatal violence	165,330	6.1
Rape/Sexual assault	3,280	0.12
Robbery	40,950	1.5
Total assault	121,100	4.5
Aggravated assault	34,050	1.3
Simple assault	87,050	3.2
Personal theft	46,090	1.7
Number of persons age 65 or older	31,296,350	
Property crimes	2,481,870	92.1%
Household burglary	623,790	23.2
Motor vehicle theft	124,930	4.6
Theft	1,733,160	64.3
Households heads age 65 or older	21,161,850	

Source: *Crimes Against Persons Age 65 or Older, 1992-97*, Bureau of Justice Statistics, Washington, DC, 2000

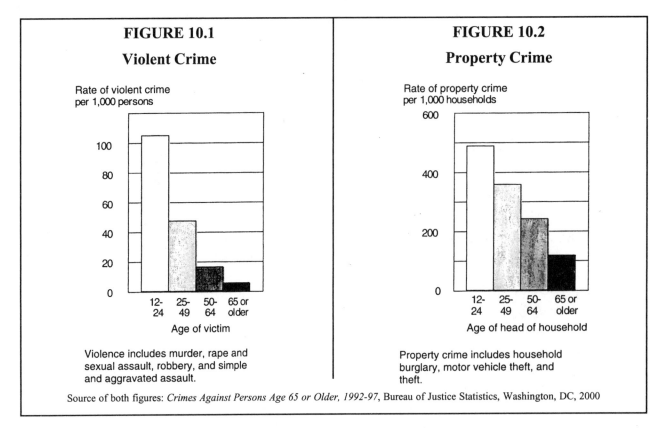

FIGURE 10.1

Violent Crime

Rate of violent crime
per 1,000 persons

Age of victim

Violence includes murder, rape and
sexual assault, robbery, and simple
and aggravated assault.

FIGURE 10.2

Property Crime

Rate of property crime
per 1,000 households

Age of head of household

Property crime includes household
burglary, motor vehicle theft, and
theft.

Source of both figures: *Crimes Against Persons Age 65 or Older, 1992-97*, Bureau of Justice Statistics, Washington, DC, 2000

The consequences of victimization, however, can be much more severe for the elderly. Speaking before the House Select Committee on Aging in 1995, Irwin I. Kimmelman, Attorney General for the New Jersey Department of Law and Safety, noted that it is not the number of crimes, but the "terrible and tragic impact that crime has on [the elderly] that is significant. Crime causes much more fear among the elderly and has a far more deleterious impact on the quality of their lives."

Crimes against the elderly are particularly devastating because older people are often less resilient than younger people. They may not be able to cope with the trauma and "get on with their lives," especially if their lives are static, with few new pleasant experiences to replace the memory of painful ones. Even so-called non-violent crimes, such as purse snatching, vandalism, and burglary, can be devastating. Stolen or damaged articles and property are often irreplaceable, either because of

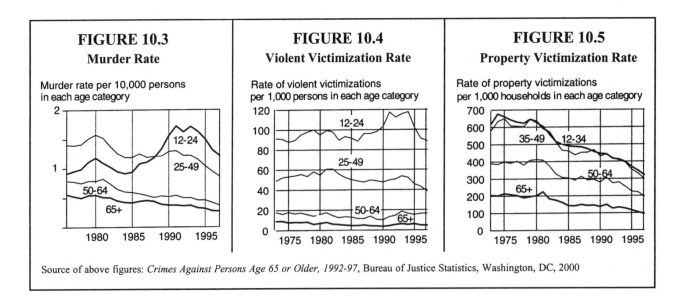

FIGURE 10.3
Murder Rate

Murder rate per 10,000 persons
in each age category

12-24
25-49
50-64
65+

FIGURE 10.4
Violent Victimization Rate

Rate of violent victimizations
per 1,000 persons in each age category

12-24
25-49
50-64
65+

FIGURE 10.5
Property Victimization Rate

Rate of property victimizations
per 1,000 households in each age category

35-49   12-34
50-64
65+

Source of above figures: *Crimes Against Persons Age 65 or Older, 1992-97*, Bureau of Justice Statistics, Washington, DC, 2000

172

TABLE 10.2
Victim-Offender Relationship

Type of violence and victim-offender relationship	Age of victim	
	65 or older	12-64
Murder	100.0%	100.0%
Nonstranger total	50.1	45.8
Relative, intimate	26.4	13.5
Other known	23.7	32.3
Stranger	14.6	14.3
Unknown relationship	35.3	39.9
Total nonlethal violence	100.0%	100.0%
Relatives or intimates	9.1	15.0
Well known	12.9	15.3
Casual acquaintances	14.5	18.0
Strangers	56.2	48.4
Unknown relationship	7.4	3.3

Note: "Other known" murder victims includes a wide variety of relationships These data cannot be classified into "well known" and "casual acquaintances." For nonlethal violence, the victim identified the nature of the relationship as "well known" or "casual acquaintance."

Source: *Crimes Against Persons Age 65 or Older, 1992-97*, Bureau of Justice Statistics, Washington, DC, 2000

the sentimental or monetary value. Even non-violent crimes leave victims with a sense of violation and vulnerability.

Once victimized, older people may become obsessed with the idea that they will be victimized again (a common reaction in younger victims, as well). They may develop a negative outlook on life and even alter their lifestyle, resorting to extreme precautionary measures. Fear of strangers can make an elderly person reluctant to leave his or her home. Only 14.6 percent of murders of the elderly between 1992 and 1997 were committed by a person who was a total stranger to them, as were 56.2 percent of nonlethal violence incidents (Table 10.2).

CHARACTERISTICS OF ELDERLY CRIME VICTIMS

Among the elderly, certain groups are generally more likely to experience a crime than others. More than 60 percent of the elderly live in metropolitan areas, and many live in inner cities where crime rates are the highest. From 1992 to 1997, 43 percent of violent, nonlethal crimes against older people occurred in or near their homes (compared to 26 percent for younger victims) (Figure 10.6). For the elderly, the homes and neighborhoods where they generally spend most of their time do not necessarily offer escape from victimization, but, in fact, may make them especially vulnerable.

As a group, the elderly are more dependent on walking and public transportation, which increases their exposure to possible criminal attack. People 65 and older were about six times more likely than younger persons to "never" go out at night. Crimes against the elderly were far more likely to occur

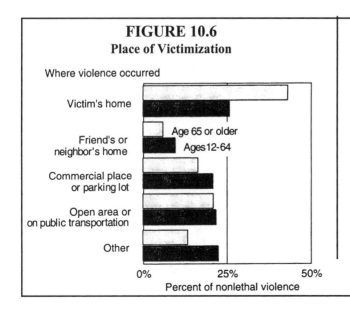

FIGURE 10.6
Place of Victimization

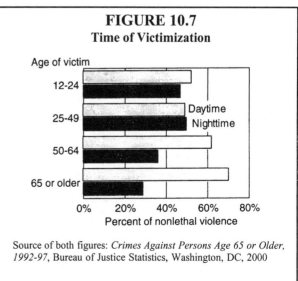

FIGURE 10.7
Time of Victimization

Source of both figures: *Crimes Against Persons Age 65 or Older, 1992-97*, Bureau of Justice Statistics, Washington, DC, 2000

173

FIGURE 10.8

Property Victimization Rate and Income

Annual household income

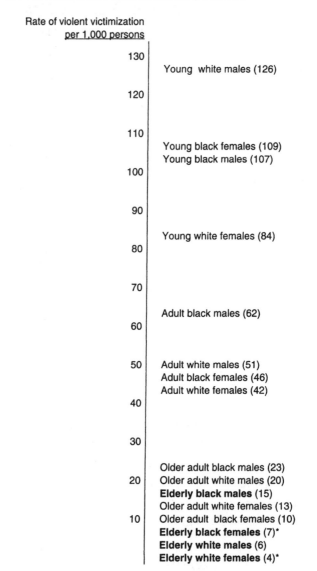

Source: *Crimes Against Persons Age 65 or Older, 1992-97*, Bureau of Justice Statistics, Washington, DC, 2000

FIGURE 10.9

White women age 65 or older had the lowest rate of nonlethal violent victimization, 1992-97

Rate of violent victimization per 1,000 persons

Young white males (126)

Young black females (109)
Young black males (107)

Young white females (84)

Adult black males (62)

Adult white males (51)
Adult black females (46)
Adult white females (42)

Older adult black males (23)
Older adult white males (20)
Elderly black males (15)
Older adult white females (13)
Older adult black females (10)
Elderly black females (7)*
Elderly white males (6)
Elderly white females (4)*

Note: This report applies the following age categories: ♦ Young (ages 12-24) ♦ Adult (ages 24-49) ♦ Older adult (ages 50-64) ♦ Elderly (age 65 or older)

*The apparent difference between elderly females is not statistically significant.

Source: *Crimes Against Persons Age 65 or Older, 1992-97*, Bureau of Justice Statistics, Washington, DC, 2000

during the day (70 percent) than at night (30 percent) (Figure 10.7). Most personal theft from elderly persons took place in stores or other businesses and occurred during the day.

Crimes of violence were highest for those who lived in the city, rented their homes, were divorced or separated, were Black or Hispanic, and had incomes below $7,500. Crimes of theft were greatest for those elderly with incomes over $25,000, those who lived in cities, and those who were divorced or separated. Property crime rates were highest for those with incomes above $50,000 (Figure 10.8). Elderly Whites had both the lowest violent crime (Figure 10.9) and property crime rates (Figure 10.10).

Elderly persons were about as likely as younger persons to sustain serious injuries from violent crimes. Among people 65 and older who were victims of violence, 22 percent were injured, approximately half required treatment at the scene or in a doctor's office or hospital, and about 1 percent were hospitalized overnight (Figure 10.11).

Weapons were somewhat more likely to be used against elderly victims of violence (32 percent) than against younger victims (28 percent). Firearms comprised 42 percent of weapons used against the elderly. Knives accounted for 17 percent; other or unknown for the remainder.

They Often Report

People 65 and older were more likely to report violence (52 percent), personal theft (45 percent), and property crimes (36 percent) to the police than were younger victims, who reported 43 percent of violent crimes, 29 percent of personal thefts, and 32 percent of property crimes (Figure 10.12).

Older People Are Considered Easy Prey

Because of their physical limitations, older people are often considered easy prey. The elderly usually do not resist a criminal attack. They are aware that they may lack the strength to repel a younger aggressor and that they are particularly susceptible to broken bones and fractured hips, which could permanently cripple them. The Bureau of Justice reports that victims age 65 and older take protective measures in about half of their victimizations, compared to 73 percent of younger victims. Those over 65 who try to protect themselves most often use nonphysical action, such as arguing, reasoning, screaming, or running away. Younger victims are more likely to use physical action, such as attacking, resisting, or chasing the offender. Most criminals are likely less concerned about nonphysical defenses than they are about physical resistance.

TREATMENT BY THE COURTS

Elderly victims are sometimes poorly treated by the criminal justice system. Because of physical impairments such as poor hearing and vision and slowness of movement and speech, older persons can encounter impatience and insensitivity when they attempt to report a crime. This kind of treatment adds to their frustration and sense of helplessness.

FIGURE 10.10

Households with a white female head of household age 65 or older had the lowest property crime rates, 1992-97

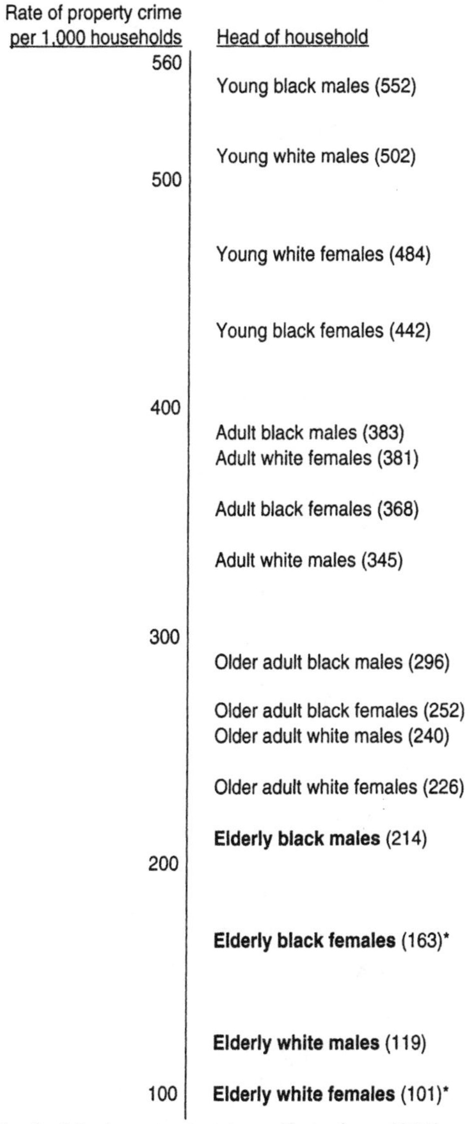

Rate of property crime per 1,000 households	Head of household
560	Young black males (552)
500	Young white males (502)
	Young white females (484)
	Young black females (442)
400	Adult black males (383)
	Adult white females (381)
	Adult black females (368)
	Adult white males (345)
300	Older adult black males (296)
	Older adult black females (252)
	Older adult white males (240)
	Older adult white females (226)
	Elderly black males (214)
200	
	Elderly black females (163)*
	Elderly white males (119)
100	**Elderly white females (101)***

Note: This report applies the following age categories: ♦ Young (ages 12-24) ♦ Adult (ages 24-49) ♦ Older adult (ages 50-64) ♦ Elderly (age 65 or older)

*The apparent difference between elderly females is not statistically significant.

Source: *Crimes Against Persons Age 65 or Older, 1992-97*, Bureau of Justice Statistics, Washington, DC, 2000

175

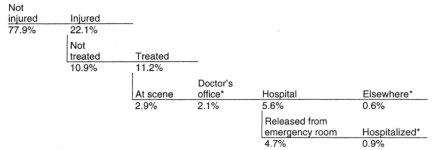

FIGURE 10.11

On average each year 1992-97, of persons age 65 or older who reported being a victim of violence, 22% were injured and 1% were hospitalized overnight

Not injured	Injured			
77.9%	22.1%			
	Not treated	Treated		
	10.9%	11.2%		
		At scene	Doctor's office*	Hospital	Elsewhere*
		2.9%	2.1%	5.6%	0.6%
				Released from emergency room	Hospitalized*
				4.7%	0.9%

*Based on 10 or fewer cases.

• More than three-fourths of elderly nonlethal violence victims were not injured.
• About 11% of all nonlethal violence against the elderly resulted in medical treatment.
• About 6% of all elderly victims of nonlethal violence went to the hospital for emergency room care or other type of treatment.

Source: *Crimes Against Persons Age 65 or Older, 1992-97*, Bureau of Justice Statistics, Washington, DC, 2000

The National Center on Elder Abuse reported 117,000 incidents in 1986. By 1996, 293,000 were reported, an increase of 150 percent over the 10 years. (See Figure 10.13.)

The NCEA (National Center on Elder Abuse) estimated, however, that in 1996, approximately 1.01 million elders were victims of domestic abuse. Another 1.15 million elders are believed to have been victims of self-neglect, bringing the total number of abuse victims to 2.16 million individuals that year. With enhanced public awareness and improved reporting systems, experts anticipate reports of elder domestic abuse will continue to increase.

Victim compensation for crimes against the elderly is currently provided on the state level, and amounts vary from state to state. Most states compensate for medical, counseling, and physical therapy expenses associated with the crime and reimburse for lost wages, loss of support to dependents, and for funeral expenses.

DOMESTIC ABUSE AND MISTREATMENT AGAINST THE ELDERLY*

Domestic violence against the elderly is a phenomenon that has only recently gained public attention. It is impossible to determine exactly how many elderly people are the victims of domestic violence. As with child abuse, the number of actual cases is larger than the number of reported cases. However, experts agree that elder abuse is far less likely to be reported than child or spousal abuse. Definitions of abuse and reporting methods vary greatly both between states and among different government agencies.

Nationwide, reports of domestic elder abuse have increased steadily in the past several years.

Types of Mistreatment

Research on domestic elder abuse is still in its infancy, but studies conducted over the past 10 years have revealed several recurring forms of abuse. Federal definitions of elder abuse, neglect, and exploitation appeared for the first time in the 1987 Amendments to the Old Americans Act. Broadly defined, there are three basic categories of abuse: (1) domestic elder abuse, (2) institutional elder abuse (see below), and (3) self-neglect or self-abuse.

Domestic elder abuse generally refers to any form of maltreatment of an older person by someone who has a special relationship with the elder (a spouse, sibling, child, friend, or caregiver). Most sources have identified the following categories of domestic elder mistreatment.

---

* For a complete discussion of domestic violence against the elderly, see *Violent Relationships — Battering and Abuse Among Adults*, Information Plus, Wylie, Texas, 1999.

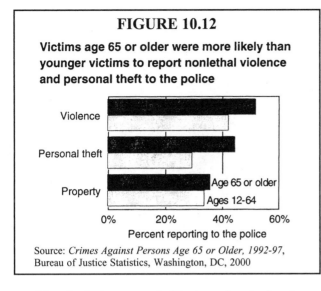

FIGURE 10.12

Victims age 65 or older were more likely than younger victims to report nonlethal violence and personal theft to the police

Percent reporting to the police

Age 65 or older
Ages 12-64

Source: *Crimes Against Persons Age 65 or Older, 1992-97*, Bureau of Justice Statistics, Washington, DC, 2000

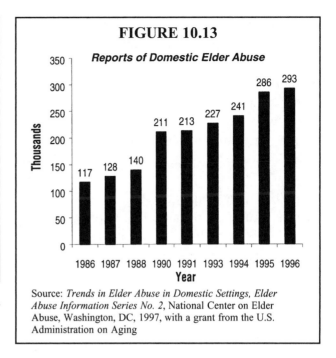

FIGURE 10.13

Reports of Domestic Elder Abuse

Year

Source: *Trends in Elder Abuse in Domestic Settings, Elder Abuse Information Series No. 2*, National Center on Elder Abuse, Washington, DC, 1997, with a grant from the U.S. Administration on Aging

- Physical abuse — inflicting physical pain or injury.

- Sexual abuse — non-consensual sexual contact of any kind with an older person.

- Emotional or psychological abuse — inflicting mental anguish by, for example, name calling, humiliation, making threats, or isolation.

- Neglect — willful or unintentional failure to provide basic necessities, such as food and medical care due to caregiver indifference, inability, or ignorance.

- Material or financial abuse — exploiting or misusing an older person's money or assets.

- Abandonment — the desertion of an elderly person by an individual who has physical custody of the elder or by a person who has assumed responsibility for providing care to the elder.

- Self-neglect — behaviors of an elderly person that threaten the elder's health or safety.

The NCEA reported that most of the confirmed cases, or about 55 percent of all reports of elder abuse in 1996, turned out to be self-neglect or self-abuse. The remaining types of domestic elder maltreatment in 1996 were physical abuse, 15 percent; sexual abuse, 0.4 percent; emotional

abuse, 8 percent; financial exploitation, 12.4 percent; all other types, 6 percent; and unknown, 4 percent (Figure 10.14).

Financial Abuse — Theft by Kin and Friends

Criminal justice professionals are finding that money and property are being stolen from today's elderly at alarming rates and that a large portion of the crimes are being committed not by professional criminals but by relatives, friends, health aides, household workers, and neighbors.

Like child and sexual abuse crimes, many crimes against the elderly are not reported because the victims are physically or mentally unable to summon help or because they are reticent or afraid to publicly accuse relatives or those they are dependent upon. In-home care for elderly persons often allows other persons access to the financial and property assets of those cared for. Officials suspect that fully 80 percent of financial theft cases go unreported.

Medical advances are lengthening lives and resulting in greater numbers of older and, in many cases, infirm persons. Increasing numbers of these elderly people have substantial bank and investment accounts. Those too sick to manage even their Social Security or pension checks are particularly vulnerable. Financial exploitation is likely to grow as the number of older Americans who are most vulnerable to it, the lonely and those in poor health, rises.

Women are frequent victims of such crimes, primarily because there are so many more elderly women. Loneliness causes many victims not to report the crimes, even when they are aware of them, simply because they are afraid to lose the companionship of the perpetrator. When a case of financial abuse is reported, the source of the information is likely to be someone other than the victim — a police officer, ambulance attendant, bank teller, neighbor, or other family member.

Most states require doctors and other social service professionals to report evidence of abuse. The most common outcome of intervention is that the victim is moved to an institution. Many elderly, however, refuse to be removed from an abusive situation in order to be put in an alternative setting, and without the victim's cooperation, little can be done.

Who Are the Abusers of the Elderly?

The NCEA reports that adult children were the most frequent abusers of the elderly. This category increased from 30 percent in 1990 to 37 percent in 1996. Other family members, such as siblings, grandchildren, and spouses, ranked as the second most likely abusers. Other family members accounted for 16 percent of reports in 1990 and 10.8 percent in 1996, while spouses were 16 percent of reports in 1990 and 12.6 percent in 1996. In addition, professional caretakers in the home sometimes abuse the elderly in their care. There may be a significant number of elderly who are abused by two or more people.

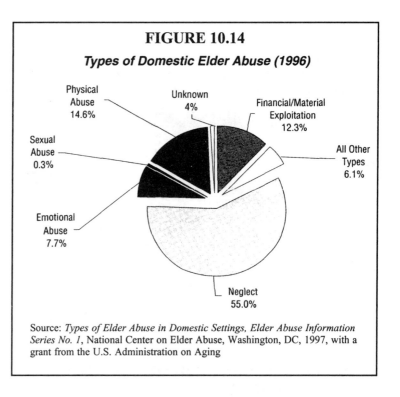

FIGURE 10.14

Types of Domestic Elder Abuse (1996)

Source: *Types of Elder Abuse in Domestic Settings, Elder Abuse Information Series No. 1*, National Center on Elder Abuse, Washington, DC, 1997, with a grant from the U.S. Administration on Aging

Sex of Perpetrators

The NCEA reported that, in 1990, the majority — 54.7 percent — of perpetrators were male. By 1996, there was no significant difference between the sexes in likelihood of elder abuse — 47.4 percent of perpetrators were male, and 48.9 percent were female.

Who Are the Abuse Victims?

The NCEA reported that about two-thirds of elder abuse victims in domestic settings are female. Data from 36 states showed that 67.4 percent of the elderly who were abused in 1996 were females. In addition, older elders are more likely to be victims. Elderly over the age of 80 made up more than one-third of victims in 1996. The median age of these victims was 77.9 years. The NCEA reported that 62.4 percent of self-abusers were women. The median age of these self-neglecting elders was 77.4 years.

By race, in 1996, 66.4 percent of the victims of domestic elder abuse were White, while 18.7 percent were Black. Hispanic elders accounted for 10.4 percent of the victims; Native American and

178

Asian American/Pacific Islanders were each less than 1 percent.

Reporting of Elder Abuse

In most states, certain professionals — adult protective service/human service workers, social service workers, law enforcement agencies, medical workers — are required to report domestic elder abuse, neglect, and exploitation. The NCEA reported that, in 1996, 22.5 percent of all reports came from physicians and other health-care professionals. Another 15.1 percent came from service providers, and family members and relatives of victims reported 16.3 percent of suspected elder abuse cases. Friends, neighbors, law enforcement personnel, clergy, banks/financial institutions, and abuse victims made the remainder of reporters. (See Figure 10.15.) The NCEA reports that most of elder abuse reports were substantiated after being investigated. In 1996, 64.2 percent of all reports were proven.

Causes of Elder Abuse

The National Center on Elder Abuse reports that no single theory can explain why older people are abused. The causes of elder abuse are diverse and complicated. Some relate to the personality of the abuser, some reflect the relationship between the abuser and the abused, and some are reactions to stressful situations. While some children truly dislike their parents and the role of caregiver, many others want to care for their parents or feel it is the right thing to do, but sometimes they may be emotionally or financially unable.

Stress

Most experts agree that stress is a contributing factor in abuse of the elderly. Meeting the daily needs of a frail and dependent elderly

relative may be overwhelming for some family members. When the elderly person lives in the same household as the caregiver, crowding, differences of opinion, and constant demands often add to the strain of providing physical care. If the elderly person lives in a different house, the added pressure of having to commute between two households, doing extra housekeeping chores, and being on call at a moment's notice may be too much for the caregiver to cope with.

The Financial Burden

In many cases, caring for an elderly person places a financial strain on a family. Elderly parents may need financial assistance at the same time that their children are raising their own families. Instead of an occasional night out, a long-awaited vacation, or a badly needed new car, families may find themselves paying for ever-increasing medical care, prescription drugs, physical aids, special dietary supplements, extra food and clothing, or therapy. Saving for their children's college education, for a daughter's wedding, or for retirement becomes difficult. Resentment can build quickly, and it can lead to emotional if not outright physical abuse of the elderly by the caregiver.

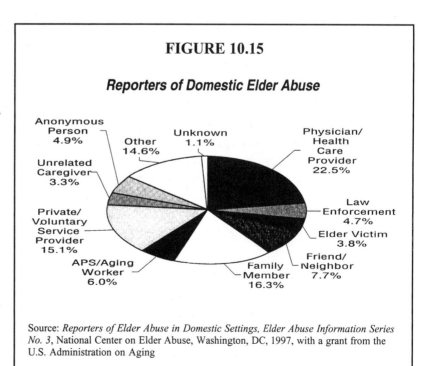

FIGURE 10.15

Reporters of Domestic Elder Abuse

Anonymous Person 4.9%
Other 14.6%
Unknown 1.1%
Physician/Health Care Provider 22.5%
Unrelated Caregiver 3.3%
Private/Voluntary Service Provider 15.1%
APS/Aging Worker 6.0%
Family Member 16.3%
Friend/Neighbor 7.7%
Elder Victim 3.8%
Law Enforcement 4.7%

Source: *Reporters of Elder Abuse in Domestic Settings, Elder Abuse Information Series No. 3*, National Center on Elder Abuse, Washington, DC, 1997, with a grant from the U.S. Administration on Aging

The Cycle of Abuse

Some experts believe that persons who abuse an elderly parent or relative were themselves abused as children. Dr. Suzanne K. Steinmetz, Director for Resources for Older Americans at the University of Delaware and a recognized expert on domestic violence, found such a pattern in her studies of elderly abusers. She found that only one out of 400 children treated non-violently when they were raised attacked their elderly parents; on the other hand, 1 out of 2 children who was violently mistreated as he or she grew up abused his or her elderly parents.

Chicago psychiatrist Mitchell Messer, who treats adults who care for elderly parents, notes, "We find parent beatings when the parents set the example of solving problems through brutality when the children were growing up.... The response is simply following the example his parents set." As adults, formerly abused children often have financial, marital, or drug problems which they blame on their parents and which make them even more abusive.

Invasion of Privacy

Most Americans believe that home is a place a person should be able to call his or her own. When that home must be shared, there is an inevitable loss of a certain amount of control and privacy. Movement may be restricted, habits may need to be changed, rivalry frequently develops between generations over decision-making, and young children may play the adults against each other to get what they want. Frustration and anxiety result as both parent and supporting child try to suppress angry feelings, sometimes unsuccessfully.

Loss of Freedom

An adult child may be obligated to care for an adult parent just at the time when his or her own children are leaving home. The resentment of being once again tied to the home, this time to care for a frail, perhaps bedridden, parent pushes many caregivers to the breaking point. To make matters worse, they may feel guilty and ashamed of their negative feelings. The dependent parent, in turn, often senses this resentment and may respond by withdrawing or becoming even more demanding. The average length of home care for a severely dependent person who is over 70 is between five and six years. In many cases, it is much longer.

Additionally, an adult child (usually a daughter) with children still in the home may find herself in the position of caring also for an elderly parent. The term "sandwich generation" (those persons who have both a younger generation and an older generation to care for) has been coined to describe these caregivers who may have anticipated enjoyment of their own interests at exactly the same time they are required to assume care for an aged parent. At the same time, it should be emphasized that the overwhelming majority of caregivers who suffer these many types of stress do not abuse the elderly people they are caring for.

Reverse Dependency

Some sources believe that people who abuse an elderly person may actually be quite dependent on that person. Some experts have found that abused elderly were no more likely to have had a recent decline in health or be seriously ill or hospitalized previously than the non-abused elderly. In fact, as a group, the abused elderly were more self-sufficient in preparing meals, doing ordinary housework, and climbing stairs than were the non-abused elderly.

On the other hand, abusing caregivers often seem more dependent on their victims for housing, financial assistance, and transportation than were nonabusing caregivers. They often seem to have fewer resources and are frequently unable to meet their own basic needs. Rather than having power in the relationship, they are relatively powerless. From these observations, some authorities have concluded that abusing caregivers may not always be driven to violence by the physical and emotional burden of caring for a seriously disabled elderly person but may have emotional problems of their own that can lead to violent behavior.

The Abusive Spouse

The high rate of spousal abuse among the elderly is possibly the result of the fact that many elderly people live with spouses, so the opportunity for spousal violence is great. Violence against an elderly spouse may be the continuation of an abusive relationship that began years earlier — abuse does not end simply because a couple gets older. Sometimes, however, the abuse may not begin until later years, in which case it is often associated with alcohol abuse, unemployment, post-retirement depression, and/or loss of self-esteem.

Intervention and Prevention

All 50 states and the District of Columbia have laws dealing specifically with adult abuse, but as with laws concerning child abuse and spousal abuse among younger couples, they are often ineffective. The effectiveness of laws and the enforcing agencies vary from state to state and even from county to county within a given state. No standard definition of abuse exists among enforcement agencies. In many cases, authorities cannot legally intervene and terminate an abusive condition unless a report is filed, the abuse is verified, and the victim files a formal complaint. An elderly person could understandably be reluctant, physically unable, or too fearful to accuse or prosecute an abuser. At the present time, 42 states and the District of Columbia operate "mandatory reporting systems," making it mandatory for certain professionals to report suspected abuse. In eight states, reporting is voluntary.

The best way to stop elder abuse is to prevent its occurrence. As noted above, researchers have identified specific situations where abuse is likely to occur and the type of person that is likely to be an abuser. Older people who know that they will eventually need outside help should carefully analyze the potential difficulties of living with a child and, if necessary and possible, make alternate arrangements. In any event, they should take care to protect their money and assets to ensure that their valuables cannot be easily taken over by someone else.

Young families or persons who must care for an older person, voluntarily or otherwise, must realize that their frustration and despair do not have to result in abuse. Social agencies can often work with families to help relieve anger and stress. Sometimes there are ways to offset the financial burden of elder care, for example, through tax deductions or subsidies for respite care. (See Chapter IX.)

Elder Shelters

In 1999, Rosalie S. Wolf, of the Institute on Aging, in *Elder Shelters: United States, Canada, and Japan*, reported that little study had been done on the subject of sheltering elderly abuse victims. Virtually no listing of shelters for the elderly existed. She was able to identify 17 programs — eight in operation, six in the planning stage, and three closed. The oldest program dated from 1986; the newest opened in May 1998. Since the original count, three additional shelters have been identified, two in Tokyo, Japan, and one in Montreal (it opened in 1992 but closed in 1995). The Japanese shelters had opened earlier than any of the others, in 1981.

Dr. Wolf's study found that few older women have been served in battered women's shelters although age was never a criterion for eligibility. Shelters typically cannot accept anyone who cannot take care of themselves. They rarely provide 24-hour supervision, and they often close during the daytime.

INSTITUTIONAL ABUSE — A FORGOTTEN POPULATION?

The greatest threat that many older Americans face is not a criminal armed with a gun but a telemarketer armed with a deceptive rap. And our most defenseless seniors, those who are sick or disabled and living in nursing homes, cannot lock the door against abuse and neglect by people paid to care for them. — President Bill Clinton, 1999

Abuse of the elderly can also occur outside the private home in nursing homes charged with the care of the aged and ill patient. Institutional abuse generally refers to the same forms of abuse mentioned as domestic abuse but perpetuated by persons who have a legal or contractual obligation to provide elders with care and protection. Despite the fact that, by law, nursing homes must take steps to attain or maintain the "highest practicable physical, mental, and psychosocial well-being of each resident," too many of such residents are the victims of neglect or abuse by these facilities or their employees.

Because data on nursing home residents' complaints are not compiled on a national level, information is scarce regarding abuse occurring in institutional settings. Critics believe the abuse of frail and ill patients occurs because there are no uniform regulations governing the facilities and no appropriate way to monitor them. Approximately 1.6 million people live in 16,700 nursing homes in the United States, and by 2023, the number of Americans age 85 and over is expected to double.

Brian Payne and Richard Cikovic studied 488 cases of nursing home abuse reported to Medicaid Fraud Control Units ("An Empirical Examination of the Characteristics, Consequences, and Causes of Elder Abuse in Nursing Homes," *Journal of Elder Abuse & Neglect*, vol. 7, no. 4, 1995). Forty-two states have Medicaid Fraud Control Units responsible for detecting, investigating, and prosecuting Medicaid fraud and abuse. The study found that 84.2 percent of the abuse was physical, including slapping; hitting with an object such as a hairbrush, wet towel, or spatula; kicking; and spitting. The remaining acts were sexual (8.8

TABLE 10.3

Occupations of Nursing Home Personnel Accused of Abuse

Occupation	n	%
Nurses' Aide	302	61.9
Licensed Practical Nurse	32	6.6
Direct Care Worker	15	3.1
Supervisor	15	3.1
Certified Nurse's Technician	11	2.3
Registered Nurse	9	1.8
Maintenance/Housekeeping	7	1.4
Orderly	6	1.2
Resident Counselor	6	1.2
Mental Health Caseworker	5	1.0
Licensed Caretaker	4	0.8
Human Service Worker	2	0.4
Developmental Trainer	2	0.4
Other/Missing	72	14.8
Total	**488**	**100.0**

TABLE 10.4

Gender of the Accused by Gender of the Victim

Gender of Victim	Gender of Accused			
	Male		Female	
	n	%	n	%
Male	126	(66.0)	48	(41.4)
Female	65	(34.0)	68	(58.6)
Total	**191**		**116**	

chi-square 17.66, phi = .24, p = .01

Source of both tables: Brian K. Payne and Richard Cikovic, "An Empirical Examination of the Characteristics, Consequences, and Causes of Elder Abuse in Nursing Homes," *Journal of Elder Abuse and Neglect*, vol. 7, no. 4, 1995, pp. 61-74, Copyright 1995, Haworth Press, Inc., Binghamton, New York.

percent), monetary (1.4 percent), or duty-related, in which an employee misperformed specific duties, such as removing bandages in a rough manner. The most recent statistics from the U.S. Department of Aging reported there were 548 complaints of sexual abuse between October 1, 1995 and September 30, 1996.

Although nurses' aides comprised the largest group of abusers (62 percent), they were also the single most numerous employee group in nursing homes (Table 10.3). Of the 488 incidents, 63 percent involved a male employee. Males were also slightly more likely to be victims (57 percent). Male employees tended to abuse male residents; female employees tended to abuse female victims (Table 10.4).

In an effort to improve the quality of care and eliminate abuse in nursing homes, government regulations and laws are requiring greater supervision of nursing homes. In 1987, then-President Ronald Reagan signed into effect a landmark law, the Omnibus Budget Reconciliation Act (PL 100-203), which included sections that protected patient rights and treatment. The law went into effect October 1990. Compliance with the law varies from state to state and from one nursing facility to another. Families are increasingly filing (and winning) court suits against irresponsible nursing facilities. New York state enacted "Kathy's Law," which created the new felony-level crime of "abuse of a vulnerable elderly person." In 1999, President Clinton announced a crackdown on nursing homes and states that do a poor job of regulating them.

Types of Abuse and Neglect

Nursing home neglect and/or abuse can take many forms including

- Failure to provide proper diet and hydration.

- Failure to assist with personal hygiene.

- Over-medication or under-medication.

- Failure to answer call lights promptly.

- Failure to turn residents in their beds to promote circulation.

- Slapping or other physical abuse.

- Leaving the resident in soiled garments or beds or failure to take them to the toilet.

- Use of unwarranted restraints.

- Emotional or verbal abuse.

- Retaliation for making a complaint.

- Failure to provide appropriate medical care.

- Sexual assault or rape of the resident.

- Theft of the resident's property or money.

Some experts suggest that in an attempt to squeeze more profit from the operation, too many nursing homes do not hire adequate numbers of qualified staff. Poorly qualified, untrained, or overworked staff are often unable to cope with the demands of nursing home residents. Exposing abuse in those situations is often more difficult than in other health care environments because the victims are sometimes unable to communicate their abuse or neglect because of their physical or mental disabilities.

CHAPTER XI

THE "AGE WAVE" — TRENDS AND PROJECTIONS

America is no longer "young." By the year 2030, one-third of the population will be over 55. Significant changes in age composition can have dramatic political, economic, and social effects on a nation.

INCREASING DIVERSITY

The United States is becoming more diverse. Among the elderly, racial and ethnic diversity will continue to increase. Although races other than White now constitute about 1 in 10 of the elderly, by 2050, that proportion is expected to increase to 2 in 10. The elderly Black population will likely increase from 8 to 10 percent, and elderly Hispanics from 4 percent to 15 percent.

Tomorrow's elderly will be more educated and wealthier than today's elderly, just as today's older Americans are better educated and more well-to-do than their grandparents. In addition, with the variety of living arrangements needed and the differences between individuals in health and personality, the older generation will reflect more variation than ever before. Growing age and racial and ethnic diversity will change the everyday social, cultural, and language interactions among Americans.

It is increasingly likely that more and more people in their 50s and 60s will have surviving parents. The four-generation family will become common, with children knowing grandparents and even great-grandparents, especially their great-grandmothers.

THE CYCLIC LIFE

Dr. Ken Dychtwald, in *Age Wave: The Challenges and Opportunities of an Aging America* (Bantam, New York City, 1990), likened the increasing numbers of elderly to an awakening giant. This wave of age, especially with baby boomers "in the wings," affects not only American institutions, but individuals as well. Added longevity often causes people to rethink the pace and plan for their lives as well as the purposes, goals, and challenges of its various stages.

Throughout human history, the average length of life was short. In a world where most people did not expect to live longer than 40 or 50 years, it was essential that certain key personal and social tasks be accomplished by specific ages. Traditionally, important activities, such as getting an education, job training, parenthood, and retirement, not only were designated to particular periods of life but also were expected to occur only once in a lifetime. The path from childhood to old age was linear: it moved in one direction.

This pattern of life was maintained not only by tradition, but by law. Government regulations and institutional rules and traditions prescribed the ages at which a person should go to school, begin and end work, or receive a pension. This approach to life was based on the assumptions that 1) the activities of life were to be performed on time and in sequence, and 2) most of life's periods of growth occurred in the first half of life, while the second half was, in general, characterized by decline and disinvestment.

Many people believe that as humans live longer, this traditional linear path is evolving into a more flexible pattern, a "cyclic life plan." Having the luxury to choose how people arrange their various life tasks is becoming commonplace. For example, some people are opting to pursue careers throughout their 20s, 30s, and even 40s, followed by marriage and childrearing activities, a reversal of traditional roles. Formal learning was once the province of the young; today, middle-aged and older people are increasingly returning to school. Advances in medical technology and knowledge are making it possible to bear children later in life.

People once pursued a single career in their lifetimes; today, workers change jobs and even careers many times. The RAND Corporation, a California-based think-tank, predicted that by the year 2020, the average worker will need to be retrained up to 13 times in his or her lifetime. Except for a few specified professions (such as airline pilots), mandatory retirement has become illegal. Many older workers want to continue working (or return to work), and some must do so for financial reasons. (For more discussion of retirement, see Chapters IV and XI.)

While the linear plan generally included education, work, and recreation/retirement, in that order, a cyclic plan could be a blending, reordering, and repeating of activities, as desired. Although not everyone will choose to do things differently than in the past, he or she increasingly has the option to do so.

Lydia Bronte, in *The Longevity Factor* (HarperCollins, New York City, 1993), followed a group of 150 people who chose to work into their 70s, 80s, 90s, and in a few cases, beyond the age of 100. Many had major achievements after age 60. Three-quarters reported that growing old was a positive experience. Bronte suggested that, while scientists in 1900 believed people could not be productive and creative over the age of 40, Americans can expect, a century later, a productive and creative "second middle age" between 50 and 75, and even beyond, that has not existed before.

QUESTIONS POSED

An aging nation raises many social and political challenges for American society. Among the questions posed are

- Can the country afford the tens of millions of septuagenarians and centenarians?

- Who will pay for long-term care?

- Will existing entitlement programs survive long enough for Americans to reap even part of what they have paid in?

- With increasing longevity, should new definitions of "old" be considered and a new age set for receiving benefits?

- Can the current health care system handle the increasing numbers of chronic degenerative diseases, such as Alzheimer's?

- How will Americans come to terms with increasing "right to die" issues?

- Can the country reengineer many of the products and services to meet the needs of mature consumers?

- How can the aging nations of the Americas, Europe, and Asia continue to be productive with so many dependent elderly and fewer and fewer young to support them?

"GRAY POWER" — A POLITICAL BLOC?

People ages 55 to 74 vote more than any other age group (see Chapter V), and therefore, the increasing number of Americans in this age group will have a growing political impact. Organizations such as the American Association of Retired Persons (AARP), which claims membership of about half of persons over age 50, already exercise considerable influence in lobbying and in educating political leaders on issues pertinent to older Americans. The AARP, with 32 million members and an annual budget of about $550 million, is the world's second-largest nonprofit organization after the Catholic Church. That influence will undoubtedly grow as lawmakers, many of whom may themselves be older, respond to the increasing voting power of the elderly. Most economists predict that growing proportions of the American budget will be dedicated to spending for the elderly.

Issues such as age discrimination, quality of care in nursing facilities, Medicare and "medigap" coverage, nontraditional living arrangements, and reform in pension plans and Social Security are vital topics for older Americans. Other areas that must be addressed are expansion of senior citizen benefits and discounts, changes in traffic and architectural design, and ethical questions raised by medical technology.

Silver-Haired Legislatures

About half the states now have "Silver-Haired Legislatures." Their members, who must be 55, although the average age is 80, include former teachers, judges, doctors, business owners, and even legislators. They take over the House and Senate chambers to consider issues of concern to the elderly. In many cases, they function to educate the real legislators about issues.

One of the largest and most active groups is Florida's 20-year-old Silver-Haired Legislature. It is a working example of grass-roots politics. For a week every year, the members pick top priority issues and take those to churches, civic clubs, mobile home park organizations, and condominium boards to enlist support. Then they promote these ideas to real state legislators. The members claim that more than 100 of the issues they have promoted have gone on to become state law. Their greatest achievement was the creation in 1988 of a State Department of Elder Affairs. The members have also pushed for bills to eliminate waste, fight consumer fraud, and press for adequate health care. It also filed a friend-of-the-court brief on physician-assisted suicide.

A SHIFTING ECONOMY

Older Workers

The increasing numbers of older Americans will change the work force as industry seeks both to accommodate the elderly and to profit from their attributes. With the declining number of younger workers, the work force will age, as will society in general. Many older Americans will find themselves needing to work for financial reasons, and many will want to remain active and employed. The first baby boomer will turn 60 in 2006, so most of the changes in the work force will not begin until late in the first decade of the twenty-first century.

Marketing to the Older Consumer

People now see themselves as 10 to 15, maybe 20 years, younger than their real age.... A person turning 50 may still have half of his or her adult life ahead. There may be as many years of life after 50 as there were between 18 and 50. — Charles Allen, *Modern Maturity,* 1999

Ken Dychtwald, in *Age Power — How the 21st Century Will Be Ruled By the New Old* (1999), enumerates the economic power of the Americans 50 and older. Today's mature consumers

- Control in excess of $7 trillion in wealth — 70 percent of the total.

- Own 77 percent of all financial assets.

- Comprise 66 percent of all stockholders, own 40 percent of all mutual funds and 60 percent of annuities, and represent 50 percent of IRA and Keogh holders.

- Seventy-nine percent own their own homes; they own 46 percent of home equity loans and transact more than 5 million car loans per year.

- Represent almost half the credit-card use — 40 million card-owners.

186

- Buy 41 percent of new cars sold and 48 percent of all luxury cars, totaling more than $60 billion.

- Account for 51 percent of all over-the-counter drug sales and consume 74 percent of all prescription drugs.

To appeal to this group, publications targeting those over 50, such as *Modern Maturity* and *New Choices*, have redesigned their magazines to make them cleaner, brighter, and more youthful. *Modern Maturity* announced a new design featuring two editions of its magazine — one for readers who work and one for those who are retired.

The already growing retirement-related industries are expected to increase as businesses seek to fill the needs of the older population. Health and fitness concerns will demand additional geriatricians (physicians specializing in the treatment of elderly persons), physical therapists, cataract and hearing specialists, and nutritionists. A market has emerged for pagers, remote controls, and monitoring devices for those living alone.

Comfort and security become more important as people age; they are more likely to purchase products based on comfort, value, and ease of use. Older adults are more likely to be attracted to products and appliances that they believe to be "user friendly," that is, easily understandable and useable (for example, easy-to-open medicine containers).

Most recreation centers and community programs have expanded their post-55 services. The hotel and travel industries now offer discounts and accommodations tailored to the needs of the increasingly mobile mature market and its discretionary income. Some restaurants have responded by offering smaller food portions and lowering prices on senior citizen menus. Many rural towns, indeed states, have found it profitable to attract retirees, with their pensions and savings, who make fewer demands on expensive local public services, such as schools.

ON THE ROAD

During the past decade, the number of licensed drivers 70 or older has grown by nearly 50 percent. As the nation's population grows older, more older persons are on the streets, both as drivers and as pedestrians. In 1998, there were 24.8 million licensed drivers over 65 in the United States, and their ranks are expected to reach 30 million by 2020. In 1998, they accounted for 14 percent of all drivers, up from 10 percent in 1980.

The Insurance Institute for Highway Safety reports that drivers over 65 have a higher crash rate per mile driven than all other motorists, except those under 25. Those over 75 have the second-highest fatality rate per mile driven of all drivers after teenagers. Older people who are injured in motor vehicle crashes are more likely to die of their injuries than are people in other age groups. About half of fatal crashes involving drivers 80 and older occur at intersections and involve more than one vehicle. Drivers over 65 have a particularly high accident rate when making left turns. Experts attribute that to the fact that older drivers take longer to make the turns, increasing the risk of a crash.

Reduced vision, especially night vision, slower reflexes, reduced hearing, and less flexibility of the head and neck are common problems of aging that can impair driving performance. However, although crash rates are high among older drivers, the actual number of crashes and deaths are relatively low because seniors usually cut down on their driving. In 1998, John Eberhard, senior researcher at the National Highway Traffic Safety Administration (NHTSA), claimed, "If you look at the number of accidents per licensed drivers, those in the 65-and-above group are the safest around."

Vision Problems

A 1999 study at Johns Hopkins University School of Medicine (*Journal of American Medi-*

cal Association, vol. 282, no.17), which studied a variety of visual changes in older drivers, found that visual field was highly correlated with crash risk. (Cognitive or thinking process deficiencies are believed to increase crash risk by 50 to 60 percent.) People with restricted visual field (peripheral vision) were about 30 percent more likely to have been in a crash. Visual field is not measured by motor vehicle bureaus, which test only visual acuity (sharpness). The most dramatic age-related vision changes involved sensitivity to glare and the time it takes the eyes to readjust to normal light after exposure to glare.

In studies of patients 55 and older with cataracts, researchers at the University of Alabama at Birmingham found that those with cataracts were two and one-half times more likely to have been in a crash in the previous five years than those without cataracts. Half the patients with cataracts had surgery to remove them; three years after surgery, their crash rates had leveled off, at a rate of 4.9 crashes per million person-miles of travel. Among those who chose not to have surgery, crash rates increased from 4.8 to 8.3 per million miles of travel in three years.

Ensuring the Safety of Older Drivers

The trend now is more toward helping those who need it and less toward regulating them out of their cars. — William Barnhill, *AARP Bulletin*, 1998

Officials are wrestling with how to get hazardous older drivers off the roads without penalizing able ones. At what age should a person give up driving? It is a hard decision for an older person to make because the automobile is the chief means of mobility and, just as important, a sense of autonomy for most people. Studies show that the driver's state of general health and fitness is important. Only three states — Illinois, Indiana, and New Hampshire — and the District of Columbia require age-based road tests for license renewal. Seven other states offer shorter renewal periods for older drivers. In addition, some require physical examina-

tions, others require physicians to report patients who have impairments that could affect driving safety, and many specify a wide variety of medical and mental conditions for which licenses can be suspended. Some states do not require vision tests at all.

While officials must deal with the necessity of getting some older drivers off the road, they also are struggling to find ways to enable others to continue to drive, especially since increasingly more of American society will be older. A growing number of states now try to keep older drivers behind the wheel as long as possible. Some states, such as California, Oregon, and Texas, offer special driver assessments on request, counseling for those with impairments, and advise on how to stay mobile afterward.

One reason states have not clamped down harder is that older drivers as a group generally regulate themselves quite effectively. Principal health reasons reported for stopping driving were macular degeneration of the eye and other eye conditions, stroke, hospitalization within the previous year, and Parkinson's disease. The total number of illnesses reported was the most important factor in the decision to stop driving. Age and sex were not important predictors of traffic accidents.

In 1993, a study of 1,470 elderly drivers, funded by the American Automobile Association (AAA) Foundation for Traffic Safety, reported that 20.9 percent of women and 9.8 percent of men between 65 and 90 had voluntarily stopped driving because of recognized functional impairment. Nine percent of the females and 11 percent of the males reported they had been in a traffic accident in the previous five years. Women were more likely to voluntarily stop driving than men. The average age for women deciding to stop driving was 80.9 years, while the average for men was 82.5 years.

Many states are upgrading inadequate highway lighting, signs, and markings, improvements that will aid drivers of all ages. Older drivers are encouraged to upgrade their skills with training, such

TABLE 11.1

People 18 Years and Older by Computer and Internet Use: October 1997

[Numbers in thousands. Civilian noninstitutional population]

Characteristics	Total people 18 years and over	Computer at home Yes Number	Computer at home Yes Percent[1]	Computer at home Use computer at home Percent[2]	Computer at home Use Internet at home Percent[2]	Employed Yes Number	Employed Use computer at work Percent[3]	Employed Use Internet at work Percent[3]	Enrolled in school Yes Number	Enrolled in school Use computer at school Percent[4]	Enrolled in school Use Internet at school Percent[4]	Use computer anywhere Percent[1]	Use Internet anywhere Percent[1]
TOTAL	195,689	79,594	40.7	70.9	35.2	128,198	49.8	16.6	16,918	62.3	36.0	47.1	22.1
AGE													
18 to 24 years	24,929	10,788	43.3	70.1	36.5	16,178	37.1	9.4	10,559	70.3	42.9	58.1	31.6
25 to 34 years	39,248	16,442	41.9	79.4	42.8	31,995	53.1	18.2	3,370	54.2	29.4	57.2	27.3
35 to 44 years	44,027	22,609	51.4	73.9	36.7	36,443	53.9	18.8	1,798	43.6	19.9	58.0	27.1
45 to 54 years	33,718	16,854	50.0	69.3	34.4	27,075	54.1	18.7	965	45.5	19.9	55.3	25.1
55 years and over	53,766	12,901	24.0	57.4	23.0	16,508	39.8	12.2	225	31.7	11.7	20.7	7.9
GENDER													
Male	93,897	39,646	42.2	72.1	39.5	68,801	44.1	17.5	7,706	65.6	40.3	47.0	24.8
Female	101,792	39,948	39.2	69.6	31.0	59,397	56.5	15.5	9,211	59.6	32.5	47.3	19.6
RACE													
Non-Hispanic White	145,672	66,179	45.4	72.6	36.8	96,371	53.9	18.4	12,014	61.9	37.7	51.4	24.9
Non-Hispanic Black	22,232	4,875	21.9	65.6	26.4	13,665	40.0	11.2	2,193	66.1	33.0	34.3	12.8
Hispanic (of any race)	19,459	4,313	22.2	59.6	25.9	12,733	30.2	7.7	1,554	59.3	26.1	28.9	10.5
EDUCATIONAL ATTAINMENT													
Less than high school diploma	33,789	4,500	13.3	41.5	15.4	13,820	11.9	1.5	1,669	58.7	19.5	11.1	3.2
High school diploma/GED	65,968	20,397	30.9	58.0	22.4	42,324	36.4	6.6	2,522	60.9	34.1	34.9	10.9
Some college	52,324	26,031	49.7	73.3	36.2	37,291	55.6	16.1	9,557	65.8	40.8	61.6	29.2
Bachelor's degree or more	43,609	28,667	65.7	82.4	46.6	34,762	75.0	35.3	3,170	54.6	31.8	76.3	45.1
FAMILY INCOME													
Under $25,000	58,312	10,024	17.2	68.1	29.2	28,457	29.0	6.4	4,896	62.9	36.8	23.9	9.2
25,000 to 49,999	54,727	22,017	40.2	68.5	30.5	39,083	47.6	13.3	4,203	59.9	32.1	48.9	19.7
50,000 to 74,999	31,650	19,282	60.9	72.2	36.5	25,501	61.3	21.7	3,063	62.4	35.7	67.7	33.4
75,000 and over	27,910	21,438	76.8	75.0	43.7	22,335	71.0	31.2	3,221	63.9	40.5	77.9	46.5
Not reported	23,090	6,832	29.6	66.0	29.2	12,821	43.4	13.4	1,534	63.2	35.5	36.2	15.2
HOUSEHOLD SIZE													
1 person	26,350	5,279	20.0	89.4	46.6	13,950	54.5	21.0	1,303	57.8	36.0	36.0	17.0
2-3 people	103,165	39,681	38.5	71.9	36.3	65,987	51.0	17.0	7,762	60.0	34.8	46.0	21.4
4-5 people	55,250	30,014	54.3	68.3	33.4	41,292	49.3	15.7	6,601	65.5	38.0	56.4	26.8
6-7 people	8,754	3,889	44.4	58.8	26.2	5,650	35.0	10.1	1,013	63.5	32.8	40.4	17.6
8 or more people	2,170	731	33.7	52.4	18.2	1,318	23.1	5.7	239	67.7	36.4	31.1	12.0
REGION													
Northeast	38,340	15,308	39.9	68.2	34.7	24,337	49.7	15.9	3,112	65.2	38.0	45.6	21.3
Midwest	45,427	18,751	41.3	70.3	33.3	31,063	49.8	15.8	4,001	68.8	42.7	48.6	22.1
South	69,025	25,508	37.0	72.0	36.3	44,480	48.6	15.9	5,562	64.1	35.0	44.9	20.6
West	42,897	20,027	46.7	72.0	36.1	28,318	51.9	19.1	4,243	51.7	29.6	50.5	25.2

[1] Among all adults.
[2] Among adults with a computer in the home.
[3] Among employed adults.
[4] Among those adults enrolled in school.
Source: U.S. Census Bureau, Current Population Survey, October 1997.

Source: *Computer Use in the United States 1997*, Bureau of the Census, Washington, DC, 1999

as is offered by the American Association for Retired Persons (AARP) in its 55 ALIVE driver refreshment program, from which 5 million Americans have graduated since 1979. Insurance companies are now offering reduced premiums to elderly who enroll in driver's safety classes.

As a group, older drivers are more likely than any other age group except infants and preschool children to wear safety belts. Older drivers tend to drive when conditions are safest. They generally limit their driving during bad weather and at night, and they drive fewer miles than younger drivers do. Older drivers are also less likely to drive and drink. The National Center for Health Statistics reported that, in 1996, drivers younger than 70 who died in crashes were five times more likely than those 70 and older to be intoxicated (blood alcohol concentration of at least 0.10 per deciliter).

Some measures that could benefit older drivers as well as other age groups include

- Improvements in automobile design that simplify driving and increase crash protection, such as reduced-glare headlights, improved head restraints, knee bars, and side-impact protection.

- Improvements in road design, such as wider lanes and shoulders, more one-way streets, better lighting and signs, and lower speed limits where complex maneuvers are required.

- Greater use of public transportation.

- Restricted driving when conditions warrant, such as to particular times of day, geographic location, or road type.

- Physician reporting — many states already require that doctors report to a state licensing agency certain medical conditions, such as diabetes, seizure disorders, etc., that could affect a person's ability to drive.

COMPUTER USE

Although computer usage is most frequently associated with the young, many older persons are increasingly using computer technology. The U.S. Census, in its *Computer Use in the United States: 1997* (1999), reported that 24 percent of those 55 and older — the lowest of any age group — had a computer in their homes. Some of these computers may be used by the children of those over-55 persons who head the households, although by the age of 55 (and older), most parents do not have children residing in the home. Of those 55 and older with computers in the home, 57.4 percent used the computer at home, and 23 percent used the Internet. Of adults 55 and older who were employed, 39.8 percent used a computer at work, and 12.2 percent used the Internet. (See Table 11.1.)

In 1998, SeniorNet, a nonprofit organization that helps the elderly with computers, and Charles Schwab, a discount stockbroker with a large online trading business, conducted a survey, *The 1998 SeniorNet Survey*, to determine computer use among older Americans. The study found that only 18 percent of those 70 and older had ever used a computer, and most said they probably would not do so. Between 50 and 70, however, computer ownership rose to 51 percent. Among those 50 and older with a college degree, ownership approached 64 percent. SeniorNet found that older residents were the fastest-growing segment of the computer world.

Fifty-six percent of seniors who were investors had a computer at home. Almost 40 percent of those over 50 had access to the Internet either at home, work, or another site. Nearly 80 percent of those had logged on in the previous month and spent an average of five hours per week online. One-quarter of seniors who used the Internet said they checked a stock quote the first time they went online. Nevertheless, only one-fifth of senior investors with Internet access used the Internet for financial or investment purposes.

Computer companies are focusing new attention on the over-55 population. Dell Computers has found that older Americans would be even more inclined to purchase a home computer if they knew someone would be there to help them if they encountered problems. Service and support concerns apparently prevent many of them from "taking the plunge." Dell found that 46 percent of seniors would use computers to e-mail friends and family, 33 percent would play computer games, and 26 percent would surf the Internet.

THE GRAYING OF THE NATION

Campuses

The speed of technological innovation guarantees that you can't be alive for eight or nine decades without needing to retrain multiple times throughout your work life.
— Ken Dychtwald, *Age Power*, 1999

Universities report an increase in the age of students. According to the National Center for

Education Statistics, 1 in 3 Americans over 50 were engaged in some sort of adult education in 1998, more than double the number involved in 1990-91. This "graying" of the campus reflects the influx of older students, some of whom are elderly, who have enrolled in response to a changing job market, as well as increased free time, discretionary income, and vitality among older people.

This new population has prompted changes in college life, especially at two-year schools, including more flexible class schedules and greater demands on faculty, since the older student is often more demanding. It is no longer unusual to read about an elderly person going to college and getting the degree he or she had always wanted or had never completed. Experts expect study among older students to continue to skyrocket as baby boomers retire and live longer and healthier lives.

For these reasons, a thriving adult education industry has grown exponentially, including magazines, books, audio, video, Internet-based programs, workshops, and seminars. Colleges and universities across the nation have begun to pursue older students. They often offer credit for life and work experience.

In addition to traditional institutions of learning, many new learning environments have originated that target older persons. In 1989, two dozen institutes for learning were affiliated with Elderhostel, a national travel education group. Today, there are 272 such groups. There are even a number of retirement communities being built in association with universities.

Lifelong Learning — A Model Program

Well-educated retirees often enjoy the chance to return to the classroom. They can concentrate on those "elective" topics of personal interest they had to forego during their work lives. Quest, affiliated with the City College of New York, the Center for Worker Education, and the Elderhostel Network, offers study groups for and by its well-educated members. These include men and women with careers as teachers, accountants, librarians, dentists, secretaries, business executives, lawyers, publishers, scientists, writers, public administrators, and social workers.

Annual dues entitle a member to take as many of the 42 courses offered as desired and to attend special guest lectures. Members create and lead their own courses in what is termed "peer learning." Courses include musical theater, Plato, recreational mathematics, current ethical dilemmas, the American West, nutrition and health, crafts, languages, Shakespeare, drawing, the Islamic world, biography, God and science, Jewish authors, the Thirties, and cultural anthropology.

The members of Quest are part of a growing trend toward recreational education and educational vacations. Such learning institutions provide an alternative to stereotypical retirement activities, such as playing golf or bridge. In addition, peer learning programs foster social networks and give reason to get up and go out every day, both of which are crucial to good health.

Prisons

Another institution affected by the age of our society is the penal system. Eighty-one-year-old Viva LeRoy Nash, believed to be the nation's oldest death-row inmate, at Arizona State Prison, has suffered numerous heart attacks over the past 17 years. Like many others his age, he takes many medications each day and requires a low-fat diet. He is part of a growing number of older inmates. Some experts believe stricter sentencing laws mean prisons will be housing more elderly convicts and paying more money to do so. With the increasing introduction of "three strikes and you're out" programs that sentence habitual felons to life sentences, the 1987 abolition of parole for federal crimes, and the growing use of mandatory life sentences, the problems of the elderly will become a major problem for the nation's prisons. Approximately 11 percent of today's inmates have been behind bars for more than 30 years. The proportion of 30-year prisoners will undoubtedly balloon in decades ahead.

As the inmate population grows older, prisoners require additional medical, dietary, and psychological services that will further stretch the already huge cost of inmate care. Surveys of the elderly population have found that among those over 65, 80 percent have one or more chronic illnesses or diseases, and 60 percent have at least three medical problems. Prisons are increasingly being asked to provide long-term medical care for an aging population.

Older inmates often suffer from more health problems than the general aged population. They are more likely to be infected with HIV and tuberculosis and have histories of drug abuse. They are often less mobile, and prisons are not designed for "easy access." Aged inmates are more affected by violence within the prison. Experts estimate that caring for aging convicts can be two to three times as expensive as caring for younger prisoners. In addition, when elderly inmates are released, where do they go? Who will care for them?

Others have questioned the value of incarcerating older inmates. Many criminologists claim that most prisoners become less violent with age. They contend that the money spent to imprison a 60-year-old who is likely no longer a threat to society could be better spent to incarcerate an 18-year-old with a budding career in crime. Taxpayers may ask themselves if they are willing to pay out of their pocket to maintain older offenders in prison for their lifetimes as corrections take a growing proportion of public money.

Other critics observe that retaining prisoners in prison for years creates people who are conditioned to being told what to do and who have no support systems outside. They often have no skills with which to support themselves. For some of them, their only friends are fellow inmates. They may be out of touch with the outside world and unable to adjust to life as free persons. Some of those who have lived much of their adult lives inside prison walls actually prefer to be kept in confinement at government expense to having to forge new lives in freedom.

Rural Areas Turning Gray — Young People Leave; the Elderly Stay

In rural America, as generations of young people have sought jobs and opportunity elsewhere, parents, grandparents, and great-grandparents remain. The result is a transformation across the farm belt — Nebraska, Illinois, Indiana, Kansas, and other Midwestern states, as well as in rural areas of other states, especially the Sunbelt.

As the number of births has dropped, so has the number of students in rural schools. Hospitals stopped delivering babies, and in some places, hospitals, schools, and malls have closed completely. Residents have to go to nearby cities to shop or receive medical care. Some towns have died, and others are but small retirement communities of elderly, many of them in nursing homes. Many of those residents, primarily widows, help one another in what is considered the small town version of Social Security — volunteering in church, cooking for the sick, being good neighbors. As one senior explained, "There is no forced retirement here. Everyone's labor is needed." Those who are able deliver mail, drive snowplows, and serve on county boards.

Town Councils

Across the nation, particularly in small and medium-size towns, more and more older people are being elected to civic positions. There are many reasons for this trend, including the growing demands on council members' time, something retired persons often have in abundance, the increased numbers of older people, and the growing interests older people have in protecting their resources. One advantage older people offer councils is their greater life experience and long-term perspective.

HELP IN AN INCREASINGLY COMPLEX SOCIETY

The increasing complexity of American society and the growing needs of the aged who have no one to assist them have led to the emergence of two new types of service professions — private care managers and claims companies — that provide, for a fee, what family members may once have provided. Private care (or case) managers are social workers who provide one-to-one assistance in arranging care or housing or referral to government agencies that serve the elderly. Care managers oversee home-health staffing needs, monitor the quality of in-home services and equipment, and act as liaison with families living far away. Private care managers can be expensive ($50 to $150 per hour), but they may well be worth the cost. Medical claims companies assist the aged in filling out complicated insurance forms — for a charge or a percentage of the benefits received.

An estimated 500,000 U.S. elderly people need help with financial affairs. In response, new daily money management (DMM) programs have emerged, which provide help to the elderly in paying bills, filling out medical insurance forms, balancing checkbooks, making bank deposits, preparing tax returns, and budgeting. Some managers can even sign checks. There is, unfortunately, ample opportunity for abuse. Because some elderly may be confused or forgetful, it is easy for them to be taken advantage of. The American Association of Retired Persons (AARP) offers free DMM services to low-income families through community agencies. In 1986, the National Association of Professional Geriatric Care Managers was started in Tucson, Arizona, with 30 members. Today, 1,200 of the nation's estimated 4,000 care managers belong to the organization. Many care managers are now advocating certification.

Elder Law

The legal profession has seen the emergence of a new specialty — elder law, which covers the issues that often affect the senior population. The field of elder law includes a wide and growing range of topics. In addition to traditional work in probate, wills, and trust and estate planning, elder law specialists are now involved in such diverse areas as:

- Planning for disability or incapacity through living wills and durable power of attorney.

- Establishing eligibility for Social Security, Medicare, and Medicaid benefits.

- Long-term care, including patient rights, quality of care, and long-term care insurance.

- Elder fraud and abuse.

- Grandparents' visitation rights.

- Age discrimination at work.

- Housing problems (mortgages, housing discrimination).

- Conservatorships and guardianships.

- Retirement and pension benefits.

Driving Services

I gave up driving this year because my eyes are going. I can't take the bus because I can't see the numbers. I won't take taxis because they smell of smoke and they cost too much. You have to reserve a week in advance for a Regional Transport van, and the seats are tough on my bad back. I'm not frail enough to qualify for some other services. I don't want to impose on my friends or my family. Am I just supposed to sit at home? — Elderly woman, Portland, Maine

Many aging Americans face the dilemma of being unable to drive and yet, despite being otherwise healthy, find themselves prematurely lodged or housed in a nursing facility, simply because they cannot get around their communities to accomplish simple tasks, such as shopping for necessities and keeping doctors' appointments. Two-thirds of the elderly live in suburban and rural areas, and most of their homes are more than two miles from a public transportation stop. There is a large network of individual transportation services, public and private, that will pick up the elderly and disabled at their homes. But these services, known as "paratransit," do not cover the entire country. Most paratransit services rely on vans and paid drivers and run on fixed schedules to specific sites, such as senior centers. They are limited as to whom they can take and where and when they can go.

As the number of car-less elderly people has multiplied, federal agencies and organizations devoted to the aging have begun paying attention. AARP's Connections for Independent Living pilot project, using a mix of volunteer and paid drivers, and cars, not vans, is providing on-demand service to the elderly and disabled in Portland, Maine. Clients make a monthly payment or set up an account against which they can draw to pay for service. The network will sell the cars the elderly no longer use and start accounts with the money. Entrepreneurs in American communities might also find a market for transporting the elderly.

efits. (Table 11.3 shows expenditures for veterans' benefits from 1980 to 1998.) With the growth in the number and proportion of older veterans, an additional strain on the Veterans Administration medical system will likely result, putting further pressure on community resources.

NONTRADITIONAL LIFESTYLES

The increasing diversity of the aging population and the shortage of caregivers to provide long-term care for them will demand different ways of living and increased use of formal community services. The disabled will still need nursing facilities. Hospices have established themselves as an alternative and humane solution to dying in the hospital.

Minimally physically impaired elderly may need new kinds of home care or adult day care. With more multi-generational families, a growing number of people will face the obligation and ex-

WAR VETERANS

The Department of Veterans Affairs reported that, in 1980, about 2 million American men over 65 were veterans. By 1998, there were close to 9.3 million veterans over 65 (Table 11.2). About 4 percent of those were women. Because of the deaths of many of the World War II veterans, the number is expected to peak around 2000 and then decline. The number of veterans is projected to decline after 2000 to about 8.5 million by 2010.

About 60 percent of all elderly men today are eligible for veterans' ben-

TABLE 11.2

Veterans Living in the United States and Puerto Rico, by Age and by Service: 1998

[In thousands, except as indicated. As of July, 1. Estimated. Excludes 500,000 veterans whose active military service of less than 2 years occurred since Sept. 30, 1980. See headnote, Table 600]

Age	Total veterans	Wartime veterans						Peace-time veterans
		Total [1]	Persian Gulf	Vietnam era	Korean conflict	World War II	World War I	
All ages.	25,188	19,300	2,048	8,166	4,179	6,319	5	5,888
Under 30 years old . . .	914	831	831	-	-	-	-	83
30-34 years old	1,150	493	493	-	-	-	-	657
35-39 years old	1,427	257	230	27	-	-	-	1,170
40-44 years old	1,740	896	205	767	-	-	-	844
45-49 years old	2,537	2,357	179	2,323	-	-	-	181
50-54 years old	3,369	3,155	79	3,137	-	-	-	214
55-59 years old	2,373	1,187	24	1,164	17	-	-	1,186
60-64 years old	2,396	1,154	7	328	927	-	-	1,242
65 years old and over .	9,281	8,971	2	421	3,235	6,319	5	310

- Represents zero. [1]Veterans who served in more than one wartime period are counted only once.

TABLE 11.3

Veterans Benefits—Expenditures, by Program: 1980 to 1998

[In millions of dollars ($23,187 represents $23,187,000,000). For fiscal years ending in year shown; see text, Section 9, State and Local Government. Beginning with fiscal year 1990, data are for outlays]

Program	1980	1985	1990	1993	1994	1995	1996	1997	1998
Total	23,187	29,359	28,998	35,460	37,401	37,775	36,915	39,277	41,776
Medical programs	6,042	9,227	11,582	14,603	15,430	16,255	16,337	16,900	17,575
Construction.	300	557	661	622	695	641	698	597	515
General operating expenses . . .	605	765	811	904	906	954	961	1,063	877
Compensation and pension. . . .	11,044	14,037	14,674	16,882	17,188	17,765	17,056	19,284	20,289
Vocational rehabilitation and education	2,350	1,164	452	863	1,119	1,127	1,212	1,287	1,310
All other [1]	2,846	3,609	818	1,586	2,062	1,034	652	145	1,209

[1] Includes insurance and indemnities, and miscellaneous funds and expenditures. (Excludes expenditures from personal funds of patients.)

Source of both tables: Bureau of the Census, Washington, DC, 1999

pense of caring for old or frail parents since so many people now live long enough to face multiple, chronic illnesses.

Accessory apartments, shared housing, and housing designed for the elderly will become more available. Home equity conversion and reverse mortgages, in which an aged person "sells back" his mortgage to the lender in a gradual liquidation (as opposed to selling the house and living on the proceeds or leaving an estate for payment of debts upon one's death), may ease the housing problem for some elderly.

For the poorer elderly, the possibility of homelessness may remain all too real. American society remains challenged by an economy that forces growing numbers of aged, infirm, mentally impaired, and unemployed residents to live in its streets. (For more information on housing, see Chapter III.)

"QUITTING TIME" — RETIREMENT BECOMES AN INSTITUTION

A longer lifespan gives people the opportunity to spend more time in all the major activities of life — education, work, and retirement. In fact, retirement has become as much an institution in American life as education and work. For those who choose to retire, the retirement years can be a period to relax and do many things they have never done. On the other hand, for older persons who need or want to continue working, unemployment and age discrimination can pose serious hardships.

What do the elderly do with their time? The differences in time use between the elderly and the general population result from less time spent working. Men are likely to increase the amount of time spent on traditionally female tasks such as cooking and housework. In addition to travel, study, and socializing, the media claim the largest share of the elderly person's day, with television consuming more than half the newly available time. Loss of employment income may limit the pastime activities possible for some older Americans.

CHANGING FORMS OF RECREATION

Many recreation and leisure companies already recognize that their industry will need to customize products and services to take advantage of a potentially significant exercise market. — Kathie Davis, executive director, IDEA (fitness organization), 1998

Today's baby boomers and elderly are more healthy and active than ever before. They participate in recreational and exercise activities to a far greater degree than in the past. And that trend will likely continue with successive generations. However, as the current crop of Americans in their 50s to 70s age, they will likely switch to less vigorous sports.

The recreation industry has experienced fluctuations depending on the abilities and interests of the huge cohort of boomers. At one time they jogged and played tennis. Today, more of them are walking and playing golf. Although today's motorcyclist on the Harley is more likely to be a middle-aged guy than someone in his 20s or 30s, that will likely change. Aided by their considerable economic power, boomers are the core constituent of the recreation market now, although industry experts predict a switch to "softer" forms of exercise and socializing.

Recreation industry experts do not believe the drop in physical activity will be as steep as for previous generations. They have, however, already noticed some growth in safer sports designed to cater to aging bodies. Many popular fitness activities, such as walking, swimming, bicycling, birdwatching, hiking, fishing, motor-boating, and camping, are relatively easy on muscles, joints, and bones and may continue to be popular with aging Americans. There will likely be added interest in massages, steam baths, and saunas. Mind/body activities, such as tai chi, yoga, and martial arts, which focus on flexibility and body awareness rather than strength and speed, are already growing and will likely continue to grow. And whatever older Americans choose to do, there will be plenty of involvement on the part of the recreation and fitness industries to market to those needs.

DEATH AND DYING

By far, the most frequent beneficiaries of the advances in medical technology are the elderly. Unfortunately, while technology can enhance life in certain circumstances, it may prolong life (as well as dying) at the expense of quality of life and without regard for individual wishes. The legal, ethical, religious, and economic questions raised by such technology have yet to be resolved and will certainly touch the lives of an ever-growing number of older Americans.

Among those technologies at issue are cardiopulmonary resuscitation (CPR), respiratory ventilation, organ transplants, dialysis, nutritional support and hydration, antibiotics, and recently, euthanasia and suicide-enabling paraphernalia and procedures.

Controversy involving medical technology generally centers around terminology such as "quality versus quantity (longevity)" of life, the "high cost of dying," "living wills," and "the right to die." Court cases increasingly challenge accepted procedure. Under the Patient Self-Determination Act, part of the Omnibus Budget Reconciliation Act (PL 101-508) that went into effect in 1991, all individuals receiving medical care in hospitals, nursing homes, and certain other facilities receiving Medicare and Medicaid funds must be advised of two rights, (1) the right to make decisions about their care — including the right to refuse that care, and (2) the right to prepare binding documents stating whether they desire life-sustaining intervention in the event of their incapacitation — a "living will."

Extending a patient's life by technology is not necessarily a benefit for the person. Although today's elderly are healthier and more affluent than previous generations, the suicide rate among the elderly remains high. According to the National Center for Health Statistics, in 1997, the suicide rate among persons 65 and older was 17.4 per 100,000 people, compared to an overall national rate of 10.8 per 100,000. Among those older than 75, the rate was more than 20 per 100,000 people, twice that of the general population. (See Chapter VII.) Because older persons constitute the fastest-growing age group in the United States, the number of suicides will probably continue to rise. (See also *Death and Dying — Who Decides?*, Information Plus, Wylie, Texas, 1998.)

IMPORTANT NAMES AND ADDRESSES

Alzheimer's Disease Association
919 N. Michigan Ave., Suite 1000
Chicago, IL 60611
(800) 272-3900
FAX (312) 335-1110
www.alz.org

American Association of Homes and
Services for the Aging
901 E St. NW, Suite 500
Washington, DC 20004
(202) 783-2242
FAX (202) 783-2255
www.aahsa.org

American Association of Retired Persons
601 E St. NW
Washington, DC 20049
(202) 434-2277
FAX (202) 728-4573
www.aarp.org

Assisted Living Federation of America
10300 Eaton Pl., Suite 400
Fairfax, VA 22030
(703) 691-8100
FAX (703) 691-8106
www.alfa.org

Children of Aging Parents (CAPS)
180 Howard St., First Floor
San Francisco, CA 94105
(415) 474-1278
FAX (415) 474-1353
www.careguide.com

Eldercare Locator Directory
(800) 677-1116

Family Caregiver Alliance
690 Market St., Suite 600
San Francisco, CA 94104
(415) 434-3388
www.caregiver.org

Gerontological Society of America
1030 15th St. NW, Suite 250
Washington, DC 20005
(202) 842-1275
FAX (202) 842-1150
www.geron.org

Jewish Council for the Aging
11820 Parklawn Dr., #200
Rockville, MD 20852
(301) 255-4200
FAX (301) 231-9360
www.jcagw.org

National Academy of Elder Law Attorneys
1604 N. Country Club Rd.
Tucson, AZ 86716
(520) 881-4005
FAX (520) 325-7925
www.naela.org

National Alliance for Caregiving
4720 Montgomery Ln., Suite 642
Bethesda, MD 20814
(301) 718-8444
FAX (301) 652-7711
www.caregiving.org

National Alliance for Senior Citizens
1744 Riggs NW, Third Floor
Washington, DC 20009
(202) 986-0117
FAX (202) 986-2974

National Association for Home Care
228 7th St. SE
Washington, DC 20003
(202) 547-7424
FAX (202) 547-3540
www.nahc.org

National Caregiving Foundation
(800) 930-1357

National Caucus and Center on Black Aged
1424 K St. NW, Suite 500
Washington, DC 20005
(202) 637-8400
FAX (202) 347-0895
www.hcba-blackaged.org

National Center on Elder Abuse
1225 I St. NW, Suite 725
Washington, DC 20005
(202) 898-2586
FAX (202) 898-2583
NCEA@nasua.org
www.gwjapan.com/NCEA

National Council on the Aging
409 3rd St. SW, Suite 200
Washington, DC 20024
(202) 479-6653
FAX (202) 479-0735
www.ncoa.org

National Family Caregivers Association
10400 Connecticut Ave., Suite 500
Kensington, MD 20895
(800) 896-3650
FAX (301) 942-2304
www.nfcacares.org

National Hispanic Council on Aging
2713 Ontario Rd. NW
Washington, DC 20009
(202) 265-1288
FAX (202) 745-2522
www.nhcoa.org

National Hospice and Palliative Care
Organization
1700 Diagonal Rd., Suite 300
Arlington, VA 22314
(703) 243-5900
FAX (703) 525-5762
www.nhpco.org

National Institute on Aging
31 Center Dr., Room 5627
Bethesda, MD 20892
(301) 496-1752
FAX (301) 496-1072
www.nih.gov/nia

National Respite Locator Service
(800) 773-5433

National Senior Citizens Law Center
1104 14th St. NW, Suite 400
Washington, DC 20005
(202) 289-6976
FAX (202) 289-7224
www.nsclc.org

National Urban League
120 Wall St.
New York, NY 10005
(212) 558-5300
FAX (212) 344-5332
www.nul.org

Older Women's League
666 11th St. NW, #700
Washington, DC 20001
(202) 783-6686
FAX (202) 638-2356
www.owl-national.org

Pension Rights Center
1140 19th St. NW, #602
Washington, DC 20036
(202) 296-3776
FAX (202) 833-2472

Quest
City College Center for Worker Education
99 Hudson St., 6th Floor
New York, NY 10013
(212) 925-6625, Ext. 229
FAX (212) 925-0963

Service Corps of Retired Executives
409 3rd St. SW, 6th Floor
Washington, DC 20024
(800) 634-0245
FAX (202) 205-7636
www.score.org

U. S. Department of Health and Human
Services
Administration on Aging
200 Independence Ave. SW, Rm. 309F
Washington, DC 20201
(202) 401-4634
FAX (202) 401-7741

Veterans Affairs Department
810 Vermont Ave. NW
Washington, DC 20420
(202) 273-5700
www.va.gov

RESOURCES

The Bureau of the Census of the U.S. Department of Commerce in Washington, DC, is the major source of statistics on American life. Many of its publications were essential for the preparation of this book, including *Marital Status and Living Arrangements: 1998* (1999), *Asset Ownership of Households: 1993* (1995), *Americans with Disabilities 1994-95* (1997), *Voting and Registration in the Election of November 1996* (1998), *Housing Vacancies and Homeownership 1998* (2000), *Consumer Expenditures: 1998* (1999), *Health Insurance Coverage: 1998* (1999), *Resident Population Estimates of the United States by Age and Sex: 1990-1999* (1999), *Aging in the Americas into the XXI Century* (1999), *Aging in the United States — Past, Present, and Future* (1997), *Computer Use in the United States, 1997* (1999), *Educational Attainment in the United States: 1998* (1999), *Centenarians in the United States, 1990* (1999), and *Global Aging into the 21st Century* (1999).

The Social Security Administration, an agency of the U.S. Department of Health and Human Services (HHS), is responsible for the financial security of millions of older Americans. *Fast Facts and Figures About Social Security* (Washington, DC, 1999) answers the most commonly asked questions about Social Security benefits, the Supplemental Security Income program, and Medicare. The Bureau of Labor Statistics' *Employment and Earnings* (January 2000) provided data on work and earnings of the elderly.

The Health Care Financing Administration (HCFA) of the U.S. Department of Health and Human Services prepares the *Health Care Financing Review* and the *Medicare and Medicaid Supplement*, which were the sources of much of the material on health care coverage. The HCFA also published *National Health Expenditures 1998* (2000) and *A Profile of Medicare Chartbook* (1998).

The Centers for Disease Control and Prevention (CDC) of the U.S. Public Health Service supplied statistics on health issues in its *Advance Data* and *Mortality Trends for Alzheimer's Disease* (1996), *Vital and Health Statistics — Access to Health Care, Part 3: Older Adults* (1997), and *Morbidity and Mortality Weekly Reports*. The Public Health Service publishes its annual *Health*, which gives information on disease issues.

The U.S. Department of Justice is the major source of information concerning crime and justice in America. *Crime Against Persons Age 65 or Older, 1992-1997* (2000), *Age Patterns of Victims of Serious Violent Crime* (1997), and *Change in Criminal Victimization 1994-95* (1997), prepared by the Federal Bureau of Investigation (FBI) and the Bureau of Justice Statistics (BJS), were helpful in providing information on elderly victims.

The National Center for Education Statistics compiles data on U.S. education. Its annuals *Digest of Education Statistics 1997* (1998) and *The Condition of Education 1998* (1999) were useful in understanding educational attainment and continuing study among the elderly.

"The Older Workforce: Recruitment and Retention" (1993), a study by the American Association of Retired Persons (AARP) and the Society for Human Resource Management, includes valuable material on employment of older Americans. Another helpful study was "Americans over 55 at Work Program," conducted by ICF, Inc., for the Commonwealth Fund. The AARP also allowed use of its *AARP/Modern Maturity Sexuality Survey* (1999), *Comparisons of Grandparent Visitation Statutes Nationwide* (January 2000), and *Out-of-Pocket Spending on Health Care by Medicare Beneficiaries Age 65 and Older* (1999).

Family Caregiving in the United States (1997), prepared by the National Alliance for Caregiving (Bethesda, Maryland) and the American Association of Retired Persons, was the source of much invaluable data on elder care. *The MetLife Study of Employer Costs for Working Caregivers* (1997), published by the National Alliance for Caregiving and Metropolitan Life Insurance Company, was most helpful regarding costs to business for caring for elderly relatives of employees. The Alzheimer's Association (Washington, DC) and the National Alliance for Caregiving published *Who Cares: Families Caring for Persons with Alzheimer's Disease* (1999). The National Alliance for Caregiving also prepared *The Caregiving Boom: Baby Boomer Women Giving Care* (1998).

Elder Abuse: Questions and Answers (1996) and *Elder Abuse Information Series* (1999), prepared by the National Center for Elder Abuse, provided much helpful information on abuse of the nation's elderly. Information Plus thanks the American Heart Association (Dallas, Texas) for use of data on cardiovascular disease from its *2000 Heart and Stroke Statistical Update*. *PREVENTION Magazine's* "The Prevention Index: 1996 Summary Report" (1996) provided data on nutrition and alcohol consumption among the elderly. The Independent Sector graciously allowed use of its *America's Senior Volunteers* (1998), and Project Hope (Bethesda, Maryland), in *Health Affairs* (March/April 1999), discussed the economic value of caring for elder Americans. *Older Women: The Economics of Aging*, published by the Women's Research and Education Institute (New York, New York, 1998), offered material on the financial condition of women as they age. As always, Information Plus appreciates the use of polls conducted by the Gallup Organization.

INDEX

INDEX (Continued)